Representations of Euro
since 19

Stefanie Pukallus

Representations of European Citizenship since 1951

palgrave
macmillan

Stefanie Pukallus
University of Sheffield
United Kingdom

ISBN 978-1-137-51146-1 (hardcover)   ISBN 978-1-137-51147-8 (eBook)
ISBN 978-1-349-70235-0 (softcover)
DOI 10.1057/978-1-137-51147-8

Library of Congress Control Number: 2016936773

© The Editor(s) (if applicable) and The Author(s) 2016, First softcover printing 2018
The author(s) has/have asserted their right(s) to be identified as the author(s) of this work in accordance with the Copyright, Designs and Patents Act 1988.
This work is subject to copyright. All rights are solely and exclusively licensed by the Publisher, whether the whole or part of the material is concerned, specifically the rights of translation, reprinting, reuse of illustrations, recitation, broadcasting, reproduction on microfilms or in any other physical way, and transmission or information storage and retrieval, electronic adaptation, computer software, or by similar or dissimilar methodology now known or hereafter developed.
The use of general descriptive names, registered names, trademarks, service marks, etc. in this publication does not imply, even in the absence of a specific statement, that such names are exempt from the relevant protective laws and regulations and therefore free for general use.
The publisher, the authors and the editors are safe to assume that the advice and information in this book are believed to be true and accurate at the date of publication. Neither the publisher nor the authors or the editors give a warranty, express or implied, with respect to the material contained herein or for any errors or omissions that may have been made.

Printed on acid-free paper

This Palgrave Macmillan imprint is published by Springer Nature
The registered company is Macmillan Publishers Ltd. London

For Jackie

Preface

The European Commission is not usually associated with anything sentimental, consisting as it does of well-educated elite bureaucrats and technocrats. However, it is possible and certainly plausible to describe the account I offer of the European Commission's attempts to communicate the meaning and significance of European citizenship as a story of wishful thinking. It is important wishful thinking because it is in essence the history of the European Commission's ideals and hopes for a Civil Europe or, more forthrightly, what the European Commission would have wanted Europeans to be like. This history is also a story of unrequited hopes—since, quite simply, what the European Commission dreamt of bore little relationship to how most Europeans felt. For those who take a realistic line and have a bias towards results, the European Commission's communicative efforts in representing the European citizen in a compelling manner and in such a way as to persuade us all to adopt the mantle of urbane, cosmopolitan Europeans enjoying the benefits of European integration can count amongst its more extravagant undertakings. However, wishful thinking and unrequited hopes form a historical judgement that I think is worth understanding via the detail of the European Commission's communicative efforts with the European peoples. Although the detail is in the story of what some think is from the start a ridiculous idea: European citizenship. Representing European citizens, giving them their place in the European integration process, informing them of the benefits they might derive from being European, creating their European civil identity and encouraging a civil consciousness of belonging to Europe has been a core activity in the public communication policy of the European Commission since the early 1950s. In order to tell this story of wishful thinking and unrequited hopes, it is necessary to interpret the European Commission's discourse concerning European citizens, the stories it told about them and the ideals it articulated in brochures and speeches as deeply meaningful. In short, one needs to regard this discourse as an uninterrupted (since 1951), serious and considered attempt to bring about a Civil Europe.

In this book, I unashamedly take the European Commission's discourse regarding European citizens at face value. This is not to say that we should not avail ourselves of a critical attitude but rather that only by analysing and interpreting this discourse in its various historical, political and institutional contexts of European integration can historically sensitive meaning-making be undertaken. There is nothing new in this idea. Indeed, the Cambridge School of Historiography believe in the importance of the performative nature of what was said and in which context it was said—no matter how silly, contradictory, inconsistent or naïve these discourses might appear. Making sense of discourse is not a matter of intuition but of a detailed historical analysis of what was said in which context and why, how these messages were publicly communicated, how consistently they were expressed and the reasons for change. The discourse on European citizenship that I examine in this book can be found in a combination of three sources. First, the European treaties—Treaty of Paris (1951), Treaty of Rome establishing the European Community (1957), Single European Act (1986), Treaty of Maastricht (1992), Treaty of Amsterdam (1997), Treaty of Nice (2001), Constitutional Treaty (2004, not ratified) and the Treaty of Lisbon (2009)—are important because each of them reflects a different stage and focus of European integration and as such, provides the framing context for the Commission's understanding of European citizenship at a certain period in the European integration process. Second, my analysis includes three kinds of documents: (a) public communication policy papers which determine the scope of information programmes, note communication priorities and define the understanding and value of public communication, and (b) EU citizenship reports. I also used reports that are (c) related to the identity of the European Community in relation to European citizens and their civil identity, to the relevance of the European Community for European citizens in their daily lives, to the relationship between the European Community and European citizens and to the value of public communication for this relationship. The third source is public communication outputs such as public communication brochures and speeches given by European Commission and

High Authority officials. Both enabled the European Commission, particularly during the 1950s and 1960s, to publicly communicate to a broad European public despite its then very limited civil competences. Official speeches have remained a crucial source for analysis because they are helpful in understanding the nuances and subtleties of the representations of European citizenship.

One important caveat needs mentioning: Although I focus on the European Commission as the main protagonist in the representations of European citizenship and their public communication, it is relevant and critical (and therefore) justified to include reports from the European Parliament and other EU institutions. The reason for including non-European Commission authored reports is twofold: first, the European Commission's public communication strategies have often been the result of inter-institutional cooperation and negotiations from the beginning of the ECSC, and second, the over 30 interviews I have conducted with past and present senior European Commission officials revealed that reports such as the Tindemans Report (1975) and the Adonnino Reports (1985) are vital to the understanding of the meaning of European citizenship and have been used by the European Commission. As such, they are included in my analysis.

The result of the analysis of the European Commission's discourse shows that the European Commission has depicted European citizenship in five different but related ways. I call these representations Homo Oeconomicus (1951–1972), A People's Europe (1973–1992), Europe of Transparency (1993–2004), Europe of Agorai (2005–2009) and Europe of Rights (2010–2014). Their names capture the essence and focus of each version of European citizenship.

One further point needs to be made. I use European integration history only for the purpose of being able to provide some context to each representation. The choice of what counted as critical context was informed by and discussed in interviews with past and present European Commission officials who had key roles in the formulation and execution of European citizenship and public communication policies. Their positions range from Director General for Information and Communication policy to spokespersons and Commissioners. They include key Commission officials involved in European citizenship and public communication policies, such as J.R. Rabier, J. Lastenouse, P. Adonnino, A. Vitorino, J. Santer and M. Wallström. Recent or current key Commission officials came from Directorate-General (DG), Communication (COMM) and DG Justice

(JUS). Interviewing these key officials enabled me to fill historical gaps, to verify and obtain historical detail and importantly, to test the theoretical analysis against the practical experience of these interviewees. In this way I try to combine a formal historical approach (events, policy developments, etc.) with an informal and personal historical approach (the insights obtained from my interviewees).

As for my wishful thinking, I hope that this combination enables some new insights into the history of the European Commission's changing understandings of European citizenship and that this history, in turn, casts a little light on one aspect of the history of an idea that has been spoken about with varying degrees of enthusiasm since 1951. In summary, I wish to bring to my readers' attention the European Commission's consistent civil aspirations and concomitantly its tireless and myriad attempts to bring about a Civil Europe.

Acknowledgments

I would like to thank my family, friends and colleagues for being there when it was important, and my interviewees for their time and valuable insights which, I hope, made the story this book tells come alive. I have also had the great good fortune to benefit from N. Piers Ludlow's intellectual guidance, personal kindness and encouragement to publish, and from Sven Carnel's patience and generosity—Sven was my companion in the archives who answered any question, found documents I had asked for and brought to my attention those I didn't know existed. As a source of inspiration, historical knowledge and unique insight, I extend my warmest gratitude to my wonderful friend and mentor Jacques-René Rabier, who with charm and grace gave me so much of his time and advice, shared personal anecdotes and insights and more than anyone imbued in me a sense of the European adventure. Finally, and most of all, my deepest debt is to Jackie, who in so many ways made everything possible. I dedicate this book to her.

Contents

1 A Civil Europe   1

2 Homo Oeconomicus (1951–1972)   39

3 A People's Europe (1973–1992)   93

4 Europe of Transparency (1993–2004)   135

5 Europe of Agorai (2005–2009)   169

6 Europe of Rights (2010–2014)   217

7 Summary   259

Bibliography   269

Index   271

CHAPTER 1

A Civil Europe

1   The European Commission and the Stimulation of a European Civil Consciousness

The European Commission (henceforth Commission) has been a continuing driving force for European integration.[1] It has been characterised as having two main characteristics: first, it is independent in that it has to treat the opinions of the member states with parity and respect. In short, 'it must be impartially politically and indifferent as to nationality'.[2] Second, and importantly for the civil narrative described in this book, the Commission 'must also be European, meaning that it must discern the common interest clearly and accurately and promote it energetically. In this sense it must be partisan and protagonistic'.[3] According to Haas[4] '(…) Monnet was reported to consider the Commission as 'the repository of the European General Will'. As the 'motor of the Community',[5] it envisaged 'politics [as] the art of the possible'.[6] What this meant was that the Commission provided the dynamism necessary to bring European integration forward—in fact, Hallstein argued that 'no feature of the Community is as spectacular, as thrilling as its progressiveness'.[7] In short, the Commission interpreted its competences in the Treaties widely and was therefore able to define the scope and depth of European integration in distinct policy areas. From the start, the Commission's vision of what European integration was to become included European civil integration and concomitantly, European policy areas extended beyond economic and political policies to include specifically civil policies. In other words, the Commission (and before that the High Authority[8]) has shown a persistent interest in fostering European civil integration since the 1950s. By European civil integration I mean the Commission's ambitions and subsequent efforts to stimulate greater European civil unity and solidarity through a range of civil initiatives in the cultural and educational fields such as the building of European schools, University programmes and collaborations, the production of European films and documentaries as well as the organisation of art and music festivals; civil-spatial policy which included the use of symbols, statues and the organisation of European exhibitions; and social policy where the Community attempted to create a European social security system, developed housing projects and provided funding for further education and training. Importantly, public communication was a policy in its own right[9] but also supported the raising awareness efforts of the other civil initiatives and, so it was hoped, the stimulation of a European civil consciousness.

Indeed, already in the first generation of European civil servants—'enlightened and purposeful politicians'[10]—there was a group of influential officials who firmly believed in the value of, the potential for and the necessity of European civil integration. The members of this group included René Mayer, Max Kohnstamm, Michel Gaudet, Pierre Uri, Jacques-René Rabier, François Fontaine, all of whom worked closely with one of the main protagonists of European integration, Jean Monnet, who was the driving force behind the High Authority's early civil initiatives. Indeed Monnet, his collaborators (as well as their successors, which included, notably, Walter Hallstein[11] and Jean Rey[12] but also Sicco Mansholt,[13] Robert Marjolin)[14] showed a steadfast conviction and political perseverance, not to say political courage,[15] in their attempts to pursue a persistent civil aim: the stimulation of a European civil consciousness favourably disposed towards the Community's federal ambitions.[16] Specifically, such a civil consciousness referred to the Commission's view of an ideal European public perceived of in terms of its own universalising solidarity which extended beyond a specific nationally based political or economic milieu. This was a European public perceived of as a 'solidary sphere' which would '[unite] individuals dispersed by class, race, religion, ethnicity'[17] and sustain civil society in the working out of its own identity and boundaries.

What the following chapters will show is that the early European civil servants naturally encouraged the development of civil institutions.

It was as if they instinctively understood their value and the necessity to build them. And whilst they did not use a specifically modern and sociological vocabulary when it came to articulating European civil society and its institutions, their vision corresponded to the way the sociologist Jeffrey Alexander understood the history and development of modern civil society. As Alexander argued, 'Civil society is not merely an institutional realm. It is also a realm of structured, socially established consciousness, a network of understandings creating structures of feeling that permeate social life (…)'[18] and, as I will show, early European officials emphasised the need for the emergence of a European civil consciousness. In this sense, Alexander provides a useful vocabulary able to capture what the early European officials were doing in terms of facilitating a Civil Europe. Indeed, Alexander's terminology can, without anachronism, help us to reveal and name early European civil aims and efforts. And whilst Alexander wrote about the development and nature of civil society in North America, he admitted that 'there is no principled reason (…) why the concept of civil society cannot be applied to the supranational plane'.[19] In other words, the concept 'civil society' can be used independently from a national setting because it is a value-concept much in the same way that Weber understood the nation: both belong to what Weber[20] called the 'sphere of values'. Understood as a value-concept, European civil society would be based on common European values such as the 'principles of freedom, of human dignity, of a constant and unremitting search for peace'[21] rather than being geographically, linguistically or ethnically fixed. Subsequently, civil solidarity would arise through the sharing of these common values by the members of civil society. As such, the solidarising 'we' of civil society can be Europeanised, and this was what the European Commission intended to stimulate, as can be illustrated by Hallstein's claim that 'solidarity is not only a matter of political convenience, it is part of our political conviction',[22] and such solidarity or European civil 'unity (…) is not something that can be imposed from above'.[23] In other words, 'Europe's unity, which cannot be a technocratic achievement or the result of a plethora of regulations, will be brought about by the freely expressed will of its people'.[24] Correspondingly, the emergence of a European civil society and its attendant institutions could only be stimulated by the Community, but not imposed. Thus, as Alexander argued, civil society was best understood 'as a solidary sphere, in which a certain kind of universalizing community comes to be culturally defined and to some degree institutionally enforced'.[25] The defining feature of any civil society is civil solidarity which, in turn, is 'exhibited and sustained by public opinion, deep cultural codes, distinctive organizations—legal, journalistic and associational—and such historically specific interactional practices as civility, criticism, and mutual respect'.[26] Civil society as a concept is analytically distinct (although in reality the distinction is not always clear-cut) from the so-called non-civil spheres. The non-civil spheres include the political sphere (the state), education, family life, religion and others. Structurally, civil society is supported by regulative institutions and by communicative institutions. Whereas regulative institutions are composed of voting, party, office and law and its attendant legal institutions, communicative institutions include the factual and the fictional media, civil associations and public opinion polls. The existence of these two kinds of civil institutions ensures the autonomy and independence of the civil sphere from the non-civil sphere and indicates the degree to which a society is democratic. Or as Alexander put it: 'To the degree that civil society becomes independent (…) marks the degree to which there is a democratic social life'.[27]

According to Ludlow, Hallstein believed that 'the Commission was the most 'striking' and innovative of the four principal European institutions'[28] and as such had the capacity to act towards facilitating the development of both a European identity and with it a solidary European public marked by a unity of interests and civil dispositions within its own plurality. In other words, the emergence of such a European civil consciousness was seen as a precondition for widespread support for the European public's active participation in the realisation of the Community's federal aim, which in the long run would enable the European public to act as a European civil society 'beyond the borders of nationality'.[29] It was thought by the Commission that appealing to the European public in inclusive terms such as 'Europeans',[30] 'citizens',[31] 'men and women',[32] 'every man',[33] 'citizens of the European Community',[34] 'individuals and peoples',[35] 'entire population',[36] a 'human Community',[37] 'a new society',[38] a 'European civilisation',[39] and a 'Europe of free and equal men'[40] would stimulate this 'civil consciousness'. Such a consciousness was not incommensurate with nationally based citizenship, as the Commission was at pains to point out primarily through its public communication policy and in official speeches. Quite simply, the peoples of Europe could see themselves as both European and nationals of their home country, and as such they encouraged these 'neonate' European citizens to, in Sandel's terms, 'think and act as multiply situated selves'.[41] Alternatively expressed, the Commission somewhat prudentially emphasised that national identity and a feeling of belonging to Europe were considered complementary and not exclusive of each other. Hallstein, for example, insisted that 'no one is asked to disown its country' and that, instead, 'a double allegiance is required of our citizens, so that the new Europe may be built with the nations for its foundation'.[42] Mayer, in an address at the Council on Foreign Relations in New York, attempted to show the complementary character of national identity and being European by taking himself as an example: 'Tonight I address you as a European. It is not to say that I have ceased being a Frenchman—indeed that would be quite impossible—but rather I am a Frenchman and something more',[43] to which he added, 'I shall never be persuaded that in seeking to become a better European one becomes a worse Frenchman'.[44]

As 'some old hands of an institution who were there at the birth and watched it grow'[45] wrote, in the early days of the European Community, the Commission believed that 'the sense of a shared identity [Mayer appealed to] would not be long in spreading through the hierarchy from top to bottom [meaning from European civil servants to the European public], mobilising its creativity and energy in the service of the European ideal'.[46] What this pointed to was an atmosphere of openness, adventure and excitement and a belief that a 'Civil Europe' was possible. With regard to the working environment and specifically under the leadership of Jean Monnet (and later of René Mayer, Walter Hallstein and Jean Rey and others), Commission officials developed a feeling of belonging to the European Community and of making significant contributions to the common undertaking of ensuring peace and fostering European unity, starting with the Commission officials. Indeed, Monnet 'generated [an atmosphere of permanent emergency which] drove people of different and stubborn traditions to overwork together and, almost without knowing it, to develop a corporate identity and pride'.[47] He was characterised by 'his experience, imagination, tenacity [and] enormous capacity for work'.[48] In fact, according to van Helmont,[49] Monnet was disciplined, would go for a walk in the morning and work until late. He did not like weekends or holidays (except when he left for the mountains), as he felt that they interrupted his projects. He was perseverant, committed to make Europe a success; he was imaginative and warm, and according to Kohnstamm, 'tous ceux qui eurent la chance de le connaitre en gardent l'empreinte'.[50] Or as Brugmans put it: 'No one who lived in his entourage during the initial period in the decrepit building in the Place de Metz will ever forget those years of fervour and of inspiring work'.[51] Monnet and his successors understood that for the success of European integration it was 'of vital importance' to create 'an organizational common culture based mainly on a sense of shared adventure and common commitment to European unity',[52] and it appeared that this newly established 'common culture (...) lasted even after the partisan phase of the Commission had passed and beyond the early years of pioneering, purposive commitment to getting the Community off the ground'.[53] However, the intercultural dialogues and relationships were not confined to the workplace. Rather, a variety of sport clubs, charitable associations and other groups were founded by Community officials for Commission officials in order to facilitate contact between them in their free time. Indeed, Commission officials developed a curiosity about other nationalities, histories and visions for the future of Europe.[54] It was this new 'European way of life' and direct involvement in the future of Europe that provided Commission officials with confidence in the future of Europe and particularly in the easy stimulation of a European civil consciousness amongst a wide European public. Today, however, Rabier admits that while being enthusiastic about the possibility of a Civil Europe, the Commission might have been naïve in thinking that a European civil consciousness would spread as easily and as quickly as they hoped. He also feels that it proved more difficult than expected to show Europeans the tangibility of Europe and its concrete significance for their own lives.[55] The failed projects of the European Defence Community (EDC) and the European Political Community (EPC) showed that political integration was a slow process and that sometimes the enthusiasm of the Commission officials wasn't shared by the European people. In fact, when Monnet was informed about the failure of the EDC, he said that the committee that prepared the EDC project had been too quick and hasty.[56] What this rejection showed was that public opinion had not been ready yet to agree to further European political integration. Alternatively expressed, the idea of a federal Europe had not yet provided sufficient 'identitive power'[57] for Europeans to accept such change. Although the early European civil servants were enthusiastic and confident about the future of European integration—Monnet said that he couldn't help being optimistic[58]—they also wondered about the depth of the European public's agreement to European integration. For example, Rabier thought that the European public agreed with European integration per se but wasn't sufficiently interested or passionate about European integration to take an active role in its building, to critically engage with it or to accept major changes just yet.[59]

Nevertheless, attempts to promote a European civil consciousness were felt to be tenable because they were based upon the assumption that the member states and the European Community collectively shared certain values. These values were mostly appealed to in speeches by senior Commission officials[60] and included such things as a 'European' pacific destiny;[61] a commitment to liberal democracy; an understanding of specific freedoms, most notably, assembly, expression and mobility; the rule of law; safeguarding human dignity and promoting civil equality. These values or principles of the modern liberal state have, according to Israel,[62] their intellectual origin in the radical Enlightenment[63] and in this sense the radical Enlightenment could be seen as an integral part of a European history and cultural heritage that both the European Community and the member states shared (whether they were always aware of this or not).[64] It was upon these values that a European civil society, so the Commission hoped, could be based. The persistent hope that was at the heart of Commission civil initiatives and attempts to stimulate a European civil consciousness was that one day 'in a sense of participation, in an order based on the approval of all Europeans, it can be said with no less pride [than it was the case for Roman citizenship] but with awareness of sharing a great responsibility: "Civis Europaeus sum"—"I am a citizen of Europe"'.[65] In the light of the above, claims such as Schulz-Forberg's,[66] that European integration was dominated by a distant anti-democratic technocratic or a hypocritically democratic elite can only be seen as incorrect.

Despite the Commission's enthusiasm about the possibilities of European political and economic integration and the emergence of a European civil consciousness, there was an atmosphere of uncertainty due to the fact that the Commission was, unlike other institutions, 'not rooted in any tradition or prior experience but [had] to invent [its] role as [it] went along'.[67] Politically, the Commission was 'faced with an all-powerful and overbearing Council' and as such it found itself in constant negotiation with the member states about the extent of its competencies. In other words, the Commission had 'to fight every step of the way for the prerogatives which were, after all, its by right under the Treaty, engaging in difficult battles on every subject. But at every turn it was in danger of sparking a major political crisis, another 'empty chair', which would have jeopardised everything it had achieved'.[68] As such, the Commission operated in a dialectic of prudence and risk and of pragmatism and opportunism, especially when it came to civil initiatives for which the Commission had no explicit mandate. In other words, since the beginning of European integration there has been a recognisable tension between the Commission's ambitions and convictions with regard to Civil Europe and the pragmatic adjustments to circumstances that was required.[69] In short, and as put by a Commission official: 'Everything one does is a compromise'.[70] Nevertheless, the Commission and their successors persevered in the attempt to facilitate a Civil Europe by attempting to 'bend the rules' discreetly, and it is art. 5 of the Treaty of Paris (ToP) that offered a welcomed opportunity to unofficially broaden its scope of intervention. Specifically, art. 5 read: 'The Community shall accomplish its mission, under the conditions provided for in the present Treaty (…). To this end, the Community will (…) enlighten and facilitate the action of the interested parties by collecting information, organizing consultations and defining general objectives.' By interpreting 'all interested parties' as the entire European public, the Commission made sure that it could develop a public communication policy that was unrestrained by matters of competence and therefore could address a wide European public. Maybe surprisingly for some, it was Monnet who was the driving force behind the Community's early public communication policy. He believed that 'Our Community will only come to true realization if the actions it takes are made public, and explained publicly (…) to the people of our Community'.[71] Accordingly and from the start, the Community used its public communication policy to stimulate a European civil consciousness.[72] Indeed, since the beginning of European integration it focused on the public communication of one of the most important concepts in the definition and stimulation of European civil integration, European unity and a European civil consciousness: European citizenship.

The question of what European citizenship is and how it can be understood has been the focus of academic research and has been a continuous concern for the European institutions. In recent times, the Eurozone crisis, austerity measures, youth unemployment and civil protests – especially in Greece, Portugal and Spain – along with the refugee crisis have raised questions about what the EU stands for and what it means to be a European citizen. As such, the debate of who we are as Europeans and what we might actually belong to is as relevant today as it was in the 1950s. At the same time, the questions of how European citizenship is best understood, how its meaning has been contingent on historical and political circumstances, and what it means to be a European citizen at different times remain pertinent.

2 EUROPEAN CITIZENSHIP

Whilst undertaking research for this book, I had the opportunity to interview over 30 senior Commission officials, past and present. Amongst the many things I learnt was the remarkably imprecise way European citizenship was spoken about, and when asked how it was defined, just how many different views there were. This prosaic and casual imprecision simply reflected what has been very well known: that there is little consensus on what European citizenship actually means. Indeed, some Commission officials used the terms 'EU citizenship' and 'European citizenship' interchangeably, with one Commission official noting: 'I don't see a distinction. I think we use the terms in the same way. It is only for communication purposes (…) [where] 'European' is more easily understood and identified with'[73] whereas other officials were punctilious in the distinction: 'We must first distinguish between Union citizenship and citizenship in a wider sense. While the former is legally defined in the Treaties and is limited to holders of the citizenship of the 27 Member States (…), the latter is more inclusive and reaches out to all people [non-EU or EU citizens] living in the EU (…)' as one official[74] put it. She described European citizenship as much more broadly conceived than in the Maastricht Treaty; she described it as consisting of fundamental and non-discrimination rights, consumer rights, socio-economic rights, rights in the internal market, to which are added the societal dimension of European citizenship, civil responsibilities and shared values.[75] Another Commission official[76] described European citizenship as related to certain social, economic and cultural conditions which had legal, political and societal dimensions. Thus, even the most basic operational and working definition of European citizenship has been open to ambiguity.

Such ambiguity is not uncommon. Indeed, it is inherent in the very idea of a European citizen itself if for no other reason than because the idea is not fixed in any philosophical, historical, geographical, cultural, constitutional or quotidian civil way. As such, its ambiguity has 'historical depth' and is not merely 'the result of conceptual confusion'.[77] European citizenship is a complex concept which is, like any other complex concept, 'difficult to dissolve, difficult to analyse, and, it must be emphasized, utterly *undefinable*'.[78] Accordingly, and instead of attempting to give a static definition, it is preferable to 'try to give an 'analysis' of the contingent synthesis of "meaning"[79] that European citizenship represented during a certain period of European integration. At any given point in the European integration process, European citizenship will be 'a 'synthesis' of the various different 'meanings' imposed on it in the past'.[80] Consequently, anyone who takes up the challenge of studying European citizenship needs to find a way to understand and accommodate its retained and changing meanings. The question is not so much 'what is European citizenship?' than 'how has European citizenship been spoken of and known throughout a period of time?'[81] Thus far, the malleable features and different representations of European citizenship have not been adequately captured by any of the three main approaches to European citizenship that I have identified: first, the national approach; second, the socio-historical policy analysis approach and third, the cosmopolitan post-national approach. To take each in turn:

The National Approach to European Citizenship

The national approach to European citizenship has relied on Marshall's[82] triadic conception of national citizenship as comprising political, civil (which is to be understood as including rights giving citizens access to justice) and social rights. Numerous European scholars have appropriated Marshall's concept and based their evaluation of the substance of EU citizenship[83]—as defined in the Maastricht Treaty (1992)—on their analysis of its legal,[84] political[85] and social dimensions.[86] They have concluded that—compared to national citizenship—EU citizenship has been merely decorative and unsubstantial. They have pointed to the 'unbearable lightness of European citizenship'.[87] Overall, the shortcomings of this national approach have been threefold: first, it has confined European citizenship to the few articles on Citizenship of the Union as legally codified in the Maastricht Treaty (1992) rather than acknowledging that European citizenship has been a persistent concern for the European Community since 1951. Second, it has treated European citizenship as a static and essentialist concept and failed to acknowledge that its meaning and scope are not fixed. Third, and directly linked to the second, it has failed to show the connection between the context of European integration and the contingently changing meanings of European citizenship. Rather, European citizenship needs to be understood as a 'moveable feast' that has changed in meaning and scope. In turn, these changes need to be understood as relating in different ways to the economic, political and institutional context of European integration. As Shaw put it: '[T]he development of citizenship is related in different ways to other changes of both an institutional and an ideational nature which can be seen within the scope of European integration processes'.[88] As such, the definition of European citizenship—as many other areas in which the Commission worked—'demands (...) pragmatic adaptation to ever-changing reality'.[89]

The Socio-Historical Policy Analysis Approach

The socio-historical policy analysis approach, which was developed by Wiener, Magnette and Kostakopoulou and more recently adopted by Maas and Olsen,[90] has acknowledged the contingent nature of the meaning of European citizenship and its relationship to the European integration context. It has operated according to three main premises: first, that the meaning of European citizenship has changed over time. Specifically, Olsen characterised European citizenship as a concept that 'varies diachronically over time'[91] and Wiener spoke of European citizenship and its 'historical variability'[92] as 'an expression of changes'.[93] Second, that these historical changes in meaning have occurred according to and in direct relation to the political, economic and institutional circumstances of the European integration process. Magnette emphasised that European citizenship was conceived of as a 'dynamic status whose content was to evolve in parallel to the key stages of European integration',[94] whilst Maas argued that 'European citizenship developed through a continuing series of political junctures spanning the entire history of European integration'.[95] Third, that the meaning of European citizenship can be understood through an analysis of discourse. And yet whereas I accept that these three premises are historiographically correct in trying to understand the history of the idea of European citizenship, I would further add the premise that the Commission has been the key institution in attempting to define European citizenship (within the framework set by the Treaties) and that it has used public communication policy and outputs since 1951 to make European citizenship comprehensible and concrete for European citizens.

Based on the recognition of this premise, my approach is different in two ways from the one described above: first, I have prioritised different sources. Whereas Wiener looked at '(1) dossiers and minutes of the EC/EU institutions' meetings; (2) routine by-products of organizational work (...) and (3) records and reports of interactions between governments and members of the Euro-polity (...)',[96] Olsen focused on the 'content of relevant Treaty provisions, policies, policy documents, reform proposals, and actors' perception on citizenship at given instances over the course of European integration'.[97] Magnette adopted a right-based approach to European citizenship (similar to Maas) and analysed treaties, ECJ jurisprudence, policy reports, citizen-related documents and intergovernmental conferences, whilst Kostakopoulou, similarly, focused on citizenship laws and immigration policies. In contrast, I have prioritised public communication policy papers and outputs (such as brochures and speeches) for two reasons: first, already in the 1950s and 1960s the Commission used its public communication policy and outputs to overcome the initial lack of explicit civil competences[98] and as such, it was through its public communication policy that the Commission was able to play out its understanding of European citizenship; and second, public communication policy and outputs need to be understood as the Commission's voice with which it has addressed the European citizenry. Correspondingly, it is in the Commission's public communication policy and outputs that I have located the clearest understanding of the mundane meaning of European citizenship[99] and therefore our greater understanding of the meaning that European citizenship was to have practically for 'real' Europeans.

The second difference from Wiener, Olsen, Magnette and Kostakopoulou concerns the kind of discourse that has been analysed. I argue that there have been five representations of European citizenship which reflect contingent shifts of meaning and the Commission's changing preferences for emphasising different constituent features of European citizenship at various times. Accordingly, and rather than analysing the 'contextualised discourse' of policy and government actors and the discourse of those negotiations that led to construction of citizenship (Wiener and Olsen), I have focused on those terms and concepts that the Commission used to describe European citizens, their European setting and their role in the European integration process in its public communication policy and outputs. In this, my approach is close to that of Magnette, who also focused on the discourse on European citizenship itself by examining how the rhetorical register employed by the European Community changed over time and to what extent the European Community adopted different ways of 'marketing' European citizenship. However, and by extending Magnette's analysis, it was possible to discern the three constituent elements of the representations of European citizenship, which I will turn to below.

The Cosmopolitan Post-national Approach to European Citizenship

With regard to the third, scholars who have taken a cosmopolitan post-national approach to European citizenship are more or less in agreement that the current institutional design of Europe is insufficient to meet the basic necessities of a new form of post-national citizenship, which Europe needs if European citizenship was to be at all meaningful (although some scholars have been more optimistic than others with regard to the future of Europe). Where cosmopolitan citizenship has been extended beyond simply consisting of a political-economic identity to include legal, constitutional, civil, cultural, and social matters[100] Europe has been described as 'moving towards' a 'new' form of cosmopolitanism. For example, Beck argued that 'a new cosmopolitanism is in the air' and that a new cosmopolitan Europe 'would be a social Europe of workers and citizens in the making, a Europe that would encompass the struggles for democratic legitimacy and political responses to global problems in a way that is transparent and of existential importance for the people in their everyday life. And the reason they would give their vote for it'.[101] To this he added that 'horizontal Europeanization is giving rise to new shadow realities that are lived in the blind spots of the aliens' registration office: multilingualism, multinational networks, bi-national marriages, multiple residences, educational mobility, transnational careers, and linkages between science and the economy'.[102]

However, what Beck et al. have failed to realise is that civil and social Europe, a Europe of workers, democratic legitimacy and the Europeanising effect of the Single Market, have all been emphasised at different times since 1951 in the way the Commission has variously understood and represented European citizenship. Indeed, it would be more accurate to say that the issues he referred to have been long-standing and intrinsic to the Commission's representations of European citizenship. As such, and contrary to what Beck might have thought, cosmopolitan Europe has never been an 'excluded third way'.[103] Similarly, Stevenson, who argued that cosmopolitan 'citizenship needs to become as concerned with questions of imagination, identity, recognition and belonging as it has been traditionally with entitlements and obligations'[104] and that 'a democratic identity will have to forge itself in opposition to consumerist inclinations (…)',[105] failed to realise the extent to which non-consumerists' European anxieties and sensibilities have been included in the various representations of European citizenship communicated by the Commission. These anxieties and sensibilities ranged from a concern with perpetual peace, 'hospitality', a rights-based civil-legal order, shared moral standards, civil-spatial policy concerned with history, memory and reconciliation, a vast array of cultural policies concerned with art, sport and music and policies concerned with democratic and civil identity as well as the promotion of 'dialogue and debate'. Indeed, some of these themes sound more like late eighteenth-century Enlightenment concerns than those of a modern Europe conceived of as a Single Market inhabited by consumers. And yet the European Community has persistently concerned itself with these pacific, democratic and civil matters.

It has, in fact, been concerned with identifying in very concrete terms what exactly a European citizen is since 1951,[106] and I argue that the different understandings of European citizenship are best captured as representations.

3   Five Representations of European Citizenship

Skinner argued that the idea of representations was not new but that in fact, visual images have long been considered as being able to exercise powerful effects on the audience. In fact, visual eloquence (i.e. 'matching word and image'[107]) and the tradition of emblem books emerged as part of the humanist tradition in the sixteenth century. As Skinner showed, Thomas Hobbes was enthusiastic about representing his political ideas and arguments visually. He elaborated a 'spectacular emblematic frontispiece'[108] for his translation of Thucydides. His works *De Cive* and *Leviathan* were both accompanied by 'frontispieces of fascinating complexity'.[109] These representations of the works' political ideas, main actors or key events can be seen as an expression of the idea that 'the most effective means of moving and persuading an audience will always be to supply its members with an *imago* or picture of whatever we want them to hold in their minds'.[110]

Skinner (referring to Quintilian) further noted that the force of images was deeply believed in so much so that orators have attempted to turn auditors into spectators by employing language 'with so much vividness and immediacy that our audience comes to 'see' what we are trying to describe'[111]. They have attempted to help the audience form "mental pictures"—'visiones or, adapting the Greek term fantasias' so that 'images of things absent come to be present to the mind, in consequence of which we appear to see them before our very eyes' (here Skinner quotes Quintilian). Skinner further explained that the 'indispensable talent is that of 'fancying', creating a fantasia of the scene or action we wish to describe'.[112] Accordingly and in this book, by representation I mean a portrait of the European civil identity the Commission imagined European citizens to have at a certain period of European integration.

These representations can be understood as the Commission's '"plastic power", its own way of actively and creatively interpreting'[113] European citizenship. The force of these representations is their synoptic simplicity, their evocative resonances and promissory narrative. The representations are my attempt to contribute some visual imagery to the history of European civil integration and European citizenship. The representations of European citizenship capture the mundane meaning of European citizenship for 'real' Europeans. What I have attempted to achieve is an evocation in the reader's mind of the different ways in which European citizens were imagined[114] and subsequently represented in public communication. These representations ranged from the first representation of the European coal and steel workers who, seeing a chance of employment in another member state, used their newly acquired European citizens' rights and moved from Italy to the Ruhr area, from Belgium to the Saarland and from Germany to the Campine region and took (encouraged by the Community) their families with them, to the most recent representation of the European citizen as a consumer and user of the Single Market who is worried about his cross-border rights in diverse areas of life—shopping online or offline, marriage and divorce, birth and death, writing a will and inheriting, travelling, studying, working, founding a business, health care, law, diploma recognition and car registration. I have discussed each of the five representations analytically and in terms of the way each can be sketched. Each sketch is a quasi-fictional summative representation which, when linked together, form an uninterrupted civil narrative of who the European citizen was imagined to be during a specific period of the European integration process. To borrow Alexander's terms, 'while their materiality is an illusion, their factuality is not: it is useful'.[115] They are quasi-fictional if for no other reason than there was (and arguably still is) simply no European civil society European citizens could belong to nor was there *then* an institutional basis that would have structurally supported any potentially emerging European civil society. Nevertheless, by writing about these five representations, they enter 'into history as meanings'.[116]

Analytically, each representation was composed of three elements: first, a distinct lexicon which framed the civil identity of the European citizen; second, a specific spatial story or narrative through which the Commission represented the environmental setting the imagined European citizen lived in; and third, the use of different styles of public communication. I will take each of these three elements in turn before giving an overview of how these three elements combined in each representation.

First, with regard to the linguistic element of each of the five representations of European citizenship, I identified five corresponding lexica: first, the economic-social lexicon; second, the political-federal lexicon; third, the political-dialogical lexicon; fourth, the civil-spatial lexicon and fifth, the civil-legal lexicon. Each of these lexica comprised of specific terms, concepts, metaphors, symbols and phrases and it was through the use of these lexica that the Commission discursively shaped the meaning of European citizenship during a specific period of European integration. In other words, and to borrow Schrag Sternberg's[117] words, the lexica helped to 'historically [reconstruct] changing discursive landscapes of competing ideas on what constitutes' European civil identity in various contexts.[118] I return to each of these lexica in their particular and differential detail when analysing the representations in the following chapters.

With regard to the second element, space, in each representation the Commission promoted and depicted a particular spatial story or narrative,[119] which I have captured by adopting Ruggie's conception of space as either 'single-perspectival' or 'multiperspectival'.[120] The spatial conception of each representation reflected the Commission's changing understanding and use of Community space in the public communication of European citizenship. Simply put, single-perspectival space can be understood as a uniquely horizontal territory. In other words, the single-perspectival conception of Community space was exclusively concerned with the Community level and excluded vertical levels such as the national, regional and local levels. Multiperspectival space, on the other hand, was defined across two essential characteristics. First, space was understood as a network of different levels. These levels included the Community level as well as the national, regional and local levels. Second, multiperspectival space was not only conceived of in terms of physical space but also included virtual spaces such as audiovisual space and the Internet.

The third element to the Commission's representation of European citizenship consisted of how the representation was publicly communicated. When publicly communicating the representations of European citizenship the Commission used three different styles of public communication in order to effectively engage with European citizens. These three styles were the factual style of public communication, the affective style of public communication and the deliberative-rational style of public communication. They were discernible and used in each representation in varying combinations depending on the Commission's conceptions of how to 'teach', 'educate', 'engage with', 'debate with', 'dialogue with' or 'deliberate with' European citizens about issues of European integration. To take each style in turn:

The factual style of public communication was—as the term indicates—primarily concerned with providing facts about the European integration process and unambiguous information (statistical and descriptive). Through the factual style of public communication, the Commission provided European citizens with what it referred to as 'descriptive accounts', 'illustrated descriptions', 'illustrated chronological accounts' and 'comprehensive guides'. The factual style of public communication had the straightforward purpose of informing European citizens about the existence, historical development and the function of the European Community and its institutions. Accordingly, public communication outputs in the factual style of public communication (brochures, pamphlets, reports) frequently presented historical timelines to describe key events and significant developments of the European integration process. To do this, the Commission used short texts, information boxes, simple and clear statistics, and sometimes cartoons or pictures of photos of significant moments in the history of the Community or of Community symbols to illustrate historical developments (see chapter "Homo Oeconomicus (1951–1972)" for more detail and examples). The factual style of public communication can be considered overall as an attempt to provide a truthful, detached account of European integration. As such, these accounts also allowed for some self-criticism, such as having been 'overambitious', acknowledging 'failures' and pointing to difficulties and disagreement between key actors on certain policy areas. At the same time, they informed European citizens about successfully completed initiatives. The language used in the factual style of public communication was clear, plain and simple. Sentences were kept short, were clearly structured (for example, sentences without sub-clauses or dependent clauses) and avoided extensive use of adjectives and adverbs.

The affective style of public communication was characterised by its partiality and emotional tone: value judgements were made explicitly and implicitly in favour of the European Community and of European integration per se. The affective style of public communication had the intention of stimulating a 'common fondness' for European integration and an appreciation of the benefits it brings. Specifically, it was most frequently been used in relation to several recurring themes such as solidarity, mutual understanding between European citizens, a feeling of belonging to the Community and European identity based on European culture, common values and shared symbols.[121]

This style was used in three discrete ways. First, the Commission tried to stimulate a feeling of belonging and civil solidarity through the use of political-federal symbols. These included such things as the Community flag, the anthem, the emblem, European driving licences and the uniform passport[122] as well as the paraphernalia attached to Community sports events and youth events. Second, the affective style of public communication was characterised by its use of possessive pronouns and value-laden terms suggesting civil solidarity and unity. Both were used in slogans, brochure titles and the Commission's discourse on European citizenship to stimulate an emotional linkage, an almost personal and affective relationship, of European citizens to Europe. Examples of possessive pronouns included: '**your** rights', 'Europe and **its** citizens', '**our** peoples', '**your** Europe', 'a people's Europe' and 'Citizens' Europe', which were found in texts and in the titles of public communication brochures.[123] Related to this, the affective style of public communication also made use of solidary terms such as 'together' or 'togetherness' and references to the Community as a 'home' and to the European citizenry as the 'great European family'. The affective style was most evident in the De Clercq Report, which emphasised that 'Europe must be presented with a human face: sympathetic, warm and caring' and it 'must be brought to the people, implicitly evoking the maternal, nurturing care of "Europa" for all her children'[124] through using an affective vocabulary and emphasising terms such as 'warm', 'caring,' 'maternal' and 'sympathetic'. In parallel, the De Clercq Report (1993) rejected the factual style of public communication as 'boring, irrelevant and "cold"'[125] and promoted a form of public communication that would 'reassure'[126] and 'emotionally involve the citizens of Europe in the building of Europe'.[127] It was badly received by the press when it was released at a press briefing—so badly that for the first time journalists 'staged a mass walkout in protest'.[128]

Third, the Commission used personal stories which again had the purpose of stimulating a feeling of civil solidarity amongst European citizens. The use of these stories was based upon the belief that European civil solidarity would arise when European citizens realised they had the same questions with regard to exercising their citizens' rights regardless of wherever they were in the EU. An example of these personal stories was found in the EU citizenship Report of 2010 and 2013: 'Chiara, who lives in Italy, has found a digital camera on the website of a Bulgarian electronics shop at a much lower price than in her home town. However, she is reluctant to buy it online from Bulgaria. She wonders: 'What happens if the camera gets lost or damaged during delivery?' Will she be able to send it back to the seller if she doesn't like it, as she could do in Italy? How long does she have to send it back?'[129]

The deliberative-rational style of public communication was rarely used between 1951 and 1992 but became increasingly important in the Commission's public communication efforts after the difficult ratification process of the Maastricht Treaty (1992) and what was perceived as a failure of the affective style of public communication (see chapters "A People's Europe (1973–1992)" and "Europe of Transparency (1993–2004))". It was a style which depended upon the deliberate conflation of the medium and the message. In other words, the deliberative-rational style of public communication existed at two levels: its advocacy and its use through both the Commission and European citizens' participation in it. Basically, the Commission advocated idealisations of informed Commission–public democratic deliberation and then sought to facilitate these deliberations and communicative opportunities to 'engage with', 'debate with', 'dialogue with' or hold an 'enlightened and reasonable debate'. These collaborative forms of mutual engagement between the Commission and the European citizen sought to take advantage of the Internet and the possibilities it offered for online consultations and debate and dialogue. The deliberative-rational style of public communication was premised on the Commission's belief that informed European citizens are more likely to be disposed towards Europe than those who are not so well informed. Accordingly, the deliberative-rational styles of public communication and the factual style of public communication go hand in hand, since it was believed by the Commission that public debates, dialogues and deliberations which took place amongst European citizens or between European citizens and the EU institutions depended per se upon factual information presented in a clear and simple way. In other words, the deliberative-rational style placed great value on the idea of promoting and establishing forms of immediate two-way communication between European citizens and the EU institutions. It was believed that this two-way communication could be realised in a combination of face-to-face debates in physical spaces on Community, national, regional or local levels or in virtual spaces such as Internet fora.

These three elements of the representations of European citizenship—the lexica, the spatial conception and the style of public communication—were found in the sources I consulted. It should be made abundantly clear, however, that none of the five representations was found in its entirety in a single document and that the titles I ascribe to them are my own descriptors.

As to how these three elements of each of the five representations of European citizenship combined, it is necessary to provide a schematic overview of the five representations of European citizenship:

- Representation 1: **Homo Oeconomicus: economic-social citizenship (1951–1972)**
  This baseline representation emphasised economic and social rights. It described the civil identity of the European citizen through the use of an economic-social lexicon. It used a single-perspectival conception of European space and was communicated using an essentially factual style of public communication.

- Representation 2: **Political-federal citizenship in 'A People's Europe' (1973–1992)**
  This representation emphasised political participation, European identity and culture. It described the civil identity of the European citizen through the use of a political-federal lexicon. It used a single-perspectival conception of European space and was communicated using an affective style of public communication.

- Representation 3: **Political-dialogical citizenship in a 'Europe of Transparency' (1993–2004)**
  This representation emphasised political dialogue as well as the right to civil scrutiny of the European institutions and governance. It described the civil identity of the European citizen through the use of a political-dialogical lexicon. For the first time, the Commission represented European space as multiperspectival and introduced the deliberative-rational style of public communication.

- Representation 4: **Civil-spatial citizenship in a 'Europe of Agorai'** (2005–2009)
  This representation emphasised political deliberation, the establishment and the use of European public spaces and the development of civil communicative institutions. It described the civil identity of the European citizen through the use of a civil-spatial lexicon. It used a more sophisticated multiperspectival conception of European space and was communicated using a combination of the deliberative-rational and factual styles of public communication.

- Representation 5: **Civil-legal citizenship in a 'Europe of Rights'** (2010–14)
  This representation emphasised Single Market consumer rights. It described the civil identity of the European citizen through the use of a civil-legal lexicon. This representation showed a return to the use of a single-perspectival conception of European space. It was communicated using the factual style of public communication with some affective elements.

These five representations of European citizenship only acquire their full meaning through their contextualisation within the political, institutional and historical contexts of European integration. In this way, each representation is time-specific. Accordingly, each of the following chapters begins with an examination and analysis of the context in which the representation of European citizenship emerged. The context presented is vital to understanding why a particular representation of European citizenship emerged at the time it did and what it meant to be a European citizen in these specific circumstances.[130]

Overall, my argument in this book is simply this: With each representation of European citizenship and its subsequent public communication, the Commission attempted to portray European citizens in such a way that the peoples of Europe could come to recognise themselves as European. This was important for the Commission because it believed that successful European integration depended on Europeans identifying with the European project. In other words, the Commission continuously pursued a single civil aim: to stimulate a European civil consciousness which was seen as a precondition for the emergence of an active European civil society. It was the Commission's unchanging civil aim that provided the premise for the representations of European citizenship which together in turn, I hope, go some little way to explicate a continuous but little-appreciated European civil narrative.

Notes

1. Cini (1996), Nicoll and Salmon (1997), Nugent (2001), Van Oudenaren (2005).
2. Coombes (1970: 78).
3. Ibid.
4. Haas (1958: 456 cited in Schrag Sternberg 2013: 29).
5. I have used the term European Community to refer to the EU and all previous European Communities since 1951. Throughout European Community and Community and Europe have been used as synonyms. I have used the term EU for the period post-Maastricht.
6. Lerner and Gordon (1969: 281).
7. Hallstein (1970, cited in Loth 2007: 89)
8. The High Authority (HA) can be seen as the precursor to today's Commission. The term 'High Authority' has been used to refer to the period 1951–1958 of the European Community and 'European Commission' to refer to (a) the European Commission from 1958 on, or (b) when making overall historical judgements about the period 1951–2014 or periods where the existence of the High Authority and the Commission overlapped. As such, the use of the term 'Commission' has sometimes been used anachronistically for reasons of simplicity and clarity.
9. I have used the term public communication to refer to the information policy and the communication policy of the Commission. Historically, the Commission did use the term 'information policy' exclusively until the 1980s, when a distinction between 'information' and 'communication' began to be made (on the definition of information and communication see EP 1998).
10. Kaiser (2011: 392).
11. On Hallstein, his life and personality and European vision, see Hallstein (1962a, 1972), Fragnière (1995), Loth et al. (1998), Zuleeg (2003), Loth (2007), Calliano (2012) and Piela (2012).
12. See Lukaszewski (1984), Balace et al. (2004) and Conrad (2007) on Jean Rey.
13. See Van der Harst (2007).
14. On 'personalities of European integration', see Gouzy (1968), which included a historical account of the beginnings of the European Community between WWII and the Messina Conference; Jansen and Mahncke (1981) and Bossuat (1994).
15. The High Authority faced stiff resistance in their attempts to publicly communicate European citizenship by, notably, the Council and some of the member states, especially France (see Dumoulin 2007).
16. In fact, this aim was articulated in various reports, especially throughout the 1960s and 1970s (EP 1960, Caron 1963, Commission 1963, 1964,

1965, 1967, 1968). See also Pourvoyeur (1981) and Rabier (personal communication, 20.4.2012).
17. Alexander (2006: 43).
18. Alexander (2006: 54)
19. Alexander (1997: 123).
20. For example Weber (1949, 1978).
21. Hallstein (1959: 6).
22. Hallstein (1960: 1).
23. Hallstein (1962b: 18).
24. See Dumoulin (2007: 131).
25. Alexander (2006: 31).
26. Ibid.
27. Alexander (2006: 83).
28. Ludlow (1998: 1).
29. Rabier, personal communication, 20.4.2012.
30. Monnet (1952).
31. Coppé (1956), Monnet (1962), Hallstein (1964a, b ,c).
32. Mayer (1957), Hallstein (1962c, e).
33. Hallstein (1958).
34. Hallstein (1969).
35. Hallstein (1962d).
36. Levi Sandri (1962).
37. Levi Sandri (1964).
38. Hallstein (1963: 3).
39. Monnet (1954: 48).
40. Hallstein (1965: 12).
41. Sandel (2005: 34). See especially EP (1960, 1962, 1972).
42. Hallstein (1964c: 7), also Hallstein (1972).
43. Mayer (1956: 1).
44. Ibid.: 5. This complementary character was to be understood in the way that Rabier described Monnet: as a provincial cosmopolitan citizen with deep roots (1998 in an interview with Bossuat).
45. The 'some old hands…' (2007: 16) were cited as the authors of the foreword to Dumoulin (ed.) (2007) 'The European Commission, 1958–1972—History and memories'.
46. See also Monnet (1962).
47. Seidel (2010: 17).
48. Spierenburg and Poidevin (1994: 56).
49. Van Helmont (1981).
50. Kohnstamm (1982: 9).
51. Brugmans (1966: 172, cited in Coombes 1970: 21)
52. Coombes (1970: 309).

53. Ibid.: 309f.
54. Seidel (2010).
55. Rabier, personal communication, 26 May 2013. On the crises of the 1960s, see Ludlow (2006).
56. Rabier, personal communication, 18 June 2012.
57. Etzioni (1965).
58. Monnet (1964).
59. Rabier (1965).
60. See, for example, Monnet (1952, 1962), Coppé (1956), Hallstein (1959, 1964a). Interestingly, these shared values started to become a part—albeit indirectly—of the European Treaties. The preamble of the Treaty of Rome (1957) establishing the European Economic Community (EEC) references the Charter of the United Nations, which emphasised the same values the Commission was promoting in official speeches: human rights, the dignity and worth of the human person, equal rights of men, justice and respect and freedom.
61. The achievement of peace amongst the nations of Europe has been a recurrent theme in all of the preambles to the European Treaties since 1951.
62. Israel (2011).
63. The European movement appealed to the same values Europeans have in common.
64. It needs to be noted, however, that no explicit references to the Enlightenment were found in either the Treaties or official Commission speeches.
65. Hallstein (1964a: 26).
66. See Schulz-Forberg (2012).
67. 'Some old hands of an institution who were there at the birth and watched it grow' (2007: 11; authors of the foreword to Dumoulin (ed.)).
68. Ibid.: 13.
69. This was also reflected in the way these early Commission officials could be characterised. Seidel (2010) divided Commission officials into three opposing pairs, one of which was the 'realistic idealist' and the 'pragmatist'.
70. Cited in Seidel (2010: 148).
71. Monnet (1955: 46 cited in Petit 2006: 664).
72. On the importance of public communication policy since 1951, see Harrison and Pukallus (2015).
73. Interview, Commission official, DG JUS (name of interviewee and date of interview are confidential).
74. Sophie Bernaeerts (then Head of Unit at European Commission, DG Communication—Citizens' Policy Unit C2 of Directorate), personal communication, 11 October 2011.

75. Ibid.
76. Joachim Ott, personal communication, October 2011.
77. Kalmo and Skinner (2010: 11).
78. Geuss (1994: 282) quoting from Nietzsche's Genealogy of Morals (GM) 11.13 (emphasis in the original).
79. Ibid.
80. Ibid.
81. I have borrowed this question from Bartelson (1995), who posed it with regard to sovereignty. Schrag Sternberg (2013) asked a similar question with regard to European legitimacy and argued that the meaning of legitimacy was constructed in discourse and that its meaning depended on context. See also Bostanci (2013).
82. Marshall (1992 [1949]).
For various accounts of EU citizenship, see Close (1995), Rosas and Antola (1995) (eds.), Schnapper (1997), Wiener (1997), Follesdal (2001, 2007), Magnette (1998, 1999, 2007), Delgado Moreira (2000), Lehning (2001), Prentoulis (2001), Jamieson (2002), Schuster and Solomos (2002), Shore (2004), Vink (2005), Bellamy (2006, 2008), Kostakopoulou (2005, 2007, 2008), Weale (2005), Besson and Utzinger (2007), Beata (2007), Epinay (2007), Goudappel (2010).
83. D'Oliveira (1995), O'Leary (1996), Meehan (1993, 1996, 2000); Cheneval (2007).
84. Neunreither (1995), Bauböck (1997), Roche (1997), Schmitter (2000), Bellamy (2001), Warleigh (2001).
85. Dunkerley et al. (2002), Dwyer (2004).
86. Title of Vink's (2004) paper.
87. Shaw (2007: 41).
88. Hallstein (1958, cited in Loth and Bitsch 2007: 57).
89. Wiener (1998), Magnette (1999), Kostakopoulou (2001), Maas (2007), Olsen (2008, 2012).
90. Olsen (2012: 4).
91. Wiener (1998: 42).
92. Ibid.: 12.
93. Magnette (1999: 205).
94. Maas (2007: 8). See Maas (2013) on his understanding of citizenship as multilevel rather than exclusively nation-based.
95. Wiener (1997: 15).
96. Olsen (2012: 9/10).
97. Harrison and Pukallus (2015).
98. This is not to say that all citizenship policies only emerged in public communication policy. Rather, I agree with Wiener (1998: 42) that citizenship 'cannot be located in just one policy area'—nevertheless, public

communication policy papers and outputs brought all citizenship-relevant policy areas together.

Offe (2000, 2002), Habermas (2001), Stevenson (2003, 2005), Beck (2006) and Eriksen (2008)—for a categorisation of cosmopolitanism see Held (2010).

99. Beck (2005).
100. Ibid., also Beck (2011).
101. Beck (2011).
102. Stevenson (2003: 35f.).
103. Ibid.: 41.
104. Although it can be argued that the actual term 'European citizenship' was only rarely used in the first two decades of European integration, the concept of European citizen was understood and appealed to from the very beginning of the ECSC (1951).
105. Skinner (2008: 7).
106. Ibid.
107. Ibid.: 13.
108. Ibid.: 7.
109. Ibid.: 183.
110. Ibid.
111. See Mahon (1992: 96).
112. Hooghe (2001) used the idea of 'images' with regard to European governance. Her approach was more technical than mine and looked at binary images such as 'Intergovernmentalism or supranationalism', 'Europe as ends or means' or 'Political mobilization or exploiting institutional asymmetry'. Bottici and Challand (2014) focused on how the way in which Europe has been imagined and understood has changed over time as well as how and why some historical narratives have turned into what one could refer to as 'political' myth. Their analysis extended beyond the European Community. On European political myths, see Bostanci (2013) and the Journal of Common Market Studies special issue (2010, 48(1)) on Political Myth, Mythology and the European Union edited by Vincent della Sala.
113. Alexander (2011: 3).
114. Ibid.
115. Schrag Sternberg (2013: 2).
116. Of course, I am not suggesting—to borrow Hopf's (2002: 3) words—'that identities are intentionally or deliberately chosen, used, and/or strategically manipulated' but am recognising the fact that the identities of both Europe and European citizens are not fixed (Bee 2008, also Pantel 1999). In a similar vein, Delanty (1995: 1) wrote 'the book [Inventing Europe] is about how every age invented the idea of Europe in the mirror

of its own identity', a view which is similar to my claim that European citizenship mirrors a certain period of European integration and the way the Commission understood the EU at a particular moment. Delanty (ibid.: 3) further argued that 'Europe is more than a region and polity, it is also an idea and an identity' and 'also a geo-political reality' (ibid.: 7) and that 'the sociological concept of a "discourse" [that] can help to explain this' (ibid.).

117. I am suggesting that the Commission, whether it knew it or not, showed an understanding of space which seems to me similar to Massey's (2005) definition of space. Massey (2005: 9) argued that there were three defining characteristics of space. These were first, space as the product of interrelations; second, space as the 'sphere of the possibility of the existence of multiplicity in the sense of contemporaneous plurality' and third, space as 'always under construction', as a set of 'stories-so-far'. As for the first characteristic, the Commission conceived of space as being able to provide European citizens with the increased possibility of greater 'interrelations' across historically and culturally defined borders. With regard to the second characteristic, plurality, the Commission has pursued a pluralist identity policy in which a plurality of citizens from different nations (28 at the time of writing) were always conceived of as 'united in diversity'. So conceived by the Commission, European spaces—as distinct from purely national, regional and locally defined spaces—have literally been the setting where the European slogan 'Unity in Diversity' could be concretely played out and performed both immediately (physically) and remotely (communicatively). With regard to the third characteristic, open-endedness of space, I argued that European citizenship is a dynamic and diachronically evolving concept. As such, the spatial story that accompanied the identity narrative of European citizenship was subject to the same dynamics and as such both European citizenship and European space have always been 'under construction'.
118. Ruggie (1993, 1998).
119. On European symbols, see Shore (2000), Foret (2003, 2008, 2010), Theiler (2005), Sonntag (2010), Manners (2011), Fornäs (2012), Krumrey (2013) and chapter "A People's Europe (1973–1992)".
120. Other ideas included postage stamps and a European identity card.
121. European employment and social policy: a policy **for people** (2000), It's **your** Europe—Living, learning and working anywhere in the EU (2003), Freedom to move and live in Europe—A guide to **your** rights as an EU citizen (2010b) and **your** guide to the Lisbon Treaty (2010c). All emphases are mine.
122. EP (1993: 9).
123. Ibid.: 10.

124. Ibid.: 47.
125. Ibid.: 19.
126. Podkalicka and Shore (2010: 98).
127. Commission (2010a: 13).
128. In this way, my approach is close to Wæver (2009) because it takes up the key question of the meaning and representation of European citizenship in the context of the relevant period of European integration.

REFERENCES

Alexander, J. (1997). The paradoxes of civil society. *International Sociology, 12*(2), 115–133.

Alexander, J. (2006). *The civil sphere.* Oxford: Oxford University Press.

Alexander, J. (2011). *Performative revolution in Egypt: An essay in cultural power.* London: Bloomsbury.

Balace, F., DeClercq, W., & Planchard, R. (2004). *Jean Rey: liégeois, européen, homme politique. Actes de la commémoration Jean Rey 1902–2002.* Liège: Éditions de l'Université de Liège.

Bartelson, J. (1995). *A genealogy of sovereignty.* Cambridge: Cambridge University Press.

Bauböck, R. (1997). *Citizenship and national identities in the European Union.* Harvard Law School, Jean Monnet Chair (Working Papers Series 4/1997).

Beata, S. (2007). *European citizenship: Past, present and future.* Saarbrücken: VDM Verlag Dr. Mueller e.K.

Beck, U. (2005). Re-inventing Europe: A cosmopolitan vision. Talk given at the Centre de Cultura Contemporania de Barcelona on 27th October. http://www.publicspace.org/en/text-library/eng/b004-re-inventing-europe-a-cosmopolitan-vision. Accessed 17 Oct 2011.

Beck, U. (2006). *The cosmopolitan vision.* Cambridge: Polity.

Beck, U. (2011). Cosmopolitanism can set Europe aright. *Die Zeit* 11.7.2011. http://www.presseurop.eu/en/content/article/751391-cosmopolitanism-can-set-europe-aright. Accessed 13 Nov 2011.

Bee, C. (2008). The institutionally constructed European identity: Public sphere and citizenship narrated by the Commission. *Perspectives on European Politics and Society, 9*(4), 431–450.

Bellamy, R. (2001). The 'right to have rights': Citizenship practice and the political constitution of the EU. In R. Bellamy & A. Warleigh (Eds.), *Citizenship and governance in the European Union* (pp. 41–70). London: Continuum.

Bellamy, R. (2006). Between past and future: The democratic limits of EU citizenship. In R. Bellamy, D. Castiglione, & J. Shaw (Eds.), *Making European citizens: Civic inclusion in a transnational context* (pp. 238–265). New York: Palgrave Macmillan.

Bellamy, R. (2008). Evaluating Union citizenship: Belonging, rights and participation within the EU. *Citizenship Studies, 12*(6), 597–611.
Besson, S., & Utzinger, A. (2007). Introduction: Future challenges of European citizenship—Facing a wide-open Pandora's box. *European Law Journal, 13*(5), 573–590.
Bossuat, G. (1994). *Les fondateurs de l'Europe.* Paris: Belin.
Bostanci, A. (2013). Making the mythical European: Elucidating the EU's powerful integration instrument of discursive identity construction. *Perspectives on European Politics and Society, 14*(2), 172–184.
Bottici, C., & Challand, B. (2014). *Imagining Europe.* Cambridge: Cambridge University Press.
Brugmans, H. (1966). L'idée européenne, 1918–1965, Cahiers de Bruges, N-S 12. Bruges.
Calliano, O. (2012). La supranationalitè, kainologisme institutionnel pour la création du consensus au processus d'intégration européenne. In D. Preda & D. Pasquinucci (Eds.), *Consensus and European integration. An historical perspective [sic]* (pp. 41–54). Brussels: Peter Lang.
Caron, G. (1963, Janvier 28). *Comment informer l'Europe des problèmes du marché commun?* Expose de M. Giuseppe Caron, Vice-President de la Commission de la Communauté économique européenne à l'Université de Liège.
CCE (Commission des Communautés Européennes). (1963, Juin 26). *Mémorandum sur la politique des Communautés en matière d'information à l'attention des Conseils* (COM (63) 242).
CCE (Commission des Communautés Européennes). (1964, Février 3). *Programme d'activité pour 1964* (Doc no. 1383/PI/64-F).
CCE (Commission des Communautés Européennes). (1965, Avril 9). *Document de travail sur les activités prioritaires d'information à développer en 1965–1966* (Doc no. 5044/PI/65-F).
CCE (Commission des Communautés Européennes). (1967, Juin 1). *Mémorandum sur la politique d'information de la Commission.*
CCE (Commission des Communautés Européennes). (1968). *Document sur la politique d'information de la Commission* (Doc no 4279/1/PI/68F), (no date).
CCE (Commission des Communautés Européennes). (2003). *It's your Europe—Living, learning and working anywhere in the EU.* Luxembourg: Office for Official Publications of the European Communities.
CCE (Commission des Communautés Européennes). (2010a, October 27). *EU citizenship report 2010. Dismantling the obstacles to EU citizens' rights* (COM (2010) 603 final).
CCE (Commission des Communautés Européennes). (2010b). *Freedom to move and live in Europe—A guide to your rights as an EU citizen.* Luxembourg: Publications Office of the European Union.

CCE (Commission des Communautés Européennes). (2010c). *Your guide to the Lisbon Treaty*. Luxembourg: Publications Office of the European Union.

Cheneval, F. (2007). Caminante, no hay camino, se hace camino al andar: EU citizenship, direct democracy and treaty ratification. *European Law Journal, 13*(5), 647–663.

Cini, M. (1996). *The European Commission: Leadership, organisation and culture in the EU administration*. Manchester: Manchester University Press.

Close, P. (1995). *Citizenship, Europe and change*. Basingstoke: Palgrave Macmillan.

Conrad, Y. (2007). Jean Rey, moderate optimist and instinctive European. In M. Dumoulin (Ed.), *The European Commission, 1958–72. History and memories* (pp. 109–123). Luxembourg: Office for Official Publications of the European Communities.

Coombes, D. (1970). *Politics and bureaucracy in the European Community*. London: George Allen and Unwin.

Coppé, A. (1956). Speech by Albert Coppé, Vice-President of the High Authority, *ECSC on efforts toward European unity*.

D'Oliveira, H. U. J. (1995). Union citizenship: A pie in the sky? In A. Rosas & E. Antola (Eds.), *A citizen's Europe. In search of a new order* (pp. 58–84). London: Sage.

Delanty, G. (1995). *Inventing Europe: Idea, identity, reality*. London: Macmillan.

Delgado Moreira, J. M. (2000). Cohesion and citizenship in EU cultural policy. *Journal of Common Market Studies, 38*(3), 449–470.

Dumoulin, Michel (Ed.). (2007). *The European Commission, 1958–72. History and memories* (pp. 125–151). Luxembourg: Office for Official Publications of the European Communities.

Dunkerley, D., et al. (2002). *Changing Europe: Identities, nations and citizens*. London: Routledge.

Dwyer, P. (2004). *Understanding social citizenship: Themes and perspectives for policy and practice*. Bristol: Policy Press.

EP. (1960, November 18). *Bericht im Namen des politischen Ausschusses über die Probleme der Information in den Europäischen Gemeinschaften* (Berichterstatter Schuijt). Europäisches Parlament Sitzungsdokumente 1960–1961 (Dokument 89).

EP. (1962, November 14). *Bericht im Namen des politischen Ausschusses über die Tätigkeit der Informationsdienste der Europäischen Gemeinschaften* (Berichterstatter Schuijt). Europäisches Parlament Sitzungsdokumente 1962–1963 (Dokument 103).

EP. (1972, Februar 7). *Bericht im Namen des politischen Ausschusses über die Informationspolitik der Europäischen Gemeinschaften* (Berichterstatter Schuijt), Europäisches Parlament Sitzungsdokumente 1971–1972 (Dokument 246/71).

EP. (1993) *Reflection on Information and Communication Policy of the European Community* (De Clercq Report) OP-EC/3240, March.

EP. (1998, Mai 5). *Rapport sur la politique d'information et de communication dans l'Union européenne de Peter Pex en Commission de la culture, de la jeunesse, de l'éducation et des médias (Pex Report)* (A4-0115/98).
Epinay, A. (2007). The scope of article 12 EC: Some remarks on the influence of European citizenship. *European Law Journal, 13*(5), 611–622.
Eriksen, E. (2008). The EU: A cosmopolitan vanguard? Paper to the ECPR fourth pan-European conference on EU politics, University of Latvia, Riga. http://www.jhubc.it/ecpr-riga/virtualpaperroom/038.pdf. Accessed 13 Mar 2012.
Etzioni, A. (1965). *Political unification*. New York: Holt, Rinehart and Winston.
Follesdal, A. (2001). Union citizenship: Unpacking the beast of burden. *Law and Philosophy, 20*(3), 313–343.
Follesdal, A. (2007). If Union citizenship is the right answer, what is the question? In S. Piattoni & R. Scartezzini (Eds.), *European citizenship: Theories, arenas, levels* (pp. 123–134). Baden-Baden: Nomos. http://www.follesdal.net/publ.htm. Accessed 12 Sept 2011.
Foret, F. (2003). L'Europe comme tout: La représentation symbolique de l'Union européenne dans le discours institutionnel. In S. Saurugger (Ed.), *Les modes de représentation dans l'Union européenne* (pp. 177–204). Paris: L'Harmattan.
Foret, F. (2008). *Légitimer l'Europe. Pouvoir et symbolique à l'ère de la gouvernance*. Paris: Sciences Po.
Foret, F. (2010). European political rituals: A challenging tradition in the making. *International Political Anthropology, 3*(1), 55–77.
Fornäs, J. (2012). *Signifying €urope*. Bristol: Intellect.
Fragnière, G. (1995). *Walter Hallstein ou…une pédagogie politique pour la Fédération européenne*. Bruxelles: Presses interuniversitaires européennes.
Geuss, R. (1994). Nietzsche and genealogy. *European Journal of Philosophy, 2*(3), 274–292.
Goudappel, F. (2010). *The effects of EU citizenship: Economic, social and political rights in a time of constitutional change*. The Hague: T.M.C. Asser Press.
Gouzy, J. P. (1968). *Les Pionniers de l'Europe communautaire*. Lausanne: Fondation Jean Monnet pour l'Europe et Centre de recherches européennes.
Haas, E. (1958). *The uniting of Europe: Political, social, and economic forces 1950–57*. Stanford: Stanford University Press.
Habermas, J. (2001). Why Europe needs a constitution. *New Left Review, 11*, 5–26.
Hallstein, W. (1958, July 3). Address by Professor Walter Hallstein, President of the Commission of the European Economic Community, at the opening of the conference of the member states of the European Economic Community. Stresa.
Hallstein, W. (1959, November 10). *Europe is on the move: Political and economic policies*. Speech by Professor Dr. Walter Hallstein, President of the Commission, European Economic Community, delivered to the Royal Institute of International Relations. Brussels.

Hallstein, W. (1960, June 24) Speech at the Joint session of the EP and the Consultative Assembly of the Council of Europe

Hallstein, W. (1962a). *United Europe: Challenge and opportunity.* Cambridge, MA: Harvard University Press.

Hallstein, W. (1962b, April 17). *The economics of European integration.* The William L. Clayton Lecture Series, 1961–1962. Delivered by Professor Walter Hallstein, President of the Commission of the European Economic Community, at the Fletcher School of Law and Diplomacy, Tufts University. Medford, Massachusetts.

Hallstein, W. (1962c, October 22). *The European communities as the foundation of the political union of Europe.* Address by Professor Dr. Walter Hallstein, President of the Commission of the European Economic Community, before the Europa-Union. Bad Godesberg.

Hallstein, W. (1962d, December 10). Address by Professor Dr. Walter Hallstein, President of the Commission of the European Economic Community, delivered at the opening of the European conference on social security. Brussels.

Hallstein, W. (1962e, April 2). *The establishment of European unity.* Summary of an address by Professor Walter Hallstein, President of the Commission of the European Economic Community, to Dutch students. The Hague.

Hallstein, W. (1963, April). *The European Community, a new path to peaceful union.* Lectures given by Prof. Walter Hallstein, President of the Commission of the European Economic Community, to the Indian Council for Cultural Relations in memory of Maulana Abul Kalam Azad.

Hallstein, W. (1964a). *The unity of the drive for Europe.* Address by Professor Dr. Walter Hallstein, President of the Commission of the European Economic Community, at the opening session of the seventh conference of European local authorities. Rome, 15 October.

Hallstein, W. (1964b, March 19). Speech on the occasion of the ceremony of laying the inaugural stone of the new building made available to the European School by the Belgian government. Brussels.

Hallstein, W. (1964c, December 4). *Some of our 'faux problemes'.* Speech by Walter Hallstein, President of the Commission of the European Economic Community. Fourteenth Sir David Stevenson memorial lecture of the Royal Institute of International Affairs, Chatham House, Community Topics 17. London.

Hallstein, W. (1965, April 24). Address given at the opening of the Hanover Fair by Professor Dr. Walter Hallstein, President of the Commission of the European Economic Community. Hanover.

Hallstein, W. (1969, May 5). Speech (on European integration) delivered by Professor Dr. Walter Hallstein, President of the European Movement, to the European Luncheon Club. London.

Hallstein, W. (1972). *Europe in the making.* London: Allen and Unwin.

Harrison, J., & Pukallus, S. (2015). The European Community's public communication policy 1951–1967. *Contemporary European History, 24*(2), 233–251.

Held, D. (2010). *Cosmopolitanism: Ideals and realities.* London: Polity Press.
Hooghe, L. (2001). *The European Commission and the integration of Europe. Images of governance.* Cambridge: Cambridge University Press.
Hopf, T. (2002). *Social construction of international politics: Identities and foreign policies.* Ithaca/London: Cornell University Press.
Israel, J. (2011). *A revolution of the mind.* Princeton: Princeton University Press.
Jamieson, L. (2002). Theorising identity, nationality and citizenship: Implications for European citizenship identity. *Sociológia, 34*(6), 507–532.
Jansen, T., & Mahncke, D. (Eds.). (1981). *Persönlichkeiten der Europäischen Integration. Vierzehn Biographische Essays.* Bonn: Europa Union Verlag GmbH.
Kaiser, W. (2011). From great men to ordinary citizens? The biographical approach to narrating European integration in museums. *Culture Unbound, 3*, 385–400.
Kalmo, H., & Skinner, Q. (2010). Introduction: A concept in fragments. In H. Kalmo & Q. Skinner (Eds.), *Sovereignty in fragments. The past, present and future of a contested concept* (pp. 1–25). Cambridge: Cambridge University Press.
Kohnstamm, M. (1982). *Jean Monnet ou le pouvoir de l'imagination.* Lausanne: Fondation Jean Monnet pour l'Europe et Centre de recherches européennes.
Kostakopoulou, D. (2001). *Citizenship, identity and immigration in the European Union.* Manchester: Manchester University Press.
Kostakopoulou, D. (2005). Ideas, norms and European citizenship: Explaining institutional change. *The Modern Law Review, 68*(2), 233–267.
Kostakopoulou, D. (2007). European Union citizenship: Writing the future. *European Law Journal, 13*(5), 623–646.
Kostakopoulou, D. (2008). The evolution of European Union citizenship. *European Political Science, 7*, 285–295.
Krumrey, J. (2013). *Staging Europe. The symbolic politics of European integration during the 1950s and 1960s.* PhD thesis, European University Institute.
Lehning, P. (2001). European citizenship: Towards a European identity? *Law and Philosophy, 20*(3), 239–282.
Lerner, D., & Gordon, M. (1969). *Euratlantica: Changing perspectives of the European elites.* Cambridge, MA: MIT Press.
Levi-Sandri, L. (1962, June 14). Address by M. Levi Sandri, President of the Social Affairs Group of the Commission of the European Economic Community, to the 46th International Labour Conference, Geneva.
Levi-Sandri, L. (1964). Address (on social security) by M. Lionello Levi Sandri, Vice-President of the EEC Commission, President of the Social Affairs Group, before the XVth General Assembly of the International Social Security Association.
Loth, W. (2007). Walter Hallstein, a committed European. In M. Dumoulin (Ed.), *The European Commission, 1958–72. History and memories* (pp. 79–90). Luxembourg: Office for Official Publications of the European Communities.

Loth, W., & Bitsch, M. T. (2007). The Hallstein Commission 1958–67. In M. Dumoulin (Ed.), *The European Commission, 1958–72. History and memories* (pp. 51–78). Luxembourg: Office for Official Publications of the European Communities.

Loth, W., Wallace, W., & Wessels, W. (Eds.). (1998). *Walter Hallstein: The forgotten European.* Basingstoke: Palgrave Macmillan.

Ludlow, N. P. (1998). *Frustrated ambitions: The European Commission and the formation of a European identity, 1958–1967,* obtained via personal communication.

Ludlow, N. P. (2006). *The European Community and the crises of the 1960s: Negotiating the Gaullist challenge.* London: Routledge.

Lukaszewski, J. (1984). *Jean Rey.* Lausanne: Fondation Jean Monnet pour l'Europe et Centre de recherches européennes.

Maas, W. (2007). *Creating European citizens.* Lanham/Plymouth: Rowman & Littlefield.

Maas, W. (2013). Varieties of multilevel citizenship. In W. Maas (Ed.), *Multilevel citizenship* (pp. 1–21). Philadelphia: University of Pennsylvania Press.

Magnette, P. (1998). European citizenship from Maastricht to Amsterdam: The narrow path of legitimation. *Journal of European Integration, 21*(1), 37–69.

Magnette, P. (1999). *La Citoyenneté européenne: droits, politiques, institutions.* Bruxelles: Editions de l'Université de Bruxelles.

Magnette, P. (2007). How can one be European? Reflections on the pillars of European civic identity. *European Law Journal, 13*(5), 664–679.

Mahon, M. (1992). *Foucault's Nietzschean genealogy: Truth, power and the subject.* Albany: State University of New York Press.

Manners, I. (2011). Symbolism in European integration. *Comparative European Politics, 9*(3), 243–268.

Marshall, T. H. (1992). *Citizenship and social class.* London: Pluto Press.

Massey, D. (2005). *For space.* London: Sage.

Mayer, R. (1956, February 16). Address (on progress toward European integration) delivered by M. Rene Mayer, President of the High Authority of the European Community for Coal and Steel, at the New York Council on Foreign Relations, New York.

Mayer, R. (1957, May 14). Address (on the annual report) by M. Rene Mayer, President of the High Authority [ECSC] to the Common Assembly, Strasbourg.

Meehan, E. (1993). *Citizenship and the European Community.* London: Sage.

Meehan, E. (1996). European integration and citizens' rights: A comparative perspective. *Publius, 26*(4), 99–121.

Meehan, E. (2000). Citizenship and the European Union. *ZEI Discussion Paper C 63.*

Monnet, J. (1952, Avril 30). *Allocution de monsieur Jean Monnet au National press club,* Washington, DC.

Monnet, J. (1954). *A living reality*, The United States of Europe has begun. The European Coal and Steel Community—Speeches and addresses by Jean Monnet, 1952–1954.

Monnet, J. (1962). A ferment of change. *Journal of Common Market Studies, 3*(1), 203–211.

Monnet, J. (1964). *L'Europe et l'organisation de la paix*. Lausanne: Fondation Jean Monnet pour l'Europe et Centre de recherches européennes.

Neunreither, K. (1995). Citizens and the exercise of power in the European Union: Towards a new social contract? In A. Rosas & E. Antola (Eds.), *A citizens' Europe: In search of a new order* (pp. 1–18). London: Sage.

Nicoll, W., & Salmon, T. (1997). *Building European Union: A documentary history and analysis*. Manchester: Manchester University Press.

Nugent, N. (2001). *The European Commission*. Basingstoke: Palgrave macmillan.

O'Leary, S. (1996). *The evolving concept of community citizenship: From the free movement of persons to Union citizenship*. London: Kluwer Law International.

Offe, C. (2000 Manuscript, Sept). Is there, or can there be, a 'European society'? http://www4.soc.unitn.it:8080/poloeuropeo/content/e64/e385/e395/offe-Europeansociety_ita.pdf. Accessed 14 Oct 2011.

Offe, C. (2002). The democratic welfare state: A European regime under the strain of European integration. http://www.eurozine.com/articles/2002-02-08-offe-en.html. Accessed 4 Apr 2015.

Olsen, E. D. H. (2008). The origins of European citizenship in the first two decades of European integration. *Journal of European Public Policy, 15*(1), 40–57.

Olsen, E. D. H. (2012). *Transnational citizenship in the European Union: Past, present and future*. London/New York: Continuum Books.

Pantel, M. (1999). Unity-in-diversity: Cultural policy and EU legitimacy. In T. Banchoff & M. Smith (Eds.), *Legitimacy and the European Union: The contested polity* (pp. 46–65). London: Routledge.

Petit, I. (2006). Dispelling a myth? The fathers of Europe and the construction of a Euro-identity. *European Law Journal, 12*(5), 661–679.

Piela, I. (2012). *Walter Hallstein—Jurist und gestaltender Europapolitiker der ersten Stunde: Politische und institutionelle Visionen des ersten Präsidenten der EWG-Kommission (1958–1967)*. Berlin: Bwv Berliner-Wissenschaft.

Podkalicka, A., & Shore, C. (2010). Communicating Europe? EU Communication policy and cultural politics. In C. Valentini & G. Nesti (Eds.), *Public communication in the European Union: History, perspectives and challenges* (pp. 93–112). Newcastle upon Tyne: Cambridge Scholars.

Pourvoyeur, R. (1981). La Politique de l'information de la Communauté européenne. *Revue du Marché Commun, 246*, 192–204. Paris.

Prentoulis, N. (2001). On the technology of collective identity: Normative reconstructions of the concept of EU citizenship. *European Law Journal, 7*(2), 196–218.

Rabier, J. R. (1965). *L'information des Européens et l'integration de l'Europe. Leçons données le 17 et 18 février 1965*. Bruxelles: Université Libre de Bruxelles.
Roche, M. (1997). Citizenship and exclusion: Reconstructing the European Union. In M. Roche & R. Van Berkel (Eds.), *European citizenship and social exclusion* (pp. 3–22). Aldershot: Ashgate.
Rosas, A., & Antola, E. (Eds.). (1995). *A citizens' Europe: In search of a new order*. London: Sage.
Ruggie, J. G. (1993). Territoriality and beyond: Problematizing modernity in international relations. *International Organization, 47*(1), 139–174.
Ruggie, J. G. (1998). *Constructing the world polity: Essays on international institutionalization*. New York: Routledge.
Sandel, M. (2005). *Public philosophy: Essays on morality and politics*. Cambridge, MA: London: Harvard University Press.
Schmitter, P. (2000). *How to democratize the European Union ... and why bother?* Oxford: Rowman and Littlefield.
Schnapper, D. (1997). The European debate on citizenship. *Daedalus, 126*(3), 199–222.
Schrag Sternberg, C. (2013). *The struggle for EU legitimacy. Public contestation, 1950–2005*. Basingstoke: Palgrave Macmillan.
Schulz-Forberg, H. (2012). On the historical origins of the EU's current crisis or the hypocritical turn of European integration. In E. Chiti et al., (Eds.), *The European rescue of the European Union? ARENA Report*, 3, 12, 15–36.
Schuster, L., & Solomos, J. (2002). Rights and wrongs across European borders: Migrants, minorities and citizenship. *Citizenship Studies, 6*(1), 37–54.
Seidel, K. (2010). *The process of politics in Europe: The rise of European elites and supranational institutions*. London: IB Tauris.
Shaw, J. (2007). *The transformation of citizenship in the European Union: Electoral rights and the restructuring of political space*. Cambridge: Cambridge University Press.
Shore, C. (2000). *Building Europe: The cultural politics of European integration*. London: Routledge.
Shore, C. (2004). Whither European citizenship? Eros and civilization revisited. *European Journal of Social Theory, 7*(1), 27–44.
Skinner, Q. (2008). *Reason and rhetoric in the philosophy of Hobbes*. Cambridge: Cambridge University Press.
Sonntag, A. (2010). Political symbols, citizenship and communication, paper presented at the communicating European citizenship conference, 22 March, London. http://www.uaces.org/pdf/papers/1002/Sonntag.pdf. Accessed 25 July 2012.
Spierenburg, D., & Poidevin, R. (1994). *The history of the High Authority of the European Coal and Steel Community. Supranationality in operation*. London: Weidenfeld and Nicolson.

Stevenson, N. (2003). *Cultural citizenship: Cosmopolitan questions*. Maidenhead: Open University Press.
Stevenson, N. (2005). European cosmopolitanism and civil society: Questions of culture, identity and citizenship. http://eprints.nottingham.ac.uk/751/2/euroeuroarticle11.pdf. Accessed 12 June 2012.
Theiler, T. (2005). *Political symbolism and European integration*. Manchester: Manchester University Press.
Van der Harst, J. (2007). Sicco Mansholt: Courage and conviction. In M. Dumoulin (Ed.), *The European Commission, 1958–72. History and memories* (pp. 165–180). Luxembourg: Office for Official Publications of the European Communities.
Van Helmont, J. (1981). *Jean Monnet comme il était*. Lausanne: Fondation Jean Monnet pour l'Europe et Centre de recherches européennes.
Van Oudenaren, J. (2005). *Uniting Europe: An introduction to the European Union* (2nd ed.). Lanham/Oxford: Rowman & Littlefield.
Vink, M. (2004). The unbearable lightness of European citizenship. *Citizenship, Social and Economics Education*, 6(1), 24–33.
Vink, M. (2005). *Limits of European citizenship: European integration and domestic immigration policies*. Basingstoke: Palgrave Macmillan.
Waever, O. (2009). Discursive approaches. In A. Wiener & T. Diez (Eds.), *European integration theory* (2nd ed., pp. 163–180). Oxford: Oxford University Press.
Warleigh, A. (2001). Purposeful opportunists? EU institutions and the struggle over European citizenship. In R. Bellamy & A. Warleigh (Eds.), *Citizenship and governance in the European Union* (pp. 19–40). London: Continuum.
Weale, A. (2005). *Democratic citizenship and the European Union*. Manchester: Manchester University Press.
Weber, M. (1949). "Objectivity" in social science and social policy. http://anthropos-lab.net/wp/wp-content/uploads/2011/12/Weber-objectivity-in-the-social-sciences.pdf. Accessed 14 Oct 2014.
Weber, M. (1978). *Economy and society* (Vols. 1 & 2, Eds. G. Roth, & C. Wittich). Berkeley: University of California Press.
Wiener, A. (1997). Making sense of the new geography of citizenship: Fragmented citizenship in the European Union. *Theory and Society*, 26(4), 529–560.
Wiener, A. (1998). *European citizenship practice: Building institutions of a non-state*. Oxford: Perseus.
Zuleeg, M. (2003). *Der Beitrag Walter Hallsteins zur Zukunft Europas: Referate zu Ehren von Walter Hallstein*. Baden-Baden: Nomos Verlagsgesellschaft.

CHAPTER 2

Homo Oeconomicus (1951–1972)

1   All Things Fall and Are Built Again[1]

Whenever a story is told a beginning needs to be found. For European integration, some have taken Churchill's appeal for a United Europe in 1946[2] as a starting point, some chose to start with the Hague Summit of 1948, others found that the Treaty of Paris marked the official beginning of European integration and some considered 9 May 1950, the day of the Schuman Declaration, the date of the birth of the European Community. These are all plausible and reasonable starting points. Indeed, in 1985 the European Council declared 9 May 'Europe day' to annually celebrate European peace and unity. I propose, however, to begin the story this book tells about the public communication of European citizenship a few weeks before the Schuman Declaration was announced and that was sometime in late March 1950.

March 1950 might seem an odd time, and I owe an explanation about what made it significant. In the spring of 1950, several political conflicts intensified and put the newly established European peace in danger. The Cold War was omnipresent, and the United States thought that only if Germany was granted an early rearmament could Western Europe defend itself against the Soviet Union.[3] However, Monnet—who has often been described as a lucid observer and analyst of circumstances[4]—knew that France was suspicious of Germany and wouldn't support its early rearmament. In fact, Germany's quick industrial development and its emerging

© The Editor(s) (if applicable) and The Author(s) 2016
S. Pukallus, *Representations of European Citizenship since 1951*,
DOI 10.1057/978-1-137-51147-8_2

economic superiority over France, especially in the coal and steel sector, reinforced France's distrust and suspicion of Germany. Monnet believed that peace couldn't be established if people were suspicious of and distrusted each other. On the contrary, only if there was trust and equality could there be peace. As such, it was necessary to devise a plan that would allow France to trust Germany and Germany to be an equal partner. Monnet did not have much time, as the international conference at which the USA wanted to obtain Britain's and France's agreement to German rearmament was scheduled for 10 May.[5]

Aware of the need to act promptly, but not yet clear about what action best to take, Monnet[6] did what he always did when he had to make important decisions: he went walking. This time he left Paris for the mountains. He used to say that after about an hour his mind was clear and he was able to concentrate on a specific problem during the rest of his walk. The question he had to address was how to square three key concerns: 'paix, Europe, Franco-Allemagne' and he realised that it was necessary to direct Germany's economic and political development in such a way as to allow for peaceful collaboration between free peoples. In other words, public perceptions of Germany as a threat needed to be transformed into perceptions of Germany as a reliable and equal partner who any nation, but particularly France, could collaborate with peacefully, both economically and politically. This was difficult. WWII had hardened the minds of Europeans to such an extent that it was no longer possible to bring about change and give people hope through mere words and official declarations. Rather, it was necessary to start an undertaking that was profound, real, immediate and dramatic—dramatic in the sense that it would enter people's minds and give them hope. Monnet was convinced that '[o]nly a hopeful—but realistic—projection of [the people's] future could subsume and surpass the bitter events of recent memory and the abundant evidence for present doubts'.[7] What was required, so Monnet believed, was to put the French and German coal and steel industries under a common supranational authority. Monnet trusted the power of institutions more than people's capacity to change. Following the Swiss philosopher Amiel, he argued that only institutions become wiser as they gain experience. The acquired experience and expertise would put people under common rules to help them to gradually change their behaviour rather than their nature.[8] The idea of common supranational European institutions was indeed new, and as Monnet said himself, he couldn't find any historical examples of such institutions that would have helped him to work out the details about their role, organisation and functioning. Therefore, it was necessary to consult, but it had to be done quietly because too much publicity in these early stages could have been fatal.[9] As such, the period between late March and 9 May 1950 revealed a mixture of idealism and pragmatism—Collowald called it audacity and realism, of aspiration and opportunism and of confidence and doubt.[10] The atmosphere was marked by hope and optimism and urgency and tension at the same time—the sword of Damocles seemed to be hanging over Monnet's and his colleagues' heads, as it was imperative to keep the project secret in order to avoid anyone plotting against it. There was an awareness of the fact that any badly chosen term or wording in the Declaration itself could have put an end to the greatest peace endeavour ever to be undertaken before it actually began.[11] It is important to capture this tension and constant negotiation between what was aspired to, desired and imagined, and what could realistically be achieved step by step with regard to a lasting pax Europa and Monnet's scenario of the 'Etats-Unis d'Europe', because it was characteristic of and set the scene for at least the next two decades of European integration. It reflected the way and the context in which the public communication of European citizenship and the continuous reinterpretation of the meaning of European citizenship would take place.[12]

The Schuman Declaration would officially suggest that the French and German coal and steel industries be pooled and placed under a common supranational authority. This economic programme was seen as the first step to ensure that future war was made impossible and that peace on the European continent would last. The team that was involved in the preparation of the Schuman Declaration was small and mainly included four people: Monnet, Etienne Hirsch, Pierre Uri and Paul Reuter, who together engaged in what we can call, following Allen, 'democratic writing'.[13] Hirsch was an engineer who knew the primary and secondary industrial sectors well and could therefore offer expert advice. Uri was an economist who had previously worked for the French Commissariat général du Plan, which was established by De Gaulle in 1946 and was responsible for the planning of French economic strategies and policies. Reuter was a professor of law and introduced to Monnet by Rabier initially to advise Monnet on antitrust legislation.[14] It was the relationship between Reuter and Monnet that was to be decisive. When Reuter met Monnet on 12 April 1950, Monnet showed him a note Adenauer wrote about the necessity of French–German reconciliation and asked for Reuter's opinion on how to bring about such reconciliation. Monnet suggested a French–German

Parliament or the establishment of a political union composed of Belgium, Luxembourg, Alsace, Lorraine, Saarland—in fact all those who, as Monnet claimed, were neither really French nor German. Reuter rejected this idea because he believed that the border population had suffered enough during the past decades and that it would not be wise to do anything related to their political status. Instead Reuter suggested that French–German reconciliation should start in the economic sector and possibly be quite narrow at first. It is at this point that the idea of pooling the French and German coal and steel industries started to take shape.[15] Finally, and after two meetings that included Uri and Hirsch, Monnet[16] asked Reuter to draft the first version of the Schuman Declaration on 15 April.[17] It took nine drafts to arrive at the final version of 9 May 1950. Each iterative draft testified to the felt need by those involved for very carefully chosen words that carried a clear message acceptable to both France and Germany,[18] and possibly other European nations.

The opening sentence, which remained the same throughout the nine drafts, can be seen as the Declaration's foundation. It read: 'La paix mondiale ne saurait être sauvegardée sans des efforts créateurs à la mesure des dangers qui la menacent. La contribution qu'une Europe organisée et vivante peut apporter à la civilisation est indispensable au maintien des relations pacifiques.'[19] Monnet believed that lasting peace could only be achieved if all partners were equal, and this thought was visible in the first seven drafts of the declaration, which emphasised that Germany needed to be able to collaborate as an equal partner. However, in draft eight and in the final version this wording disappeared and instead the following was added to the end of the declaration: 'In the exercise of its functions, the common High Authority will take into account the powers conferred upon the International Ruhr Authority and the obligations of all kinds imposed upon Germany, so long as these remain in force'. We can only speculate about the reasons for this change, but it appears that the team had to be mindful of international agreements and couldn't just overrule those by single-handedly giving back Germany its sovereign status. Monnet was also cautious not to raise France's suspicion about Germany's position or role. What the change in wording did do, however, was to turn the German problem into a European one (Monnet 1976)—one that would need to be solved if European integration was to go forward and peace was to be ensured. Monnet's team was also anxious to portray France as the initiator and creator of this new Europe. Whereas the first five drafts said that the French government was taking the initiative, drafts six and seven no longer contained this sentence, and drafts eight and nine focused on the proposition of the French government to pool the French and German coal and steel industry. This wording allowed for the understanding of Europe being built by and around France rather than Germany. The idea of building a European federation was expressed in all nine drafts and was considered essential to the safeguarding of peace. However, there existed amongst European nations deep distrust which could have jeopardised the possible success of the Schumann Declaration. As noted above, Monnet and his team were optimistic, though at the same time they were acutely aware of the diplomatic realities. Their realistic outlook recognised the extent of the difficulties facing them. Indeed, the first seven drafts talked about obstacles which hindered the immediate creation of a European federation and needed to be overcome. Drafts eight and nine abandoned the term 'obstacles' and introduced the following sentence: 'Europe will not be made all at once, or according to a single plan. It will be built through concrete achievements which first create a de facto solidarity'. The rewording came with a shift of emphasis from difficulties and possible failure to achievability and success in little steps. In short, the solution to reconciling France and Germany was, so Monnet and his team believed, to be found in somehow pooling the French and German coal and steel industries.

Schuman, then French Minister of Foreign Affairs, was handed a copy of a draft of the Declaration on 29 April 1950 which featured this proposed solution for reconciling France and Germany. Schuman was pleased with the draft, as it seemed to him that Monnet and his team had found a possible answer to this seemingly intractable problem: how to create a French–German partnership?[20] He enthusiastically endorsed the Declaration and used, as Lejeune argued, all his tactical skills in his attempt to obtain the French government's endorsement of the proposed pooling of the French and German coal and steel industries.[21] Importantly, the Declaration was kept secret. Indeed, according to Gerbet the team decided not to inform the Ministry of the Interior, the Ministry of Defence or the Ministry of Industrial Production. Neither did it inform the relevant authorities, administrators and managers of the coal and steel industry.[22] In addition to this, the importance of the Declaration was downplayed. At the first meeting at which Schuman had the opportunity to present the Declaration (to the Conseil des Ministres on 3 May 1950), he minimised its significance by 'saying a lot without really saying anything'. After this first meeting and before the second meeting of the Conseil des Ministres, scheduled for 9 May 1950, Schuman met with René Mayer, Minister of Justice, and René Pleven, Minister of Defence. He asked them to unhesitatingly endorse the Declaration during the session of the Conseil des Ministres on 9 May, which they duly agreed to. The scheduled meeting of the Conseil des Ministres was therefore nothing short of a set-up. As agreed, Mayer and Pleven endorsed the Declaration with such conviction that the other ministers had not much to say. In fact, they were too surprised to react.[23] Lejeune judged Schuman's diplomatic efforts as having the ability to manipulate without deception and to manoeuvre without mischief.[24]

The Schuman Declaration stood for 'a vision, a document and for a common political will'.[25] In its final version it proposed that the 'Franco-German production of coal and steel as a whole be placed under a common High Authority within the framework of an organisation open to the participation of the other countries of Europe'. It was intended that the High Authority would be a supranational European institution which would impartially regulate and oversee the production of coal and steel independent of national interests, thereby creating a European 'solidarity in production'. Pragmatically, the Schuman Declaration set out to achieve two things: first, as the Declaration unambiguously stated, that 'any war between France and Germany becomes not merely unthinkable, but materially impossible', simply because the raw materials to manufacture munitions for military purposes would no longer be controlled by nation-states alone. Second, establishing economic solidarity between France and Germany required 'the elimination of the age-old opposition', and overcoming the long-standing enmity between the two countries was considered to be the essential basis for achieving a lasting pax Europa. It was a point that Schuman emphasised in no uncertain terms. Indeed, when he was asked how many countries would be necessary to make his plan work, he simply replied: 'If necessary, we shall go ahead with only two'.[26]

In conclusion, the creation of the European Coal and Steel Community 'was made possible only by the catastrophe of the Second World War and the looming disaster of the Cold War, which finally succeeded in banging French and German heads together'.[27] What this points to is that context and circumstances mattered and continue to matter. Adam argued that Monnet was acutely aware of the importance of circumstances and foresaw that much in the European integration process would depend upon how contexts were interpreted and seized as opportunities to act[28]—this was true for the elaboration of the Schuman Declaration as it was, as we will see, for the definition and public communication of European citizenship. Straightforwardly put, there was an awareness that, to borrow Runciman's words, 'context trumps everything'.[29] Monnet and his collaborators were able to master and act according to circumstances: as is well known, not two but six countries—France, Germany, Belgium, the Netherlands, Luxemburg and Italy[30]—signed the Treaty of Paris on 18 April 1951 and thereby established the European Coal and Steel Community (ECSC), and it was in the context of the Schuman Declaration, its acceptance by France and Germany and the birth of the fledgling ECSC that the first representation of European citizenship emerged.

2 Economic Pragmatism, a Political Vision and Civil Aspirations: The Emergence of Homo Oeconomicus Within the Context of the ECSC

European integration was driven by the need to achieve the economic pragmatic objectives laid out in the Treaty of Paris (ToP) and later the Treaty of Rome (ToR), which established the EEC in 1957.[31] However, the political vision of establishing a European federation carried forward in the ECSC was as much a driving force as economic objectives. As Coppé pointed out '(…) the Schuman Plan means, and will always mean, more than just a common market. It is, and will always be, the first step towards United Europe'.[32] Accordingly, the ECSC created the institutional foundations for a European federation: it established supranational political and legal institutions. As Hallstein stated, the 'Community itself was organized along lines which were plainly federal',[33] to which the Commission added that 'the Community is a political entity through its institutions, which are not already taking political decisions, but which are also organized in such a way as to form the basis for a system of government'.[34] In short: some 'sort of government building' [35] was happening. As such the ECSC represented an embryonic political union ostensibly formed in the economic domain.[36] However, and as I will show, the ECSC also created circumstances in which its civil aspirations (see chapter "A Civil Europe") could be gradually concretised and realised.

The ECSC's political character was immediately apparent in the design of the four supranational institutions that shared the task of operationalizing the Common Coal and Steel Market and of ensuring that no one member state enjoyed structural or strategic competitive economic advantages over another.[37] These four institutions were the High Authority, the Council of Ministers, the Assembly and the Court of Justice. Combined they held European-wide powers, though their working relationships were somewhat attenuated by different responsibilities and tasks. Thus, the independent collegiate executive, the High Authority, was responsible for achieving the objectives laid down by the Treaty, thereby accruing a degree of real sovereignty over the member states' indigenous coal and steel industry and attendant economic policies. At the same time, the High Authority's sovereignty was itself subject to, as noted in the previous chapter, 'an overbearing' Council of Ministers which constantly attempted to restrict the scope of the High Authority's powers, even though the High Authority had legitimately acquired these powers through the stipulations of the ToP. Added to this, there was the Assembly, which was comprised of representatives of the national parliaments and had a supervisory role with regard to the High Authority (it acquired its legislative role later). The High Authority and the Assembly engaged in a good working relationship and would collaborate often more than the Treaties required. Rabier and his counterparts in the Assembly, and later the European Parliament, would collaborate with regard to public communication strategies. Collaboration was seen as a means to avoid 'bureaucratic inertia'.[38] Mayer, in particular, was 'anxious to maintain good relations with the Common Assembly and seized every opportunity to explain his actions to it (…)'.[39]

From the outset, the Community wanted the Assembly to evolve into a directly elected Parliamentarian Assembly (ToP, art. 21)—today's European Parliament.[40] This was an intention that was clearly apparent in the democratic electoral vocabulary both the ToP and later the ToR operated with. This vocabulary included expressions such as 'representation of the peoples of the member states' (ToP, art. 6 and 20) and references to proposals for universal suffrage of the Assembly (ToP, art. 21 and ToR, art. 138) which, as Hallstein observed, would come about when 'the time will be ripe'.[41] The precondition for the existence of a European Parliament that could be elected and therefore directly legitimised by the European citizenry was the existence of European political parties. In Alexander's theory of civil society, political parties represent a powerful regulative civil institution, and the desire to transform the Common Assembly into a directly elected Parliament showed that the early European officials recognised intuitively that there would be a need for political parties at some point in the future. It was Burke who first pointed out the importance of political parties, which he defined as 'a body of men united, for promoting by their joint endeavours the national interest, upon some particular principle in which they are all agreed'.[42] Burke distinguished between factions and parties and argued that the latter would defend the common good rather than be driven by private consideration and egoism.[43] To this, Alexander added that political parties consist of 'those who wish to assume state power' and 'must persuade their fellow members of civil society that they are deserving their votes, that they will represent their values and their interests [and] exercise state power in their name'. As such, elections allow citizens to construct and deconstruct political power and 'parties form the containers in within which [citizens'] votes are cast'.[44] With the establishment of European-wide political parties would come, if we accept Burke and Alexander's understanding of parties, various forms of political legitimation and various forms of political manifestos. In short, democratic contestation would emerge in what would appear to be a familiar political setting, namely a parliament.

Finally, the Court of Justice was trusted to ensure that new European law, the 'acquis communautaire', was observed in the interpretation and implementation of the Treaty. It, then as now, seemed somewhat semi-detached from the prosaic nature of economic policy and political ambition. Even so, and in spite of the tension between the four supranational institutions, the transference of a very limited range of sovereign powers, accompanied by the establishment of overarching European institutions, symbolically as well as practically, indicated the first major European-wide adjustment to the Westphalian ideal of the nation-state as politically sovereign. Krasner argued that sovereignty is comprised of three core elements: first, international legal sovereignty, which implies 'international recognition which, [for example, ascribes] the right to enter into contracts or treaties with other states'; second, Westphalian/Vattelian sovereignty, which describes 'the absence of submission to external authority structures, even structures that states have created using their international legal sovereignty'; third, domestic sovereignty, which means 'more or less effective control over the territory of the state including the ability to regulate trans-border movements'.[45] If we follow Krasner's analytical distinction then we can argue that the member states gained in international legal sovereignty but compromised to a certain extent, but of course not entirely, their Westphalian/Vattelian and domestic sovereignties. In other words, what was being accepted, as well as what would be subsequently and constantly contested by the member states, was ultimately nothing short of the principle of the transference of political power to a European federal body that didn't yet exist (the empty chair crises addressed below is a prime example of this[46]). Correspondingly, implicit or otherwise, the member states' showed support for an integrative economic-political ideal. The experience of the two world wars, as well as the Cold War, led Monnet[47] to realise that a mythic belief in national sovereignty and national superiority was the cause of conflict and needed to be addressed.[48] Accordingly, the Schuman Declaration introduced a new form of sovereignty, one that Monnet judged capable of addressing contemporary problems more adequately than nation-states because it was based on the idea of European unity rather than the primacy of national interests. Hallstein unambiguously and unhesitantly admitted that 'there [was] no aspect of European politics more important to us than political unity'.[49]

However, the Community's concern for solidarity and unity went beyond the political and extended to the civil realm. Monnet's conviction was to not only join States together economically and politically but more importantly to unite people in a peaceful civil association. He famously claimed that 'Nous ne coalisons pas des Etats, nous unissons des hommes'—'We do not build a coalition of States but unite men'. Kohnstamm explained that Monnet believed that the opportunity to unite men was most rewarding and emphasised that Monnet was, throughout his efforts for European integration, concerned with 'men' and their flourishing, liberty, responsibilities and dignity.[50] Accordingly, the European integration process needed to be understood as more than 'a concert of the powerful' (Konzert der Mächte): it was a 'Community of citizens' [51] and as such, the Community was concerned from the beginning to define in concrete terms who a European citizen was and represented European citizenship accordingly in its public communication policy. The first representation of European citizenship was a form of economic-social citizenship represented as 'Homo Oeconomicus'.

3   Homo Oeconomicus: An Economic-Social Representation of European Citizenship

An Economic-Social Lexicon

The first indication of who the Community imagined the European citizen to be can be found in the provisions of the Treaty of Paris (ToP 1951) and later the Treaty of Rome (ToR 1957). The Treaty of Paris referred to the representation of homo oeconomicus as the neonate European citizen as follows: 'The member States bind themselves to renounce any restriction based on nationality[52] against the employment in the coal and steel industries of workers of proven qualifications for such industries who possess the nationality of one of the member States; this commitment shall be subject to the limitations imposed by the fundamental needs of health and public order' (art. 69). In economic terms, the membership criteria for European citizenship were defined by as few as five key terms: workers (ToP, art. 46); wages (ibid., art. 68), mobility, coal and steel industry; and proven qualifications (ibid., art. 69). Underlying these few articles was an image of the European citizen as essentially a male coal and steel worker with proven qualifications. He had the nationality of any of the member states and could with his newly acquired right to freedom of movement and establishment seek employment in any of the member states. In other words, the relationship to Europe of the European citizen was regarded as being fashioned through a set of employment (and social) opportunities, and was described in the Treaties in terms of both an economic and a social lexicon which I will disaggregate for reasons of clarity.

Economically, European citizenship was conditioned upon proven qualifications in the coal and steel industry. In this sense, the representation of European citizenship as homo oeconomicus was admittedly narrow and exclusive because, as Baldoni pointed out, art. 69 'explicitly refer[red] only to qualified workers in the indicated sectors and not to the whole workforce'.[53] As I will show below, this changed with the ToR in 1957 when the representation homo oeconomicus was extended to include essentially the whole European workforce. The requirement to have 'proven qualifications' meant, according to Maas, that 'only approximately 300,000 of the Community's 1.4 million coal and steel workers qualified for the permits that allowed these workers to seek employment in other member states (...)'.[54] These permits were 'Labour Cards' which could be seen as embryonic European identity cards[55] and as the precursor of the uniform European passport (introduced in the mid-1980s for all Community nationals). As a political symbol, the Labour Card did two things: first, it showed an emerging spatial conception of Community space as the territory of a federal European Community whose geo-political scope was symbolised by the Labour Card, and second, it identified the members of a particular and restricted Community in what Billig[56] referred to as a 'banal' fashion. I will return to the significance of political symbols in the next chapter. At this point, it suffices to say that the Community hoped that such political symbols would help reinforce a sense of the uniqueness of being a member of the European Community (an idea taken further when the Community acquired its own first flag in 1958) and would ultimately help facilitate the emergence of a European civil consciousness, albeit only for a relatively low number of qualified workers.

Whereas the right to free movement and establishment only applied to a limited number of coal and steel workers, other stipulations of the Treaty of Paris (1951) provided for an extension of this economic European citizenship by including those who were concerned by the coal and steel industries—and these were consumers[57] as well as representatives of consumers and workers.[58] It was this recognition of representatives of diverse groups that established the first European civil-legal rights and led to the emergence of the first European civil association—the Consultative Committee.[59]

The Consultative Committee was a very restricted form of civil association and limited in its concerns to the economic realm. Membership of the Consultative Committee was almost exclusively confined to a small elected economic elite. The ToP read: 'There shall be created a Consultative Committee, attached to the High Authority. It shall consist of not less than thirty and not more than fifty-one members, and shall include producers, workers and consumers and dealers in equal numbers' (art. 16). The members of this Committee were to be appointed by the Council: 'the members of the Consultative Committee shall be designated in their individual capacity. They shall not be bound by any mandate or instruction from the organizations which proposed them as candidates'. As such, the earliest conceptions of civil institutions that served 'homo oeconomicus' did not emerge from a citizens' initiative or 'out of the people' but came together as prescribed by the Treaty and on the initiative of the High Authority: 'The High Authority may consult the Consultative Committee in any case it deems proper. It shall be required to do so whenever such consultation is prescribed by the present Treaty' (ToP, art. 19). As such, the Consultative Committee was at least able to express 'functional interests', though not yet any 'broader civil concerns', nor did it have very much 'civil potential'. This limited version of European civil power continued when the Consultative Committee evolved into a 'social and economic committee with consultative capacity' (ToR, art. 4).

What is common to all civil associations in mature Western democracies is, as Alexander argued, that 'they have stepped outside the role structures of noncivil institutions—outside of economic organisations, families, churches, and local communities—to press their argument in the 'court of public opinion'. [60] More specifically, they 'translate the codes of civil society into specific claims for, and against, the expansion of rights, the execution of new government policies, and the undertaking of news social actions. They may do so by creating conflict and intensifying opposition, or by trying to create greater cooperation and political or social harmony'. [61] In short: they address broad civil concerns with a communicative intent. It is clear that the Consultative Committee was in no way a full-fledged civil association. It was not independent from the non-civil political sphere as prescribed by the Treaty and did not have any of the spontaneous character that civil associations can be characterised by. Rather, the existence of the Consultative Committee was dependent upon the 'goodwill' of the ECSC, and its form, purpose and composition was set.[62]

However, and regardless of its lack of civil power, the Consultative Committee represented an attempt of the Community to encourage the building of European civil associations, which are still seen as an important feature of any independent and autonomous civil society.[63] The Consultative Committee as an embryonic civil association was important—more symbolically than practically, of course—because it stood for the Community's civil-democratic aspiration which centred on a conception of an active European citizen. The fact that the Treaty of Paris legally codified the first European civil-legal rights in the form of a consultation mechanism for an economic-social European civil association was equally important. As I noted above, the Court of Justice had the responsibility to monitor respect for, and implementation of, the Treaties. Consequently, and at a very early stage, there existed a willingness to establish legal protection for civil associations and their possible regulation by the Court of Justice.

This is significant for the boundary maintenance of any civil society whether aspired to, emerging or fully-fledged. It is particularly when these boundaries are 'fortified by law' that states, or in this case a supranational entity, are compelled 'to enforce civil obligations'.[64] To this Alexander added that 'the aspiration toward which democratic law aims is civil society. In fact, to the degree that the civil sphere gains authority and independence, obedience to law is seen not as subservience to authority (...) but as commitment to rules that allow solidarity and autonomy'.[65] And this is exactly what the Community aspired to achieve when it introduced civil-legal rights which were to act as the basis for the conception of the first representation of European citizenship 'Homo Oeconomicus'. With the ToR establishing the EEC (1957), the Commission's conception of European citizenship moved away from the narrow definition of the European citizen as merely a coal and steel worker. The right to accept offers of employment made in another country, to reside and move freely within the territory of the member states, subject to employment in the paid labour market (ToR, art. 48), was no longer granted exclusively to qualified coal and steel workers but was extended to a large part of the European workforce. Correspondingly, the economic lexicon of 'homo oeconomicus' expanded to include other general terms such as worker, wage-earning workers (art. 54 al. 3d), migrant workers (art. 121), men and women workers (art. 119) and young workers (art. 50). Further, the expanded lexicon included terms referring to specific professions and employees of the medical, para-medical and pharmaceutical professions (art. 57) and the industrial, commercial, artisan and liberal professions (art. 60) as well as to producers, agriculturists, transport operators, workers, merchants, artisans, the liberal professions (art. 193). With the widening of the scope of European citizenship to a majority of professions, civil-legal associations were equally extended. Accordingly, an Economic and Social Committee[66] composed of representatives of producers, agriculturists, transport operators, workers, merchants, artisans, liberal professions, general interest (art. 193), trade union law as well as employers' associations (art. 117) was created.

The conception of the economic dimension of 'homo oeconomicus' evolved from a coal and steel worker with proven qualifications who was given the right to free movement and establishment to an employed worker who—independently of any specific qualification—was given the right to free movement and establishment in any of the six member states of the Community. This economic dimension of the representation 'homo oeconomicus' was also supported by the right to belong to a representative association—a right best described as civil-legal which, admittedly, did not extend very much beyond economic considerations. Yet this civil-legal right alongside the civil nature of the European Court of Justice and the Consultative Committee (and subsequently the Economic and Social Committee) combined to represent the first recognition of a European civil society, albeit one in a singularly direct relationship to the economic realm.

However, as noted above, despite the predominant economic attributes circumscribing the first representation of the European citizen 'homo oeconomicus', it would be wrong to say that 'homo oeconomicus' was nothing more than a one-dimensional economic actor and that European citizenship was purely functional.[67] In this vein, Hallstein argued that '[f]or if, in setting up a common market, our only aim were to unleash powerful economic forces and move masses of men to the place where their labour would be most rapidly transformed into economic gain, we should be forgetting that Man is not merely a homo oeconomicus or a homo faber'[68], and Moravcsik acknowledged that '(...) naked economic preferences would probably have led to a highly institutionalized pan-European free trade area with flanking policies of regulatory harmonization and monetary stabilization (...)'.[69] And yet it is clear that both historically and empirically the Community extended far beyond such a purely and idealistically conceived of free trade area. Europe demonstrably had an established political and legal dimension with some limited social and civil-cultural aspects (though of increasing significance) attached to it. This can be illustrated by the fact that the Community considered 'homo oeconomicus' to be more than 'a factor of production' and showed responsibility for 'homo oeconomicus' outside the economic realm. This will become clearer when we examine the social provisions ascribed to 'homo oeconomicus'.

The Treaty of Paris (1951) defined 'homo oeconomicus' through economic and through social attributes. What this showed was that labour policy and social policy were closely linked. [70] Here we can see that from the beginning European social policy differed in two basic aspects from national social policy. First, European social policy did not cover the traditional core domains of social policy such as redistribution of income, social welfare, education policy and pension but was instead concerned with and has developed to include worker mobility and employment, jobs and working conditions, gender equality, social protection schemes, a protective legal framework for European citizens, youth unemployment and poverty and social exclusion.[71] Second, with the Community lacking the competences of a nation-state, it was 'tightly constrained by legal provision, a protectionist stance towards their own social territory on the part of the member states and the dominant market character of the [European] project'.[72] Therefore, the Community was only able to be operational in a limited scope of competences and subsequently struggled to develop a social policy that applied to the European citizenry as a whole and did not focus on the social environment of the worker.

To return to the ToP and its social lexicon: The preamble referred to the objective of raising the standard of living conditions. To this, added in art. 3, was the improvement of the working conditions of the labour force.

Although not explicitly stated in the ToP, social concerns were extended to the workers' families. This extension became particularly clear in brochures, as I will show in more detail later, which showed how the ECSC, starting off as a predominately economic entity, quickly expanded its interventions into the social realm of the worker's family through housing projects set up by the High Authority in order to guarantee better housing to the miners and their families[73] and other financial bonuses that would help to set up a new life under the new conditions of free movement and travel. The intervention by the High Authority into the social and civic domain were announced and legalised by art. 2, which is concerned with improvement of the workers' living conditions. This increasing inclusion of the workers' families, albeit at that stage more or less only rhetorically and symbolically, foreshadowed the far-reaching impact a formal extension to the workers' family would have for the meaning of belonging and the scope of European integration and the conception of a European public. Levi Sandri,[74] for example, with regard to the social realm, talked about the need to gradually broaden the scope of social security to embrace the entire population.

During the six years that lay between the Treaty of Paris (1951) and the Treaty of Rome (1957) the social realms of the Community expanded increasingly and progressively, which was also reflected in the public communication brochures (see ahead). Spierenburg and Poidevin argued that the 'High Authority's social policy had been somewhat sketchy under Monnet's Presidency because preliminary enquiries were complicated and therefore slow; but they took a leap forward under Mayer'[75], and the Community paid more and more attention to turning the social provisions of the Treaties into concrete reality for workers and their families. The expansion of the social realm was accompanied by a broadened social lexicon and an increase in the publication of brochures addressing social policy.

The ToR itself approached social policy in two ways: first, more generally, by simply stating the importance of economic and social progress, of improving the living and working conditions of their people and of accelerating a rise in the standard of living (preamble) and second, by social provisions specifically related to the worker (and his family). With regard to the latter, the ToR introduced the European Social Fund (ESF), a 'social philosophy' according to Ronan,[76] whose purpose was to improve the possibilities of employment for workers and to contribute to the raising of their standard of living (art. 2) and to improve employment facilities and to improve geographical and occupational mobility of workers (art. 123). The Treaty explicitly recognised labour legislation, working conditions, occupational and vocational training, the protection of occupational accidents and social security as 'social fields' (art. 117). In this emerging European social policy, it was notably the concern for social security that affected not only the worker himself but was extended to his beneficiaries. The objective with regard to this aspect was the harmonisation of the social system and the introduction of a social security system which would permit assurance to migrant workers and their beneficiaries (art. 51 and 120). Social welfare became increasingly important and was expressed through art. 125, which provided for occupational retraining, aids for the settlement of workers and resettlement allowances. Art. 92 provided for aids of social character granted to individual consumers.[77]

As noted above, the Treaties did not refer to the worker and his family but used rather the technical term 'beneficiaries'. The concern for the family at this time did not extend beyond social security and was intrinsically linked to the worker exercising his right of movement and establishment. Although the Treaties did not take a position with regard to the status of the workers' family, they did nevertheless lead to a 'reflection process' on which status to give to the workers' families that resulted in 1968 in a directive on the abolition of restrictions on movement and residence within the Community for workers of Member States and their families.[78] This directive read as follows: 'Whereas freedom of movement constitutes a fundamental right of workers and their families; whereas mobility of labour within the Community must be one of the means by which the worker is guaranteed the possibility of improving his living and working conditions and promoting his social advancement, while helping to satisfy the requirements of the economies of the Member States (...)'[79] and distinguished between freedom of movement as a means of ensuring labour mobility and the conception of freedom of movement as a fundamental right. With freedom of movement starting to be considered as a fundamental right, the question of how to integrate the families into the social life of the host state became an important question, not only with regard to new policies regarding the schooling of the workers' children,[80] vocational[81] and linguistic training.

The existence of a social lexicon was of crucial importance for two reasons. First, these Treaties witnessed the emergence of the first attempt at developing a European social policy. This social policy was defined through the economic competences of the Community and was therefore attached to economic provisions, particularly to the right of free movement and establishment, and the area of employment. Second, the Community's conception of 'homo oeconomicus' extended beyond considering him as a worker or as a pure factor of production. On the contrary, it showed that the coal and steel worker was as much a worker as he ('or she' from 1957 on) was a European citizen with a family and limited social and civil-legal rights. Although these rights for these workers and their families were limited—a pan-European social security scheme, for example, did not exist—the Community nevertheless demonstrated its willingness to make the workers' and their families' life as socially protected as possible. Ronan put it as follows: 'The Community developed a responsibility for the social consequences of its economic decisions (...)'[82] to which the EC added that the 'Community has contributed to the well-being of certain groups of workers, and thus indirectly to the well-being of the Community's citizens as a whole'.[83]

I said in the previous chapter that the analysis of each representation will reveal an image of what the European citizen was meant to look like and what kind of European life this citizen was meant to live. It is here that words turn into image and the first representation of European citizenship is best encapsulated in the following sketch:

Homo oeconomicus was a male qualified coal and steel worker (from 1957 a worker *per se*) of French, German, Dutch, Luxembourgian, Italian or Belgium nationality. He was a worker, husband and father and chances are that the war had left him unemployed and unable to provide for his family. The Community provided him with both hope and concrete possibilities to find work and to secure a descent quality of life for himself and his family by doing two things. First, the Community created about 100.000 new jobs to address the pressing problem of unemployment in the coal and steel industry, and contributed to better housing provisions for miners, and second, the Community provided qualified European coal and steel workers (from 1957 a worker *per se*) with the rights to free movement and to establishment in any of the member states. And so, in order to find work, European coal and steel workers from across the Community packed their bags and used their newly acquired European citizens' rights by moving from Italy to the Ruhr area, from Belgium to the Saarland and from Germany to the Campine. However, the Commission understood that homo oeconomicus would only move across Europe if he could take his family with him and be sure that the Community also provided for his wife and children. In fact, homo oeconomicus was portrayed as a responsible family man who was concerned with achieving a comfortable standard of living for himself and his family. And in order to show him that moving to another member state would not threaten his standard of living, the Community concerned itself with the harmonisation of social security schemes across Europe where necessary. The Community also provided for the workers' families through housing initiatives and by enabling the workers' children to get enrolled in local schools[84], and by facilitating language education for the workers' wives (amongst other things). Once homo oeconomicus and his family had become familiar with their new European way of life and settled in their new home, the Community expected homo oeconomicus to become more curious about the European Community and his fellow European citizens. Accordingly, the Community provided homo oeconomicus and his family with a financial bonus to go travelling across Europe. The new opportunities the European Community offered to homo oeconomicus would, so the Community hoped, encourage him to inform himself about the Community, to develop a curiosity and ultimately acquire a European 'civil consciousness' facilitated through the auxiliary use of explicitly European economic-social symbols such as the labour card and the ECSC flag.

The Community's Early Public Communication Policy and Homo Oeconomicus

In order to understand how the representation 'homo oeconomicus' was publicly communicated, it is necessary to contextualise and situate the Community's public communication policy, which started in 1952 when the Information Service of the High Authority was founded.

As pointed out in chapter "A Civil Europe" the Community's civil competencies were limited in the early days of European integration. Realising the importance of informing the European public about the European integration process, its successes and failures, its objectives and purpose, the early European officials had to be creative in finding opportunities to devise a public communication strategy despite the lack of official consequences. One of the first things they did was, as noted previously, to use the rather ambiguous 'brief' as concerns informing the public of art. 5 ToP to their own advantage. By interpreting the mission this article referred to as stimulating a European civil consciousness amongst an inclusive European public, the Community was able to conduct a public communication policy that was not constrained by matters of competence.

Indeed, Monnet thought that in order for the High Authority to fulfil its legal obligation of consulting with interested parties, it needed to develop a public communication policy directed at *all* interested parties[85] and that meant in practise the requirement to address a European public comprised of 160 million people[86] and to target 'all levels of the population'.[87] In 1960, the European Parliament confirmed this early interpretation of the Commission's public communication competencies by insisting that the Community had competences in the field of information policy *pactum de contrahendo*,[88] as it wouldn't be able to fulfil the Treaties' stipulations otherwise.

The importance the Community gave to informing a wide European public of which homo oeconomicus was part was reflected in the budget allocation of the Commission for public communication. Between 1950 and 1960 the budget allocated to information activities addressed at the European general public were consistently higher than that for workers and trade unions (see Table 1 below).

Correspondingly, in 1958 the ECSC noted that the Community's public communication policy efforts 'had long ceased to be confined to the admittedly most important fields of economic and social information work and of daily press releases, and was bringing all appropriate technical sources to bear in an endeavour to reach the various circles which make up European public opinion'.

At this point, it is already possible to correct two historical claims made by scholars about the early Community information/public communication policy. First, the above shows that Valentini and Nesti[89] were wrong to claim that information policy wasn't felt to be a binding institutional priority until 2005. This will become even clearer in the following. Second, it is incorrect to argue that the information policy was uninterested in

Table 1 The Commission's information policy budget for 1955–60[a]

	General public	*Workers and trade unions*
1955/56	2.75m FB	1m FB
1956/57	4.64m FB	2.2m FB
1957/58	5.1m FB	2.3m FB
1958/59	n/a	n/a
1959/60	5.0m FB	3.0 FB

[a]Source: Amorin-Fulle, G. (1995: 133–136).

the general public.[90] Terra has provided a misleading account about the scope of the Community's information activities of the 1950s and 1960s when she claimed that the 'sphere of action' of the Press and Information Service consisted of 'disseminating information amongst designated 'multipliers' drawn from the political, academic, economic and media elites in order to foster support for European integration'.[91] The general public was the dominant audience for the Community's public communication policy and information activities in the 1950s and 1960s. The reason for addressing opinion leaders rather than an 'elite' from 1963 onwards was that the Community thought that it could reach a wider audience more effectively through them.[92]

From the 1950s onwards the Community's public communication strategy had two objectives: first, to inform the European public about European integration and raise awareness amongst this European public that a 'new Europe' was being built and second, it was necessary to show the neonate European citizens—homo oeconomicus—what European integration concretely meant and what benefits homo oeconomicus could derive from it. The Community believed that a public communication policy was the *sine qua non* for the eventual emergence of a European civil consciousness. Only if, so the Commission believed, Europeans were provided with information about the Community could they identify with it and develop a feeling of belonging to it. As such, homo oeconomicus, as a narrow representation of European citizenship, found its place amongst the wide European public in a public communication policy that was more oriented by the vision of moving towards the establishment of a federal Europe to which all Europeans would belong and could identify with. It is clear, however, that some public communication material was more general and orientated towards a wide audience, whereas some of the material was more technical and related to the employment and social environment of homo oeconomicus. Some public communication outputs combined both.

What characterised all public communication outputs was the use of a factual style of public communication. Through this style of public communication the Commission sought to inform Europeans about the value and significance of European citizenship, the European integration process, the existence of the Community, its successes and failures, the utility of the Community method and its contribution to the preservation of peace and the achievement of prosperity in Europe.[93] That informing the European public was a priority was also clearly expressed by the European Parliament, which argued that the short-term objective of the Commission's information policy was to inform the public about the existence of the Community's institutions, to provoke interest and to inform the European public about the problems and the achievements of the Community.[94] This short-term objective was considered imperative if the Community was to exist as a democratic entity,[95] if a European public opinion was to emerge and if the Community was not to turn into some 'technocratic monster' disconnected from the European citizenry.[96] Or as Hallstein put it: 'Nor, indeed, was it ever the intention of the Schuman Plan, or of the countries that accepted it, to establish in Europe a kind of remote technocracy ruling by ukase from some supranational Kremlin'[97] but to '(…) to associate the citizens of Europe with the building of our Community'.[98]

The concern to inform an inclusive European public brought with it a concern for public communication in a clear and simple language. Monnet continuously insisted on the use of simple but powerful language. According to him, Europeans would be suspicious about Europe if it was not able to clearly talk about itself and its policies, its objectives, plans, successes and failures.[99] In fact, Monnet's concern for simple language extended beyond the general public to include his own projects and speeches that he needed to present. He would practise in front of his chauffeur and his wife, and only if they agreed that what he said was easily comprehensible would he go ahead and present it formally.[100] One of the reasons Monnet expressed for his insistence on simple language was that people will only trust you are being sincere if they understand what you say and see that you tell everyone the same thing.[101] Van Helmont, a European official, said that Monnet was fond of clarity and precision. When he wrote, he would always use simple words and avoid sophisticated and only rarely used terms.[102]

In accordance with this conviction, official documents concerned with the Information Service of the High Authority pointed out the importance of simple and non-technical language.[103] Equally, Hallstein realised the need to show that 'Europe was for all'. He argued that 'the average citizen—and this must be a matter of concern to us—feels somewhat lost when confronted with an edifice whose structure appears to him complicated; he easily imagines that Europe is a matter exclusively for technicians, economists and a few political figures upon whom it is difficult for him to exercise any influence. This opinion is obviously erroneous (…)'.[104]

Overall, the factual style of public communication was applied in all the Community's public communication activities, which can essentially be categorised into first, the national factual mass media and second, quasi-fictional material such as brochures and film.[105]

Factual Mass Media

The Commission realised the value of establishing a presence in the national mass media (radio, TV, print)[106] and of establishing good relationships with the press, in particular. Monnet, for example, paid constant attention to the establishment of good press relations with journalists—he would often invite them to discuss current affairs and ask for their advice[107]—and was at the same time quite instrumental in his use of them to inform the European public about the Community's affairs.[108] The Commission also encouraged national and regional newspapers to send correspondents to Luxembourg to cover the workings of the ECSC and the EEC, invited journalists to visit the Community institutions, gave regular press conferences and sent out daily information bulletins to European news agencies.[109] However, and at the same time, Monnet realised the fragility of European integration and particularly of the Community's newly established institutions and was afraid that public discussions about European matters that were in the process of being decided could threaten the successful continuation of European integration.[110] It is in this context that the famous anecdote about Monnet telling Gazzo, the founder of the press agency Agence Europe, to stop reporting about the European Community needs to be reinterpreted as Monnet objecting to against Gazzo reporting while matters were still being deliberated but his welcoming reporting after decisions had been taken.[111]

The Commission saw a threefold benefit in maintaining good relations with the media, especially the press: first, the press was seen as a way of reaching a large audience of Europeans with information about the Community; second, it was hoped that a press which reported European news would help Europeans to collectively feel more (and not less, as is sometimes the case in the UK today) European. Quite simply, Monnet, his collaborators and successors hoped that the generation of European news would show that national identity and European identity were compatible. In other words, it was hoped that European news would frame neonate *European* invariant civil concerns and make Europeans aware of the existence of common civil concerns[112] and third, it was hoped that in the medium term the media would fulfil a scrutinising function (its fourth-estate function[113]) which was estimated crucial, as Hallstein pointed out: 'If our great task [of establishing a democratic political union] is to be carried through to success, we need (…) the criticism and the encouragement of the organs of public opinion'.[114] Indeed the Community, comparing itself to other Western liberal democracies,[115] felt that it had the democratic duty to inform the future European citizens about the Community and that the European citizen had a right to information.[116] Whereas the EP stated that it was necessary to sell one's ideas as well in politics as in the advertising business,[117] it equally emphasised that only morally justified means can be used in public communication activities or outputs addressed to the European public about European integration. It was clearly stated that the Community rejected propaganda in the sense of muzzling the media, as it has been used in totalitarian regimes, but that it encouraged the propagation of the European idea in a democratic framework.[118]

From the above we can draw two conclusions: first, and linked to early public communication policy, it is fair to argue that the early European officials cannot be understood as 'proponent[s] of arcane policy'[119] or 'spin-doctors'[120] and that it is misleading to argue, in the light of the Gazzo anecdote, that they were primarily concerned with stifling debate[121] or that they intended to avoid the reporting of European affairs[122] and preferred to hide where integration was going and how it was undertaken.[123] Second, the public communication activities of the Community pointed to an early understanding of the importance of factual mass media—and especially the news media—for what would later by termed an autonomous civil society. News is important, as it has the ability to 'represent the public to itself' and because it provides citizens the 'only source of firsthand experience (…) about their fellow citizens [and] about their motives for acting the way they do (…)'.[124] The Community realised the importance of independent media since the beginning of European integration and has since attempted to establish a European public service broadcaster—however, each attempt failed. The value of the news media also lay in the fact that it revealed public opinion and that if it acted according to its ideal democratic function, it would be able to expose government corruption and hold power holders accountable. This is the news' essential democratic role by which it contributes to the maintenance of an autonomous civil society.[125] At this point it is worth mentioning, and I will return to this in more detail in the following chapter, that the

Community was interested in public opinion polls from the beginning of European integration.

Quasi-Fictional/Quasi-Factual Mass Media

The Community used a variety of quasi-fictional/quasi-factual mass media, including contributions to national magazines such as *Ihre Freundin* and *Heimat und Familie* as well as documentaries. The first documentary 'Histoire d'un Traité' (1954) was translated in several Community languages. In France, it was shown in approximately 500 cinemas, reaching an audience of two million viewers. Three other documentaries were produced in 1956, two more in 1958 and between 1958 and 1963 at least five more short films were produced.[126]

The main public communication tool was brochures—both in black-and-white and in colour—that were appropriate to inform European citizens about European integration in an accessible style. Unfortunately, we can't be sure about how many of these brochures the Community produced, as my archival work revealed that the inventories have been lost. We do have, however, some indication about circulation figures. Caron claimed that in 1962 the circulation figure of publications such as brochures and leaflets was of 3,125,000 copies.[127] With regard to the style it is fair to say that the Community translated Monnet's emphasis on the need for an easy and simple language into practise: sentences were short and straightforward and jargon was altogether avoided.[128] The brochures were intended to be read by a wide European public[129] and combined both factual and fictional elements.

The factual elements had an informative and explanatory purpose. Often the brochures provided historical background with timelines on key events[130] and included questions such as 'how' and 'why',[131] portrayed European key actors such as Monnet, Schuman, Hallstein, Adenauer and Rey,[132] included pictures of official European events such as the signing of a Treaty and the commemoration of it[133] as well as the photographs of the buildings housing the official European institutions.[134] The brochures equally put a focus on explaining what the new institutions were and how they worked.[135] The Community emphasised the teleological aim of the European Community, which was to move towards a European federation, a politically unified Europe and a fully democratic union.[136] It highlighted both success and failure (the latter according to Foret[137] was presented in a quite modest way) on the way to European political integration[138] and emphasised in the case of the latter that failure did not mean that European integration lost its objective of becoming a political union but merely that a change in the way to achieve it was necessary. In other words, the Community attempted to show that it was able to adapt to circumstances and to come up with a Plan B when needed[139]—an ability that Runciman[140] sees as a defining feature of modern democracies. The brochures were also concerned with European economic development and economic growth in terms of the GNP (which was portrayed to be increasing quicker for the Community than the USA or the UK, for example), imports and exports and wages.[141] Facts and figures were either directly incorporated in the text and/or rendered more accessible to the reader by presenting them in graphs and tables,[142] and often maps were used[143] as illustrations. Information about economic integration and progress was sometimes combined with more detailed information about attendant policy areas such as social policy or transport policy,[144] and it was explained how these policy initiatives impacted and improved Europeans lives in terms of greater consumer choice, freedom of movement, working conditions and living standards and conditions, including social security issues[145]—the latter was, as I have argued throughout, from the start (intended to be) extended to workers and their families.

These factual elements were often combined with quasi-fictional ones in an attempt to render European integration more 'human' and 'individually relevant', less technocratic[146] and in some ways more fun. In this sense, the Community can be seen to have attempted to provide the European public with a factual but also emotional point of orientation in the complex landscape of Community policies and their evolving nature. Specifically, the quasi-fictional elements included the more 'decorative' aspects[147] such as photographs of children, women and families (...) which were often embedded in the tale of a 'Europe for all' and a 'Europe for the future',[148] photos of workers[149]; cartoons and caricatures of individuals, the relationship between Europeans, the new 'European way of life', economic progress and developments with regard to the Common Market[150] as well as tales about a European peace, growth and stability illustrated by pictures showing a destructed post-war Europe and pictures that showed that the Community is 'building' and 'creating' a new Europe.[151] In this way, the brochures sometimes represented a simplified and romanticised version of European integration history.

Overall, quasi-fictional/quasi-factual public communication tools provided the Commission with the opportunity to tell stories about Europeans in a 'fictional and ahistorical way'[152] and to 'provide a continuous flow about ongoing social events and actors'.[153] Such stories can have civil force because they interpret some events, plots and characters as 'typical' and place them 'into revealing and easily interpretable situations that represent civil and uncivil motives and relations'.[154] What the Commission hoped to achieve through the use of brochures and quasi-fictional/quasi-factual accounts was to provide European citizens with a self-understanding of their encouraged European identity and belonging to a newly established European (civil) society. The European public was hoped to believe that the 'narrative accounts', to borrow from Alexander, told in brochures and films 'describe faithfully not only the present but also the past'[155] and, importantly for the Community, the future. Brochures and films can be seen as the Commission's intuitive attempt to provide a not-yet-emerged or existent European civil society with a civil discourse it could identify with. Quasi-fictional/quasi-factual media broadcasted these events and characters in relation to our civil identity, to who we are as a civil society. They showed us the significance of European integration in relation to who we, as Europeans, were and are.

However, the Community's public communication policy, and its aim to stimulate a European civil consciousness and feeling of belonging to Europe amongst a wide European public, soon experienced a setback. De Gaulle was against Hallstein's federal ambitions for European integration.[156] Hallstein, President of the Commission, considered the European institutions, notably the Commission, sovereign and almost independent supranational federal institutions. Hallstein himself also behaved like a sovereign, demanding the same attention as a head of state,[157] and the public communication policy he pursued became increasingly political in that it actively promoted European political integration. Instead of factual information, affective and emotive messages aiming at fostering a European identity amongst European citizens were included. De Gaulle was in particular against the Commission acting independently from the member states in its public communication initiatives.[158] Accordingly, his minister of foreign affairs, Maurice Couve de Murville, proposed the following point as a matter of discussion at the first extraordinary session of the Council in Luxembourg on 17 and 18 January 1966: 'Information policy should not be planned and implemented by the Commission alone but jointly by the Council and the Commission. The Council should exercise effective, and not only budgetary, control over the Joint Information Service of the Communities'. This was particularly because the Treaties did not provide explicitly for the Community to have competences in the field of information policies. In the aftermath of the empty chair crisis and the Luxembourg compromise, the Commission attempted to act in a neutral manner and to only release factual information related to issues that fell within the Community's scope of competences as defined in the Treaties. It tried to avoid antagonising the French. Accordingly, the Commission no longer mentioned the Community's objective of forming a European political federation.[159] This changed, however, when Pompidou succeeded de Gaulle as French President.[160]

4 From 'Homo Oeconomicus' to 'A People's Europe'

In the late 1960s and the early 1970s the representation of European citizenship began to change. This change was triggered by newly emerging possibilities to push European political integration forward.

In 1968 the Community's main objective of completing the customs union was successfully achieved and so the Commission began to spell out the Community's objectives for the future in a wide-ranging programme. This programme included, for example, further progress towards federal institutions, to give the Commission executive powers, to introduce majority voting in the Council, to extend the democratic powers of the Parliament and to enable European citizens to participate in Community life through direct elections of the European Parliament.[161] The resignation of de Gaulle and the arrival of George Pompidou as French President in 1969 eased the relation between the Community and France, and gave hope for an easier collaboration between the member states and the Community and progress of European political integration along the lines of 'completion/deepening/enlargement'.[162]

However, the most significant event in the late 1960s was the Hague Summit (1969),[163] which, despite some disappointments, can be seen as the revival of European political integration. Revival here needs to be understood as a re-emerging optimism. According to Griffiths, the 'late 1960s and the early 1970s started with a new sense of optimism about the future of the Community'.[164] This optimism emerged despite the difficulties the Community faced, such as the budgetary crisis, inflation and economic stagnation.[165] Rey expressed this kind of optimism at the Hague summit as follows: 'The recent events will enable us all to celebrate this great anniversary [of the Schuman Declaration] without a feeling of remorse towards the great figure and political initiative of Robert Schuman, since the Community is on the way to recover the creative drive which had been missing in recent months. On 9 May 1970, the Parliament, Council and Commission will together demonstrate with a better conscience and renewed energy, their will to hasten the building of Europe'.[166] Hastening 'the building' of Europe meant essentially to push European political integration forward. According to Rey 'it was essential to make clear to European and world opinion that after twenty years the Community had abandoned none of its political aims',[167] to which the final communiqué of the Hague Summit (1969) added: 'The Heads of State or Government therefore wish to reaffirm their belief in the political objectives which give the Community its full meaning and scope, their determination to carry their undertaking through to the end, and their confidence in the final success of their efforts'. Following the Hague Summit (1969), the foreign ministers of the Six drafted the Davignon Report (1970),[168] which emphasised the understanding of Europe as a political union and the need for the Community to learn to speak with one voice on the international scene in matters of foreign policy.

The increasing understanding of the Community as a political entity on the way to greater political integration and potentially a European federation affected the Commission's conception of the European citizen because the Community realised that such a federation required of itself a commitment to meet the liberal standards of citizen autonomy and democratic scrutiny and that in this respect homo oeconomicus's political and civil-legal rights were too narrowly conceived. In other words, and again reifying the representation homo oeconomicus, we can say that homo oeconomicus lacked sufficient civil power to legitimise and scrutinise the European institutions and thereby he was unable to fulfil the citizens' political and civil role, as imagined by the Community, in a European federation. This 'deficit' of homo oeconomicus was to be addressed in the second representation of European citizenship 'A People's Europe'.

Notes

1. From Lapis Lazuli by W.B. Yeats.
2. According to Rabier (personal communication, 26 December 2014), Churchill did not consider Britain to be part of the United States of Europe and was talking about continental Europe.
3. Warner (1985).

4. For insights into Monnet's life, personality and way of working, see Rieben et al. (1971), Fondation Jean Monnet pour l'Europe et Centre de recherches européennes (ed.) (1978), van Helmont (1981), Kohnstamm (1982, 1989), Fontaine (1988), Uri (1989), Duchêne (1994) and Adam (2011), amongst others.
5. In September 1949 US Secretary of State Dean Acheson and British Secretary of State for Foreign Affairs Ernest Bevin asked Schuman to devise a plan on how to reintegrate Germany and overcome the German problem. Acheson, Bevin and Schuman were to meet again at the conference on 10 May 1950 to discuss Schuman's proposition. Not having written this proposition, Schuman welcomed Monnet's plans outlined in the first few drafts of what was to become the Schuman declaration. Schuman was handed a copy on 29 April 1950 and after studying it in detail he agreed to pursue this project further.
6. This account draws from Monnet's memoirs published in 1978.
7. Lerner and Gordon (1969: 170).
8. See Coombes (1970: 21).
9. Monnet (1978).
10. Collowald (2014).
11. Monnet was involved in the League of Nations and experienced that plans for peace can flounder swiftly because of national self-interest and hapless idealism (see Runciman 2013).
12. At this point it is worth pointing out that my understanding of the preparation of the Schuman Declaration, its significance and the importance of individual actors, including Monnet, differs from Milward et al. Milward (1992, 2000), known as having provided a revisionist account of European integration, argued three things that are at odds with my account. First, he argued that the Schuman Declaration aimed at strengthening and protecting nation-states and that in some ways the Schuman Declaration was a continuation of the Monnet Plan and simply intended to strengthen France's economic recovery and allow for its economic superiority. In fact, Milward (2000: 4) understood European integration as 'a part of that post-war rescue of the European nation-state'. I believe this complete reliance on a 'state-centric rationale for European integration' (Dinan 2014: 347) to be a simplification. Of course, each of the nation-states was concerned with its own survival (economic and otherwise), its own interests and the issue of security, but such concerns are not incommensurable with a European outlook, federal ambitions and the transfer of certain sovereign powers to a supranational level. All throughout the first two decades of European integration in particular, Commission officials emphasised time and time again that they did not attempt to dissolve nation-states but rather to unite them in a common European undertaking based on a cer-

tain degree of solidarity. Second, Milward claimed that the role of Monnet, Schuman and others involved in the writing of the Declaration has been overstated in historical accounts. He (2000: 318) emphasised that these actors had been misleadingly referred to as 'saints' and incorporated in 'legends of great men' and insisted on them being 'busy politicians' rather than 'theorists'. The position that these actors were unimportant is not tenable and is not supported by archival evidence such as documents, interviews or testimonies. Monnet surely had a crucial role in the development of the Schuman Declaration and even Milward acknowledged at some point that Schuman was a key player. Of course, these actors were not 'saints', but they were not simply pragmatists or hypocrites. In fact, they had a shared vision which can be found particularly in official speeches. Milward further claimed that Monnet was in favour of a bureaucratic state rather than a democratic arrangement—a claim which again finds no support in archival material, testimonies, biographies or speeches and as such it is a charge that has remained unsubstantiated.

13. Essentially, Allen (2014: 47) understood democratic writing to mean 'group writing' which, according to her, 'is not easy, but, when done well, it heads the ranks of human achievement. It even stands in front of works of individual genius, because it involves a far greater degree of difficulty'.
14. Bernard Clappier, Head of Schuman's Cabinet, also supported the preparation of the Schuman Declaration but is not referred to as a 'permanent' member (Collowald 2014).
15. According to Gerbet (1962), the idea of pooling the French and German primary industries was not new but emerged in the late 1940s. In fact, in August 1949 the Consultative Assembly of the Council of Europe discussed the idea of integrating the coal, iron and steel industries of Luxembourg, Belgium, Lorraine, Great-Britain and the Ruhr and to put it under the control of a supranational authority. However, the suggestion was perceived as too audacious (the failure of the 1933 London conference might still have been vivid) and was therefore not pursued.
16. Politicians across the world recognised the importance of the European project and the importance of one man in its creation: Jean Monnet. It was Monnet who juggled and who was able to combine courage, analytical skills, timing and a bit of audacity successfully. For his 90th birthday, various politicians paid tribute to him and it is worth citing some of the contributors. I will leave the citations in French as I have found them in Fondation Jean Monnet pour l'Europe et al. (ed.) (1978). My apologies to those who find this inconvenient, but I believe they capture more than my translations would how Monnet was perceived and described. Valery Giscard d'Estaing refers to Monnet's 'lucidité de l'analyse, l'ardeur de l'imagination et la force de la volonté' (ibid.: 9) and Helmut Schmidt, in a

similar way, describes Monnet's 'clairvoyance, courage et [sa] ferme volonté' (ibid.: 14). Monnet's was driven by an 'esprit d'idéal', according to Adolfo Suarez, to which Jimmy Carter adds 'l'esprit d'innovation' et 'l'énergie'. Carter continues to say that 'Peu d'hommes ont marqué leur temps d'une empreinte aussi profonde' and are seen as 'le pionnier de toute une génération d'Européens' (Hans Dietrich Genscher in CREL 1978: 19). M CA Vanderklaauw (ibid.: 25) expressed a 'sentiment de profonde gratitude' for, as Willy Ritschard (ibid.: 28) adds, 'votre inestimable contribution à la construction de l'Europe'. For other accounts of Monnet's personality and his contribution to European integration see Reuter (1980), van Helmont (1981), Kohnstamm (1982, 1989), Fontaine (1988), Küsters (1989), Rieben et al. (2004), Fontaine (2013).
17. This account draws from Reuter (1980).
18. For details on the preparation of the Schuman Declaration, including how Schuman secured Germany's agreement, see Gerbet (1962), Massip (1980), Beyer (1986), Poidevin (1986), Lejeune (2000), Rieben et al. (2000) and Roth (2008).
19. English translation: World peace cannot be safeguarded without the making of creative efforts proportionate to the dangers which threaten it. The contribution which an organised and living Europe can bring to civilisation is indispensable to the maintenance of peaceful relations.
20. For written exchanges between Schuman and Monnet between 1947 and 1953, see Fondation Jean Monnet pour l'Europe (1986).
21. Lejeune (2000). For biographies and insights into Schuman's personality, see Schuman (1963), Fondation Jean Monnet pour l'Europe et al. (1964), Brugmans (1965), Poidevin (1986), Borella et al. (2006), Roth (2008) and Benning (2013).
22. Gerbet (1962).
23. See Gerbet (1962).
24. Lejeune (2000). Monnet (1978) endorsed a similar approach and emphasised that it was necessary to be strategic but not calculating and that creating distrust was to be avoided at all times. Featherstone (1994) has interpreted such statements and the way Monnet undertook his role in the first few years of European integration as undemocratic and characterised Monnet's approach as elitist and technocratic, to which Haller (2008: 59) added that more or less all of the early European officials need to be understood as having 'autocratic tendencies'. Schulz-Forberg and Stråth (2010) equally suggested that in the 1950s there existed no understanding by the 'founding fathers' of the EU as a democracy. Majone (2009) also understood European integration as an elite conception with little concern for democracy. However, these judgements cannot be supported by historical evidence and are misleading, as they were made without considering the context of the time (also Harrison and Pukallus 2015).

25. Collowald (2014: 67).
26. Cited in Urwin (1995: 44).
27. Runciman (2014: 154).
28. Adam (2011).
29. Runciman (2014: 121).
30. Just as Germany and France had economic and political motives, the other joining states did too. Italy joined the ECSC for economic reasons: After the Second World War, Italy had an unemployment rate of almost 10%. Freedom of movement for workers was therefore seen as a key factor in diminishing unemployment and was a key factor in Italy's participating in the ECSC. Moreover, about 70,000–80,000 Italian coal and steel workers were already prospective member states at that point. The Netherlands and Belgium, relatively small countries next to Germany and France, in particular, were in rather weak positions. The coal industry of the Netherlands accounted for only 5.6% of the total output of negotiating states, and Belgium, albeit a significant producer of both steel and coal, suffered from high production costs and was burdened with inefficient coal mines (see Stirk and Weigall 1999; also Dedman 2010). For an account of how Monnet managed to handle the Six and their different views and demands, see von Simson (1989).
31. On the 1955 Messina conference leading to the creation of the EEC, see Moravcsik (1998) and for testimonies of the negotiations leading to the Treaties of Rome, see Melchionni et Ducci (ed.) (2007).
32. Coppé (1956: 4).
33. Hallstein (1972: 23).
34. European Communities (1971a: 24).
35. Hallstein (1963: 14).
36. To which Caron (1963) and Hallstein (1962a: 29) added a social domain. Also Spierenburg and Poidevin 1994.
37. Monnet (1955).
38. Spierenburg and Poidevin (1994: 244)
39. Ibid.
40. On the debate about the powers of the European Parliament in the 1960s/1970s, see Schrag Sternberg (2013).
41. Hallstein (1959: 201). In fact, Rabier (1964) noted insufficient opportunities for citizens to participate in Community matters—an aspect which is picked up by Olivi (1971), who emphasised the need to involve the public and to be in close contact with the people. This is because, according to Olivi (1971), the Community had responsibility over people's lives and has therefore to have a real meaning for the man in the street (see also HA 1954a).
42. Burke ([1770] 1981: 317).

43. In the current European Parliament we have what can only be described as factions based upon national party outlooks, allegiances and priorities. We do not have as yet genuine EU parties that resemble the organisational and political agendas of nationally based parties.
44. Alexander (2006: 123).
45. Krasner (2010: 96).
46. The UK government's (2010–15) stand on EU immigration policy represents both a discourse of contestation and a nostalgic lament over the loss of national sovereignty with regard to border controls.
47. Monnet (1978).
48. Here again, Milward would disagree.
49. Hallstein (1970 cited in Loth 2007: 82).
50. Kohnstamm (1982).
51. Wessels, personal communication, 23 November 2011.
52. Non-discrimination on the grounds of nationality is nowadays considered the cornerstone of European citizenship and EU fundamental rights.
53. Baldoni (2003: 5).
54. Maas (2007: 16). In fact, there had been a discussion about whether the right to free movement should be given to all coal and steel workers, but whereas 'Italy and the High Authority had strongly urged that the definition of worker qualifications be interpreted broadly, other governments succeeded in limiting free movement to certain skilled workers' (ibid.).
55. In 1961 the idea of a European identity card (see EP 1961) to be issued to all member state nationals emerged. However, this project was never put into practise.
56. Billig (1995).
57. Art. 3 ToP, EC (1961b).
58. Art. 48 ToP, EP (1961).
59. I treat these in this section as part of the economic aspect attached to 'homo oeconomicus', because the civil-legal rights are conditioned by economic stipulations and as such do not exist independently of the economic aspects.
60. Alexander (2006: 92). On early pressure groups in the European Community, see Meynaud and Sidjanski (1971) and Tilly (2014). The idea of the court of public opinion goes back to Jeremy Bentham and his thought-experiment—the Public Opinion Tribunal. See also Cutler (1999).
61. Ibid.
62. Levi-Sandri (1964b, c) recognised the value of and need for trade unions/workers' associations in a democratic Europe.
63. Alexander (2006).
64. Alexander (2006: 151).
65. Alexander (2006: 152).

66. In 1957, the European Economic and Social Committee (EESC) 'was set up (...) in order to involve economic and social interest groups in the establishment of the common market and to provide institutional machinery for briefing the European Commission and the Council of Ministers on European Union issues' (see European Economic and Social Committee 2010).
67. Olsen (2006, 2008, 2012).
68. Hallstein (1964a: 3).
69. Moravcsik (1998: 6).
70. EC (1961b).
71. See Commission (2012).
72. Daly (2007: 2).
73. Also Levi-Sandri (1962, 1964a).
74. (1962: 3).
75. Spierenburg and Poidevin (1994: 325).
76. Ronan (1975).
77. The EC (1969a) criticised the provisions on social policy in the Treaty as insufficient, as the Treaty lacks an agreement of how to interpret the social provisions. In this sense, the EC (1969a) argued that what the Treaty did not say on social policy is actually as important as what it stipulated.
78. Council Directive 68/360/EEC of 15 October 1968.
79. Ibid.
80. Council Directive 77/486/EEC of 25 July 1977.
81. See Geyer (2000) and Walkenhorst (2008) on aspects of European vocational training.
82. Ronan (1975). Levi-Sandri (1963) in fact argued that it was necessary to develop a European social policy if the objectives of the Treaties were to be achieved. He (1964b) argued, and I believe it is worth quoting at length, that 'the achievement of social objectives must be considered today as a means of giving form and substance to the principles of freedom and equality enunciated by constitutions. Citizens must not only equal before the law but must also have an equal start as regards the basic minimum requirements of existence. And freedom must also be safeguarded by protection vis-à-vis these minimum requirements (...). The role of social policy in a modern state is therefore clear (...). The role of social policy in European integration cannot, mutatis mutandis, be any different or be situated on a different plane'. To this he added (ibid.) that 'If the aim is really to build that vaster and deeper Community between peoples who were for so long divided by bloody combat, that is to say if we really wish to build a United States of Europe it is not sufficient to ensure stability, expansion, balanced trade and fair competition. Above all, the European peoples must also accept and will this union and recognise it as the best

means of political and social organisation. In other words, the European ideal must (...) be the common patrimony of our generation and our peoples. For this purpose a social policy (...) is a sine qua non. The European Community must be a genuine instrument of social justice and must be seen to be such by the working masses, who form the great majority of our population'. Only two years later Levi-Sandri (1966) appeared disillusioned about the possibilities for a genuine European social policy and disappointed about the unwillingness of European officials to follow the narrow possibilities the Treaty offers rather than interpreting the Treaty more widely.

83. EC (1969a: 5).
84. From the early 1950s onwards, the ECSC started to further initiatives within the field of education (see particularly Henderson 1965). For example, the employees who relocated to Luxembourg needed to school their children. Even though Luxembourg had agreed to school these children, the problem of multilingualism made it impossible for the children to simply go to a Luxembourg school. The Community took the opportunity to create European kindergarten, primary and secondary schools (the latter out of necessity once the children had almost finished primary school) and thereby progressively entered the field of education policy, which it judged important for European civil integration since: 'Being brought up in contact with each other, and freed at an early age from the prejudices which divide, and initiated into the beauties and values of the various cultures, they will as they grow up become conscious of their solidarity. While retaining love for and pride in their country, they will become Europeans in spirit, well prepared to complete and consolidate the work undertaken by their fathers to establish a prosperous and united Europe' (Henderson 1965: 189). However, these schools touched only a very limited number of school children (about 5000 pupils in 1964—Henderson 1965: 181, inscriptions on foundation stones of schools). On European education policy see, for example, Commission (1973c, 2006), Corbett (2005), Petit (2005, 2007).
85. HA (1956a: 1 emphasis in the original).
86. HA (1955b).
87. ECSC (1958: 101).
88. EP (1960:6).
89. Valentini and Nesti (2010).
90. Nesti (2010) has argued this.
91. Terra (2010: 50), also Reinfeldt (2012).
92. Harrison and Pukallus (2015). Reinfeldt (2012) acknowledged that elites were targeted due to a lack of financial and personal resources but neglected to realise that the Community had attempted to directly target the general

public before turning to elites understood as opinion-multipliers in 1963. As such, and contra Reinfeldt (2012), it was not the case that the Community targeted primarily elites throughout the 1950s/1960s.

At this point it is worthwhile mentioning what can be referred to as a 'eurosphere', a term coined by Rabier and Meynaud in the 1950s. This term designated the different people and groups that participate actively in the European integration movement. According to Meynaud and Sidjanski (1965, see also Sidjanski 1996: 282), the eurosphere comprised of three sub-spheres. First, the promoters of European integration (Schuman, Monnet etc.); second, the 'eurocrats' and third, other spheres on the European and national level (media, administrations etc.). As such, the eurosphere can be said to be inhabited rather by actors than by citizens per se (Collowald interview 22 February 2012). It is remarkable that this notion of a 'eurosphere' emerged directly out of the European Community and that was before Habermas published his work on the public sphere in the early 1960s, from which then later, allegedly, the notion of a European public sphere was derived. According to Sidjanski (1996: 297), the members of the eurosphere created a network of organisations at the Community level. It was the interactions of these groups that built the grounds for civil participation and the emergence of a European civil society.

93. HA (1954a), ECSC (1957, 1958).
94. EP (1960), also Commission (1970) and EP (1972).
95. EP (1972).
96. EP (1960).
97. Hallstein (1962b: 18).
98. Hallstein (1959: 201).
99. Rabier 1998, in an interview with Bossuat.
100. Rabier, personal communication, 10 December 2011, also HA (1954a).
101. See Monnet (1978).
102. Van Helmont (1981). The emphasis Monnet put on the use of simple language showed that Monnet was concerned about the general public and the way European integration was conveyed to them.
103. In fact, Monnet believed that confining the activities of the Information Service to the provision of technical information addressed at the economic sector would mean that the European public would stay largely unaware of the European integration process and consequently would not be able to feel part of a common destiny (see Lastenouse 2008: 2–3 and HA 1954a: 2). This twofold approach to the Commission's information policy was reflected in the Information Service's structure, which from the start was divided into two divisions. The first was responsible for all information addressed to the coal and steel sector (notably employers and companies) and the second division was concerned with providing information

to the European public 'in its widest extension' (HA 1954a, 1956a). And as such, even the High Authority's early information policy cannot be regarded as confined to speaking to 'the industrials and the unionists' (Rabier, personal communication, 29 January 2012) or describing 'homo oeconomicus' alone.

The structure of the Information Service, which was organised by subject and by milieu, developed continuously. By 1960 six different sections were created, and in 1961 two further sections were added: one concerned with the media, including TV and radio, and another concerned with general affairs (Gramberger 1997: 104). This organisation had the role of enabling the Information Service to issue specialised information to specific target groups. These target groups included women, youth, higher education, primary and secondary education and trade unions.

On information activities for the university sector, see Lastenouse (2003). Lastenouse was recruited in the 1960s by Rabier into the Press and Information Service 'Youth, Universities and adult education'. She is the founder of the University Jean Monnet programmes. With regard to the importance of information policy directed at the University sector, she argued (personal communication, 22 February 2012) that it was particularly the academic sector that turned to the Commission in order to obtain information about the European Community. In other words, the information policy addressed to the academic sector was the direct result of the academy 'pressuring' the Community to issue information on its own functioning and structures etc. (Community information was particularly relevant for academics and students in economy, political sciences and law) but it was not a top-down initiative of the Commission. Bourdon (2010) thus misrepresented information actions in the university sector when she argued that these information activities were elitist and top-down strategies and were, as such, following Monnet's elitist vision of Europe. For more information on the information initiatives in the academic sector, see Lastenouse (2008, historical account of information activities), see Petit (2005, 2006, 2007) and particularly Deshormes (2004, in an interview with Dumoulin and Cailleau), who worked in this same division as Lastenouse.

On information activities for trade unions, see Giro (1993), Chittolina (1993) and Collowald (2003 in an interview with Conrad and Rancon). According to Lastenouse, Collowald and Rabier (personal communication, 22 February 2012), the two most important target groups, besides the general public, were the trade unions and the university sector in the 1950s/1960s.

104. Hallstein (1959: 200).
105. For more information on public communication tools used by the Community, see Ludlow (1998), Pasquinucci (2010), Harrison and Pukallus (2015).

106. HA (1954a, b, c, 1955b, c, 1956a). In fact, from 1958, in each of the reports about the activities of the Information Service, there was a section about in which national media the Community was represented, reported and talked about (see HA 1958a, b, c, d, e, f, g).
107. This was how Monnet attempted to establish a relationship of trust between him and the journalists (Rabier, personal communication, 12 December 2011).
108. Rabier (1993), Guichaoua (1998), Casini (2012).
109. HA (1954a, b, c, 1955b, c, 1956a, 1958a, b, c, d, e, f, g). In 1955, the first 'Association des Journalistes accredités auprès de la C.E.C.A.' was established. The number of accredited journalists increased from 23 in 1956 to about 100 in the 1960, and in 1958 the post of a spokesperson was created. The first spokesperson was Giorgia Smoquina (1959–1961), who was followed by Beniamino Olivi (1961–1968). The creation of the post of a spokesperson also led to more regular press briefings—the Thursday lunchtime one became particularly important—and in order to ensure that as many journalists as possible attended, the Commission attempted to facilitate the journalists' job by providing office space with phones, fax and stationery (see Bastin 2007).
110. Monnet (1978: 367) wrote '(…) I thought it wrong to consult peoples of Europe about the structure of a Community of which they had no practical experience. It was another matter, however, to ensure that in their limited field the new institutions were thoroughly democratic (…)'.
111. Rabier (2000).
112. This is not an entirely unreasonable expectation in light of current communications research on the 'civil power of the news'. For example, Harrison (forthcoming) argues that the civil power of the news lies in the news' ability to undertake boundary maintenance through the framing 'our' invariant civil concerns (ICCs) of identity, legitimacy and risk in relation to what is civil and what is anti-civil. In so doing, the news may ignore, listen to, amplify or influence public sentiment. Whilst Coleman (2012) talked of the news as capable of generating 'civil efficacy', Cushion (2012) regarded the news as sometimes enabling civic and democratic activism. Also see Schudson (2008).
113. The term 'Fourth Estate' goes back to Edmund Burke, according to Thomas Carlyle (1901: 152) and referred to the idea of the press acting as a counterweight to the other three estates, which were then the Church, the aristocracy and the judiciary. In more modern terms, the press is seen to act as a fourth estate and to ensure that citizens receive the information necessary to hold politicians and power holders accountable. The press can only fulfil this function if it acts with complete freedom and is not constrained. It need to be able to take part in society's 'antagonism of opinion'

to use JS Mill's words. Tocqueville (2000[1835]: 210) also supported the idea of the press as conducting itself as a Fourth Estate simply because a free press provides citizens with the 'power of discriminating between different opinions' and 'the sovereignty of the people and the liberty of the press may therefore be looked upon as correlative institutions; just as censorship of the press and universal suffrage are two things which are irreconcilably opposed (…)'.

114. Hallstein (1964a: 26). The Commission has from the start been interested in knowing what Europeans thought about the European Community, whether they agreed with European integration, whether they were hesitant towards it, whether they identified with the new Europe and whether their consensus was one that merely tolerated European integration or proactively supported it (see Haute Autorité (1954a, 1955a, d, e); European Parliament (1960, 1962); Commission (1973a, b)).

For literature on the importance of public opinion for the Community, see Rabier (1965, 1966, 1993, 2000), Guichaoua (1998), Ludlow (1998) and Pasquinucci (2010).

115. The Community does so also with regard to a budget for information policies. By this I mean that the Community was, according to the EP and the Commission, to have a budget dedicated to information policy as have nation-states (EP 1960: 2). This comparison to nation-states which implicitly represented the Community as a federal entity was not appreciated by De Gaulle and this was why France would not take part in votes on the Community's budget for information policy (see also later text on the empty chair crisis).

116. In fact, Hallstein (1961: 16) argued that 'economic integration is a matter for democratic [information] policy. Because it concerns the cause of the citizen, a responsibility to the citizen must be organised which is in line with democratic traditions'.

117. Given this statement and Monnet's time spent in the States, the birthplace of the advertising industry and Madison Avenue (see also Packard 1957), it is fair to assume that the first European politicians were aware of professional information and communication. Accounts of whether professional communication or advertising companies were used in the information policy of the Community vary. Whereas Vanhaeverbeke (2003 in an interview by Dumoulin and Legendre) claimed that no agencies were hired for information purposes until the campaign for the first direct elections of the European Parliament (1979), Sélys (1996) wrote that the Information Service of the High Authority hired a public relations company as early as 1954. Collowald (2003 in an interview by Conrad and Rancon) explained how Hallstein was able to give a speech on the common market in front of an assembly of corporate executives through the Bleustein-Blanchet's con-

tacts. Bleustein-Blanchet was head of 'Publicis', which was the first in France (beginning of the 1960s) to specialise in institutional information or publicity.
118. See EP (1960: 1). See also Commission (1977).
119. Brüggemann (2005).
120. Haller (2008).
121. Gramberger (1997).
122. Brüggemann (2005, 2010). See also Brüggemann (2008) on the European public sphere and European information policy.
123. Gramberger (1997). On misconceptions about the early Community's public communication policy, see Harrison and Pukallus (2015).
124. Alexander (2006: 80).
125. Harrison (forthcoming).
126. See ECSC (1957, 1958). Interestingly, I have been able to compile a list of over 90 short films and documentaries that were produced by the Community between 1955 and 1973. I am currently analyzing these and am researching their production history, which is unknown.
127. Caron (1963); for publication and circulation figures see also ECSC (1957, 1958) and EEC (1962, 1963, 1964).
128. See also Harrison and Pukallus (2015).
129. Also Foret (2001).
130. HA (1956a), EC (1960a, b, 1961b, 1965b, 1969d, 1971a, b).
131. HA (1955f, g, 1956b), EC (1960a, 1961a, 1962, 1965b, 1971b).
132. HA (1957), EC (1960a, 1961a, b, c, 1963c, 1971a, b).
133. HA (1957), EC (1960a, 1961b, 1963c, 1971a, b).
134. EC (1963c, 1971a, b).
135. HA (1955f, g, 1956b, 1957), EC (1959, 1960a, b, 1961a, b, 1962, 1963c, 1969b, d, 1970).
136. HA (1955f, g, 1956b), EC (1959, 1960a, 1961a, 1963b, c, 1964a, b, 1971a).
137. Foret (2001).
138. EC (1960a, 1961b, 1962, 1971a).
139. EC (1960a, 1962, 1963a).
140. Runciman (2013).
141. HA (1955f, g, 1956b, 1957), EC (1959, 1961a, b, 1962, 1963a, 1966, 1969d, 1971a, b).
142. HA (1955f, 1956b, 1957), EC (1959, 1960a, 1961b, 1962, 1969a, d, 1971a, b).
143. HA (1955f, g, 1957), EC (1959, 1960b, 1961a, b).
144. HA (1955f, g), EC (1961a, c, 1962, 1963b, 1965a, 1966, 1969a, c, 1970, 1971b).
145. HA (1955f, g, 1956b), EC (1960b, 1961a, 1962, 1963a, b, c, 1965a, 1966, 1969a).

146. Rabier 1998 interviewed by Bossuat.
147. Also Pourvoyeur (1981).
148. EC (1960b, 1961b, 1969a).
149. HA (1957), EC (1960b, EC 1962, 1963c).
150. HA (1956b, 1957), EC (1960a, b, 1961a, c, 1969a, 1971a).
151. Especially EC (1963c).
152. Alexander (2006: 76).
153. Ibid.: 75.
154. Ibid.: 76.
155. Ibid.: 63.
156. Gramberger (1997), Dinan (2014).
157. Jouve (1967), Gramberger (1997), Rabier (personal communication, 12 December 2011).
158. Rabier (2000).
159. EP (1972: 19).
160. Gramberger (1997). On the empty chair crisis see Ludlow (2006b).
161. BAC 1.7.1968 referred to in Bitsch (2007: 127).
162. Bitsch (2007: 129).
163. The Hague Summit also advanced the economic and monetary union and laid the foundation for the Werner Plan (1970). For a detailed analysis of the Hague Summit (1969) see Ludlow (2003: 1), who showed that the 'Commission pleasure, anticipation and relief, while genuine, coexisted with a degree of discontent'. Ludlow (2003, 2006a) gave a detailed overview of the successes and agreements reached at the Summit and the reasons the Commission had to be disappointed about certain outcomes at the same time.
164. Griffiths (2006: 172).
165. On this, see Griffiths (2006), Ludlow (2006a), Dinan (2010).
166. Rey (1969).
167. Ibid.
168. The Davignon Report was approved by the foreign ministers in Luxemburg on 27 October 1970 and is therefore also known as the Luxemburg Report. I use the term Davignon Report.

References

Adam, M. (2011). *Jean Monnet. Citoyen du Monde. La pensée d'un précurseur.* Paris: L'Harmattan.

Alexander, J. (2006). *The civil sphere.* Oxford: Oxford University Press.

Allen, D. (2014). *Our declaration. A reading of the Declaration of Independence in defense of equality.* New York: W. W. Norton & Company.

Amorin-Fulle, G. (1995). *Médias et construction européenne, généalogie d'une dynamique*. Bachelor's dissertation, History Department, Université Catholique de Louvant-La-Neuve, Louvain-la-Neuve.
Baldoni, E. (2003, July). *The free movement of persons in the European Union: A legal-historical overview* (PIONEUR Working Paper, No. 2).
Bastin, G. (2007). Une politique de l'information ? Le « système Olivi » ou l'invention des relations de presse à la Commission européenne. *La communication sur l'Europe, regards croisés* (pp. 125–136). Strasbourg: L'ENA.
Benning, H. J. (2013). *Robert Schuman: Leben und Vermächtnis*. Wien: Neue Stadt Verlag GmbH.
Beyer, H. (1986). *Robert Schuman. L'Europe par la reconciliation franco-allemande*. Lausanne: Fondation Jean Monnet pour l'Europe et Centre de recherches européennes.
Billig, M. (1995). *Banal nationalism*. London: Sage.
Bitsch, M.-T. (2007). The development of the Single Commission (1967–1972). In M. Dumoulin (Ed.), *The European Commission, 1958–72. History and memories* (pp. 125–151). Luxembourg: Office for Official Publications of the European Communities.
Borella, F., Clément, R., et al. (2006). *Robert Schuman: Homme d'Etat, citoyen du Ciel*. Paris: François-Xavier de Guibert.
Bossuat, G. (1998). *Entretien avec Jacques-René Rabier*, juin, http://www.eui.eu/HAEU/OralHistory/pdf/INT609.pdf. Accessed 15 Jul 2013.
Bourdon, M. (2010). Genèse d'une identité communautaire européenne à l'Université de Grenoble (des années 1960 à nos jours). In M. Boers & J. Raflik (Eds.), *Cultures nationales et identités communautaires. Un défi pour l'Europe* (pp. 125–134). Bruxelles: Peter Lang.
Brüggemann, M. (2005). How the EU constructs the European public sphere: Seven strategies of information policy. *Javnost/The Public, 12*(2), 57–74.
Brüggemann, M. (2008). *Europäische Öffentlichkeit durch Öffentlichkeitsarbeit*. Wiesbaden: VS Verlag für Sozialwissenschaften.
Brüggemann, M. (2010). Public relations between propaganda and the public sphere: The information policy of the European Commission. In C. Valentini & G. Nesti (Eds.), *Public communication in the European Union: History, perspectives and challenges* (pp. 67–91). Newcastle upon Tyne: Cambridge Scholars.
Brugmans, H. (1965). *Le message européen de Robert Schuman*. Lausanne: Fondation Jean Monnet pour l'Europe et Centre de recherches européennes.
Burke, E. ([1770]1981). Thoughts on the cause of the present discontents. In P. Langford (Ed.), *The writings and speeches of Edmund Burke*. Oxford: Clarendon Press.
Carlyle, T. (1901). *Heroes, hero worship and heroic history*. London: Chapman and Hall.

Caron, G. (1963, Janvier 28). *Comment informer l'Europe des problèmes du marché commun?* Expose de M. Giuseppe Caron, Vice-President de la Commission de la Communauté économique européenne à l'Université de Liège.
Casini, F. (2012). The role of information policy in the development of consensus towards European integration (1952–1958). In D. Preda & D. Pasquinucci (Eds.), *Consensus and European integration. An historical perspective [sic]* (pp. 267–278). Brussels: Peter Lang.
CCE (Commission des Communautés Européennes). (1970, Janvier 30). *Organisation de la politique d'information pour 1970* (SEC (70) 378).
CCE (Commission des Communautés Européennes). (1973a, June 18). *Information policy programme for 1973* (SEC (73) 2200).
CCE (Commission des Communautés Européennes). (1973b, Décembre 12). *Programme d'information 1974–1975* (SEC (73) 4660 final).
CCE (Commission des Communautés Européennes). (1973c, October). *For a community policy on education* (Summary of the Janne Report). (Information Memo P-53/73).
CCE (Commission des Communautés Européennes). (1977, Juillet 27). *Politique d'information et principales activités de 1976—Activités des Bureaux* (SEC (77) 2754).
CCE (Commission des Communautés Européennes). (2006). *The history of European cooperation in education and training*. Luxembourg: Office for Official Publications of the European Communities.
CCE (Commission des Communautés Européennes). (2012). EUROPA—Employment and social policy. http://europa.eu/legislation_summaries/employment_and_social_policy/index_en.htm. Accessed 15 Mar 2012.
Chittolina, F. (1993). Quelques réflexions sur l'information syndicale des années 80. In F. Dassetto & M. Dumoulin (Eds.), *Naissance et développement de l'information européenne* (pp. 57–66). Bern: Peter Lang.
Coleman, S. (2012). Believing the news: From sinking trust to atrophied efficacy. *European Journal of Communication, 27*(1), 35–45.
Collowald, P. (2014). *J'ai vu naître l'Europe: De Strasbourg à Bruxelles, le parcours d'un pionnier de la construction européenne*. Strasbourg: La Nuée bleue.
Conrad, Y., & Rancon, M. (2003). *Entretien avec Paul Collowald*. Histoire interne de la Commission européenne 1958–1973. http://www.eui.eu/HAEU/OralHistory/pdf/INT707.pdf. Accessed 12 Mar 2012.
Coombes, D. (1970). *Politics and bureaucracy in the European Community*. London: George Allen and Unwin.
Coppé, A. (1956). Speech by Albert Coppé, Vice-President of the High Authority, *ECSC on efforts toward European unity*.
Corbett, A. (2005). *Universities and the Europe of knowledge*. Basingstoke: Palgrave Macmillan.
Cushion, S. (2012). *The democratic value of news: Why public service media matters*. Basingstoke: Palgrave.

Cutler, F. (1999). Jeremy Bentham and the public opinion tribunal. *Public Opinion Quarterly*, 63(3), 321-346.

Daly, M. (2007). Whither EU social policy? An account and assessment of developments in the Lisbon social inclusion process. *Journal of Social Policy*, 37(1), 1-19.

Dedman, M. J. (2010). *The origins and development of the European Union, 1945-95: A history of European integration* (2nd ed.). London: Routledge.

Dinan, D. (2010). *Ever closer union: An introduction to European integration* (4th ed.). Basingstoke: Palgrave Macmillan.

Dinan, D. (2014). The historiography of European integration. In D. Dinan (Ed.), *Origins and evolution of the European Union* (2nd ed., pp. 345-375). Oxford: Oxford University Press.

Duchêne, F. (1994). *The first statesman of interdependence*. New York: W. W. Norton & Company.

Dumoulin, M., & Cailleau, J. (2004) Entretien avec Fausta Deshormes née la Vallé. Histoire interne de la Commission européenne 1958-1973. http://www.eui.eu/HAEU/OralHistory/pdf/INT726.pdf. Accessed 12 Mar 2012.

Dumoulin, M., & Legendre, A. (2003). Entretien avec Guy Vanhaeverbeke. Histoire interne de la Commission européenne 1958-1973. http://www.eui.eu/HAEU/OralHistory/pdf/INT698.pdf. Accessed 12 Mar 2012.

EP. (1960, November 18). *Bericht im Namen des politischen Ausschusses über die Probleme der Information in den Europäischen Gemeinschaften* (Berichterstatter Schuijt). Europäisches Parlament Sitzungsdokumente 1960-1961 (Dokument 89).

EP. (1961). *Création d'une carte d'identité européenne*, A0-0136/61.

EP. (1962, November 14). *Bericht im Namen des politischen Ausschusses über die Tätigkeit der Informationsdienste der Europäischen Gemeinschaften* (Berichterstatter Schuijt). Europäisches Parlament Sitzungsdokumente 1962-1963 (Dokument 103).

EP. (1972, Februar 7). *Bericht im Namen des politischen Ausschusses über die Informationspolitik der Europäischen Gemeinschaften* (Berichterstatter Schuijt), Europäisches Parlament Sitzungsdokumente 1971-1972 (Dokument 246/71).

European Coal and Steel Community (ECSC). (1957, April 13). 5th General on the activities of the Community (9 April 1956 – 13 April 1957). *No doc no.*

European Coal and Steel Community (ECSC). (1958, April 13). 6th General report on the activities of the Community. *No doc no.*

European Economic and Social Committee. (2010). About the Committee. http://www.eesc.europa.eu/?i=portal.en.about-the-committee. Accessed 19 Dec 2011.

European Communities. (1959). *Le marché commun* (Communauté européenne). Bruxelles: Service d'information des Communautés européennes.

European Communities. (1960a). *L'Europe a dix ans. Les Cahiers de Communauté Européenne*. Paris:Service d'information des Communautés européennes.

European Communities. (1960b). *The common market at work. The common market after two years 1958–1959*. No place: European Community Information Service.
European Communities. (1961a). *The common market*. Brussels/Luxembourg: European Community Information Service.
European Communities. (1961b). *The European Community 1950–1960: Ten years' progress towards unity*. London: Press and Information Services of the European Communities.
European Communities. (1961c). *Sur le chemin de l'intégration européenne. Huit années de marché commun charbon-acier*. Luxembourg: no publisher.
European Communities. (1962). *The European Coal and Steel Community*. No place: Information Service of the European Communities.
European Communities. (1963a). *1952–1962: Ten years of ECSC. Community topics* 8. London: European Community Information Service.
European Communities. (1963b). *The common market's action program*. Community topics 10. London: European Community Information Service.
European Communities. (1963c). *Ten years of the coal-steel common market*. No place: Publication Service of the European Community.
European Communities. (1964a). *La Communauté Européenne—les faits, les chiffres 1964*. Bruxelles: Service de presse et d'information des CE.
European Communities. (1964b). *Towards political union*. Presented by the European Parliament. Community topics 25. London: European Community Information Service.
European Communities. (1965a). *La politique sociale de la C.E.C.A.* Les documents Communautés européennes 32, mai 1965. Paris: Service de presse et d'information des Communautés européennes.
European Communities. (1965b) *Comunidad europea—Los Hechos. Mercado común-c.e.c.a.-euratom*. Servicio de información y presa. Bruselas: Servicio de información de las CE.
European Communities. (1966). *Social policy in the ECSC 1953–65* (Community topics 20). London: European Community Information Service.
European Communities. (1969a). *The common market and the common man: Social policy and working and living conditions in the European Community*. Brussels: European Communities Press and Information Service.
European Communities. (1969b). *How the European Economic Community's institutions work* (by Emile Noël). *Community topics* 27. London: European Community Information Service.
European Communities. (1969c). *Le programme d'action de la Communauté européen*. Les documents communauté européenne, supplément au No 132–juillet 1969 de « communauté européenne ». Paris: Direction générale de la presse et de l'information des Communautés européennes.
European Communities. (1969d). *La communauté européenne en marche 1950–1968*. Paris: Bureau d'information des Communautés européennes.

European Communities. (1970). *La Communauté européenne en 1970*. Bruxelles: Commission européenne, Direction générale presse et information.
European Communities. (1971a). *Uniting Europe. The European Community since 1950*. Brussels: European Communities Press and Information Office.
European Communities. (1971b). *European Community—The facts*. Brussels: European Communities press and information Service.
European Council. (1968). Council directive 68/360/EEC of 15 October 1968 on the abolition of restrictions on movement and residence within the Community for workers of member states and their families.
European Council. (1977). Council directive 77/486/EEC of 25 July 1977 on the education of the children of migrant workers. http://eur-lex.europa.eu/LexUriServ/LexUriServ.do?uri=CELEX:31977L0486:EN:HTML. Accessed 26 May 2011.
European Economic Community (EEC). (1962) Fifth general report on the activities of the European Communities. 1 May 1961 - 30 Apr 1962.
European Economic Community (EEC). (1963) Sixth general report on the activities of the Community. 1 May 1962 - 31 Mar 1963.
European Economic Community (EEC). (1964) Seventh general report on the activities of the Community. 1 Apr 1963 - 31 Mar 1964.
Featherstone, K. (1994). Jean Monnet and the democratic deficit in the European Union. *Journal of Common Market Studies, 32*(2), 149–170.
Fondation Jean Monnet pour l'Europe et Centre de recherches européennes (Ed.). (1964). *Hommage au Président Robert Schuman*. Lausanne: Fondation Jean Monnet pour l'Europe et Centre de recherches européennes.
Fondation Jean Monnet pour l'Europe et Centre de recherches européennes Lausanne (CREL) (Ed.). (1978). *Messages à Jean Monnet*. Lausanne: Fondation Jean Monnet pour l'Europe et Centre de recherches européennes.
Fondation Jean Monnet pour l'Europe et Centre de recherches européennes. (1978). *Jean Monnet—Robert Schuman. Correspondance 1947–1953*. Lausanne: Fondation Jean Monnet pour l'Europe et Centre de recherches européennes.
Fontaine, P. (1988). *Jean Monnet. L'inspirateur*. Paris: Jacques Grancher.
Fontaine, P. (2013). *Jean Monnet. Actualité d'un bâtisseur de l'Europe unie*. Lausanne: Fondation Jean Monnet pour l'Europe et Centre de recherches européennes.
Foret, F. (2001). Dire l'Europe. Les publications grand public de la Commission européenne: entre rhétoriques politique et bureaucratique. *Pôle Sud*, numéro sur « La Commission européenne et la politique », no 15, 77–92.
Gerbet, P. (1962). *La genèse du plan Schuman*. Lausanne: Fondation Jean Monnet pour l'Europe et Centre de recherches européennes.
Geyer, R. (2000). *Exploring European social policy*. Cambridge: Polity.
Giro, G. (1993). Treize années au Service de l'information syndicale (1961–1973). In F. Dassetto & M. Dumoulin (Eds.), *Naissance et développement de l'information européenne* (pp. 49–56). Bern: Peter Lang.
Gramberger, M. (1997). *Die Öffentlichkeitsarbeit der Europäischen Kommission 1952–1996: PR zur Legitimation von Integration?* Baden-Baden: Nomos.

Griffiths, R. (2006). A dismal decade? European integration in the 1970s. In D. Dinan (Ed.), *Origins and evolution of the European Union* (pp. 169–190). Oxford: Oxford University Press.

Guichaoua, E. (1998). Jean Monnet, l'information et l'opinion publique. In E. du Réau (Ed.), *Europe des Elites? Europe des peuples: la construction de l'espace européen 1945–1960* (pp. 317–338). Paris: Presses de la Sorbonne Nouvelle.

Haller, M. (2008). *European integration as an elite process: The failure of a dream?* London: Routledge.

Hallstein, W. (1959, November 10). *Europe is on the move: Political and economic policies*. Speech by Professor Dr. Walter Hallstein, President of the Commission, European Economic Community, delivered to the Royal Institute of International Relations. Brussels.

Hallstein, W. (1961, June 28). *Economic integration as a factor of political unification*. Written by Professor Dr. Walter Hallstein, President of the Commission of the European Economic Community, as a contribution to a volume of essays presented to Professor Dr. Alfred Muller-Armack, under Secretary of State in the Ministry of Economic Affairs of the Federal Republic of Germany to mark his sixtieth birthday.

Hallstein, W. (1962a). *United Europe: Challenge and opportunity*. Cambridge, MA: Harvard University Press.

Hallstein, W. (1962b, April 17). *The economics of European integration*. The William L. Clayton Lecture Series, 1961–1962. Delivered by Professor Walter Hallstein, President of the Commission of the European Economic Community, at the Fletcher School of Law and Diplomacy, Tufts University. Medford, Massachusetts.

Hallstein, W. (1963, April). *The European Community, a new path to peaceful union*. Lectures given by Prof. Walter Hallstein, President of the Commission of the European Economic Community, to the Indian Council for Cultural Relations in memory of Maulana Abul Kalam Azad.

Hallstein, W. (1964a). *The unity of the drive for Europe*. Address by Professor Dr. Walter Hallstein, President of the Commission of the European Economic Community, at the opening session of the seventh conference of European local authorities. Rome, 15 October.

Hallstein, W. (1972). *Europe in the making*. London: Allen and Unwin.

Harrison, J. (forthcoming). The civil power of the news. Unpublished manuscript.

Harrison, J., & Pukallus, S. (2015). The European Community's public communication policy 1951–1967. *Contemporary European History*, 24(2), 233–251.

Haute Autorité. (1954a, Juin 10). *Note sur l'organisation du Service d'Information de la Haute Autorité* (Doc no 3903/54f CEAB 1 no 940).

Haute Autorité. (1954b). *Compte rendu d'activité*. Doc no 4258/54 f, CEAB 3 no 708, no date.

Haute Autorité. (1954c, September 1). *Rapport d'activité du service de presse et d'info pour la période du 15 juin au début d'août 1954* (Doc no 5681/54 f, CEAB 3 no 708).

Haute Autorité. (1955a). *Rapport sur l'évolution de l'opinion publique en ce qui concerne l'intégration européenne et l'action de la Communauté dans les milieux syndicaux* (Doc no 8997/55f. CEAB 13 no 69), (no date).
Haute Autorité. (1955b, Février 1). *Rapport d'activité du service d'information du 1er août au 31 décembre 1954* (1.2.1955. 329/55 f, CEAB 3 no 708).
Haute Autorité. (1955c, Février 18). *Rapport d'activité du service d'information du 1er août 1954 au 15 février 1955* (Doc no 329/1/55 f, CEAB 3 no 708).
Haute Autorité. (1955d, November 26). *Rapport sur l'évolution de l'opinion publique dans la République fédérale d'Allemagne au sujet de la C.E.C.A. et de l'intégration européenne* (Doc no 8867/55f. CEAB 13 no 69).
Haute Autorité. (1955e, November 30). *Rapport sur l'évolution de l'opinion publique en ce qui concerne l'intégration européenne et l'action de la Communauté en France* (Doc no 8919/55. CEAB 13 no 69).
Haute Autorité. (1955f). *The European Coal and Steel Community.* Luxembourg: Information Service of the High Authority.
Haute Autorité. (1955g). *The European Community for Coal and Steel—The facts political, institutional, economic, financial and social.* Luxembourg: Information Service of the High Authority.
Haute Autorité. (1956a, Janvier 19). *Les moyens de l'action de la Haute Autorité dans le domaine de l'information* (No doc no).
Haute Autorité. (1956b). *What is the European Community?* (1st ed). Luxembourg: Information Service of the High Authority.
Haute Autorité. (1957). *United Europe. The first step.* Luxembourg: Information Service of the High Authority.
Haute Autorité. (1958a, Février 12). *Rapport d'activité 1–31 janvier 1958* (Doc no1330/58 f. CEAB 3 no 1217).
Haute Autorité. (1958b, Mars 27). *Rapport d'activité 1–28 février 1958* (Doc no 2567/58 f. CEAB 3 no 1217).
Haute Autorité. (1958c). *Rapport d'activité du 1er mars au 30 avril 1958* (Doc no 3764/58 f. CEAB 3 no 1217), (no date).
Haute Autorité. (1958d, Mai 27). *Aide-mémoire sur les principales activités du service d'information pour la période de juin/août 1958* (Doc no 3829/58 f. CEAB 3 no 1217).
Haute Autorité. (1958e, Août 8). *Rapport d'activité du 1er au 31 juillet 1958* (Doc no 5652/58 f. CEAB 3 no 1217).
Haute Autorité. (1958f, November 21). *Rapport d'activité du 1er août au 31 octobre 1958* (Doc no 7874/58 f. CEAB 3 no 1217).
Haute Autorité. (1958g, Juin). *Rapport d'activité—période du 1er janvier au 30 avril 1959* (Doc no 3766/59. CEAB 3 no 1320).
Henderson, J. L. (1965). The schools of the six. *Journal of Common Market Studies, 4*(2), 178–190.
Jouve, E. (1967). *Le Général de Gaulle et la construction de l'Europe, 1940–1966.* Paris: LGDJ.

Kohnstamm, M. (1982). *Jean Monnet ou le pouvoir de l'imagination*. Lausanne: Fondation Jean Monnet pour l'Europe et Centre de recherches européennes.

Kohnstamm, M. (1989). Jean Monnet face à l'Union européenne. In G. Majone, E. Noël, & P. Van den Bossche (Eds.), *Jean Monnet et l'Europe d'aujourd'hui* (pp. 39–44). Nomos: Baden-Baden.

Krasner, S. (2010). The durability of organized hypocrisy. In H. Kalmo & Q. Skinner (Eds.), *Sovereignty in fragments. The past, present and future of a contested concept* (pp. 96–113). Cambridge: Cambridge University Press.

Küsters, H. J. (1989). Jean Monnet and the European Union: Idea and reality of the integration process. In G. Majone, E. Noël, & P. Van den Bossche (Eds.), *Jean Monnet et l'Europe d'aujourd'hui* (pp. 45–59). Baden-Baden: Nomos.

Lastenouse, J. (2003). *La Commission Européenne et les études universitaires sur l'intégration européenne 1960–2000*, obtained via personal communication.

Lastenouse, J. (2008). *Hommage au professeur Paulo Pitta e Cunha*. Faculté de droit de l'Université de Lisbonne, obtained via personal communication, unpublished speech.

Lejeune, R. (2000). *Robert SCHUMAN. Père de l'Europe 1886–1963* (La Politique, chemin de sainteté). Paris: Fayard.

Lerner, D., & Gordon, M. (1969). *Euratlantica: Changing perspectives of the European elites*. Cambridge, MA: MIT Press.

Levi-Sandri, L. (1962, June 14). Address by M. Levi Sandri, President of the Social Affairs Group of the Commission of the European Economic Community, to the 46th International Labour Conference, Geneva.

Levi-Sandri, L. (1963). Interview de M. Lionello Levi Sandri. (no further information).

Levi-Sandri, L. (1964a). Address (on social security) by M. Lionello Levi Sandri, Vice-President of the EEC Commission, President of the Social Affairs Group, before the XVth General Assembly of the International Social Security Association.

Levi-Sandri, L. (1964b, April 15). European democracy, social policy and role of the trade unions. Address, Strasbourg.

Levi-Sandri, L. (1964c, 17 June–9 July). Address at the International Labour Conference, 48th session, Geneva.

Levi-Sandri, L. (1966, November 10). The social policy of the European Community, Rome.

Loth, W. (2007). Walter Hallstein, a committed European. In M. Dumoulin (Ed.), *The European Commission, 1958–72. History and memories* (pp. 79–90). Luxembourg: Office for Official Publications of the European Communities.

Ludlow, N. P. (1998). *Frustrated ambitions: The European Commission and the formation of a European identity, 1958–1967*, obtained via personal communication.

Ludlow, N. P. (2003). An opportunity or a threat? The European Commission and the Hague Council of December 1969. *Journal of European Integration History, 9*(2), 11–26.

Ludlow, N. P. (2006a). *The European Community and the crises of the 1960s: Negotiating the Gaullist challenge.* London: Routledge.
Ludlow, N. P. (2006b). De-commissioning the empty chair crisis: The community institutions and the crisis of 1965–6. In H. Wallace, P. Winand, & J.-M. Palayret (Eds.), *Visions, votes and vetoes: The empty chair crisis and the Luxembourg compromise forty years on* (pp. 79–96). Brussels: Peter Lang.
Maas, W. (2007). *Creating European citizens.* Lanham/Plymouth: Rowman & Littlefield.
Majone, G. (2009). *Europe as the would-be world power: The EU at fifty.* Cambridge: Cambridge University Press.
Massip, R. (1980). Ce jour-là, l'Europe est née.... In Fondation Jean Monnet pour l'Europe et Centre de recherches européennes (Ed.), *Ce jour-là, l'Europe est née* (pp. 5–13). Lausanne: Fondation Jean Monnet pour l'Europe et Centre de recherches européennes.
Melchionni, M. G., & Ducci, R. (Eds.). (2007). *La Genèse des Traités de Rome.* Lausanne: Fondation Jean Monnet pour l'Europe et Centre de recherches européennes.
Meynaud, J., & Sidjanski, D. (Eds.) (1965). *Science politique et intégration européenne.* Genève: Institut d'Études Européennes. http://www.dusan-sidjanski.eu/pdf/Direction_Ouvrages/65_SciencePo_IntegrationEurop_VERS2.pdf. Accessed 29 Feb 2012.
Meynaud, J., & Sidjanski, D. (1971). *Les groupes de pressions dans la communauté européenne. Editions de l'institut de sociologie.* Brussels: ULB. http://www.dusan-sidjanski.eu/pdf/Ouvrages/71_GroupesPressionCommEuro.pdf. Accessed 29 Feb 2012.
Milward, A. (1992). *The reconstruction of Western Europe, 1945–51.* London: Routledge.
Milward, A. (2000). *The European rescue of the nation-state* (2nd ed.). London: Routledge.
Monnet, J. (1955). *Les États-Unis d'Europe ont commencé.* Paris: R. Laffont.
Monnet, J. (1976). *Mémoires.* Paris: Fayard.
Monnet, J. (1978). *Memoirs.* London: Collins.
Moravcsik, A. (1998). *The choice for Europe: Social purpose and state power from Rome to Maastricht.* Ithaca: Cornell University Press.
Nesti, G. (2010). The information and communication policy of the European Union between institutionalisation and legitimation. In C. Valentini, & G. Nesti, (Eds.), *Public communication in the European Union: History, perspectives and challenges* (pp. 23–48). Newcastle upon Tyne: Cambridge Scholars.
Olivi, B. (1971, November 20). *Information policy as an instrument of international relations.* Address by Dr. Beniamino Olivi, Official Spokesman of the Commission of the European Communities, to the European Federation of Public Relations, Dublin.
Olsen, E. D. H. (2006). *Work, production, free movement and then what? Conceptions of citizenship in European integration, 1951–71* (EUI Working

Paper 2006/8). Dept. of Political and Social Sciences. San Domenico di Fiesole: European University Institute.

Olsen, E. D. H. (2008). The origins of European citizenship in the first two decades of European integration. *Journal of European Public Policy, 15*(1), 40–57.

Olsen, E. D. H. (2012). *Transnational citizenship in the European Union: Past, present and future.* London/New York: Continuum Books.

Packard, V. (2007). *The hidden persuaders.* New York: Ig Publishing.

Pasquinucci, D. (2010). « Faire les Européens » Les origins de la politique d'information communautaire. In D. Preda & D. Pasquinucci (Eds.), *The road Europe travelled along: The evolution of the EEC/EU institutions and policies.* Brussels: Peter Lang.

Petit, I. (2005). Agir par mimétisme: la Commission européenne et sa politique d'éducation. *Canadian Journal of Political Science/Revue canadienne de science politique, 38*(3), 627–652.

Petit, I. (2006). Dispelling a myth? The fathers of Europe and the construction of a Euro-identity. *European Law Journal, 12*(5), 661–679.

Petit, I. (2007). Mimicking history: The European Commission and its European education policy. *World Political Science Review, 3*(1), 1–24.

Poidevin, R. (1986). *Robert Schuman.* Paris: Imprimerie Nationale.

Pourvoyeur, R. (1981). La Politique de l'information de la Communauté européenne. *Revue du Marché Commun, 246*, 192–204. Paris.

Rabier, J. R. (1964, Mai 29). *Union des six capitales des pays de la Communauté européenne.* Bruxelles.

Rabier, J. R. (1965). *L'information des Européens et l'integration de l'Europe. Leçons données le 17 et 18 février 1965.* Bruxelles: Université Libre de Bruxelles.

Rabier, J. R. (1966). *L'Opinion Publique et l'Europe.* Brussels: Institute of Sociology.

Rabier, J. R. (1993). La naissance d'une politique d'information sur la Communauté européenne (1952–1967). In F. Dassetto & M. Dumoulin (Eds.), *Naissance et développement de l'information européenne* (pp. 21–32). Bern: Peter Lang.

Rabier, J. R. (2000). Les origines de la politique d'information européenne (1953–1973). In M. Melchionni (Ed.), *Fondi e luoghi della documentazione europea. Istruzioni per l'uso* (pp. 84–98). Rome: Université de la Sapienza.

Reinfeldt, A. (2012). Information or propaganda? Supranational and Europeanist strategies of consensus creation on European integration 1952–1972. In D. Preda & D. Pasquinucci (Eds.), *Consensus and European integration. An historical perspective [sic]* (pp. 257–266). Brussels: Peter Lang.

Reuter, P. (1980). *La naissance de l'Europe communautaire.* Lausanne: Fondation Jean Monnet pour l'Europe et Centre de recherches européennes.

Rey, J. (1969, December 11). *Address by M. Jean Rey to the European Parliament.*

Rieben, H., Monnet, J., & Chevallaz, G. A. (Eds.). (1971). *Jean Monnet.* Lausanne: Fondation Jean Monnet pour l'Europe et Centre de recherches européennes.

Rieben, H., Nathusius, M., et al. (Eds.). (2000). *Un changement d'espérance. La Déclaration du 9 mai 1950*. Lausanne: Fondation Jean Monnet pour l'Europe et Centre de recherches européennes.

Rieben, H., Camperio-Tixier, C., & Nicod, F. (2004). *A l'écoute de Jean Monnet*. Lausanne: Fondation Jean Monnet pour l'Europe et Centre de recherches européennes.

Ronan, S. G. (1975, November 7). *The information policy of the Commission*. Address by Mr. Sean G. Ronan, Director-General of the Commission of the European Communities, to the Public Relations Institute of Ireland.

Roth, F. (2008). *Robert Schuman: Du Lorrain des frontières au père de l'Europe*. Paris: Fayard.

Runciman, D. (2013). *Politics*. London: Profile Books.

Runciman, D. (2014). *The confidence trap*. Princeton: Princeton University Press.

Schrag Sternberg, C. (2013). *The struggle for EU legitimacy. Public contestation, 1950–2005*. Basingstoke: Palgrave Macmillan.

Schudson, M. (2008). *Why democracies need an unlovable press*. Cambridge: Polity Press.

Schulz-Forberg, H., & Stråth, B. (2010). *The political history of European integration: The hypocrisy of democracy-through-market*. London: Routledge.

Schuman, R. (1963). *Pour l'Europe*. Paris: Editions Nagel Briquet.

Sélys, G. de (1996). 'La machine de propagande de la Commission' dans Le Monde diplomatique juin 1996. http://www.monde-diplomatique. fr/1996/06/DE_SELYS/3753. Accessed 22 Feb 2010.

Sidjanski, D. (1996). Eurosphère—Dirigeants et groups européens. In F. D'Arcy, & L. Rouban (Eds.), *De la Ve République à l'Europe. Hommage a Jean-Louis Quermonne* (pp. 279–298). Presse de la fondation nationale des sciences politiques. http://www.dusan-sidjanski.eu/pdf/Contributions/96_Eurosphere. pdf. Accessed 29 Apr 2012.

Spierenburg, D., & Poidevin, R. (1994). *The history of the High Authority of the European Coal and Steel Community. Supranationality in operation*. London: Weidenfeld and Nicolson.

Stirk, P., & Weigall, D. (Eds.). (1999). *The origins and development of European integration: A reader and companion*. London: Pinter.

Terra, A. L. (2010). From information policy to communication policy: First steps towards reaching European citizens in the 1970s and 1980s. In C. Valentini & G. Nesti (Eds.), *Public communication in the European Union: History, perspectives and challenges* (pp. 49–66). Newcastle upon Tyne: Cambridge Scholars.

Tilly, P. (2014). Interest groups: A necessary evil? In E. Bussière, V. Dujardin, M. Dumoulin, et al. (Eds.), *The European Commission 1973–86. History and memories of an institution* (pp. 137–141). Luxembourg: Publications Office of the European Union.

Tocqueville, A. (2000[1835]). *Democracy in America*. New York: Bantam Classic.

Uri, P. (1989). Réflexion sur l'approche fonctionnaliste de Jean Monnet et suggestions pour l'avenir. In G. Majone, E. Noël, & P. Van den Bossche (Eds.), *Jean Monnet et l'Europe d'aujourd'hui* (pp. 75–82). Baden-Baden: Nomos.

Urwin, D. (1995). *The community of Europe: A history of European integration since 1945* (2nd ed.). London: Longman.

Valentini, C., & Nesti, G. (2010). Introduction. In C. Valentini & G. Nesti (Eds.), *Public communication in the European Union: History, perspectives and challenges* (pp. 1–20). Newcastle upon Tyne: Cambridge Scholars.

Van Helmont, J. (1981). *Jean Monnet comme il était*. Lausanne: Fondation Jean Monnet pour l'Europe et Centre de recherches européennes.

Von Simson, W. (1989). Reflections on Jean Monnet's skillful [sic] handling of member states and people during the first years of the community. In G. Majone, E. Noël, & P. Van den Bossche (Eds.), *Jean Monnet et l'Europe d'aujourd'hui* (pp. 29–36). Baden-Baden: Nomos.

Walkenhorst, H. (2008). Explaining change in EU education policy. *Journal of European Public Policy, 15*(4), 567–587.

Warner, G. (1985). The United States and the rearmament of West Germany. *International Affairs, 61*(2), 279–286.

CHAPTER 3

'A People's Europe' (1973–1992)

1 The Emergence of 'A People's Europe': Common European Identity and Greater Democracy

In 1973 two international events prompted the Community to increasingly act as a political union with one voice, thereby strengthening European Political Cooperation (EPC).[1] These events were, first, the Nixon-Kissinger European Year[2] and second, the oil embargo in the aftermath of the Yom Kippur War.[3] Of the two events notably the latter required the Community to coordinate the member states' foreign policies. Faced with an OPEC-inspired 5% cut in oil production, a 70% 'massive hike in oil prices'[4] and a complete oil embargo that targeted several countries, and importantly the Netherlands, a member state, the Community found itself in 'disarray as regards energy policy, and in grave danger as regards the security of its energy supplies'[5] of which 60% normally were provided by the Arab countries. The urgent need to solve this economic-political conflict led the Community to issue a common position statement on the situation in the Middle East on 6 November 1973.[6] We can neglect the details of this common statement, as the significance for the argument I am presenting was not so much its content or any political or economic effect it might have had but rather the fact that this statement represented something new and to a certain extent something special (especially in the light of the failed attempts to bring about political unity in the 1950s

© The Editor(s) (if applicable) and The Author(s) 2016
S. Pukallus, *Representations of European Citizenship since 1951*,
DOI 10.1057/978-1-137-51147-8_3

93

and 1960s): it represented the Community's first collective response to a matter of foreign policy. For the first time, and despite an atmosphere of uncertainty regarding its political direction, the Community used its 'vox Europa' and thereby acted as a political actor.[7] As such, I agree with Ifestos who wrote: '[I]f one considers the fact that the EPC was in its infant and experimental stages, that there are no other institutions to formulate a collective response to problems of this magnitude, and the fact that whatever decision one was about to take would most likely have generated reactions from many quarters, then the declaration (...) was a remarkable statement'.[8] In short, it was 'a historical novelty'.[9]

Without wanting to exaggerate or overemphasise the importance of this event or pushing for a cause-effect relationship, it is fair to argue that the common statement has stimulated a new hope in the Community's ability to become a unified political actor and concomitantly, it filled the Community with confidence to attempt once again to push European political integration forward—this time by introducing a European external identity, or a public image, to accompany and frame its emerging foreign policy. According to Gfeller,[10] the French were especially keen on strengthening the Community as a political actor and started to introduce a political language of European identity. In the same vein and only a few weeks later, the Heads of States and Government of the Nine—by this time Ireland, Great Britain and Denmark had joined the Community—wrote the so-called Declaration on European Identity (Copenhagen, 14 December 1973) which noted that the identity of Europe entailed the defence of 'the principles of representative democracy, of the rule of law, of social justice—which is the ultimate goal of economic progress—and of respect for human rights' (art. 1).[11] Whereas the Copenhagen Declaration was primarily concerned with the Community's external identity, it can nevertheless be seen as having had an impact upon the way the Community conceived of its own internal identity. More specifically, the Community's self-understanding of being primarily an economic-social entity changed. The Community's desire to become a liberal democratic Community became emphasised more than ever before. This did not mean, however, that the Community, albeit desirous of creating a united federal Europe, intended at any point to dissolve nation-states or, as pointed out in the previous chapter, national citizenship or identity. What was emphasised instead was the principle of Gleichberechtigung (equality) of the member states[12] and the compatibility of European and national citizenship and identity and of European and national politics. This view has also been supported by liberal intergovernmentalists and most prominently Moravcsik, who have argued that dominant loyalties of membership and attachment would remain with the nation-states and that 'the primary source of integration lies in the interests of the states themselves and the relative power each brings to Brussels'.[13] What this means is that 'the most fundamental source of the EU's legitimacy lies in the democratic accountability of national governments'[14] and as such, European integration is best understood a 'European Constitutional Settlement'[15] in which 'Europe may expand geographically, reform institutionally and deepen substantively, but [where] all this will take place incrementally and within the existing constitutional contours of European institutions'.[16] In other words, decisions regarding the course of European integration were made through intergovernmental negotiations and bargaining according to dominant preferences of the nation-states. Consequently, it is fair to argue that 'the [European] integration process did not supersede or circumvent the political will of national leaders [but that] it *reflected* their will'.[17]

Only one year after the Copenhagen Declaration, the final statement of the Paris Summit (1974)[18] outlined three specific propositions with regard to the Community's internal democratisation process and more importantly, to the introduction of a form of political-federal citizenship: first, art. 10 was concerned with 'the possibility of establishing a passport union and, in anticipation of this, the introduction of a uniform passport'; second art. 11 emphasised the importance 'to study the conditions and the timing under which the citizens of the nine Member States could be given special rights as members of the Community' and finally, art. 12 stated that the 'election of the European Assembly by universal suffrage (...) should be achieved as soon as possible'. In short, the final statement of the Paris Summit (1974) proposed the introduction of the three following elements traditionally associated with the features of a nation-state: a passport, citizens' rights and the election of a parliament by universal direct suffrage. It seemed as if the time to give European citizens the possibility to participate in the political processes of the Community through the direct election of the European Parliament[19] was finally, to use Hallstein's words again, 'ripe'.[20] In this sense, the Paris Summit represented a 'milestone'[21] in the Commission's reinterpretation of its original understanding of European citizenship. The representation of European citizenship as homo oeconomicus and the limited range of economic-social entitlements ascribed to it no longer coincided with the ambitious political and civil plans for the 'democratisation of Europe'.[22] Accordingly, the representation of European citizenship as homo oeconomicus evolved into a political-federal representation of European citizenship, which I call 'A People's Europe'.[23]

2 A People's Europe: A Political-Federal Representation of European Citizenship

A Political-Federal Lexicon

In the early 1970s, the Commission abandoned the distinction between 'workers' and 'the European public' and introduced a political-federal lexicon comprising inclusive terms such as 'European citizen',[24] 'peoples'/'peoples of Europe',[25] 'democratic peoples of Europe',[26] 'people of the Community',[27] 'people',[28] 'Europeans',[29] 'citizens',[30] 'Community citizens'/'citizens of the Community'[31] and for the first time explicitly 'European citizenship'[32] and finally 'Citizenship of the Union' in the Maastricht Treaty (1992) to describe the civil identity of European citizenship. In the run-up to the first direct European elections (1979)[33] this lexicon was extended to include other inclusive terms such as 'voters',[34] (direct) 'elections',[35] 'democratic contest',[36] 'political parties'[37] and 'election campaigns'.[38]

What this lexicon introduced was a conception of an integral European 'demos' which expanded upon the much narrower conception used in the representation 'homo oeconomicus' and was best understood to mean a European people or a European citizenry conceived of as rights-bearing European citizens (civil, cultural, political and social) with historically and culturally constituted common identities and with active economic and democratic-political entitlements in a Europe understood as a representative democracy. The neonate European 'demos' electoral rights were not limited to the elections of the EP but extended to include municipal elections. The right to stand and vote in local elections was first mentioned by the Commission[39] and subsequently legally codified in the Maastricht Treaty (1992).

The Maastricht Treaty strengthened the political-federal dimension of the idea of a European 'demos' through the introduction of the criteria of nationality which meant that only those citizens who had the nationality of any of the EU member states were also de facto EU citizens and could enjoy the above rights. And whilst, as noted in chapter "A Civil Europe", some scholars have argued that the political rights delineated in the Maastricht Treaty were no more than 'thin' rights, the substantive significance of electoral rights was to be found in their legal codification and the decision of who could and could not vote in these elections. This codification strengthened the idea of a European based 'demos' to mean a European politically active public with its own specific and unique identity. It rendered the concept of European 'demos' more meaningful and more 'European' by moving it away from an aggregate of nation-based publics. With regard to the introduction of a right to stand and vote in local elections, voting rights were extended to ensure that a national living in a part of Europe other than their own country could vote in the municipal elections of their place of residence. This stipulation in the Maastricht Treaty further reflected a genuine sense of a European 'demos' as something *sui generis*. It was in this confident claim to the plausible existence of a unique European 'demos' (made in the Maastricht Treaty and prior to that by the Commission) that the Commission grounded the political-federal rights attached to the second representation of European citizenship.

The equality of Community nationals as members of a common European 'demos' was further emphasised through another EU citizenship right—the 'protection by the diplomatic or consular authorities of any Member State' (Maastricht Treaty 1992, D). This right put all Community nationals on an equal footing by obligating member states to offer diplomatic protection for any of the EU nationals. And whilst this right—which had already been mentioned in several Community reports since the 1970s[40]—enhanced the Community's standing as a political entity on the world scene, it became also part of the repertoire of rights that supported the representation of European citizenship as political-federal by locating it in the idea of a European 'demos' with its own integrity. Corresponding to this integrity was a realisation of the importance of defining Europe in spatial terms, and with that the concretisation of the European demos as belonging to its own 'homeland'.

European Space: The 'Homeland' of the Political-Federal European Citizen

From 1973 onwards, the Commission became increasingly concerned with the way European citizens were conceived of as experientially linked to a geo-politically identified and bounded place in which a set of historical spatial narratives come together. It was through the manipulation of this space, in ways that represent and articulate the unity, common identity and values bequeathed by the European Community through the idea of common citizenship, that the second interpretation of European citizenship acquired an explicit historical and spatial story. Spatial articulations were both real and symbolic, and included the manipulation of the physical environment through architecture such as the Community institutions, statues and the building of public fora and symbolism which, in turn, included a common anthem, a flag, passports or acts of naming. They were both the concretisation of a common identity and set of values and an attempt to inspire European citizens in a particular 'European' way. Cohen argued that the term 'Community' in itself is a 'boundary-expressing symbol'[41] which simultaneously implies 'both similarity and difference'[42] and that the boundary is 'the element which embodies this sense of discrimination' between similarity and difference or 'us' and 'the other'. As will become more evident as we go along, boundaries can be symbolically, physically or discursively expressed. The Commission defined European space in three ways: territorially conceived, in economic-social terms and culturally.

European Political-Federal Territory

The idea of a European territory was not explicitly formulated but rather expressed through initiatives aiming at making the right to free movement more easily enjoyable through the abolition of passport control at internal borders of the Community.[43] This was done through the European uniform passport, which was first suggested at the Paris Summit (1974) and ultimately introduced in the mid-1980s.[44]

As a 'particular kind of identity document',[45] the uniform passport had two functions.[46] The first function was of rather practical nature as it helped to identify European citizens quickly and, subsequently, to accelerate their border crossing at airports through separate lines for Community passports. In addition, and as the Commission pointed out, 'such a passport might be equally justified by the desire of the nine Member States to affirm *vis-à-vis* non-member countries the existence of the Community as an entity and to obtain from each of them identical treatment for citizens of the Community'.[47] It thus represented an external sign of solidarity.[48] The second function was of symbolic nature. The uniform passport was thought 'capable of reviving the feelings of [political-federal] citizens of the Community of belonging to that entity'[49] and the concomitant abolition of internal border controls[50] was to contribute to, to borrow

Taylor's concept, a European 'imaginary'[51] of a federal state conceived of as inhabiting a single space or a territory. And it was within this territory that every five years all EU citizens would come together as a demos to directly elect the EP. According to Perrin, the 'practices that connect individuals and publics are important (...) because they constitute the cultural connection between citizens and their communities'.[52] These practises, he continued, include the 'ritual of voting "simultaneously" [which] allows us to imagine ourselves as members of an abstract national community and as effective, thinking and competent individuals'.[53] Being aware of this symbolic significance for the European demos of voting at the same time, the Community took several initiatives to introduce a uniform electoral procedure for the elections of the EP and thereby to put all Community citizens in the same position regarding these elections.[54] However, to date, all of these initiatives have failed.

The representation of 'A People's Europe' and its corresponding conception of space extended beyond an understanding of the Community as an entity conceived of in purely territorial and political terms. It included an economic and a social dimension through which the Commission hoped to demonstrate the Community's concrete relevance to the man on the street and in the daily lives of European citizens.[55] In short: to reinforce the idea of a 'People's Europe'.[56] Out of this concern for the concrete manifestation of the Community in the citizens' daily lives came an increased appreciation of defining space more deeply than simply a bounded territory.

European Space Conceived of in Economic-Social Terms

European space conceived of in economic-social terms during the representation of 'A People's Europe' was linked to economic-social rights and policies[57] in three ways. First, the European citizen was conceived of as a consumer of the Single Market; second, the European citizen was represented as a worker with social rights linked to employment and third, rights were linked to the domain of health.

With regard to European citizens conceived of as citizen-consumers in the Single Market, emphasis in the Commission's discourse on European citizenship was placed upon the common market and the deriving consumer rights because 'it is in their role as consumers that the public is especially affected by Community action'.[58] Accordingly, a 'smooth-running single market[59] in which the full benefits of lower costs of transport and travel (and associated services such as insurance) can be realized for the benefit of the Community citizen as consumer'[60] was considered a priority. To this it was added that further 'priority lies in those areas where goods or services have an obvious extra-national dimension (e.g. air, road and rail transport and telecommunications)'. As Tindemans noted, 'European consumers must be made to understand that they are being afforded real protection against the constant possibility of fraud and other real dangers'.[61] Instead of conceiving of space in a purely territorial way, the Commission defined European space through the Single Market and consumer rights and protection. Further strengthening the idea of the citizen-consumer was the introduction of common currency which was ultimately to ease consumer activity in diverse European settings such as shopping through the harmonised benchmarking of retail products, the easier use of transnational services, the rationalisation of commercial contracts, the stimulation of tourism and the introduction of easier business travel. The introduction of the common currency represented a significant shift from nation-based monetary sovereignty[62] to what we have been seeing since 2012: greater monetary and fiscal union. Symbolically, and according to Shore, '(...) coins and banknotes have traditionally defined the boundaries of kingdoms, empires and nations'.[63] Shanahan went beyond the symbolic dimension and argued that the introduction of a common currency creates an 'undeniably concrete' shared reality.[64] In this sense, the idea of a common currency ultimately strengthened and supported the political-federal conception of European space conceived of both commercially and symbolically.

With regard to the second aspect, where European citizens were conceived of as workers with social rights linked to employment, European space was defined through workers' mobility and the social rights within the domain of employment that these mobile workers were entitled to. According to the 1st Adonnino Report 'the main problems in the field of freedom of movement for workers have been dealt with by legal instruments of the European institutions. The questions of the social security of migrant workers and of the inclusion of their families also appear to have in the main been resolved satisfactorily'.[65] This idea of social rights attached to the representation of European citizens as workers with families was in some ways reminiscent of the previous representation 'homo oeconomicus' and showed how some of the elements of this baseline interpretation of European citizenship remained features of successive reinterpretations of European citizenship. The economic-social aspects defined

European space insofar as it was within the borders of the Community that the right to free movement and corresponding social rights applied.[66]

The third aspect, which is directly linked to the question of social security and free movement, was the domain of health. The Tindemans Report appealed to a 'Health Europe '[which] must be given life' and emphasises the importance of the 'simplification of procedures for refunding medical expenses incurred by Union citizens in another country of the Union'.[67] This idea of a 'health Europe' was further developed by the 2nd Adonnino Report, which evoked an 'Emergency Health Card'[68] and noted the importance of 'access to medical treatment throughout the Community'.[69]

The economic-social conception of space had a dual function. First, it defined the European territory more deeply and symbolically. Second, it was through the economic-social conception of space and particularly health policies that the Community was able to manifest its sense of responsibility and care for the entire European 'demos', thereby extending the notion of social responsibility beyond 'a workers' realm.

Culturally Conceived Space[70]

The political-federal representation of European citizenship was further characterised by a cultural conception of European space, which represented the 'romantic' idea of Europe. In other words, a culturally and civilly unified Europe: 'United in Diversity'. This slogan was chosen because it was believed that it could symbolise that the different cultures of the different member states had aspects in common and that these aspects could represent elements for cultural unification. [71] It was this attempt at representing Europe as a cultural identity where European citizens were meant to get together, to speak each other's languages and to experience other Community cultures through, for example, sports events, student exchanges, and cultural manifestations[72] that accompanied the representation that I have called 'A People's Europe' and its attendant culturally conceived European space. Its significance for the political-federal European 'demos' lay in the 'importance of stimulating the imagination' of a 'Europe which should not [uniquely] be conceived of as a Community of merchants', but which should be linked to the interests of European citizens.[73]

With regard to the domain of sport,[74] the Fontainebleau Council (1984) suggested the creation of Community sports teams and European sports events in domains such as sailing, tennis and swimming. It was particularly the 2nd Adonnino Report which developed this idea further and suggested not only the creation of European sports teams but also transborder sporting events such as cycling or running races, exchange of athletes and sportsmen between different countries. As a symbolic gesture it suggested that teams 'wear the Community emblem in addition to their national colours at major sporting events of regional or worldwide interest'.[75]

With regard to education, the Community[76] emphasised the 'importance of greater integration in educational matters by promoting student exchanges'[77] and 'foster[ing] bilateral or multilateral agreements between universities and educational institutions', because 'personal and concrete impressions of the European reality and a detailed knowledge of our languages and cultures constitute the common heritage which the European Union aims specifically to protect'.[78] In this respect, Tindemans suggested the creation of a European Foundation whose objective would be 'to promote, either directly or by assisting existing bodies, anything which could help towards greater understanding among our peoples by placing the emphasis on human contact: youth activities [such as voluntary camps where young people across the Community come together for a common social purpose or European Youth Competitions in arts and music [as suggested in the 2nd Adonnino Report (1985)], university exchanges, scientific debates and symposia, meetings between the socio-professional categories, cultural and information activities'.[79] The Commission[80] emphasised the importance of a European postage stamp and common European postal rates to make the Community more visible in the daily lives of Community citizens. It also further referred to European-wide celebrations such as the anniversary of the Schuman Declaration on 9 May, awareness-raising campaigns[81] and a European City of culture.[82]

Such representations and articulations of territorially, economic-socially and culturally conceived European space were the production of European citizens' space which, following Lefebvre,[83] we could say were an attempt to generate 'European' cultural practises through a European imaginary. As noted above, this was an imaginary which accorded with Taylor's definition of a social imaginary as '(...) something much broader and deeper than the intellectual scheme people may entertain when they think about social reality in a disengaged mode' and linked to the 'the ways in which [people] imagine their social existence, how they fit together with others, how things go on between them and their fellows, the expectations which are normally met, and the deeper normative notions and images which underlie these expectations'.[84]

It is via the way the Commission conceived of space and its stimulation of a European imaginary that an explicit attempt was made to extend Europe beyond the Westphalian settlement of a collection of nation states into a space of common European values, of which the moral and scientific outlook of the Enlightenment and the pull of the post war 'pax Europa' remain essentially dominant. It was also where the concept of European citizenship defined itself as a mixture of 'citizenship that is derivative of the nation-state and a citizenship that is defined by free movement and mobility'.[85] The former, through the political-federal conception of European citizenship, and the latter, through the 'people's Europe dimension', became attached to this political-federal representation of European citizenship. It was the political-federal representation of European citizenship in 'A People's Europe' that expressed more clearly than ever before in both discursive and spatial terms the idea of common and inclusive European citizenship.

The Public Communication of 'A People's Europe'

The second representation of European citizenship was publicly communicated in an essentially affective style of public communication that was undertaken in such a way as to enhance the feeling of belonging to the Community. The turn to the affective style of public communication, and particularly the use of political-federal symbols, was deemed necessary for three reasons: first, in the early 1970s the Community was aware of deficiencies in terms of there not being sufficiently democratic Community institutions, a long and complicated policy-making and decision-making process and, most importantly, the Community's inability to access the media in the same way as nation-states could. Second, public communication policy was evaluated as being less effective than was desirable and third, the arguments for the existence of the Community that were valid in 1950, such as peace and prosperity or economic growth in order to compete internationally, had lost some of their direct relevance. It was because of these three aspects that the Community decided to promote a new image of the Community.[86] What that meant with regard to the Community's public communication policy was best expressed by the European Parliament (1986), which openly stated that a public communication policy which exclusively relied upon factual information could only lead to indifference rather than to any affective relation with the Community. Or as Froschmeier, then Director General of DG X responsible for Communication, expressed in a note to Noël, '(...) it is clear that our information policy, as it stands, is unable to create a massively pro-Community trend (...) the focus should not be on rational argument but we should appeal more to the emotions and use psychology'.[87] In fact, the formation of an affective relationship between the Community and its political-federal European citizens guided the Commission's public communication efforts in the years 1973–1992.

During this period, the Commission's institutional discourse was characterised by the use of terms and expressions such as 'the basic aim of the Commission's information policy is to contribute to the formation, in all branches of public opinion, of a 'European consciousness',[88] 'European awareness',[89] European identity',[90] 'a positive attachment of the citizens to the Community'.[91] Further, the Commission believed that its public communication efforts would be able to contribute 'to the formation of European solidarity amongst the peoples of Europe'[92] and 'the realization that a successful Community is important for the well-being of each Community citizen',[93] 'show [the Community's] "human face"'[94] and to emphasise 'the human dimension of the undertaking'.[95] At the same time, the Commission aimed at raising 'awareness of belonging to the same Community',[96] 'populariz[ing] information on the Community'[97] and at 'reinforc[ing] and promot[ing] the Community's image to its citizens and to the world'.[98] It was evident that even suggestions about what public communication itself should do adopted the same affective and inspirational tone. The Commission explicitly wanted to strengthen and adapt its public communications policy since it believed communication to be 'essential to (...) the Community's image in the minds of its people',[99] and 'to talk to the hearts of European citizens'.[100] In short, public communication was essential in the attempt to portray a 'Europe (...) close to its citizens'.[101] To this end, the affective style of public communication also made great use of possessive pronouns such as 'our', 'yours', 'its', 'your', and so on. These terms are what Billig refers to as 'crucial words'[102] because discursive formations including possessive pronouns aren't innocent or merely decorative but in fact convey powerful meanings.[103] They had as their purpose quietly but forcefully indicating a relationship, a closeness, an intimate proximity between the Community and European citizens.

Besides the use of possessive pronouns, political-federal symbols were utilised, since it was believed by the Commission that they too possessed the ability to stimulate a feeling of belonging. In other words, political-federal symbols were seen as having the capacity to reinforce and fulfil an identity-forming role. According to O'Shaughnessy, 'a symbol (...) is something visible, something into which communication has poured meaning'.[104] It is a 'mode of communication'[105] as well as 'a way of delimitating a sphere of belonging and a perimeter of sovereignty. The flag at the border signals the limit where Otherness begins. The flag is also a way to mark places of power, when displayed on public buildings and in political rituals'.[106] Ronan, then Director-General for Press and Information, argued that the Community needed to 'be visible to its citizens and (...) capable [of] making itself intelligible to them', and it could do so through the use of visible symbols which, in nation-states, accompany us 'from the "cradle to the grave"'.[107] Accordingly, the Community introduced several political-federal symbols[108] that have usually been associated with a nation-state: a uniform passport, a flag, an anthem ('Ode to Joy' from the fourth movement of Beethoven's ninth symphony) and a Community 'holiday' (9 May in remembrance of the Schuman Declaration of 1950).[109] In addition to these nation-state type symbols, the Community also introduced its own unique form of political-federal symbols such as the European City of Culture, the promotion of European youth competitions in sport, arts and music—all of which were a means of communication designed to emphasise a common European identity.[110]

These symbols attempted to make manifest the existence of the Community for a people defined as specifically European.[111] Their role was to remind European citizens in 'A People's Europe' of the existence of the Community and their belonging to it. As such, they represented a 'definite connection with the Community'.[112] The Community flag was to be displayed (and still is) at official international and national events, at exhibitions and fairs, at the seats of the institutions or outside their information offices and delegations.[113] In addition to this, the Community emblem accompanies nowadays just about anything that is produced or supported by the European Union.[114]

Despite the wide-ranging use of the affective style of public communication, it would be a mistake to argue that from the mid-1970s the Commission neglected or ceased to use a factual style of public communication. By factually informing the European citizenry about Community history and policies and by demonstrating the concrete relevance of the Community for European political-federal citizens' daily lives, the Commission hoped to raise the level of knowledge amongst European citizens and to foster a feeling of belonging and identification with the Community.[115] Accordingly, and with regard to the first direct elections of the EP, the Commission stated that it was important to 'arouse public interest in the elections by highlighting the importance of Community activities for the day-to-day life of the man in the street and in this way to encourage voters to turn out on polling day'.[116] To this end, factual information was supposed to become 'simpler, livelier and more concrete (...) in order to give the people of the Community a better idea (...) of Community activities which affect their daily lives'.[117] Information about the Community aimed at 'explain[ing] the fundamental themes, such as historical events which led to the construction of the Community and which inspired its further development in freedom, peace and security and its achievements and potential in the economic and social field'[118] in order 'to make citizens aware of being part of a social group involved in a historical experience and of participating in the shaping of a common destiny'.[119] In other words, information policy was aiming at 'mak[ing] some 260 million Europeans understand what European unification means and how the Community affects them in their daily lives'.[120]

As such, the ancillary use of a factual style of public communication had a twofold purpose: first, to provide the political-federal European 'demos' with factual information about the Community and its policy developments (thereby fulfilling its democratic obligation of information) and second, the factual style of public communication, it can be argued, was at the service of a set of affective objectives which the Commission had set for itself and which scoped its public communication policy. In other words, by providing factual information about the Community and emphasising its relevance for the man on the street, the Commission believed, a feeling of belonging to the Community amongst the European citizenry could be triggered.

Within this logic it was the singular importance of the factual mass media that was emphasised as being critical to reach a mass audience and as such, its recognised usefulness towards this end became a consistent feature of the Commission's communication policy 1973–1992.[121]

The Factual Mass Media

According to the EP, 'mass media provide an appreciable contribution to mutual understanding between peoples and thereby create the requisite cultural context within which the common institutions could acquire a more concrete image for, and be accepted by, the European citizen'.[122] In this role the mass media could help to realise the objective of the Community's information policy, and that was to 'break down the insular resistance between the populations of Europe'.[123] The mass media, notably audiovisual media, were supposed to 'bring the peoples of Europe closer together' as 'every citizen may have access to the greatest number of programmes broadcast by the various channels of the Community countries'.[124] In this context two important developments took place. First, the aspiration to establish a multilingual European television channel became apparent and second, the Television Without Frontiers Directive (1989) was formulated. With regard to a potential European television channel, it was the 2nd Adonnino Report which recognised a TV channel's 'potential importance for the knowledge of European cooperation and development of a truly European television channel' and emphasised the 'need for broadcasting to be multilingual'.[125] In the same vein, the EP 'call[ed] on the Council to declare itself in favour of a multilingual European television channel'.[126] The TVWF Directive, the cornerstone of the European Union's audiovisual policy, 'rests on two basic principles: the free movement of European television programmes within the internal market and the requirement for TV channels to reserve, whenever possible, more than half of their transmission time for European works ("broadcasting quotas")'.[127] As such 'the Directive aims to ensure the free movement of broadcasting services within the internal market and at the same time to preserve certain public interest objectives,[128] such as cultural diversity, the right of reply, consumer protection and the protection of minors'.[129]

It is through the mass media that the Commission further and communicatively conceived of a European audience. This mass-mediated communicatively conceived audience reinforced the political-federal representation of European citizenship in 'A People's Europe' in two ways. First, public service broadcasting in the form of a genuine multilingual European television channel would, so the Commission believed, reinforce the nature of the European 'demos'. This would be informed through a Community channel and subsequently receive information from a euro-perspective and not be filtered through a national lens. Second, as expressed by the EP, in each member state citizens have a right to information.[130] Further, the Commission has conceived of public communication as a democratic mission since the establishment of the first Information Service of the High Authority of the ECSC in 1952 and has, from very early on, aspired to have a designated budget for its independent public communication policy, similar to that of nation-states.[131] The idea of establishing a European-wide television channel was reminiscent of, and complemented the objectives of, the early public communication policy papers (1950s and 1960s), and the Community's own television channel would, if organised independently from the Community, contribute to the democratic standing by empowering European civil society through information and the possibility of scrutiny of the Community institutions in the way Alexander understood the role of communicative institutions.[132] To date, such a European TV channel has still not been realised.

Public Opinion Polling

It was also during the second representation of European citizenship that the Community was given the opportunity to create its own public opinion polling tool: the Eurobarometer. The Community had had a long-standing interest in public opinion[133] as it understood it as a tool to measure and understand the depth of feeling about the Community held by the European public, to evaluate whether a European civil consciousness was emerging and to determine whether the European public had developed a curiosity about European affairs and concomitantly, felt sufficiently encouraged to be active in European affairs.[134] Linked to this, the Commission and the EP believed an autonomous and independent European public opinion[135] could only emerge if the European public was sufficiently informed about the Community to develop an interest in it.[136] In this light, European public opinion was considered a factor for increasing European integration.[137] However, and until the Eurobarometer was created, the Community had to rely on infrequent external opinion polls[138] which would not cover all member states until 1962 when Gallup conducted the first Community-wide opinion poll.[139]

In 1973 Rabier had to leave his functions as Director General of the Press and Information Service following a reshuffling of staff after the first Community enlargement. The then Commission President Ortoli offered Rabier two options: he could either retire or if he wanted to stay with the Commission he would need to think about in which capacity. Rabier, who had been talking, notably, to members of the EP about his opinion that the Community needed its own public opinion poll, took the opportunity immediately and suggested to Ortoli the creation of the Eurobarometer. Ortoli agreed but asked Rabier to develop a detailed project proposition and to present it to Scarascia-Mugnozza, then Vice-President of the Commission. Scarascia-Mugnozza accepted the project unconditionally and appointed Rabier as *conseiller spécial* for European public opinion polling. Assisted by a single secretary and another one for only one month per semester, Rabier went ahead to create the Eurobarometer.[140] As such, it was a coincidence that the creation of the Eurobarometer fell into the year 1973,[141] and not the result of political calculation or a concern about decreasing popular support for European integration, as Shore, Theiler and Paoli have misleadingly argued.[142]

With the newly created Eurobarometer, public opinion had become a persistent and systematic[143] concern for the Commission during the political-federal representation of European citizenship. The Eurobarometer[144] was intended to inform the Community about attitudes towards European integration and to potentially react to these by adapting either policy initiatives or information activities.[145] In other words, the Commission desired to measure public sentiment with regard to all aspects of European integration, to understand the effectiveness of its own public communication policy[146] and to ensure that public sentiment was recognised in terms of the formation of new policies. In fact, it saw European citizens as capable of making judgements about European integration and valued its opinions sufficiently enough to reorient European policies and public communication policy, in particular. Conceived of in such a way, the Eurobarometer helped the public communication policy unit to pay 'closest attention to the interest and attitudes of the various sectors of the population and follow their evolution by periodic opinion surveys'.[147] Symbolically, the creation of the Eurobarometer and concomitantly, systematic public opinion polling, sent an important signal to the European public. To borrow Alexander's terms: 'Polling suggests trust in the sincerity, honesty and intelligence of the people, the interviewees. When public polls are systematically conducted and publicized for the first time, it is hardly surprising that the members of a nascent civil society can experience a new sense of worth'.[148] This sense of worth, which could facilitate a feeling of belonging to Europe and of wanting to take responsibility for it, was especially important in the 1970s as the Community prepared for the first direct elections of the EP in 1979. With a political-federal European 'demos' about to exercise its electoral rights, the Community needed to raise awareness of these electoral rights through its public communication policy and highlight the political issues at stake. The Commission's concern for public opinion polling was significant because it is, so Alexander argued, the 'process of opinion polling [that] turns 'the members of civil society from a passive, voiceless, and potentially manipulable "mass" into a collective actor with a voice and an intelligence of its own'.[149] This voice, in turn, was recognised to, in Alexander's words, be able to turn into a 'specific, politically (…) powerful communicative force'.[150] And as such, the Eurobarometer cannot be understood, as Aldrin has argued, as a political instrument to manipulate European public opinion into consenting to and supporting European integration.[151]

Interestingly, the Eurobarometer introduced, albeit in an embryonic and barely recognisable way, the first form of two-way communication in the form of European surveys within the framework of the Eurobarometer. This slowly paved the way for the third style of public communication, the deliberative-rational style, which emerged after the Maastricht crisis and attempt to turn European citizens into participants rather than spectators, as we will see in the following chapter.

What, then, was the image of the European citizen that the Commission created through the use of a political-federal lexicon and its conceptions of European space and subsequently publicly communicated? I suggest that it is best summarised in the following quasi-fictional portrait of the European citizen:

In the second representation of European citizenship, the Commission imagined European citizens as citizens of a liberal democratic Community who, equipped with new electoral rights, were encouraged to make their way to the polling stations to directly elect the EP in 1979 for the first time. From the beginning of the European integration process, the Community had considered it desirable and important to provide European citizens with opportunities to actively participate in the democratic life of the Community. The introduction of European electoral rights needs to be understood as the first concrete step towards realising this. The democratic development of the Community and the attendant involvement of European citizens in its political processes meant that it became increasingly important to reveal and understand European public sentiment and accordingly, the Community systematically used its new public opinion poll: the Eurobarometer. However, and in order for public sentiment to emerge, so the Commission believed, it was necessary for European citizens to be informed about Community affairs—after all, people can only have an opinion about something they are aware of. In this sense the Commission continued to use the factual style of public communication and attempted to bring about European factual mass media.

The political-federal understanding of the Community was supported by the Commission's single-perspectival conception of space. The Commission considered the Community increasingly as a single political-federal, economic-social and cultural entity, the unity of which was supported by European economic and social rights which applied within the Community's new territory—a territory which the Commission imagined in its public communication efforts to be the new homeland of a European citizenry. This single-perspectival conception of space was further supported by an emphasis on the European dimensions of culture, communication, sport and music (amongst other things) and the introduction of European sports events which newly founded European sports teams could participate in. Symbolically speaking, the single-perspectival conception of Community space was supported by the affective style of public communication via the newly introduced political-federal European symbols such as the flag, the anthem and the emblem. By displaying these political-federal European symbols at official international and national events, at exhibitions and fairs, at the seats of the institutions, public buildings or outside the Community's information offices and delegations they would progressively but forcefully, so the Commission hoped, become part of the daily lives of European citizens and, as such, act as constant reminders of the existence of the Community as a single space and European citizens' belonging to it. In this representation of European citizenship, European citizens were encouraged to celebrate the birthday of the European Community on 9 May (the date of the Schuman Declaration in 1950), to listen with a feeling of belonging and pride to Beethoven's 'Ode to Joy', which—again, so the Community hoped—would no longer simply be a piece of music to European citizens but be recognised as the European anthem reminding them of the common cultural heritage they share and the common future they were to embark upon.

However, this understanding of European citizenship changed in the beginning of the 1990s in the context of the difficult ratification of the Maastricht Treaty.

3   From 'A People's Europe' to a 'Europe of Transparency'

The Maastricht crisis was triggered by the French petit oui and particularly the negative Danish referendum on the Maastricht Treaty (1992), which came as a shock to the European institutions.[152] The rejection was based on Danish fears with regard to their own currency and defence. In summary, the Danes, who 'had approved the 1986 Single [European] Act by a considerable majority', appeared to accept 'the Economic Community but [to] reject (…) the Union, [because it] would have jeopardised their sovereignty, with particular regard to their own currency and defence'.[153] Overall and according to Ludlow, 'the single market project, while greeted with moderate public enthusiasm, brought the integration down to a level that affected, or threatened to affect, the day-to-day lives of ordinary European citizens in a way that had not occurred previously. (…) This contributed greatly to sour the reception of the Maastricht Treaty'.[154] It seemed as if the dominantly affective style of public communication used during the period of the second representation of political-federal European citizenship in 'A People's Europe' had led to the impression, especially by the Danish and the French, that the Community was turning into an omnipresent superstate replete with political-federal symbols traditionally associated with a nation-state adorning it. The Commission's emphasis on the importance of the existence of a political-federal European 'demos', the objective of completing the Single Market and the introduction of a common currency in combination with the use of political-federal European symbols had ultimately served to confuse a significant number of European citizens about the aims of European political integration and to create the feeling of having their national identities threatened.[155] Lamassoure, member of the European Parliament, argued that the European Community never intended nor conceived of European symbols as an expression of European state-hood or sovereignty, but as a means of stimulating a feeling of belonging to Europe amongst the citizens of the Community and as a way of fighting against a technocratically-run Community.[156] In short: the Community conceived of symbols as expressions of European civil solidarity and as a means to stimulate a European civil consciousness rather than as adornments of a putative European statehood. In this light it is important to note that scholars such as Shore[157] have failed to recognise the civil and solidarising intentions behind these symbols when arguing that the Commission simply engaged in political propaganda via the use of these symbols. Rather, the Commission recognised that civil solidarity is a part itself of the very definition of civil society. Just as Alexander, it understood civil solidarity in 'universalistic terms' and not in a 'particularistic way'.[158] It is this universalising solidarity that acts as 'the kind of mutual identification that unites individuals dispersed by class, race, religion, ethnicity (…)'[159] or culture and which sustains civil society in the working out of its own identity and boundaries. In other words, without a European civil consciousness, a feeling of 'we as Europeans', the emergence of civil solidarity is unlikely and without a concomitant sense of solidarity there cannot be a European civil society. In short, the affective style of public communication, the use of political symbols and the development of cultural policies in the 1970s and 1980s hadn't stimulated a sufficiently strong solidarising affective support for the immediate realisation of a political-federal Europe through the Maastricht Treaty (1992). The Community was judged by 'Europeans' to have performed effectively with regards to its *'Kompetenzkatalog'*[160] in the economic realm, whilst the Maastricht Treaty (1992) was simultaneously judged to stand for an unnecessary extension of the Community's competences combined with increasing political power not reaching out in any effective way to the civil realm.

In the aftermath of the negative Danish referendum and the French 'petit oui', a change in the Commission's style of public communication occurred on the back of the subsequent analysis of the Danish rejection of the Maastricht Treaty. The reason for the Danish rejection was attributed to the recognition that a 'socio-cultural split was (…) apparent, depending on the voters' educational background: the 'Yes' vote was generally supported by the most well-informed citizens, capable of understanding the benefits of the European Union.' Subsequently, the Community distanced itself from an affective style of public communication and began to focus on ways that would increase the level of information of all of the European citizenry and to try to stimulate a broader debate of Community affairs amongst all European citizens and between European institutions and European citizens. The Commission's intention to focus on debate and dialogue between European institutions and the European citizenry required a reinterpretation of European citizenship. Subsequently, the third representation of European citizenship emerged as political-dialogical citizenship in a 'Europe of Transparency' (1993–2004).

Notes

1. On European Political Cooperation see CVCE (2012a, b).
2. The Nixon-Kissinger Year of Europe was a programme that was initiated in the immediate aftermath of the Vietnam War and had as its objective to 're-establish a priority in relations with the transatlantic alliance' [sic] (See Library of Congress (2003). This programme forced the European

Community to position itself with regard to the Nixon-Kissinger propositions (see e.g. Ifestos 1987). However, I consider the effect of the Yom Kippur War more significant and therefore focus on it.
3. For details on the context of the Yom Kippur War and its significance for European integration, see Ifestos (1987), Urwin (1995) and Dinan (2010).
4. Dinan (2010: 55).
5. Ifestos (1987: 175).
6. CVCE (2012c).
7. In fact, as pointed out by Gfeller (2012: 2), the French government under Pompidou saw this situation as an opportunity to 'assert the nascent European entity as a world actor vis-à-vis the United States and the Arab world'.
8. Ifestos (1987: 176).
9. Gfeller (2012: 10).
10. Gfeller (2012).
11. See also the preamble of the SEA (1986) and the preamble of the Maastricht Treaty (1992).
12. Dulphy and Manigand (2011) interviewing Collowald.
13. Moravscik (1991: 75), 1994.
14. Moravcsik (2002: 619), also 1994.
15. Moravcsik (2002, 2005a, b, 2007, 2008).
16. Moravcsik (2008: 159).
17. Moravcsik (1998: 4 emphasis in the original).
18. CVCE (2012d).
19. See Vedel Report (1972), Preamble SEA (1986). For information on the information campaign for the European Parliament elections, see Laloux (2014).
20. Hallstein (1959: 201). Also 2nd Adonnino Report (1985), Adonnino, personal communication, 22 November 2011.
21. Laloux (2014: 453).
22. De Angelis and Karamouzi (forthcoming) show how the European Parliament took the accession enquiries and subsequent enlargement negotiations of Greece, Spain and Portugal as an opportunity to discursively emphasise the democratic aspects of the European Community's identity. Ultimately, this led to the Declaration on Democracy (1978).
23. The representation of 'A People's Europe' spanned over two decades of the European integration process. European integration during this period was marked by 'ups and downs'. As I have already noted in the previous chapter, the 1970s were characterised by, for example, economic and budgetary problems and differences of opinions between Britain and the other member states (amongst others). The 1980s can be sub-divided into two

periods. The beginning of the 1980s was a period of slow European integration, sometimes also referred to as the period of stagnation. Ludlow (2006: 219) argued that the 'difficulties the EC faced between 1980 and 1985 were the prolongation of the economic difficulties of the 1970s (...)'. According to Lastenouse (interview 22 February 2012) the mid-1980s was a period characterised by confidence and almost euphoria with regard to the Community's political projects (Fontainebleau 1984, Single European Act 1986 and the Maastricht Treaty 1992). It was during this period that a 'People's Europe' was envisaged in its liveliest form (see e.g. the Adonnino Reports, the introduction of political-federal European symbols). The year 1985 was also of particular importance since Jacques Delors became President of the Commission. According to Santarelli (interview 23 February 2012) the European citizenry trusted Delors and he was welcomed and treated as a 'grand Président'. Delors was, according to Santarelli an energetic but realistic President who knew that it would take several generations to achieve a federation of states. With Delors, the 'second half of the 1980s was arguably the most active and dynamic period of the European integration process since the early 1960s (...)' (Ludlow 2006: 219). For more information on the European integration process in the 1980s, see Ludlow (2006) and Dinan (2010).
24. Commission (1973b, 1975c, 1985, 1988), Tindemans Report (1975), EP (1983, 1987).
25. Commission (1973a, b, 1975d, 1982a, 1985, 1986b, 1988), Tindemans Report (1975), Conclusions du Conseil Européen de Fontainebleau (1984), EP (1986, 1987).
26. SEA (1986, preamble).
27. Commission (1975a).
28. 1st and 2nd Adonnino Report (1985).
29. Commission (1973a, 1977b), Tindemans Report (1975).
30. Commission (1973a, 1975d, 1976b, 1978b, 1985, 1986a, b, 1988), Ronan (1975), Tindemans Report (1975), Conclusions du Conseil Européen de Fontainebleau (1984), EP (1983, 1987), 1st and 2nd Adonnino Reports 1985.
31. Commission (1973b, 1975d), EP (1980), 1st and 2nd Adonnino Report (1985).
32. Commission (1975b).
33. The majority of these terms disappeared from EU secondary law after the first direct elections of the EP, and it is interesting to note that there is no mentioning of the second direct elections of 1984 in any of the Commission's information policy papers, although the EP was concerned with an information policy for the second direct elections of the EP (see EP 1983).

With the first direct elections of the EP, the EP was the only institution that was directly legitimised by the European citizenry. Subsequently, the EP seemed to put itself in a supervisory role with regard to the Commission's information policy. Accordingly, the EP (1980: 18) stated: 'Subject to normal parliamentary supervision, the Commission's first task is to inform all Community citizens (…)'. At the same time, the EP started explicitly to criticise the Commission's information policy. It noted that it seemed as if Commission staff were largely unaware of or uninterested in the communication dimension of their role (EP 1980). This division between the information strategy of the EP and the Commission was at the origin of coordinative problems in their information policies that ultimately led to the creation of a Commissioner not only for Communication Strategy but also for Interinstitutional Relations, M. Wallström 2005.

The extent of the EP's supervisory role after the first EP elections is difficult to assess because we have fewer documents about the Commission's information policy in the 1980s; for example, in the 1980s there weren't any yearly information policy programmes—at least there are no documents indicating such annual programmes. We have a short programme indicating priority themes for the years 1985–1988 which are a lot less detailed than the information programmes of the 1970s. There are four potential reasons why there are fewer documents. First, there were simply no such information policy documents. Second, the 1980s were marked by a lot of restructuring processes of the information services. Third, according to Carnel (personal communication, 9 January 2012) there might be internal documents of this time, but these are not listed in any database, but might be hidden in the 2km long shelves of documents of this period. Fourth, apparently many documents were destroyed when DG X had to leave the Berlaymont building in the late 1980s.

34. Commission (1977a, b, c, 1978a).
35. Commission (1977a, d, 1978a, 1979a), EP (1977).
36. EP (1977).
37. Commission (1977b, d).
38. EP (1977).
39. Commission (1975d).
40. For example Commission (1975d), 2nd Adonnino Report (1985).
41. Cohen (1985: 15).
42. Ibid.: 12.
43. See Commission (1975d, 1988), Tindemans Report 1975, Conclusions du Conseil Européen de Fontainebleau (1984), particularly 1st Adonnino Report (1985).
44. See Commission (2004) for relevant documents for the introduction of the uniform passport and Laloux (2014) for more information.

45. Commission (1975d: 9).
46. Commission (1975d).
47. Commission (1975d: 10).
48. Tindemans (1975: 27).
49. Commission (1975d: 12).
50. Whereas the Commission mentioned all of these ideas regarding the European passport and the abolition of internal border controls in the 1970s, the realisation of these ideas was much slower and uneven. It was only in the early 1980s that the first concrete initiatives to establish the uniform passport were taken via two resolutions, respectively, the resolutions of 23 June 1981 and 30 June 1982 (two others were passed 14 July 1986 and 10 July 1995). The abolition of internal borders took its time too: the Schengen agreement was signed in 1985, supplemented by the Schengen Convention in 1990, and the Schengen area was created in 1995. It needs to be noted, however, that not all member states are at the time of writing members of the Schengen area and that the Schengen area extends beyond the Community to include Switzerland, Norway and Iceland.
51. Taylor (2007).
52. Perrin (2014: 73).
53. Perrin (2014: 56) referring to Allen (2004). See Allen (2004) on the idea of political friendship as a means to overcome distrust amongst citizens.
54. 2nd Adonnino Report (1985).
55. Commission (1973b, 1975a, c, 1976a, b, 1978a, 1979a, 1986b, 1988), Ronan (1975), Tindemans Report (1975), 2nd Adonnino Report (1985).
56. The Tindemans Report (1975) and the Commission (1986a) refer to a 'Citizen's Europe', 1st and 2nd Adonnino Reports (1985) and the Commission (1988) uses a 'people's Europe' instead.
57. Instead of using the term 'economic-socially conceived space' one could also use the term 'legally conceived space'. However, for reasons of clarity I shall use economic and social rights. Further, this avoids confusion with features of the fifth representation of European citizenship and that is the civil-legal representation dealt with in chapter "'Europe of Rights' (2010–2014)". It is interesting to note at this point, however, that rights—and by this I mean rights stemming from Community law—are of importance and figure in the Commission's communication strategy (see e.g. Commission 1987b). This is to some extent reminiscent of the way and the style in which Reding publicly communicated European citizenship.
58. Commission (1988: 10).
59. It is in 1985 that Delors develops the project to complete the Single Market by 1992.

60. 1st Adonnino Report (1985: 11).
61. Tindemans (1975: 27).
62. The European Central Bank with monetary sovereignty was created in 1998 through the Treaty of Amsterdam (1997). It is interesting to note that even the naming of the European Central Bank follows a national model. Usually, national banks include the state in the title, for example: Deutsche Bundesbank, Banque de France or Bank of England.
63. Shore (2000: 91). On the symbolic significance of currency, see e.g. Dyson (1994), Pointon (1998) and Jönsson et al. (2000), Servet (2003) and Shanahan (2003).
64. Shanahan (2003: 163).
65. 1st Adonnino Report (1985: 13).
66. From the 1990s onwards, this definition of space through the right to free movement is no longer limited to EU member states. Several agreements such as the agreement to allow Iceland, Norway and Liechtenstein to participate in the European common market after the establishment of the European Economic Area (EEA) in 1994 or the establishment of Schengen area (as of 1995) extend the right to free movement across EU-borders.
67. Tindemans (1975: 27).
68. In 2004 the European Health Insurance Card (EHIC) was introduced which allows EU citizens to access state-provided healthcare in all European Economic Area (EEA) countries and Switzerland.
69. 2nd Adonnino Report (1985: 28).
70. One could argue that communicatively conceived space is another conception of space. Communicatively conceived space includes the media and the use of symbols which have a communicative function. As such, I deal with communicatively conceived cosmopolitan European space within the context of the affective style of public communication.
71. Adonnino (personal communication, 22 November 2011). To this he added that '[t]here was some opposition about the proposals in the field of culture, on the assumption that this could lead to the creation of a European culture that tended to eliminate cultural specificities [of the member states]'. See Pantel (1999) for an explanation of the slogan and the Community's understanding of 'unity' and 'diversity'.
72. Cultural policy has evolved from the Treaty of Rome (1957) onward—although at that time, the EEC did not have any competences for cultural policies. Hence, cultural policy had to be framed by economic integration and is therefore limited to exportation and importation of cultural goods (EEC Treaty, art. 30, 34, 36). It was in the 1970s that a formal cultural policy emerged. The Tindemans Report (1975) included cultural aspects such as the 'rapprochement of peoples', 'shared heritage' and the appeal that the Community needs to culturally intervene in the realm of news,

education, culture and communication. From 1977 on cultural policies emerged (Commission 1977e, 1982b and 1987a). The second Adonnino Report (1985) proposed to stimulate European identity through interventions in culture and communication. The Maastricht Treaty (1992) contained the legal foundation for communication policy in art. 128. Since 1982, a 'European City for culture' has been chosen every year, and since 1999 there has been a Commissioner for Culture (see also Shore 2000, Theiler 2005, Fornäs 2012, Laloux 2014).

73. Commission (1973a: 1, 7).
74. On mega-events and their role in the growth of international culture and in identity formation, see Roche (2000).
75. 2nd Adonnino Report (1985: 26), also Commission (1987a).
76. Tindemans Report (1975: 28), alongside the 2nd Adonnino Report (1985) and Commission (1988).
77. Whereas the EU does not dispose of any competence over the member states' education curricula, it has established various exchange programmes for Higher Education such as ERASMUS and SOKRATES. See Commission (2012a) for more information on different programmes and their history.
78. It appears that the Community believed European citizens would most easily identify with Europe if they 'lived and experienced' Europe. The building of identity through a process of learning and experiencing goes back to Dewey (1997[1938] and 2011[1916]). Recently, knowingly or not, this idea has been used as the basis for research on European identity. Checkel (2015: 233) referred to this as a 'contact hypothesis' according to which 'communication and personal interactions produce a greater sense of group identification'. On this idea with regard to European identity and ERASMUS, see also Favell (2008), Sigalas (2010), Wilson (2011), Kuhn (2012, 2015) and Mitchell (2015).
79. Tindemans Report (1975: 28).
80. Commission (1988).
81. For a list of European Years, see EP (2012).
82. See Commission (2012b).
83. Lefebvre (1991).
84. Taylor (2007: 171).
85. Aradau et al. (2010: 945).
86. Internal unpublished note from Rabier to M. Carpentier dated 9.10.1973 obtained through personal communication; Adonnino, personal communication, 22 November 2011.
87. HAEC, BAC 408/1991/44, Memo from Franz Froschmaier to Émile Noël, 2 October 1984, cited in Laloux (2014: 450).
88. Commission (1975a: 2).

89. Ibid.: 5.
90. Ronan (1975: 6) and Commission (1988).
91. Commission (1973b: 4).
92. Ibid.
93. Ibid.
94. Commission (1975a: 3).
95. Ibid., Commission (1990).
96. Commission (1986b).
97. Commission (1975a: 12).
98. Fontainebleau (1984).
99. 2nd Adonnino Report (1985).
100. Commission (1986b).
101. Tindemans Report (1975: 26).
102. Billig (1995: 94).
103. Also Krizsan (2011).
104. O'Shaughnessy (2004: 101).
105. Fornäs (2012: 150).
106. Foret (2009: 314), also Cohen (1985). Rabier (2008 interviewed by Dulphy and Manigand) emphasised the Community's need to have its own symbols.
107. Ronan (1975: 3).
108. According to Grant (1994), it was particularly Delors who pushed the introduction of Community symbols by declaring the former Council of Europe flag as the official Community flag in a rather unilateral action. For the history of the Community flag, see European Union (no date). According to Collowald (2011), the first Delors Commission's cabinet in particular (1985–1988) was comprised of Europeans who wished to push European political-federal integration forward. This was a contributing factor in the revival of European integration. For more information on Delors' time as President of the European Commission, see e.g. Cutler et al. (1991), Lewis (1991), Grant (1994), Ross (1995) and Schneider (2001).
109. On European symbols, see Buch (2003), Foret (2003, 2008, 2009), Hersant (2003), Kaelble (2003), Passerini (2003) and Manners (2011), and on the importance of sport for Community identity, see Commission (1987a) and Santarelli (1993).
110. On the meaning of these symbols, see in particular Fornäs (2012).
111. See also Fontainebleau Council (1984).
112. See Commission (1975d, 1988).
113. See 2nd Adonnino Report (1985), Commission (1988).
114. See Shore (2000), Bruter (2005), Sonntag (2010).

115. The understanding that factual information has for its purpose both to inform and to foster a feeling of belonging has guided the Commission's information policy since the early 1950s. For Monnet, information was a prerequisite for any feeling of belonging amongst European citizens. However, it was during the representation 'A People's Europe' that the affective style of public communication was dominant and the factual style of public communication was used to support the affective objectives of the Commission's public communication policy.
116. Commission (1978a: 3).
117. Commission (1975a: 3).
118. 2nd Adonnino Report (1985: 22).
119. Ronan (1975: 6).
120. Ibid.: 7.
121. Commission (1973a, b, 1975a, 1976a, b, 1978a, 1979a, b, 1982a, 1986b, 1989), Ronan (1975), EP (1980).
122. EP (1986, point E: 1).
123. EP (1986: 15), also EP (1980).
124. 2nd Adonnino Report (1985).
125. 2nd Adonnino Report (1985: 22).
126. EP (1986, point 15). For further information about audiovisual policy becoming a focus of the Commission, see Laloux (2014).
127. See Commission (2008) for the source of this quote and all details on the evolution of the TWF directive of 1989. For the directive itself, see Commission (1984a), which was adopted in 1989, revised in 1997 and 2007, renamed 'The Audiovisual Media Services Directive' and codified in 2010. On EU audiovisual policy, see also Harrison and Woods (2000 and 2007), Harrison and Wessels (eds.) (2009). For public information brochures on audiovisual policy, see, for example, Commission (1984b, 1986c).
128. On the conflict between commercial interest of the EU audiovisual policy and EU audiovisual policy as cultural and civil policy, see Schlesinger (1997), Harrison and Woods (2000, 2001a, b), Ward (2002), Wheeler (2004, 2009), Humphreys (2009); on the importance of a European public service broadcaster for the emergence of a European civil society, see Harrison (2010a, b).
129. Commission (2008).
130. EP (1987).
131. See, for example, EP (1960).
132. Alexander (2006).
133. See HA (1954, 1955a, b, c), EP (1960, 1962, 1972) and Commission 1963, 1970, 1971). This long-standing concern hasn't been recognised by Paoli (2012), who argued that the leaders of the European Community

were not concerned with public opinion in the 1950s and 1960s. He further argued that Gazzo had played an important role in advocating and pushing for a more systematic form of European opinion polling. However, there is no archival evidence to support this claim. Indeed, Rabier confirmed that Gazzo played no role in the creation of the Eurobarometer but wrote a supportive editorial for the Eurobarometer first opinion poll in 1974 (Rabier, personal communication, 12 February 2015).
134. Rabier (1965).
135. See EP (1962).
136. EP (1972: 3). Rabier developed the Eurobarometer in collaboration with Inglehart (1970), who developed the so-called cognitive mobilisation theory, which in high-level terms says that the better we understand something the easier we identify with it. For a contrasting view, see Jansen (1991).
137. Rabier (2003).
138. Two examples for such opinion polls are: first, a series of opinion polls carried out between 1952 and 1957 by the United States Information Agency on several aspects of European integration (Rabier 1966) and second, an opinion poll conducted by the UNESCO Institute for Social Sciences between 1956 and 1957. In 1962 Gallup conducted the first Community-wide opinion poll.
139. Rabier (1966) for an overview of public opinion polls and surveys from 1950 to 1965.
140. Rabier, personal communication, 31 December 2014.
141. Rabier, various personal communications, December 2011.
142. Shore (2000), Theiler (2005) and Paoli (2012).
143. Commission (1973a, b, 1975a, 1977b, 1978a), EP (1980 and 1986).
144. For an excellent book on the history and dynamics of the Eurobarometer, see Reif and Inglehart (eds.) (1991) 'Eurobarometer: the Dynamics of European Public Opinion.' See also Inglehart and Rabier (1978). On public opinion in general, see Lippmann (1922).
145. Commission (1975a), EP (1986).
146. It was only after the near failure of the ratification of the Maastricht Treaty in 1992 and with the subsequent reorientation of the Commission's public communication policy that questions about the degree to which the European public was informed about relevant Community affairs were included in the questionnaires of the Eurobarometer (See Commission 2012c for the 1992 and 1993 Standard Eurobarometer surveys).
147. Commission (1973a: 4).
148. Alexander (2006: 91).
149. Alexander (2006: 85).
150. Ibid.

151. Aldrin (2010).
152. Brüggemann (2005). Whereas the French 'petit oui' (51% in favour of the Treaty and 49% against) reinforced the shock about the strength of negative European public opinion towards the Maastricht Treaty, it was nevertheless the Danish 'no' that was mostly analysed in the aftermath of the referenda (see Siune (1993) and Worre (1995); on the French referendum, see Criddle (1993)). According to Santarelli (interview 23 February 2012), the outcome of the Danish referendum was not a surprise but was expected. He argued that the membership had been complicated from the beginning of the accession negotiations, as the Danish did not want to fully adhere to the European projects. On the contrary, it was the outcome of the French referendum that was a shock, especially because France was one of the founding member state countries.

Franklin et al. (1994) discussed three potential reasons for the outcomes of the Danish, Irish and French referenda. One of these reasons (besides a change in public opinion in the run-up to the referendum and the referendum as a judgement of domestic politics) was that public opinion was misread. By this the authors meant that the Community might have misinterpreted the results of the Eurobarometer, which indicated a high general support for the Community but a lower level of support for the Maastricht Treaty. Accordingly, Franklin et al. argued that the Community might have confused general support with support for the Maastricht Treaty.

Of relevance to the apparent misreading of public opinion is Lindberg and Scheingold's (1970: 40) differentiation between a utilitarian and an affective dimension of support. The former can be defined as 'support based on some perceived and relatively concrete interest' and the latter as 'support which seems to indicate a diffuse and perhaps emotional response to some of the vague ideals embodied in the notion of European Unity' such as a common Community identity. Following these definitions it could be argued that the European citizenry historically has shown itself to be more concerned with utilitarian motives than affective ones expressed as support for the Community in terms of its economic dimension—studies such as the Eurobarometer surveys have shown that public support for the Community increases with economic success but decreases in situations of high inflation or unemployment (see also Panebianco 1996) and that European citizens are in favour of common solutions for economic issues.

On the Maastricht Treaty itself, see Eichengreen (1992), Baun (1995), Schmieding (1993), Pollack (2000) and Grieco (2005, 2006).
153. CVCE (2012a: 2).
154. Ludlow (2006: 230).
155. Ibid.

156. Lamassoure in *Le Monde*, 'A Community needs symbols' (15 July 2007). Lamassoure's (2008) view was reminiscent of the understanding of European identity among the High Authority's and Commission's officials in the period 1951–1973. Just as European civil consciousness and ultimately European identity was to complement but not to replace national identity, a political-federal Europe was not to replace the nation-states but rather to deepen their integration. Accordingly, European political-federal symbols were to symbolise the existence of the European Community but not intended to lead to the abolition of nation-state symbols.
157. Shore (2000).
158. Alexander (2006: 43).
159. Ibid.
160. Jönsson et al. (2000) 'catalogue of competences'.

References

Adonnino, P. (1985). A People's Europe. Reports from the ad hoc committee. *Bulletin of the European Communities*, Supplement 7/85.
Aldrin, P. (2010). L'invention de l'opinion publique européenne. Genèse intellectuelle et politique de l'Eurobaromètre (1950–1973). *Politix, 89*, 79–101.
Alexander, J. (2006). *The civil sphere*. Oxford: Oxford University Press.
Allen, D. (2004). *Talking to strangers: Anxieties of citizenship since Brown v. Board of Education*. Chicago: University of Chicago Press.
Aradau, C., Huysmans, J., & Squire, V. (2010). Acts of European citizenship: A political sociology of mobility. *Journal of Common Market Studies, 48*(4), 947–967.
Baun, M. (1995). *An imperfect union: The Maastricht Treaty and the new politics of European integration*. Boulder: Westview Press.
Billig, M. (1995). *Banal nationalism*. London: Sage.
Brüggemann, M. (2005). How the EU constructs the European public sphere: Seven strategies of information policy. *Javnost/The Public, 12*(2), 57–74.
Bruter, M. (2005). *Citizens of Europe? The emergence of a mass European identity*. New York: Palgrave Macmillan.
Buch, E. (2003). Parcours et paradoxes de l'hymne européen. In L. Passerini (Ed.), *Figures d'Europe. Images and myths of Europe* (pp. 87–98). Brussels: Peter Lang.
CCE (Commission des Communautés Européennes). (1963, Juin 26). *Mémorandum sur la politique des Communautés en matière d'information à l'attention des Conseils* (COM (63) 242).
CCE (Commission des Communautés Européennes). (1970, Janvier 30). *Organisation de la politique d'information pour 1970* (SEC (70) 378).

CCE (Commission des Communautés Européennes). (1971, Avril 2). *Programme d'activité d'information pour 1971* (SEC (71) 590 final).
CCE (Commission des Communautés Européennes). (1973a, June 18). *Information policy programme for 1973* (SEC (73) 2200).
CCE (Commission des Communautés Européennes). (1973b, Décembre 12). *Programme d'information 1974–1975* (SEC (73) 4660 final).
CCE (Commission des Communautés Européennes). (1975a, Janvier 17). *Programme d'information 1975* (SEC (75) 200).
CCE (Commission des Communautés Européennes). (1975b). *Towards European citizenship: The granting of special rights.* COM (75) 321 final, 2.7.1975 in: Bulletin of the European Communities, Supplement 5/75.
CCE (Commission des Communautés Européennes). (1975c, Décembre 10). *Programme d'information pour 1976* (SEC (75) 4250 final).
CCE (Commission des Communautés Européennes). (1975d, July 2). *Towards European citizenship: A passport union* (COM (75) 322 final). *Bulletin of the European Communities*, Supplement 7/75.
CCE (Commission des Communautés Européennes). (1976a, June 28). *Report on the activities of the Directorate-General of Information in 1975* (COM (76) 225).
CCE (Commission des Communautés Européennes). (1976b, Décembre 9). *Programme d'information pour 1977* (SEC (76) 4293 final).
CCE (Commission des Communautés Européennes). (1977a, Septembre 29). *Programme d'information spécial de la Commission pour 1978 pour l'élection directe du Parlement européen* (SEC (77) 3372).
CCE (Commission des Communautés Européennes). (1977b, Mars 25). *Programme d'information de la Commission pour les élections directes du Parlement européen* (COM (77) 114 final).
CCE (Commission des Communautés Européennes). (1977c, March 29). *The Commission's information programme in preparation for direct elections to the European Parliament.* Information Memo Commission.
CCE (Commission des Communautés Européennes). (1977d, September 23). *Report on the activities of the Directorate-General of Information in 1976* (COM (77) 452).
CCE (Commission des Communautés Européennes). (1977e, November 22). *Community action in the cultural sector* (COM (77) 560 final).
CCE (Commission des Communautés Européennes). (1978a, February 6). *Lignes principales du programme spécial d'information pour les élections directes* (SEC (78) 532).
CCE (Commission des Communautés Européennes). (1978b, June 5). *Organisation of the Spokesman's group and Directorate-General for Information* (SEC (78) 2386).

CCE (Commission des Communautés Européennes). (1979a, February 15). *Information programme for 1979* (COM (79) 64 final).
CCE (Commission des Communautés Européennes). (1979b, December 10). *Information programme for 1980* (COM (79) 701 final).
CCE (Commission des Communautés Européennes). (1982a, February 9). *Information programme for 1982* (COM (82) 3 final).
CCE (Commission des Communautés Européennes). (1982b, October 16). *Stronger community action in the cultural sector* (COM (82) 590 final).
CCE (Commission des Communautés Européennes). (1984a, June 14). *Television without frontiers*. Green paper. (COM (84) 300).
CCE (Commission des Communautés Européennes). (1984b, December). *Towards a European television policy* (European File 19/84).
CCE (Commission des Communautés Européennes). (1985, November 19). *Communication from the Commission to the council on A People's Europe* (COM (85) 640 final).
CCE (Commission des Communautés Européennes). (1986a, Juin 26). *Information et communication. Possibilités et obstacles* (SEC (86) 1135).
CCE (Commission des Communautés Européennes). (1986b, November 25). *Politique d'information et de communication de la Commission. Priorités et propositions de coordination* (SEC (86) 1841/6).
CCE (Commission des Communautés Européennes). (1986c, Aug–Sept). *Television and the audio-visual sector: Towards a European policy* (European File 14/86).
CCE (Commission des Communautés Européennes). (1987a, December 14). *A fresh boost for culture in the European Community* (COM (87) 603 final).
CCE (Commission des Communautés Européennes). (1987b, June–July). *New rights for the citizens of Europe* (European File 11/87).
CCE (Commission des Communautés Européennes). (1988, July 7). *A People's Europe* (COM (88) 331 final).
CCE (Commission des Communautés Européennes). (1989, May 15). *Programme d'information prioritaire 1989–orientations opérationnelles* (SEC (89) 367/3).
CCE (Commission des Communautés Européennes). (1990, March). *A human face for Europe* (European Documentation 4/1990).
CCE (Commission des Communautés Européennes). (2004, October 26). *Fourth report on citizenship of the Union (1 May 2001–30 April 2004)* (COM (2004) 695).
CCE (Commission des Communautés Européennes). (2008). Television broadcasting activities: "Television without frontiers" (TVWF) directive. http://europa.eu/legislation_summaries/audiovisual_and_media/l24101_en.htm. Accessed 17 Jan 2012.
CCE (Commission des Communautés Européennes). (2012a). Education and training. http://ec.europa.eu/education/index_en.htm. Accessed 13 Jan 2012.

CCE (Commission des Communautés Européennes). (2012b). Culture 'European capital of culture'. http://ec.europa.eu/culture/our-programmes-and-actions/doc413_en.htm. Accessed 12 Jan 2012.

CCE (Commission des Communautés Européennes). (2012c). Europa—Public opinion analysis—Standard Eurobarometer archives. http://ec.europa.eu/public_opinion/archives/eb_arch_en.htm. Accessed 5 Dec 2011.

Checkel, J. T. (2015). Identity, Europe and beyond public spheres. In T. Risse (Ed.), *European public spheres. Politics is back* (pp. 227–246). Cambridge: Cambridge University Press.

Cohen, A. (1985). *The symbolic construction of community*. Chichester: Ellis Horwood.

Criddle, B. (1993). The French referendum on the Maastricht Treaty September 1992. *Parliamentary Affairs, 46*(2), 228–238.

Cutler, T., et al. (1991). *Building Europe?: Jacques Delors and his plan for EMU*. London: Thames Polytechnic.

CVCE. (2012a). European Political Cooperation. http://www.cvce.eu/obj/European_Political_Cooperation-en-23ec8fd2-1ae6-4133-91a5-4788e2e184bf.html. Accessed 21 Jan 2012.

CVCE. (2012b). How European Political Cooperation worked in practice. http://www.cvce.eu/obj/How_European_Political_Cooperation_worked_in_practice-en-9fb43023-e923-4e92-b007-68a229758897.html. Accessed 21 Jan 2012.

CVCE. (2012c). Joint statement by the governments of the EEC (6 November 1973). http://www.cvce.eu/obj/Joint_statement_by_the_Governments_of_the_EEC_6_November_1973-en-a08b36bc-6d29-475c-aadb-0f71c59dbc3e.html. Accessed 5 Jan 2012.

CVCE. (2012d). Final communiqué of the Paris Summit (9 and 10 December 1974). http://www.cvce.eu/obj/Final_communique_of_the_Paris_Summit_9_and_10_December_1974-en-2acd8532-b271-49ed-bf63-bd8131180d6b.html. Accessed 7 Jan 2012.

Dewey, J. (1997[1938]). *Experience and education*. New York: Touchstone.

Dewey, J. (2011[1916]). *Democracy and education: An introduction to the philosophy of education*. No place of publication: Simon and Brown.

Dinan, D. (2010). *Ever closer union: An introduction to European integration* (4th ed.). Basingstoke: Palgrave Macmillan.

Dulphy, A., & Manigand, C. (2008). Entretien avec Jacques-René Rabier. Propos recueillis le 16 décembre 2008. *Histoire@Politique*, no 07 janvier – avril 2009. http://www.histoire-politique.fr/index.php?numero=07&rub=portraits&item=10. Accessed 29 Jan 2012.

Dulphy, A., & Manigand, C. (2010). Entretien avec Paul Collowald. Propos recueillis à Bruxelles le 3 juillet 2010. *Histoire@Politique*, no 13 janvier – avril

2011. http://www.histoire-politique.fr/index.php?numero=13&rub=portrait s&item=18. Accessed 29 Jan 2012.
Dyson, K. (1994). *Elusive union: The process of Economic and Monetary Union in Europe*. Harlow: Longman.
Eichengreen, B. (1992). *Should the Maastricht Treaty be saved?* Princeton: Princeton University Press.
EP. (1960, November 18). *Bericht im Namen des politischen Ausschusses über die Probleme der Information in den Europäischen Gemeinschaften* (Berichterstatter Schuijt). Europäisches Parlament Sitzungsdokumente 1960–1961 (Dokument 89).
EP. (1962, November 14). *Bericht im Namen des politischen Ausschusses über die Tätigkeit der Informationsdienste der Europäischen Gemeinschaften* (Berichterstatter Schuijt). Europäisches Parlament Sitzungsdokumente 1962–1963 (Dokument 103).
EP. (1972, Februar 7). *Bericht im Namen des politischen Ausschusses über die Informationspolitik der Europäischen Gemeinschaften* (Berichterstatter Schuijt), Europäisches Parlament Sitzungsdokumente 1971–1972 (Dokument 246/71).
EP. (1977, Mai 10). *Report on the European Community's information policy, with particular reference to the Commission's information programme in preparations for direct election of the European Parliament (rapporteur Schuijt)* (Documents de séance du Parlement européen Document 93/77).
EP (Parlement Européen). (1980, Décembre 4). *Rapport sur la politique d'information de la Communauté européenne, de la Commission des Communautés européennes et du Parlement européen (Rapport Schall)* (Documents de séance du Parlement européen, 1-596/80).
EP. (1983, January 14). *On the information policy of the European Communities for the 1984 direct elections (Beuck Report)* (Information Policy, European Parliament Working Documents 1982–1983, A1-1058/82).
EP. (1986, October 6). *Report on the European Community's information policy (Baget-Bozzo Report)* (European Parliament Working Documents 1986–1987, A2-111-86).
EP. (1987, November 10). *Report on the compulsory publication of information by the European Community (Marck Report)*. (European Session Documents 1987–1988, A2-208/87).
EP. (2012). European years. http://www.europarl.org.uk/view/en/Events/special_events/European-Years.html;jsessionid=95963BA30997630C86EB217C A2897AB0. Accessed 14 July 2012.
European Union. (no date). The European flag. http://europa.eu/about-eu/basic-information/symbols/flag/index_en.htm. Accessed 22 Jan 2012.
Favell, A. (2008). *Eurostars and Eurocities: Free movement and mobility in an integrating Europe*. Oxford: Blackwell.

Foret, F. (2003). L'Europe comme tout: La représentation symbolique de l'Union européenne dans le discours institutionnel. In S. Saurugger (Ed.), *Les modes de représentation dans l'Union européenne* (pp. 177–204). Paris: L'Harmattan.

Foret, F. (2008). *Légitimer l'Europe. Pouvoir et symbolique à l'ère de la gouvernance.* Paris: Sciences Po.

Foret, F. (2009). Symbolic dimensions of EU legitimization. *Media Culture Society*, *31*(2). http://www.sciencespo.site.ulb.ac.be/dossiers_membres/foret-francois/fichiers/foret-francois-publication29.pdf. Accessed 12 June 2012.

Fornäs, J. (2012). *Signifying Europe*. Bristol: Intellect.

Franklin, M., et al. (1994). Uncorking the bottle: Popular opposition to European unification in the wake of the Maastricht Treaty. *Journal of Common Market Studies*, *32*(4), 455–472.

Gfeller, A. E. (2014). *Building a European identity: France, the United States, and the oil shock, 1973–74*. New York/Oxford: Berghahn Books.

Grant, C. (1994). *Delors: Inside the house that Jacques built*. London: Brealey Publishing.

Grieco, J. M. (1995). The Maastricht Treaty, Economic and Monetary Union and the neo-realist research programme. *Review of International Studies*, *21*(1), 21–40.

Grieco, J. M. (1996). State interests and institutional rule trajectories: A neorealist interpretation of the Maastricht Treaty and European Economic and Monetary Union. *Security Studies*, *5*(3), 261–305.

Hallstein, W. (1959, November 10). *Europe is on the move: Political and economic policies*. Speech by Professor Dr. Walter Hallstein, President of the Commission, European Economic Community, delivered to the Royal Institute of International Relations. Brussels.

Harrison, J. (2010a). European social purpose and public service communication. In C. Bee & E. Bozzini (Eds.), *Mapping the European public sphere: Institutions, media and civil society* (pp. 99–116). Aldershot: Ashgate Publishing.

Harrison, J. (2010b). The development of a European civil society through EU public service communication. In S. Papathanassopoulos & R. Negrine (Eds.), *Towards a theory of communication policy* (pp. 81–94). London: Palgrave Macmillan.

Harrison, J., & Wessels, B. (Eds.). (2009). *Mediating Europe: New media, mass communications and the European public sphere*. Oxford: Berghahn.

Harrison, J., & Woods, L. (2000). European citizenship: Can audio-visual policy make a difference? *Journal of Common Market Studies*, *38*(3), 471–495.

Harrison, J., & Woods, L. (2001a). Defining European public service broadcasting. *European Journal of Communication*, *16*(4), 477–504.

Harrison, J., & Woods, L. (2001b). Television quotas: Protecting European culture? *Entertainment Law Review*, *12*(1), 5–14.

Haute Autorité. (1954, Juin 10). *Note sur l'organisation du Service d'Information de la Haute Autorité* (Doc no 3903/54f CEAB 1 no 940).
Haute Autorité. (1955a). *Rapport sur l'évolution de l'opinion publique en ce qui concerne l'intégration européenne et l'action de la Communauté dans les milieux syndicaux* (Doc no 8997/55f. CEAB 13 no 69), (no date).
Haute Autorité. (1955b, November 26). *Rapport sur l'évolution de l'opinion publique dans la République fédérale d'Allemagne au sujet de la C.E.C.A. et de l'intégration européenne* (Doc no 8867/55f. CEAB 13 no 69).
Haute Autorité. (1955c, November 30). *Rapport sur l'évolution de l'opinion publique en ce qui concerne l'intégration européenne et l'action de la Communauté en France* (Doc no 8919/55. CEAB 13 no 69).
Hersant, Y. (2003). Douze étoiles d'or. In L. Passerini (Ed.), *Figures d'Europe. Images and myths of Europe* (pp. 99–106). Brussels: Peter Lang.
Humphreys, P. (2009). EU audio-visual policy, cultural diversity and the future of public service broadcasting. In J. Harrison & B. Wessels (Eds.), *Mediating Europe: New media, mass communications and the European public sphere* (pp. 183–212). Oxford: Berghahn.
Ifestos, P. (1987). *European Political Cooperation. Towards a framework of supranational diplomacy?* Aldershot: Avebury.
Inglehart, R. (1970). Cognitive mobilization and European identity. *Comparative Politics, 3*(1), 45–70.
Inglehart, R., & Rabier, J. R. (1978). Economic uncertainty and European solidarity: Public opinion trends in the Europe of the nine. *Annals of the American Academy of Political Science and Social Science, 440*, 66–97.
Jansen, J. (1991). Postmaterialism, cognitive mobilization and public support for European integration. *British Journal of Political Science, 21*(4), 443–468.
Jönssen, C., Tägil, S., & Törnqvist, G. (Eds.). (2000). *Organizing European space*. London: SAGE.
Kaelble, H. (2003). European symbols 1945–2000: Concept, meaning and historical change. In L. Passerini (Ed.), *Figures d'Europe. Images and myths of Europe* (pp. 47–63). Brussels: Peter Lang.
Krizsan, A. (2011). *'The EU is not them, but us!': The first person plural and the articulation of collective identities in European political discourse*. Newcastle: Cambridge Scholars.
Kuhn, T. (2012). Why educational exchange programmes miss their mark: Cross-border mobility, education and European identity. *Journal of Common Market Studies, 50*(6), 994–1010.
Kuhn, T. (2015). *Experiencing European integration: Transnational lives and European identity*. Oxford: Oxford University Press.
Laloux, P.-O. (2014). At the service of the European citizen: Information policy, a People's Europe, culture, education and training. In E. Bussière, V. Dujardin, et al. (Eds.), *The European Commission 1973–86. History and memories of an institution* (pp. 445–464). Luxembourg: Publications Office of the European Union.

Lamassoure, A. (2008). *The citizen and the application of Community law*. Report to the President of the Republic. http://www.alainlamassoure.eu/liens/975.pdf. Accessed 13 July 2011.

Lefebvre, C. (1991). *The production of space*. Malden: Blackwell.

Lewis, R. (1991). *Master Eurocrat: The making of Jacques Delors*. London: Bruges Group.

Library of Congress. (2003). Foreign affairs in the Nixon era. http://www.loc.gov/loc/lcib/0307-8/policy.html. Accessed 22 Jan 2012.

Lindberg, L., & Scheingold, S. (1970). *Europe's would-be polity: Patterns of change in the European community*. Englewood Cliffs: Prentice Hall.

Lippmann, W. (1922). *Public opinion*. New York: Macmillan.

Ludlow, N. P. (2006). From deadlock to dynamism: The European Community in the 1980s. In D. Dinan (Ed.), *The origins and evolution of the EU* (pp. 218–232). Oxford: Oxford University Press.

Manners, I. (2011). Symbolism in European integration. *Comparative European Politics, 9*(3), 243–268.

Mitchell, K. (2015). Rethinking the 'Erasmus effect' on European identity. *Journal of Common Market Studies, 53*(2), 330–348.

Moravcsik, A. (1991). Negotiating the Single European Act. *International Organization, 45*(1), 19–56.

Moravcsik, A. (1994). Why the European Community strengthens the state: Domestic politics and international cooperation. *Harvard University Center for European Studies*, no. 52. http://www.ces.fas.harvard.edu/publications/docs/pdfs/Moravcsik52.pdf. Accessed 12 Mar 2010.

Moravcsik, A. (1998). *The choice for Europe: Social purpose and state power from Rome to Maastricht*. Ithaca: Cornell University Press.

Moravcsik, A. (2002). In defence of the 'democratic deficit': Reassessing legitimacy in the European Union. *Journal of Common Market Studies, 40*(4), 603–624.

Moravcsik, A. (2005a). Europe without illusions: A category mistake. *Prospect*, Issue 112, July. http://www.prospect-magazine.co.uk/article_details.php?id=6939. Accessed 12 Mar 2010.

Moravcsik, A. (2005b). The European constitutional compromise and the neo-functionalist legacy. *Journal of European Public Policy, 12*(2), 349–386.

Moravcsik, A. (2007). The European constitutional settlement. In S. Meunier & K. McNamara (Eds.), *Making history: European integration and institutional change at fifty: Making history* (pp. 23–50). Oxford: Oxford University Press.

Moravcsik, A. (2008). The European constitutional settlement. *The World Economy, 31*(1), 158–183.

O'Shaughnessy, N. J. (2004). *Politics and propaganda: Weapons of mass seduction*. Manchester: Manchester University Press.

Panebianco, S. (1996, December). *European citizenship and European identity: From the Treaty of Maastricht to public opinion attitudes*. (JMWP, No. 03.96).

Pantel, M. (1999). Unity-in-diversity: Cultural policy and EU legitimacy. In T. Banchoff & M. Smith (Eds.), *Legitimacy and the European Union: The contested polity* (pp. 46–65). London: Routledge.

Paoli, S. (2012). The origins of the Eurobarometer surveys (1968–1974). In D. Preda & D. Pasquinucci (Eds.), *Consensus and European integration. An historical perspective [sic]* (pp. 27–39). Brussels: Peter Lang.

Passerini, L. (2003). Dimensions of the symbolic in the construction of Europeanness. In L. Passerini (Ed.), *Figures d'Europe. Images and myths of Europe* (pp. 21–34). Brussels: Peter Lang.

Perrin, A. (2014). *American democracy. From Tocqueville to town halls to Twitter.* Cambridge: Polity Press.

Pointon, M. (1998). Money and nationalism. In G. Cubitt (Ed.), *Imagining nations* (pp. 229–254). Manchester: Manchester University Press.

Pollack, M. (2000). The end of creeping competence? EU policy-making since Maastricht. *Journal of Common Market Studies, 38*(3), 519–538.

Rabier, J. R. (1965). *L'information des Européens et l'integration de l'Europe. Leçons données le 17 et 18 février 1965.* Bruxelles: Université Libre de Bruxelles.

Rabier, J. R. (1966). *L'Opinion Publique et l'Europe.* Brussels: Institute of Sociology.

Reif, K. H., & Inglehart, R. (Eds.). (1991). *Eurobarometer: The dynamics of European public opinion.* London: Macmillan.

Roche, M. (2000). *Mega-events and modernity: Olympics and expos in the growth of global culture.* London: Routledge.

Ronan, S. G. (1975, November 7). *The information policy of the Commission.* Address by Mr. Sean G. Ronan, Director-General of the Commission of the European Communities, to the Public Relations Institute of Ireland.

Ross, G. (1995). *Jacques Delors and European integration.* Cambridge: Polity.

Santarelli, M. (1993). L'information du citoyen européen. In F. Dassetto & M. Dumoulin (Eds.), *Naissance et développement de l'information européenne* (pp. 67–75). Bern: Peter Lang.

Schlesinger, P. (1997). From cultural defence to political culture: Media, politics and collective identity in the European Union. *Media Culture Society, 19*(3), 369–391.

Schmieding, H. (1993). *Europe after Maastricht.* London: Institute of Economic Affairs.

Schneider, H. (2001). *Jacques Delors: Mensch und Methode.* Wien: Institut für Höhere Studien.

Servet, J. M. (2003). L'euro: fenêtres d'un nomadisme monétaire. In L. Passerini (Ed.), *Figures d'Europe. Images and myths of Europe* (pp. 127–146). Brussels: Peter Lang.

Shanahan, S. (2003). Currency and community: European identity and the Euro. In L. Passerini (Ed.), *Figures d'Europe. Images and myths of Europe* (pp. 159–179). Brussels: Peter Lang.

Shore, C. (2000). *Building Europe: The cultural politics of European integration.* London: Routledge.
Sigalas, E. (2010). Cross-border mobility and European identity: The effectiveness of intergroup contact during the ERASMUS year abroad. *European Union Politics, 11*(2), 241–265.
Siune, K. (1993). The Danes said no to the Maastricht Treaty. The Danish EC referendum of June 1992. *Scandinavian Political Studies, 16*(1), 93–103.
Sonntag, A. (2010). Political symbols, citizenship and communication, paper presented at the communicating European citizenship conference, 22 March, London. http://www.uaces.org/pdf/papers/1002/Sonntag.pdf. Accessed 25 July 2012.
Taylor, C. (2007). *A secular age.* Cambridge, MA: Belknap Press of Harvard University Press.
Theiler, T. (2005). *Political symbolism and European integration.* Manchester: Manchester University Press.
Tindemans, L. (1975). *European Union.* Report by Mr. Leo Tindemans, Prime Minister of Belgium, to the European Council. Bulletin of the European Communities, Supplement 1/76.
Urwin, D. (1995). *The community of Europe: A history of European integration since 1945* (2nd ed.). London: Longman.
Ward, D. (2002). *The European Union democratic deficit and the public sphere: An evaluation of EU media policy.* Amsterdam: IOS Press.
Wheeler, M. (2004). Supranational regulation—Television and the European Union. *European Journal of Communication, 19*(3), 349–369.
Wheeler, M. (2009). Supranational regulation: The EU competition directorate and the European audio-visual marketplace. In J. Harrison & B. Wessels (Eds.), *Mediating Europe: New media, mass communications and the European public sphere* (pp. 262–285). Oxford: Berghahn.
Wilson, I. (2011). What should we expect of 'Erasmus generations'? *Journal of Common Market Studies, 49*(5), 1113–1140.
Worre, T. (1995). First no, then yes: The Danish referendums on the Maastricht Treaty 1992 and 1993. *Journal of Common Market Studies, 33*(2), 235–257.

CHAPTER 4

'Europe of Transparency' (1993–2004)

1 THE EMERGENCE OF A 'EUROPE OF TRANSPARENCY': MAASTRICHT AND THE PROBLEM OF DISENGAGED EUROPEAN CITIZENS

The popular reluctance to ratify the Maastricht Treaty and thereby endorse further political integration was taken as a sign by the Commission and the EP that European citizens were becoming 'increasingly alienated from the idea of the European Community'.[1] The EP referred to a 'growing perplexity amongst citizens' and claimed that this 'perplexity seems to highlight, for the first time, a break in the traditional support of European citizens for the cause of European integration'.[2] The Commission argued along the same lines, noting that the 'public has become more vigilant, even suspicious, towards public authorities, including the European institutions'[3] and that European 'public opinion no longer accepts the Community without question'.[4] The EU therefore thought it necessary to improve the relationship between the Commission and the European citizenry by focusing on its communicative aspects as, so the Commission reasoned, 'the information deficit has become part of the democratic deficit'[5] to which the EP added that 'an information and communication policy must help to democratize politics and be aimed at reducing the gulf between citizens and politics'.[6] Or, alternatively expressed: 'The difficulties raised during the ratification of the Maastricht Treaty showed that the lack of commitment of the European citizens became deeper and the

© The Editor(s) (if applicable) and The Author(s) 2016
S. Pukallus, *Representations of European Citizenship since 1951*,
DOI 10.1057/978-1-137-51147-8_4

distance between the European Union and the citizens gradually became greater'.[7] The Commission and the EP agreed that there was a structural problem in the EU that had to be addressed and that it was pressing to improve European communication policy. In other words, it was time for the European institutions to 'repair Europe' through new structures and a different public communication policy.

New Structures and a Reorientation of the Commission's Public Communication Policy

The structural defaults of the Community lay in its opaque and complex policy and decision-making processes and were seen to be the origin of the public's negative perceptions of the European institutions. The Commission, in particular, was perceived as 'autocratic, unaccountable, invisible, faceless, distant, unresponsive (…) and impervious to the public desire for openness'.[8] Subsequently, one of the main concerns of the Commission was to render its structures less opaque and more open and accessible instead. In other words, the Commission saw the need to increase institutional transparency. And while structural reform was important, it served as the background to change in the way the Commission undertook public communication and how this affected the understanding of European citizenship.

The role that the Commission's public communication policy was to play in the process of 'repairing Europe' and establishing, what I call a 'Europe of Transparency', was first mentioned in the conclusions of the Birmingham Council of October 1992.[9] The difficult ratification of the Maastricht Treaty was blamed on the lack of information for European citizens. The Community believed that sufficient information would have helped European citizens in their voting deliberations and prevented what was perceived to be a European-wide indifferent or often even negative attitude towards the Maastricht Treaty (1992). According to the conclusions of the Birmingham Council, the task ahead was to engage European citizens more systematically with the EU institutions: 'As a community of democracies, we can only move forward with the support of our citizens. We are determined to respond to the concerns raised in the recent public debate'.[10] Correspondingly, the Birmingham Declaration suggested four courses of actions, all of which were linked to information. The Community had to first 'demonstrate to [its] citizens the benefits of the Community and the Maastricht Treaty', second, 'make the Community more open, to ensure a better informed [European] public debate on its activities', third, 'respect the history, culture and traditions of individual nations, with a clearer understanding of what Member States should do and what needs to be done by the Community' and fourth, 'make clear that citizenship of the Union brings our citizens additional rights and protections without in any way taking the place of their national citizenship'. Similarly, the Commission believed that the remedy for the 'public disaffection with politics',[11] the 'crisis of representation',[12] and the lack of 'clear public perception of the legitimacy of the European institutions'[13] lay in a reorientation of the Commission's public communication strategy. Accordingly, the European institutions were convinced that the 'communication policy of the European Institutions urgently need adaptation, a higher profile and greater effectiveness as a 'conditio sine qua non' for obtaining the support of most European citizens for the integration process'.[14] Therefore, the Commission, which had hitherto been accused of an 'arrogant detachment from the public' as pointed out by Lodge,[15] assumed that greater transparency and correspondingly greater participation in European policy by the European citizenry would result in an increase in public confidence,[16] secure public support for the upcoming projects,[17] particularly the realisation of the Economic and Monetary Union.[18] All in all, the Commission hoped, more transparency and dialogue would increase the EU's overall popular legitimacy.[19]

Accordingly, the aspiration the EU had for its future public communication policy for the period 1993–2004 was stated by the Commission at the time as follows: '[the EU's] legitimacy today depends on involvement and participation. This means that the linear model of dispensing policies from above must be replaced by a virtuous circle, based on feedback, networks and involvement from policy creation to implementation at all levels'.[20] From this it followed that 'democracy depends on people being able to take part in public debate. To do this, they must have access to reliable information on European issues and be able to scrutinise the policy process in its various stages'.[21] This points to the defining feature of the third representation of European citizenship, namely the European citizen as participative and deliberative in nature, a citizen with whom the representatives of the EU could engage in debate and dialogue. This political-dialogical European citizen could only exist (ideally) through increased institutional transparency and more opportunities to become dialogically involved in the Commission's agenda-setting, policymaking and decision-making processes.

2 'Europe of Transparency': A Political-Dialogical Representation of European Citizenship

The Political-Dialogical Lexicon

The political-dialogical lexicon, which framed the civil identity of European citizens throughout the third representation, expressed the idea of citizens' participation in Community affairs through dialogue and debate. This participation was to be facilitated through greater institutional transparency. Through the marriage of the idea of debate and dialogue to institutional transparency, the Commission opened itself up to potential civil scrutiny and civil inspection, both of which are generally dependent upon access to information. The latter was recognised as important by the Community: '[A]ccess to information about the European Union [is] crucial if people are to exercise true European citizenship'[22] in a participative and democratic Europe.

Debate and Dialogue

The idea of debate and dialogue dominated the Community's discourse between 1993 and 2004,[23] and for the first time the idea of creating opportunities to enter into a dialogue with European citizens became an essential feature of the Commission's communication policy. Whilst the Commission declared that 'Communication naturally calls for a debate',[24] the EP endorsed the view that 'information and communication activities on EU matters must be aimed at promoting public debate and awareness'.[25] The Commission was seen to have 'a responsibility to better inform the Community's citizens about its policies and to engage in an on-going dialogue with them' and realised that 'in order to inform and communicate successfully, it must listen to what the public has to say'.[26] Accordingly, a 'genuine information and communication policy at the level of the European institutions (…) must be based on the principle of direct dialogue with citizens'[27] which 'should extend to preparatory stages'[28] and 'continue throughout the policy cycle'.[29] Overall, there was a perception that it was imperative to 'involve the public more in decision-making process'[30] if Europe was to become more democratic and increase its popular legitimacy. In this vein, the Commission stated that '[t]he quality, relevance and effectiveness of EU policies depend on ensuring wide participation throughout the policy chain—from conception to implementation. Improved participation is likely [to] create more confidence in the end result and in the Institutions which deliver policies. Participation crucially depends on central governments following an inclusive approach when developing and implementing EU policies'.[31]

The Community's discourse coincided with the deliberative turn in political theory of the 1990s and resonated with arguments in favour of deliberative democracy. According to Held, deliberative democracy can be understood as '(...) enhancing the nature and form of political participation, not just increasing it for its own sake. (...) [Deliberative democrats] champion (...) informed debate, the public use of reason and the impartial pursuit of truth'.[32] To this he added that 'the major contention of deliberative democrats is to bid farewell to any notion of fixed preferences and to replace them with a learning process in and through which people come to terms with the range of issues they need to understand in order to hold a sound and reasonable political judgement'. It represents 'a commitment to politics as an open-ended and continuous learning process (...)'.[33] Dryzek noted that 'increasingly democratic legitimacy came to be seen in terms of the ability or the opportunity to participate in effective deliberation on the part of those subject to collective decisions',[34] to which Cohen added that 'at the heart of the institutionalization of the deliberative procedures is the existence of arenas in which citizens can propose issues for the political agenda and participate in debate about those issues'.[35] I will return to these statements later in this chapter when I evaluate the discrepancy between the Commission's discourse and how debate and dialogue were implemented in practise.

From a 'Demos' to a 'European Civil Society'

European deliberative democracy, even in its most embryonic version, requires political-dialogical European citizens, or in other words, an active European civil society. In the previous two chapters I have discussed how the Commission's conception of a European 'demos' evolved from a very narrow conception defined in an exclusively politically active way (voting, contesting policy formation and standing for representative office) during the representation 'Homo Oeconomicus' (chapter "Homo Oeconomicus (1951–1972)") to a broader conception during the representation of 'A People's Europe' (chapter "A People's Europe (1973–1992)"), where the European 'demos' was understood as including rights-bearing European citizens (civil, cultural, political, economic and social rights) with historically and culturally constituted common identities and with active economic and political entitlements in a European democracy.

With the emergence of the representation 'Europe of Transparency', the Commission's conception of a European 'demos' evolved and broadened even further—it acquired a deliberative nature. In so doing the European 'demos' emerged as identical to an active and deliberative European civil society.[36] According to Vitorino, then responsible for the Commission's public communication policy,[37] the Commission understood such a European civil society, at least post-2001, as including all European citizens and their potential forms of organisation and association. In other words, European civil society was conceived of as European-wide voluntary associations, pressure groups, unions and professional associations and, importantly, individual citizens. Consequently, one of the primary features of the political-dialogical representation of European citizenship was the idea of involving the European public or politically and civilly active 'individual citizens',[38] ordinary citizens,[39] Community's citizen,[40] citizens,[41] the '(general) public'[42] and simply 'people'.[43] Or as the EP put it: 'Europe is not only a matter of politicians and intellectual elites; it concerns all European citizens'.[44] In short, there was a strong desire to involve European civil society as both important in its own right and as a vehicle for involving the political-dialogical European citizenry, a view expressed clearly by Santer,[45] President of the Commission 1995–1999, when he argued that the Commission faced difficulties in reaching the general public and therefore focused on European civil society as a channel to reach a broader public. This approach can be illustrated by the Commission's claim that 'introducing change requires effort from all the other Institutions, central government, regions, cities, and civil society in the current and future Member States'.[46] 'Introducing change', the Commission argued, would be realised when 'a more systematic dialogue with representatives of regional and local governments through national and European associations at an early stage in shaping policy'[47] was established.

In this way, the Commission appeared to imagine European civil society to comprise political-dialogical European citizens who were genuinely interested in Community affairs and wanted to be actively involved in the EU policymaking cycles and decision-making processes,[48] and who would, ultimately, form a democratic counterweight to the European institutions. Linked to this was the emerging issue of transparency and access to documents, which needed to be understood as a mechanism to enable greater debate and dialogue.

Greater Institutional Transparency and Open Access to EU Documents

Weber argued that bureaucracies were inextricably inclined towards secrecy: 'The bureaucracy's supreme power instrument is the transformation of official information into classified material by means of the notorious concept of the "service secret"[49] which, as Alexander noted, is 'in the last analysis (…) a means of protecting the administration from supervision',[50] civil inspection and civil scrutiny.

Therefore, one of the most remarkable features of the third representation of European citizenship was the Commission's commitment, and its subsequent practical and concrete realisation of this commitment, to open itself up to the European public. This was an important development in the history of the Commission, particularly given that the Commission was the supreme bureaucratic manifestation of administrative control over the EU. Fishkin pointed out that the 'EU policy elites [were] perceived of as insulated and unresponsive to mass public opinion',[51] and it appeared that the Community realised that the 'complex decision making [processes] ha[d] made the workings of the Community somewhat opaque'[52] and consequently, the Commission judged it necessary to increase the institutional transparency of the workings of the Commission's policy-making structures and decision-making processes and to further facilitate European citizens' access to documents. It is somewhat surprising to find that rather than conforming to Weber's pessimistic assessment, the Commission found itself in the unusual position of advocating a policy of greater transparency post-Maastricht. And whilst this policy is quite normal today in government circles, it most certainly was not then, which is why the transparency initiatives of 1992–2004 have to be viewed as a step change in the Commission's relationship to (and involvement with) European civil society comprised of political-dialogical European citizens.

Openness and Transparency

The Commission conceived of transparency as encompassing two aspects: first, openness and access to information for European citizens and second, transparency, meaning that the information provided needed to be useful and legible to a layman.[53] In other words, the Commission went beyond the question of the availability of documents to address the problem of how to render the so-called 'eurojargon' more understandable and intelligible for the average political-dialogical European citizen.

With regard to the first aspect, openness and access to documents, the Commission (1992) believed that citizens were considerably interested in obtaining Community documents and that it was an 'increasing and legitimate [expectation] of citizens to have full and easy access to information on European affairs'.[54] Accordingly, 'the Institutions should work in a more open manner. Together with the Member States, they should actively communicate about what the EU does and the decisions it takes'.[55] Consequently, passive information rights were intended to enhance accountability, transparency and openness[56] of the EU's policymaking processes and to improve the EU's democratic standing with regard to the citizens' participation in a democratic EU.[57] To demonstrate the EU's commitment to the realisation of passive information rights, a 'Declaration (No 17) on the right of access to information'[58] was annexed to the Maastricht Treaty.

With regard to the second aspect, user-friendly information in simple language, the Commission endorsed the view that information 'must be open, complete, simple and clear'[59] because, as the EP added, 'as the beneficiaries of European Union policy and as active participants in European democracy, citizens have the right to full and impartial information about the Union in their own language, in plain language and through easily accessible channels'.[60] Accordingly, the Treaty of Amsterdam (1997) legally codified that 'Every citizen of the Union may write to any of the institutions or bodies referred to in this Article or in Article 4 in one of the languages mentioned in Article 248 and have an answer in the same language' (paragraph which was to be added to Article 8d of the Maastricht Treaty). This aspect was further developed by the White Paper on European Governance, which stated that the European institutions 'should use language that is accessible and understandable for the general public'[61] and that would be 'available in all official languages'.[62]

As pointed out before, during this period institutional transparency needed to be understood as a mechanism to enable European citizens to join in a public pan-European debate. With the idea of a European debate and dialogue, the Commission's approach to public communication changed and for the first time it attempted to deploy the deliberative-rational style of public communication in a comprehensive manner.

The Public Communication of 'Europe of Transparency'

So far it sounds as if the Commission was quite simply acceding to the democratic ideal of a fully transparent deliberative democracy—if the representation of the political-dialogical European citizen was to be taken at face value. Representing the European citizen as someone who the Commission should engage with in deliberative-rational style of public communication was intrinsically linked to deliberation through the activities of debate and dialogue and sounds as if the Commission was committed to a set of communitarian values. Indeed, the terms debate and dialogue could almost be seen as synonyms for enlightened European citizens' participation in the management of Community affairs.

However, and attendant upon this particular representation of European citizenship, was what the idea of debate and dialogue actually meant to the Commission instrumentally. The Commission's understanding of debate and dialogue was neither as discursive nor as dialogical as it might have seemed in some of the official public statements made about them. This was particularly so in two ways: first, in the way the Commission defined the purpose of debate and dialogue and second, in the way the Commission continued to set the agenda of the European debate.

The Purpose of European Debate and Dialogue During 'Europe of Transparency'

The EU, and notably the Commission, described the 'great European debate'[63] as an 'on-going',[64] 'genuine'[65] and 'informed'[66] dialogue and as an 'enlightened'[67] and 'democratic' debate[68] and 'critical dialogue'.[69] However, when looking more closely at the purpose of the debate it becomes clear that debate and dialogue were understood as a means to inform European citizens about the EU, its achievements and policies. In other words, debate and dialogue were necessary because 'many people do not know the difference between the Institutions. They do not understand who takes the decisions that affect them and do not feel the Institutions act as an effective channel for their views and concerns'[70] and equally, do not see that improvements in their rights and quality of life actually come from European rather than national decisions'.[71] To this the EP added that indeed, the 'economic advantages of the Community are not easy for the citizen to grasp'.[72]

In this sense, debate and dialogue soon became a tool to manage European citizens' perceptions of the EU. As the Commission emphasised, debate and dialogue were necessary 'to generate awareness and combat ignorance and apathy so as to lay a firm foundation for the management of public life, (…) to improve popular perceptions of the Union or (…) to boost the general awareness of the European dimension of citizenship'.[73] In short, the Commission believed that the apathy of European citizens, as well as public disaffection with regard to the Community amongst the European public, stemmed primarily from ignorance about the Community. This claim was further supported by the EP, which noted that 'large sections of the population, and in particular the least favoured, are either poorly or inadequately informed about the action and the establishment of the Union' and that it was particularly 'in these groups [that] there are negative feelings about Europe'.[74] Therefore, these groups of the population 'should be a priority target group in any new communications policy'.[75] Consequently, the Commission felt that it had 'to develop a genuine teaching position' and to educate the European citizenry about Europe.[76]

The terms 'debate' or 'dialogue' traditionally suggest the discussion of different points of view with the objective of reaching an agreement, a compromise or a common decision—one that is not predetermined but is arrived at solely through such a communicative exchange. Such an agreement would then, so political theorists have argued as I pointed out earlier in this chapter, increase an institution's legitimacy. However, here in the Commission's view, informing and dialoguing with European citizens was done with the instrumental intention of fostering popular support. In short, the purpose of debate and dialogue was to foster popular support for the Community rather than dissent or, to borrow Tocqueville's and JS Mill's terms, the 'antagonism of opinion' often considered fruitful to democracy (see chapter "Europe of Agorai (2005–2009)"). Rather, the Commission believed that European political-dialogical citizens needed to be informed about the advantages and value of European policies for them from which, it was assumed, popular support would follow.[77] One of the reasons the Commission took this route of 'advertising' Europe and its benefits was, according to Vitorino,[78] that the EP had accused the Commission of being 'too neutral' in its public communication approach. The Commission depended on the EP's collaboration (the EP votes on the budget for public communication policy) and accordingly, put an increasing effort into ensuring that factual information had a positive slant. Despite the positive slant, Vitorino argued, the public was able to determine whether they agreed with the messages. They weren't 'prescribed opinions'.

What the Commission's understanding of the purpose of debate and dialogue further demonstrated was an asymmetrical distribution of power between the Commission and the European citizenry, whereby debate and dialogue were used by the Commission to refer somewhat euphemistically to a one-way, top-down flow of information. This asymmetric power relationship could be illustrated by the Commission's assumption that if European citizens were provided with the appropriate information and could be made to understand the positive value of Europe then, to put it in simple terms, they had no choice but to agree with the European project and its policies and to offer public support. In other words, the 'problem' with the perceived crisis of public disaffection with the Community was, according to the Commission, not Europe and its projects—'Europe was still right'—but the lack of understanding and knowledge about these projects and subsequently the value of the European Community to the European citizen. Ultimately, the significance of this asymmetric power relationship between the Commission and the political-dialogical European citizenry lay in the understanding of the political-dialogical European citizen as someone who had to listen and learn. As such, the Commission saw nothing wrong with giving itself agenda-setting power for debate and dialogue.

The Commission's Agenda-Setting Power Exemplified by the PRINCE Programme

The PRINCE programme, which notably involved online consultations and debates, provides an example of how the Commission organised such debates and attempted to exercise its self-didactic role. The Official Journal of the European Communities (1998) stated that 'the Prince programme covers three information campaigns ('Citizens First', 'Euro' and 'Building Europe Together') launched jointly by the European Parliament and the Commission in October 1995 with the aim of stimulating debate on major issues' and ensuring that the public became more aware of benefits deriving from European integration.

The first campaign, 'Citizens First'[79] had the objective of informing Europeans about the rights they have in the EU and the Single Market.[80] The campaign consisted of two phases. The first phase was launched in

1996 and concentrated on the EU citizens' rights with regard to studying, living and working in another member state. The second phase put more focus on buying goods and services, travelling, equal rights between men and women, diploma recognition, and so on.[81] The 'Citizens first' initiative also included a dialogue and consultation process with citizens and businesses. With regard to this particular campaign, the Commission stated that it was addressed to the general public and was further supposed to make reference to the social and cultural dimension of belonging to the EU.[82] The second campaign, 'Building Europe Together', included 'the reactions of the European Parliament to the Amsterdam Treaty' and addressed those 'themes which European citizens, according to the polls, are most interested in and concerned with, such as consumer, environmental or cultural issues'.[83] The third campaign on the 'Euro' was concerned with the dimension of employment and its relation to the single currency. It ran until 2002 and was then followed up by another communication strategy on the 'Euro'. These three briefly described campaigns shed further light on the representation of the political-dialogical European citizen and the deliberative-rational style of public communication in the following two ways.

First, the agenda for debate and dialogue was set by the Commission and did not originate out of a discussion between European citizens and the institutions (see chapter "Europe of Agorai (2005–2009)" for a different approach). This reinforces the point made above that the political-dialogical representation of European citizenship was based upon the Commission's own view as to what debate and dialogue should consist of. In this way, the asymmetrical power relationship (noted above with regard to transparency and information flows) between the Commission and the political-dialogical European citizenry during the representation 'Europe of Transparency' was further maintained. It was the Commission that held the agenda-setting power and thereby framed the debate and decided about its focus, by which I mean the substantive issues that debate and dialogue *should* touch upon.

Second, the campaign topics for debate and dialogue were intrinsically linked to the projects for which the Commission sought to secure public support. Accordingly, the PRINCE communication campaigns concerning European citizenship (1996–2004) were directly related to economic-social topics, especially to the Euro as a single currency and the completion of the internal market. As such, the 'Citizens' First' campaign was orchestrated by the Directorate General (DG) responsible for the Single Market. The fact that none of these campaigns were permanent missions but represented only 'temporary supports to accompany an exceptional period in the process building Europe together'[84] showed that it was the Commission's agenda that determined the issues to be discussed—the topics the Commission chose might, however, not necessarily have been of direct relevance or salience to European citizens.

Moravcsik made the more general point that whilst the Commission created occasions and opportunities to include and involve civil society associations into the workings of the EU, they did not appear to be directly linked to the immediately relevant concerns of European voters, such as 'healthcare; education; law and order; pensions and social security policy and taxes',[85] which remained firmly within the competencies of the nation-states. Although we should add (following Follesdal and Hix) that it would probably be more correct to say that 'citizens form their views about which policy options they prefer through the processes of deliberation and party contestation'.[86] Even this is debatable if you accept what Moravcsik called a 'curious premise', which assumed 'that the creation of more opportunities for direct participation or public deliberation would automatically generate a deeper sense of political community in Europe'.[87] In either case, the Commission further displayed its agenda-setting power with regard to its own perception of the constitution of voter salience and the outcome of voter deliberation[88] and as such, left no space at all for citizens to engage with the EU policy issues they would have been interested in deliberating. What this also showed was that the Commission's understanding of debate and dialogue bore only little relationship to the purpose of deliberative democracy as it had been formulated by deliberative democrats.[89]

Access to Information in a Factual Style of Public Communication Through Increased Institutional Transparency

The debate the Commission desired to stimulate was (disingenuously) described as an 'enlightened' debate. It was an idealisation. More realistically, and in accordance with its instrumental thinking, the Commission judged it important to provide increasing amounts of information about the EU, its workings and its policy priorities. This information needed to be available in an accessible form with the most pressing communication priority being the use of simple non-technical language to ensure that all political-dialogical European citizens were able to understand the

Community's policies, projects and institutional process. The idea behind this was straightforward—information in a simple and clear non-technical language would enable the political-dialogical European citizen to form positive opinions on Community affairs and to ultimately participate in Community affairs through affirming the agenda set by the Commission under the rubric of debate and dialogue.

And the most appropriate form of public communication to fulfil this idea was deemed by the Commission to be the factual style of public communication that, it was thought, would generate positive opinions which would support the Commission's agenda, plans and policy priorities. The Commission hoped that, in turn, this would create a communicative environment that increasingly became more deliberative and rational and ultimately accepting of the European project. In short, once in possession of the facts, the European citizen would be able to contextualise the meaning and significance of those facts and be able to determine the benefits of Europe for themselves. Thus, a 'notionally' participative Europe was envisaged.[90] Within such a participative Europe, it was also envisaged that new structures would need to be established. This establishment subsequently triggered a new conception of European space which was to include both virtual and physical space.

Transparency and the Emergence of the Commission's Conception of Multiperspectival European Space

With regard to virtual space, the White Paper on European Governance represented the starting point for online (amongst other forms of) public consultations drawing 'on the network of over 2500 organisations and people who have already taken part in the governance debate in all parts of Europe, including the applicant countries'.[91] It further stated that 'the Commission already consults interested parties through different instruments, such as Green and White Papers, Communications, advisory committees, business test panels and ad hoc consultations' to which was added that 'the Commission is developing on-line consultation through the inter-active policy-making initiative'.[92] The Commission increasingly used the Internet as a virtual platform for debate and dialogue because 'new technologies, in particular the Internet, make it possible to reach a very wide public, notably young people, at little cost. The Commission has been using these since 1995. The multilingual Europa Internet website is known for its quality'.[93] The Commission's desire to expand online consultations and debate was also reflected in the idea of turning the EUROPA website 'into an inter-active platform for information, feedback and debate, linking parallel networks across the Union'.[94] Further EUROPA was to be 'the most up-to-date practices of the new governance in Europe, symbolised by the terms "e-Commission", "e-Europe" and "e-governance". The main features are interactivity, rapid and authentic consultations, research into support by public opinion, and a simplified administrative practice for everyone'.[95]

Additionally, the Commission developed databases such as celex, rapis and Info 92 (Commission 1992). In this respect, the Commission suggested that the 'European Institutions should jointly continue to develop EUR-LEX5, in 2002, as a single on-line point in all languages, where people can follow policy proposals through the decision-making process'.[96] Further, three services with the purpose of providing replies to citizens on Community questions were created: Eurjus,[97] Signpost[98] and Europe Direct,[99] which were also part of the virtual space, as all three services featured the possibility for European citizens to make online inquiries. Additionally, the Commission introduced more instruments in the domain of the media such as Europe by Satellite (EbS)[100] and TV and Radio Broadcasts.[101] Parallel to these changes were developments in the utilisation of physical space structures for access to information. These included institutional structures such as the European Documentation Centres (EDC)[102] and Euro Info Centres and non-institutional bodies such as 'Centres de documentation européenne', or the 'Carrefours ruraux', or the 'Chaires Jean Monnet', the European Library or the 'Info Points', and so on.[103] In short, both virtual and physical access points were developed with regard to the widespread and easily undertaken access to information that the Commission felt necessary to meet its policy objective of 'an enlightened' political-dialogical European citizenry. Importantly, the fulfilment of the widespread nature of these access points involved the Commission, progressively and increasingly, in establishing information networks and their corresponding access points across the Community at the local, regional and national level. The use of local, regional and national levels had each a different objective. With regard to the national level, the objective was to 'develop an integrated system of information on the Union using local relays. Their main functions were to act as: [first,] head of the national network for all the other relays: Info-Points and, at local level, the "guides" (information kiosks); information centres; [and second,] a document resource centre as well as producing various materials (leaflets, brochures, etc.) for the network'.[104] With regard to centres on the interregional level, the Commission noted that 'relays of this type have been set up to cater for regions considered a priority from a socioeconomic point of view (regions whose development is lagging behind) and from the point of view of their geographical or geopolitical position'.[105] Centres on the local level 'are the cornerstone of decentralised information policy. Their job is to convey the information in line with everyday reality and the local economic context. These relays are grassroots information centres par excellence'.[106]

The above shows how the single-perspectival conception of European space during the previous representation of European citizenship 'A People's Europe' slowly but progressively evolved into a multiperspectival conception of European space which would go through further sophistication in the next representation.

A sketch (albeit parodic) of the European citizen that the Commission appeared to represent through its public communication discourse can be described as follows: In a 'Europe of Transparency', European citizens were disenchanted and fed up with the secretive bureaucracy of the European Community and wished for greater and easier access to official documents so that they could hold European politicians and bureaucrats accountable. Simultaneously, they insisted on opportunities to enter into dialogue and debate with the European institutions which would, when they occurred, be informed, genuine, enlightened and ongoing. In other words, the Commission understood the 'political-dialogical European citizen' as an ideal civil actor who was both politically motivated and capable of rationally discussing the future of Europe in a fully informed and enlightened manner. The Commission thus convinced itself of the need to provide European citizens with new spaces for debate and dialogue, and created opportunities for these to occur both virtually and physically and at European, national, regional and local levels. However, beneath this sketch and its rhetoric of an ideal civil actor was what the Commission genuinely believed: that European citizens needed to be taught about Europe, that they needed to be educated into an appreciation of European political and civil policies in order that they might come to agree with European integration and above all agree with its planned future direction. Accordingly, the European citizen was conceived of and understood as educable, someone who has to learn that Europe integration is desirable and to be worked towards. This didn't mean encouraging European citizens' ability to contest and disagree but rather to selectively scrutinise and then agree and support. What the Commission wished scrutinised and put on the table for discussion were the benefits of Single Market rights and Europeans citizens' experiences of them. This, in turn, meant that the Commission saw European citizenship as being experienced and lived at the level of a consumer enjoying the benefits of the Single Market.

Conclusion on and Evaluation of 'Europe of Transparency'

With the Maastricht debacle, 'forging and maintaining the support of the citizenry for the European project had become truly pressing'[107] because institutions have, so Van Bjisterveld argued, to be able to demonstrate that they 'can reliably be expected to secure more acceptable outcomes in the future'.[108] However, without effective contestation over what constitutes, and for whom, 'more acceptable', we are left with the problem of 'benevolent but non-accountable rulers' whose 'subjects have no institutionalized mechanisms that make them trustworthy'.[109] Alternatively expressed, and as the EP argued, 'many of the citizens of Europe have the impression that something about which they know very little (...), and about which they have not been consulted, is being foisted on them '*de haut en bas*': by *Brussels*'.[110] It was on the back of these kinds of judgements (the latter specifically about the situation during the ratification period of the Maastricht Treaty) that the political-dialogical representation of European citizenship 'Europe of Transparency' emerged. This political-dialogical representation of 'European' idealised the Commission's commitment to European citizens' involvement in Community affairs through debate and dialogue and represented the Commission's attempt to 'repair Europe'.

However, in the Commission's attempt to 'repair Europe' three failings could be identified. The first failing concerned the Commission's conception of European civil society in Community affairs, and here it can be argued that the Commission publicly communicated a confusing conception of European citizenship. On the one hand, the political-dialogical European citizenry was regarded as comprised of European citizens who should and could be critically engaged with Europe, actively and responsibly contesting political power. On the other hand, we had a political-dialogical European public that merely needed a little more information in order to be able to express its support for the Commission's conception of the European project.[111] To put it bluntly, it was as if (in the Commission's mind) an active political-dialogical European citizenry was a rhetorical flourish beneath which were European citizens who only required that what was actually best for them would be explained to them (in simple terms). From this, so the Commission believed, support for the European project would follow. Clearly these two conceptions of the political-dialogical European citizen contradicted each other. In short, the first political-dialogical European citizen was critically engaged, the second was a 'political dope' who had to be shown what was in their best interest and then be led to sign up to it. The point made by Gallup and Rae that 'public opinion is critical, not submissive; experimental, not dogmatic (...) [and] in this sense, public opinion is the pulse of democracy'[112] is lost on the Commission during the third representation.

The second failing concerned the power for agenda-setting the Commission had and exercised in European debates. This agenda-setting power enabled the Commission to turn dialogue into something that simply equated to the provision of channels of institutional communication which, in turn, provided the political-dialogical European citizens with nothing other than non-interactive (in any political sense) information. The Commission simply believed that an increase of information available would help the Community to 'demonstrate to [its] citizens the benefits of the Community and the Maastricht Treaty',[113] to secure public support for the upcoming projects[114] and, generally, to obtain 'the support of most European citizens for the integration process'.[115] Given that the Commission had this agenda-setting power and was concerned with achieving greater public support for the Maastricht Treaty and its heavy economic-social agenda, which included issues such as the realisation of the economic and monetary union,[116] the European debate was limited to market-related topics and to economic-social concerns, as the PRINCE programme clearly showed. Consequently debate and dialogues as managed by the Commission did not necessarily reflect the concerns faced by the political-dialogical European citizens of this time. Equally it is hard to see how any real or substantive engagement could occur in the face of the way debates were framed and conducted.

The third failing was related to the Commission's use of European space. Whereas its conception of space was more sophisticated than previously, the Commission nevertheless failed to provide spaces for European citizens where face-to-face deliberation, considered essential by Fishkin,[117] could be held. Rather, physical space was almost exclusively conceived of as housing information centres which simply held brochures, documents and leaflets which could be looked at or taken away by passers-by, whilst virtual space via EUROPA was at its inception confusing and difficult to use and navigate. In addition, and importantly, the Internet appeared to have been an inappropriate tool as, according to the Eurobarometer,[118] only 14% of the EU population had Internet access in 1998 and only 9% of the EU population used the Internet to look for information on Europe, whereas 87.3% did not. Despite these shortcomings, the multi-perspectival conception of European space during the third representation did herald the beginning of the Commission's attempt to create genuine European 'transnational "space" where citizens from different countries could discuss what they perceive as being the important challenges for the Union'.[119] In other words, the best that can be said of the use of the idea of European space at this time was that it presaged Wallström's understanding of the creation of what at the time was referred to variously as a 'European civil area',[120] 'a public forum'[121] or a 'European public space [with] temporal, spatial and ideological points of reference'.[122]

Having pointed out these three failings, there is, however, little doubting the laudable nature of the ambition of an advanced bureaucracy trying to adopt a policy of debate and dialogue accompanied by a philosophy of transparency. Indeed contra Weber (see above), the Commission, following the Maastricht crisis, described itself (even if this concealed an instrumental agenda) as concerned to engage in civil discourse with European civil society and individual political-dialogical European citizens and as such embraced the principles (if not the practise) of fulfilling the information and communication conditions of a deliberative democracy. It would be equally unfair not to note that the Commission, as a bureaucracy, distanced itself from the secrecy Weber pessimistically believed was the natural state of advanced bureaucracies by introducing various initiatives to increase transparency.[123] The significance of the Commission's departure from bureaucratic secrecy lay, at this point in its history, in its acceptance of the principle of opening itself up to the principles of public scrutiny and civil inspection, and this was something it (a) could never reverse and (b) would herald as the representation of civil-spatial European citizenship in a 'Europe of Agorai.'

3 From 'Europe of Transparency' to 'Europe of Agorai'

For the purposes of this section only I shall divide the period of the third representation of European citizenship into two: the first period from 1993–1999 and the second period from 1999–2004. During both periods, as I have argued, the primary communicative objective was to stimulate debate and dialogue between the Commission and European citizens (which was to be facilitated through increased institutional transparency) and as such both periods can naturally be subsumed under the third representation of European citizenship. However, it is helpful to take the subdivision of the period 1993–1999 to show the major obstacles, inefficiencies and setbacks the Commission endured in its public communication strategy, because they partially explain the change from the third to fourth representation of European citizenship. The most pertinent obstacle to an effective public communication strategy for the Commission lay in the lack of appropriate structures and leadership with regard to establishing a coherent and cohesive public communication policy and to achieving its subsequent implementation.

The Period 1992–1999 and the Resignation of the Santer Commission

The period 1993–1999 was characterised by uncertainty in the Commission as to how to organise public communication structures that reflected contemporary standards of efficiency and public reach, and the policy requirements of engagement and transparency.[124] It was particularly the Commission that advocated a restructuration of public communication structures which it considered necessary to redress the lack of a coordinated overall public communication strategy.[125] Accordingly, it recommended that DG X, the Directorate General for Information and Communication, should become responsible first, for the overall coordination of information and communication activities and second, for general information and communication. It further suggested the establishment of a Steering Committee and a Strategy Group to ensure coherency and coordination with regard to information and communication activities. Along the same lines, the OJEC Special Report on Communication stated that 'It appears (…) that the Commission lacked a coordinated overall strategy in communication policy and that in order to meet the challenges in this sector there was a need for the creation of an appropriate mechanism—the information plans—to ensure that the information and communication dimension is integrated into all Commission policies with external implications'.[126] However, most of the suggestions with regard to an operational framework or restructuration were not implemented or were unsuccessful. As Santer made clear, public information and communication activities were orchestrated by each individual DG. Subsequently, until 1999 no overall public communication strategy had been developed or implemented, and therefore calls for unified operational matters with regard to public communication went unheeded. This view was also supported by the lack of public communication policy papers and the absence of communication policy papers indicating communication or information priorities. This situation marked a stark contrast with the 1970s and the 1980s, when annual information programmes and information priorities were regularly determined and communicated across the Commission.

The lack of a strong DG X and the lack of effective public communication structures were factors that played a part in the resignation of the Santer Commission in March 1999. The Santer Commission had been accused of fraud and corruption and was unable to deal adequately with an increasingly hostile press during the crisis.[127] Frequently, and farcically, journalists were not spoken to but insulted, and much of the blame for the breakdown in press relations was put down to a press service which was incapable of handling the sudden media attention. As a spokesperson explained: 'We could have squashed the story much faster if we had reacted quicker. To achieve this you would have needed a centre of power, which would have orchestrated the reaction. And this is just what was missing'.[128]

As Anderson and Price summarised, 'The importance of the Commission's relationship with the media was illustrated when its inept communications performance was a crucial factor in the collapse of the Santer Presidency following a fraud scandal in 1999'.[129] However, according to Santarelli, former Director of Communication,[130] it would be a mistake to speak of an intense collaboration amongst journalists that ultimately pressured the Commission into resignation. Santarelli argued that the approximately 1000 journalists covering Europe cannot be represented as having suddenly turned into a single pressure group with only one aim in mind. According to him, each journalist's mission was determined by the national news agenda of his/her employer and this varied from country to country and across diverse news platforms. However, what cannot be doubted is that the experience of the debacle of the Santer Commission led to a new impetus for change in the way public communication was undertaken during the Prodi Commission.

Structural Public Communication Reforms During the Mandate of the Prodi Commission 1999–2004

Whereas the Santer Commission (1995–1999) did not produce any remarkable public communication policy papers and altogether lacked an overall coordinated public communication strategy, the Prodi Commission produced three consecutive public communication policy documents[131] which established the 'first official communication strategy'.[132] With regard to structural public communication deficiencies, the Prodi Commission drew up proposals concerning structural changes and operational frameworks. These attempts to reform public communication structures were described by Anderson and Price as follows: 'The reforms also aimed to focus on a few core messages, to improve coordination of these messages, increase cooperation with national governments and provide a much greater role for the Commission's representations in the member states. The aim was to have all of this implemented by the beginning of 2003. The Commission's press service was intended to play a central role in the new strategy, coordinating other departments, EU institutions and member states'.[133] However, these reforms were not implemented in their entirety and DG X did not acquire any political power over the other DGs of the Commission which would have made it a stronger centre and therefore more capable of coordinating and steering the Commission's communication policy.[134]

In 2004, Barroso became President of the new Commission, and in this position he was able to create a post for a Commissioner who was exclusively responsible for the Commission's Communication Strategy. Consequently, the public communication reforms envisaged throughout the 1990s and early 2000s could be realistically considered. There is little doubt that Barroso felt he could remedy the shortcomings identified in the period 1993–2004: lack of coordination, unprofessional communication staff and inadequate public communication structures. With these reforms in mind, Barroso nominated Margot Wallström, 'a media-savvy' Swedish politician as Commissioner for Communication Strategy. In this role, Wallström had the political authority over DG Press and Communication, which she was allowed to restructure. From the delegated authority, specific background and personal priorities of Wallström—combined with Barroso's determination to reform public communication and to have the forthcoming ratification of the Constitutional Treaty explained positively to the people of Europe—the fourth representation of European citizenship emerged as the 'Europe of Agorai'.

NOTES

1. Lodge (1994: 330).
2. EP (1993b: preface).
3. Commission (1993a: 2).
4. Ibid.: 3. With the Maastricht crisis, European opinion became more important in the daily professional lives of the Commissioners. According to the Eurobarometer 40 (Commission 1993c), once a month the Commissioners would discuss recent European public opinion and consider public perception in the development of projects and in decision-making processes.
Commission (1993a: 30). On democratic contestation, democratic legitimacy and the democratic deficit in the EU, see Beetham and Lord (1998), Scharpf (1999, 2000a, b, 2009), Schmitter (2000), Decker (2002), Crombez (2003), Follesdal and Hix (2006), Lord and Harris (2006), Hix (2008), Schmidt (2013) and Bartl (2015). It should also be noted that there are those who argue that the EU has neither a democratic deficit nor lacks legitimacy. For the most cogent presentation of this argument, see Majone (1994, 1996, 2006) and Moravcsik (2002, 2005, 2006, 2008).
5. EP (1993a: 5).
6. EP (1998: 13).
7. Lodge (1994: 346).
8. Conclusions of the Birmingham Council (1992, Annexe I).
9. Conclusions Birmingham Council (1992, art. 2 Annexe I).
10. Commission (2002: 6).
11. Ibid.
12. Ibid.
13. EP (1998: 13).
14. Lodge (1994: 343).
15. Commission (1992).
16. Commission (1995a).
17. The EP (1998) made further reference to the then forthcoming European elections in June 1999, the information campaign of the Amsterdam Treaty and the realisation of Economic and Monetary Union.
18. On the question of EU legitimacy, see Lodge (1994), Hix (1995), Banchoff (ed.) (1999), Scharpf (1999, 2007), Moravcsik (2002), Lord and Magnette (2004), Curtin and Meijer (2006), Follesdal (2006), Ehin (2008), Innerarity (2014), Thiel (2014), Voermans et al. (2014) and Schmidt (2015).
19. Commission (2001b: 11).
20. Ibid.

21. EP (2005: C.).
22. Commission (1993a, 1995a, 2001a, b, 2002) and EP (1993b, 1998, 2001, 2003, 2005).
23. Commission (2001a: 4).
24. EP (2001: 4).
25. Commission (1993a: 3).
26. EP (1998: A.).
27. EP (1993a: 7).
28. Ibid.: 15.
29. Commission (2002: 8).
30. Commission (2001b: 10).
31. Held (2006: 232).
32. Ibid.: 233.
33. Dryzek (2002: 1).
34. Cohen (1997: 85).
35. Henceforth I will use the term 'European civil society' instead of the term European 'demos' due to the increasing emphasis on the civil aspects of European citizenship and the attendant public communication priorities.
36. Vitorino, personal communication, 14 March 2012.
37. EP (1993a).
38. Commission (2001a).
39. Commission (1993a).
40. EP (1993a, b, 1998, 2001, 2003, 2004) and Commission (1995a, 2001a, 2002).
41. EP (1998) and Commission (2001a, 2002).
42. Commission (1993a, 2001a, 2002).
43. EP (1993b: 6).
44. Santer, personal communication, 1 February 2012.
45. Commission (2001b: 3).
46. Ibid.: 4. In spite of the fact that the vast majority of EU secondary law sources operated with a lexicon which focused on civil society, there were one or two interesting exceptions, none more so than a Commission document entitled 'Increased transparency in the work of the Commission' (see Commission 1992. It was published in parallel with another document entitled 'An open and structured dialogue between the Commission and Special Interest Groups'). It advocated an information priority much more narrowly conceived, one that prioritised the information needs of professionals and academics. With regard to this prioritisation, it is interesting to note that an evaluative report on the EUROPA website in 2008 stated that the majority of visitors to EUROPA were looking for information either for professional reasons or for research (Ernst and Young 2008). This was a phenomenon also observed by Moravcsik (2005), who

argued with regard to European deliberations that 'the constitutional deliberation did not mobilise Europeans. Few citizens were aware of the '200 conventionnels' deliberations. When testimony from civil society was requested, professors turned up. When a youth conference was called, would-be Eurocrats attended'.

47. The idea of involving European citizens through dialogue and debate in Community affairs was in itself not new but can in fact be considered a long-standing concern of the Community, one that was already enshrined in art. 5 of the Treaty of Paris (1951), which read: '(...) the Community will enlighten and facilitate the action of the interested parties by collecting information, organizing consultations and defining general objectives (...)'. As argued in chapter Homo Oeconomicus (1951–1972), during the 1950s and 1960s, the involvement of the European citizenry was limited to the sectoral economic-social civil associations. With the political-dialogical representation of European citizenship, the Commission moved towards providing a range of public communication channels whose purpose was to interact with a more broadly conceived European civil society and its component individual citizens.
48. Weber (1978: 1418 cited in Alexander 2006: 133).
49. Alexander (2006: 133).
50. Fishkin (2009: 177).
51. EP (1993a: 4).
52. It is worthwhile noting that this understanding of transparency has been reflected in the academic literature. Curtin and Meijer (2006: 111), for example, argued that 'transparency not only incorporates the rather passive right of every citizen to have access to information (if they activate that formal legal right) but also the much broader and more pro-active duty of the administration itself to ensure that information about its policy and actions is provided in an accessible fashion'. This is supported by Van Bijsterveld (2004: 14), who clarified that 'transparency, we must realise, is not simply concerned with providing (massive) information, but also with presenting it in a coherent and understandable fashion (...). Transparency is not simply concerned with information, but with useful information and a sensible ordering of the information'.
53. Commission (2001a: 4).
54. Commission (2001b: 10).
55. For policy initiatives and decisions on transparency and openness as well as access to documents and a detailed historical overview on the transparency policies of the EU, see Council of the European Union (no date).
56. The concern for accessibility to documents for European citizens emerged in the mid-1980s for the first time. The EP issued resolutions on the compulsory publication of information by the European Community (EP 1984 and 1987). The access to information and documents was seen as

part of the fundamental right to information which citizens were understood to have. Both documents, EP 1984 and 1987, followed the same rationale, and that was that more access to documents and therefore more information for European citizens even during the policymaking process would ultimately lead to a possibility of the participation of European citizens in Community policies and projects.

57. The 'Declaration (No. 17) on the right of access to information' read: 'The Conference considers that transparency of the decision making process strengthens the democratic nature of the institutions and the public's confidence in the administration. The Conference accordingly recommends that the Commission submit to the Council no later than 1993 a report on measures designed to improve public access to the information available to the institutions.'
58. Commission (1993a: 4).
59. EP (2005: C).
60. Commission (2001b: 10).
61. Ibid.: 11.
62. Commission (2002: 10).
63. Commission (1993a).
64. EP (2001) and Commission (2002).
65. Commission (2001a: 6).
66. Commission (2002: 8).
67. EP (1998: 7).
68. EP (1993a: 13).
69. Commission (2001a: 7).
70. Ibid.: 7.
71. EP (1993a: 14).
72. Commission (2002: 10).
73. EP (1998: I).
74. Ibid.
75. Commission (2002: 10). As noted above, the Dutch 'Nei' and the French 'petit oui' were analysed on the back of the voters' socio-professional and educational background with the result that the more educated and well-off European citizens were, the more likely they were to vote in favour of the Maastricht Treaty. The link between the level of information or knowledge and a favourable attitude towards European integration has existed in the analysis of public opinion polls on attitudes towards European integration since the 1950s.
76. Commission (1995a).
77. Personal communication, 14 March 2012.
78. For an analysis of what kind of public debate the Commission undertook via Citizens' First and which attendant conception of the European public it expressed, see Pukallus (forthcoming).

'EUROPE OF TRANSPARENCY' (1993-2004) 161

79. Commission (1995a, b, 1997a, b, c, d, e, 1998a, b, c, d).
80. It is worthwhile noticing that this second phase of the campaign reflected exactly the same issues the Barroso 2 Commission and DG COMM (2010–2014) emphasised in their communication strategy (see Commission (2010) and chapter "Europe of Rights' (2010–2014)" later in the text).
81. Commission (1995a).
82. EP (1998: 22).
83. EP (1998: 22).
84. Moravcsik (2008: 178).
85. Follesdal and Hix (2006: 545f.).
86. Moravcsik (2002: 605).
87. It was not until Wallström's mandate and the representation 'Europe of Agorai' (chapter "Europe of Agorai (2005–2009)") that European citizens were able to set the agenda for dialogue with the Commission themselves.
88. Deliberative democrats have been concerned with the question of public debate and its potential (through deliberative processes) to increase the political legitimacy of authorities, decision-making and policy-shaping processes. On this see: Manin (1987), Cohen (1998), Dryzek (2002 and 2012), Fishkin (2009), Gutman and Thompson (2004) and Dryzek and Dunleavy (2009).
89. However, this 'neonate' form of deliberative democracy should not be compared to attempts to introduce this form of democracy during the period 2005–2009, when under the Barroso 1 Commission the communicative requirements for deliberative democracy were better understood and attempts made by Wallström (following Fishkin) to have its precepts more widely accepted were systematically pursued (see chapter "Europe of Agorai (2005–2009)").
90. Commission (2001b: 9).
91. Ibid.: 15.
92. EC (1998: 59).
93. Commission (2001b: 11).
94. Commission (2001a: 26).
95. Commission (2001b: 12).
96. 'Eurojus supplements Europe Direct and provides free advice and assistance on legal problems arising from the interpretation or application of Community law' (Commission 2001a: 27).
97. 'Signpost Service was launched in 1996. It provides a service similar to that of Eurojus but focuses exclusively on the rights of citizens or businesses in connection with the internal market' (Commission 2001a: 27).

98. 'Europe Direct helps citizens to find out about and exercise their rights and to identify all of the opportunities offered by the European Union' (Commission 2001a: 26).
99. Europe by Satellite (EbS) 'is the television news instrument of the EU institutions. [It] offers a particularly important service: basically, live coverage of the Institutions' work (…)' (Commission 2001a: 28).
100. The list of different access points for European citizens to get information on Community affairs is non-exhaustive. The purpose of giving examples is merely to illustrate the Commission's changing conception of Community space.
101. 'The EDC are key information points, mainly in universities and institutes of higher education. Their task is twofold: to help academics and the general public to access information sources and to provide information in conjunction with other centres and networks' (Commission 2001a: 30).
102. See Commission (2001a).
103. Commission (2001a: 23).
104. Ibid.
105. Ibid.: 24.
106. Van Bjisterveld (2004: 4).
107. Follesdal and Hix (2006: 545).
108. Ibid.
109. EP (1993b: 1, emphasis in the original).
110. See Rabier (1986) on this problem.
111. Gallup and Rae (1940: 8 cited in Alexander 2006: 73).
112. Birmingham Conclusions (1992, annexe I).
113. Commission (1995b).
114. EP (1998: 13).
115. Santer, personal communication, 1 February 2012.
116. Fishkin (2009).
117. Commission (1998e).
118. Commission (2001b: 11f.).
119. EP (2003: 6).
120. Commission (2002: 4).
121. Ibid.: 8.
122. For a list of transparency initiatives during the period 1992–2004, see CVCE (2012).
123. Commission (1993a, b, 1994a, b).
124. Commission (1993a).
125. EC (1998: 49).
126. See Meyer (1999), Baisnée (2007) and Anderson and Price (2008).
127. Cited in Meyer (1999: 625).
128. Anderson and Price (2008: 28).
129. Santarelli, personal communication, 23 February 2012.

130. Commission (2001a, 2002, 2004). The Commission (2004) was equally concerned with public communication structures and the implementation of the ideas evoked in the Commission (2001a, 2002).
131. The gap between the entry into power of the Prodi Commission in 1999 and the first communication policy document in 2001 can be explained, according to Carnel (2011 and interview 21 February 2012), as follows. At the beginning of the Prodi Commission's mandate, a press and communication service was created. This press and communication service became attached to the DG for Education, audiovisual policy and culture (EAC). In other words, DG X, hitherto responsible for the Commission's information and communication policy, was dissolved—until in 2000 DG X reappears (due to problems of competence and budget between the EAC and the Press and Communication Service). However, the European Parliament was not satisfied with how DG EAC under Reding (Commissioner for Culture and Education 1999–2004) approached public communication with European citizens and subsequently blocked the EP's budget (Vitorino interview 14 March 2012). Finally, the White Paper on European Governance recognised the importance of an information and communication policy. Subsequently, in 2001 the Press and Communication Service became the DG Press and Communication under the authority of the Commission President, Romano Prodi. However, Vitorino was given the special mandate for the communication and information policy of the Commission (as concerns the public communication strategy to the public at large). The three communication policy papers (Commission 2001a, 2002, 2004) during the Prodi Commission have also been referred to as Vitorino I, II and III.
132. Anderson and Price (2008: 34). For an evaluation of the weaknesses and improvements in the Commission's approach to public communication see Anderson and Price (2008).
133. According to Anderson and Price (2008) these reforms were not implemented because Prodi was essentially a weak leader.

REFERENCES

Alexander, J. (2006). *The civil sphere*. Oxford: Oxford University Press.

Anderson, P., & Price, J. (2008). An evaluation of the press and communication reforms of the Prodi Commission of 1999—2004. With particular reference to UK Europhile and Eurosceptic journalists' perceptions of their impact. *European Journal of Communication, 23*(1), 29–46.

Baisnée, O. (2007). The European public sphere does not exist (at least it's worth wondering…). *European Journal of Communication, 22*(4), 493–503.

Banchoff, T., & Smith, M. (Eds.). (1999). *Legitimacy and the European Union: The contested polity*. London: Routledge.
Bartl, M. (2015). The way we do Europe: Subsidiarity and the *substantive* democratic deficit. *European Law Journal, 21*(1), 23–43.
Beetham, D., & Lord, C. (1998). *Legitimacy and the European Union*. Abingdon: Routledge.
Carnel, S. (2011, August 18). *Origines et développement des service en charge de la politique d'information et communication des Communautés Européennes (1952–2006)* (Ref. Ares (2011) 889501).
CCE (Commission des Communautés Européennes). (1992, November 25). *La Commission plus proche du citoyen* (SEC (1992) 2274).
CCE (Commission des Communautés Européennes). (1993a, June 22). *The Commission's communication and information policy: A new approach* (Pinheiro Report) (SEC (1993) 916/9).
CCE (Commission des Communautés Européennes). (1993b, July 28). *The commission's information and communication policy: The practical implementation of the information plans* (SEC (93) 1248/3 final).
CCE (Commission des Communautés Européennes). (1993c). *Standard Eurobarometer* 40.
CCE (Commission des Communautés Européennes). (1994a, January 26). *The offices in the Community: The next steps* (SEC (94) 80/4 final).
CCE (Commission des Communautés Européennes). (1994b) *Establishing the operational framework regarding information networks*. (SEC (94) 488), no date.
CCE (Commission des Communautés Européennes). (1995a, October 7). *Grandes actions prioritaires en matière d'information*, (Communication du Président Delors et de M. Oreja) (SEC (1995) 1672).
CCE (Commission des Communautés Européennes). (1995b, May 31). Citizens' rights within the single market. Press release.
CCE (Commission des Communautés Européennes). (1997a). *General report on the activities of the European Union 1996*. Luxembourg: Office for Official Publications of the European Communities.
CCE (Commission des Communautés Européennes). (1997b, November 25). Citizens first: EU rights on equal opportunities, buying goods and services and travelling. Press release.
CCE (Commission des Communautés Européennes). (1997c). Single market news, No. 6.
CCE (Commission des Communautés Européennes). (1997d). Single market news, No. 7.
CCE (Commission des Communautés Européennes). (1997e). Single market news, No. 9.

CCE (Commission des Communautés Européennes). (1998a). Internal market—Single market news. http://ec.europa.eu/internal_market/smn/smn11/s11mn04.htm. Accessed 5 June 2011.
CCE (Commission des Communautés Européennes). (1998b). *General report on the activities of the European Union 1997.* Luxembourg: Office for Official Publications of the European Communities.
CCE (Commission des Communautés Européennes). (1998c). Single market news, No. 11.
CCE (Commission des Communautés Européennes). (1998d). Single market news, No. 13.
CCE (Commission des Communautés Européennes). (1998e). Eurobarometer flash, 59.
CCE (Commission des Communautés Européennes). (2001a, June 27). *Communication on a new framework for cooperation on activities concerning the information and communication policy of the European Union* (COM (2001) 354).
CCE (Commission des Communautés Européennes). (2001b, July 25). *European governance. A white paper* (COM (2001) 428 final).
CCE (Commission des Communautés Européennes). (2002, October 2). *Communication on an information and communication strategy for the European Union* (COM (2002) 350 final/2).
CCE (Commission des Communautés Européennes). (2004, April 20). *Communication on implementing the information and communication strategy for the European Union* (COM (2004) 196).
CCE (Commission des Communautés Européennes). (2010, October 27). *EU citizenship report 2010. Dismantling the obstacles to EU citizens' rights* (COM (2010) 603 final).
Cohen, J. (1997). Deliberation and democratic legitimacy. In J. Bohman & W. Rehg (Eds.), *Deliberative democracy* (pp. 67–91). Cambridge, MA: MIT Press.
Cohen, J. (1998). Democracy and liberty. In J. Elster (Ed.), *Deliberative democracy* (pp. 185–231). Cambridge: Cambridge University Press.
Crombez, C. (2003). The democratic deficit in the European Union. Much ado about nothing? *European Union Politics, 4*(1), 101–120.
Curtin, D., & Meijer, A. J. (2006). Does transparency strengthen legitimacy? *Information Polity, 11*(2), 109–122.
CVCE. (2012). Chronological table on transparency (1992–2004). http://www.cvce.eu/viewer/-/content/23f49e51-cebf-4f55-a581-f85292be1315/en. Accessed 2 Feb 2012.
Decker, F. (2002). Governance beyond the nation-state. Reflections on the democratic deficit of the European Union. *Journal of European Public Policy, 9*(2), 256–272.

Dryzek, J. (2002). *Deliberative democracy and beyond liberals, critics, contestations*. Oxford: Oxford University Press.
Dryzek, J. (2012). *Foundations and frontiers of deliberative governance*. Oxford: Oxford University Press.
Dryzek, J., & Dunleavy, P. (2009). *Theories of the democratic state*. Basingstoke: Palgrave Macmillan.
EC. (1998). Special Report No 23/98 concerning the Information and Communication measures managed by the Commission accompanied by the replies of the Commission. In: *Official Journal of the European Communities*, 98/C 393/03, 16 December.
Ehin, P. (2008). Competing models of EU legitimacy: The test of popular expectations. *Journal of Common Market Studies*, 46(3), 619–640.
EP. (1984). *Report drawn up on behalf of the Committee on Youth, Culture, Education, Information and Sport on the compulsory publication of information by the European Community*. Working Documents 1984-85, Document 1-223/84, Marck Report, 7 May.
EP. (1987, November 10). *Report on the compulsory publication of information by the European Community (Marck Report)*. (European Session Documents 1987–1988, A2-208/87).
EP. (1993a, July 14). *Report on the information policy of the European Community* (Oostlander Report) (A3-0238/93).
EP. (1993b, March). *Reflection on information and communication policy of the European Community* (De Clercq Report) (OP-EC/3240).
EP. (1998, Mai 5). *Rapport sur la politique d'information et de communication dans l'Union européenne de Peter Pex en Commission de la culture, de la jeunesse, de l'éducation et des médias (Pex Report)* (A4-0115/98).
EP. (2001, March 8). *Motion for a resolution on behalf of the committee on culture, youth, education, the media and sport on the information and communication strategy of the EU (by Giuseppe Gargani)* (B5-0174/2001).
EP. (2003, February 21). *Report on an information and communication strategy for the European Union, committee on culture, youth, education, the media and sport (rapporteur Juan José Bayona de Perogordo)* (A5-0053/2003).
EP. (2004, October 6). *Response to hearing of Wallström 2004* (AFCO (2004) D/41922). http://www.europarl.europa.eu/hearings/commission/2004_comm/pdf/lt_wallstrom_en.pdf. Accessed 5 Apr 2015.
EP. (2005). *Resolution on the implementation of the European Union's information and communication strategy* (2004/2238(INI)), no date.
Ernst and Young. (2008). *European Commission. DG Communication. Evaluation of the EUROPA website*. http://europa.eu/survey/feb08/results/europa_final_report_executive_summary_en.pdf. Accessed 16 Feb 2012.
European Communities. (1998, December 16). Special report No 23/98 concerning the information and communication measures managed by the

Commission accompanied by the replies of the Commission. *Official Journal of the European Communities*, 98/C 393/03.
European Union. (no date). The European flag. http://europa.eu/about-eu/basic-information/symbols/flag/index_en.htm. Accessed 22 Jan 2012.
Fishkin, J. (2009). *When the people speak: Deliberative democracy and public consultation*. Oxford: Oxford University Press.
Follesdal, A., & Hix, S. (2006). Why there is a democratic deficit in the EU: A response to Majone and Moravcsik. *Journal of Common Market Studies*, 44(3), 533–562.
Gallup, G., & Rae, S. F. (1940). *The pulse of democracy: The public-opinion poll and how it works*. New York: Simon and Schuster.
Gutman, A., & Thompson, D. (2004). *Why deliberative democracy?* Princeton: Princeton University Press.
Held, D. (2006). *Models of democracy* (3rd ed.). Cambridge: Polity.
Hix, S. (1995). Parties at the European level and the legitimacy of EU socioeconomic policy. *Journal of Common Market Studies*, 33(4), 527–554.
Hix, S. (2008). *What's wrong with the European Union and how to fix it*. Cambridge/Malden: Polity.
Innerarity, D. (2014). What kind of deficit? Problems of legitimacy in the European Union. *European Journal of Social Theory*, 17(3), 307–325.
Lodge, J. (1994). Transparency and democratic legitimacy. *Journal of Common Market Studies*, 32(3), 343–368.
Lord, C., & Harris, E. (2006). *Democracy in the new Europe*. Basingstoke: Palgrave Macmillan.
Lord, C., & Magnette, P. (2004). E Pluribus Unum? Creative disagreement about legitimacy in the EU. *Journal of Common Market Studies*, 42(1), 183–202.
Majone, G. (1994). The rise of the regulatory state in Europe. *West European Politics*, 17(3), 77–101.
Majone, G. (1996). *Regulating Europe*. London: Routledge.
Majone, G. (2006). The common sense of European integration. *Journal of European Public Policy*, 13(5), 607–626.
Manin, B. (1987). On legitimacy and political deliberation. *Political Theory*, 15(3), 338–368.
Meyer, C. (1999). Political legitimacy and the invisibility of politics: Exploring the European Union's communication deficit. *Journal of Common Market Studies*, 37(4), 617–639.
Moravcsik, A. (2002). In defence of the 'democratic deficit': Reassessing legitimacy in the European Union. *Journal of Common Market Studies*, 40(4), 603–624.
Moravcsik, A. (2005). Europe without illusions: A category mistake. *Prospect*, Issue 112, July. http://www.prospect-magazine.co.uk/article_details.php?id=6939. Accessed 12 Mar 2010.

Moravcsik, A. (2006). What can we learn from the collapse of the European constitutional project? *Politische Vierteljahresschrift, 47*(2), 219–241.

Moravcsik, A. (2008). The European constitutional settlement. *The World Economy, 31*(1), 158–183.

Rabier, J. R. (1986). *Supporteurs ou citoyens?* (obtained through personal communication via e-mail).

Scharpf, F. (1999). *Governing in Europe: Effective and democratic.* Oxford: Oxford University Press.

Scharpf, F. (2000a). Notes toward a theory of multilevel governing in Europe, MPIfG Discussion Paper 00/5. http://www.mpifg.de/pu/mpifg_dp/dp00-5.pdf. Accessed 12 Mar 2010.

Scharpf, F. (2000b). The European democratic deficit: Contested definitions or diverse domains? *European Union Studies Association, 17*(1). http://www.eustudies.org/files/eusa_review/Winter2004Review.pdf. Accessed 2 Mar 2010.

Scharpf, F. (2007). *Reflections on multilevel legitimacy* (MPIfG Working Paper 07/3). http://edoc.vifapol.de/opus/volltexte/2007/84/pdf/wp07_3.pdf. Accessed 23 Mar 2010.

Scharpf, F. (2009). Legitimacy in the multilevel European polity. *European Political Science Review, 1*(2), 173–204.

Schmidt, V. A. (2013). Democracy and legitimacy in the European Union revisited: Input, output *and* 'throughput'. *Political Studies, 61*(1), 2–22.

Schmidt, V. A. (2015). The forgotten problem of democratic legitimacy. In M. Matthijs, & M. Blythe (Eds.), The future of the Euro. Oxford: Oxford University Press. http://www.cis.ethz.ch/content/dam/ethz/special-interest/gess/cis/cis-dam/News_Events/Events_2014/2014_CIS_Colloquium/2014_FS/Schmidt_Legitimacy.pdf.

Schmitter, P. (2000). *How to democratize the European Union ... and why bother?* Oxford: Rowman and Littlefield.

Thiel, M. (2014). European civil society and the EU Fundamental Rights Agency: Creating legitimacy through civil society inclusion? *Journal of European Integration, 36*(5), 435–451.

Van Bijsterveld, S. (2004). *Transparency in the European Union: A crucial link in shaping the new social contract between the citizen and the EU.* https://www.ip-rs.si/fileadmin/user_upload/Pdf/clanki/Agenda__Bijsterveld-Paper.pdf. Accessed 13 July 2012.

Voermans, W., Hartmann, J., & Kaeding, M. (2014). The quest for legitimacy in EU secondary legislation. *The Theory and Practice of Legislation, 2*(1), 5–32.

Weber, M. (1978). *Economy and society* (Vols. 1 & 2, Eds. G. Roth, & C. Wittich). Berkeley: University of California Press.

CHAPTER 5

Europe of Agorai (2005–2009)

1 THE RATIFICATION PROCESS OF THE CONSTITUTIONAL TREATY[1]

When the Barroso I Commission (2004–09) started its mandate, the EU had a main priority and that was to secure the upcoming ratification of the Constitutional Treaty. The Commission realised that it was necessary to focus on the creation of effective public communication structures which would allow the Commission to provide European citizens with the necessary information about the Constitution and to encourage them to vote for it. Scarred by the ratification disaster of the Maastricht Treaty, the Commission was determined not to be caught unaware of public sentiment but to develop public communication strategies that would ensure successful ratification by 'selling' the Constitutional Treaty more convincingly than it had been able to do with the Maastricht Treaty. That was the plan. And in order to make this plan work Barroso created the post of a Commissioner responsible for Communication Strategy and nominated Margot Wallström, a 'media-savvy' Swedish politician,[2] for this role. This nomination and ultimately the appointment of Wallström as Commissioner for Communication Strategy was significant, as it was the first time that a Commissioner responsible for public communication had both a background in politics and media-communication. Without going into great detail, it suffices to say that Wallström had held functions in both the Swedish Parliament and Government and that she had been CEO of a regional TV network and Executive Vice-President of

Worldview Global Media. Wallström expressed the complementary character of her professional profile as follows: 'Concerning my professional experience, my background as a parliamentarian and then as a Minister in the Swedish government (in which I served as a Minister for seven years) has taught me the laws of politics. As a former Chief Executive of a regional television network and working in a media company, I have also gained a good understanding of the realities of communication outside the political sphere'.[3] Wallström's professional profile was appealing to both Barroso and the EP because they believed that it was suited to communicating the EU's ambitions and aspirations of that time: a Constitution to reinforce the EU's political standing and to adopt an approach to public communication that would make it possible to realise the objectives of the Constitutional Treaty with regard to the legitimate democratic standing of the EU.

In her newly appointed role, Wallström was '[to] help to strengthen the Community's capacity to communicate both from Brussels and in the member states' (…) as well as 'our relations with the other European institutions'.[4] Further, she was responsible for 'strengthening [the] relations with the national parliaments'[5] and additionally, she was given the responsibility of the Directorate General for Press and Communication, the Commission's public communication service created under the Prodi Commission (1999–2004). The plan failed. It failed in two ways: first, Wallström refused to undertake any campaign that would attempt to 'sell' the Treaty but instead insisted on providing sufficient information to enable European citizens to make an informed choice and second, the Constitutional Treaty was rejected by the French and Dutch referenda. To be clear, I am not suggesting a causal link between these two aspects. What I want to do instead is look a little closer at the dispute between team Wallström and team Parliament. I think this is important, because the dispute will set the scene and help us understand more deeply what motivated Wallström in her understanding of the meaning of European citizenship, public communication and ultimately the EU itself.

Wallström's Understanding of the Role of Public Communication in the Ratification Process of the Constitutional Treaty and Beyond

Opinions on how the Constitutional Treaty should best be publicly communicated varied. Whereas the EP advocated a campaign in favour of the

Constitution, Wallström refused 'to issue propaganda on the Treaty' and to sell the Constitutional Treaty to the peoples of Europe. Instead, she considered public communication (in the context of, and with regard to, the Constitution) as a means to inform 'European citizens in a clear, plain and objective way on what the Constitutional Treaty means'.[6] Wallström did not consider public communication as a means to achieve predetermined political outcomes and did not think that the Commission was in a position to publicly communicate with the EU citizens without the involvement of the member states or by contradicting the public communication on the Constitutional Treaty in the member states. Correspondingly, Wallström pointed out that 'it does not fall in the remit of the Commission to start a campaign in favour of the ratification of the Constitutional Treaty; there would be neither a legal basis nor a budget for such an action'[7] and she further emphasised that her 'role will not be (...) a spin doctor—because you cannot buy or spin democracy'.[8] The EP profoundly disagreed with this approach and subsequently sent a letter to Barroso which read: 'Members repeatedly argued the necessity of the Commission to clearly commit itself in favour of the ratification of the Constitutional Treaty, pointing out that the Commission participated in the Convention and in the Intergovernmental Conference. It therefore cannot consider itself and act as being "neutral"'.[9] In order to show the significance of the issue and to ensure that Wallström would pronounce herself clearly in favour of the Constitutional Treaty, the EP went so far as to ask Barroso to officially add 'Constitutional Affairs' to Wallström's portfolio.

Wallström, however, did not make any concessions and introduced a memo on 'Communicating the Constitution: 10 concrete actions by the Commission'[10] which outlined how the Commission was to assist the ratification process through public communication. This document stated that (a) the Commission would focus on those countries that request assistance, (b) the Commission maintained its position that it was mainly the member states' duty to communicate and ratify, (c) the Commission would ensure that factual information was provided regarding the debate on the Constitution and beyond, (d) the Commission had made it clear that it would not issue propaganda on the Constitution campaign during election periods or breach national rules on referenda or distribution of information and (e) the Commission would seek to ensure that Europe's citizens would be able to make informed choices on the Constitution.

Moreover, Wallström was in favour of an open debate[11] focused on the Constitution that would give citizens the chance to voice their opinions and concerns. She argued that it was necessary to 'try to keep the focus of the European debate over the next two years on the Constitutional Treaty itself, on what it means and what it brings to Europe and its citizens. That is the debate Europe really needs'.[12] Clearly this position, as noted above, was at variance with the EP and its desire for an explicitly pro-Constitutional Treaty public communication campaign. Although Wallström's approach was in line with the Constitution's stipulations on 'The democratic life of the European Union', which stated that the EU needed to be regarded as a representative and 'participatory democracy, based on transparency of the institutions, the maintenance of dialogue between the institutions and the citizens and (…) the possibility of a citizens' initiative (not less than one million citizens may sign an initiative inviting the Commission to draw up and submit to the Council a proposal for a Union act in a given area)', the approach Wallström took remained a sensitive issue between the EP and Wallström, and led to various disputes whose significance I will turn to at the end of this chapter.

The Rejection of the Constitutional Treaty: Moving Towards a 'Europe of Agorai'

The Constitutional Treaty was rejected in 2005 through the French referendum held on 29 May, when 54.68% voted against the Constitution and also through the Dutch referendum where 61.54% voted against the Constitution in a consultative referendum on 1 June.

The subsequent Constitutional crisis[13] led to a reconsideration of the EU's, and notably the Commission's, public communication strategies.[14] Finally, at 'the end of the European Council on 18 June 2005, Heads of State and Government adopted a declaration on "the ratification of the Treaty establishing a Constitution for Europe"' as Plan-D stated. 'This declaration called for a "period of reflection" following the negative votes in France and the Netherlands on the European Constitution'[15]. Further, Heads of State and Government gave guidance to the Member States on the type of debate that could be organised: '[T]he period of reflection will be used to enable a broad debate to take place in each of our countries, involving citizens, civil society, social partners, national parliaments and political parties. This debate, designed to generate interest, which is already under way in many Member States, must be intensified and broadened'. They also indicated that the European institutions should 'make their contribution, with the Commission playing a special role in this regard'[16] and the Commission agreed in Plan D that a 'broad and intensive debate on European policies'[17] was needed and that 'any vision of the future of Europe needs to build on a clear view of citizen's needs and expectations'.[18]

Wallström was committed to help the democratisation process of the EU through a public communication approach that she believed would help to 'build a true participatory democracy in Europe'.[19] The emphasis on participatory democracy reflected her desire for European debate and dialogue between European politicians and European citizens, and it was this understanding that would define the civil-spatial representation of European citizenship which I call a 'Europe of Agorai' and which I will now turn to in detail.

2 The Fourth Representation of European Citizenship: 'Europe of Agorai'

During this representation, the Commission sought to bring about a European deliberative democracy and was tireless in its efforts to genuinely involve European citizens in the EU's decision-making and policy-shaping processes. It showed an innovative understanding of European space and was resolute to bring about a 'Europe of Agorai' (my term). The Ancient Greeks understood an agora as a political place of assembly, debate and contestation over matters of public policy. The modern European agorai of the fourth representation extended beyond a political purpose and came to be civilly, socially and culturally significant. They represented 'democratic infrastructures' that effortlessly combined the use of physical and virtual space and fostered both face-to-face and online communication amongst European citizens, and were seen to fulfil the function of European town squares, European town halls, European civic centres and European assembly halls. It was these new European spaces that, to borrow Calhoun's terms, 'public communication takes place in, and helps to create, a space of relationships amongst citizens'.[20] In this sense, European agorai just as '(…) public spaces from the Greek agora to early modern marketplaces, theaters and parliaments all give support and setting to public life'.[21]

For Wallström, European public spaces would give European citizens the opportunity to express themselves, to debate European affairs and to find a consensus on what kind of Europe they would like to see emerge. It was time to build Europe together with European citizens in a bottom-up approach, and this understanding of Europe as a Civil Europe is reminiscent of the way the early Commission officials imagined Europe to be built. In fact, it is possible to argue that Wallström's 'Europe of Agorai' represented a revival of the early Commission official's excitement and enthusiasm about the possibility of a Civil Europe. Wallström's understanding of European citizenship was expressed through the use of a civil-spatial lexicon. Whereas we need to remember that the fourth representation of European citizenship only existed and acquired its full meaning as the amalgam of its civil and spatial elements, I will disaggregate the civil-spatial lexicon for reasons of clarity into a civil and a spatial lexicon.

A Civil Lexicon

The civil lexicon expressed two things: first, Wallström's conception of Europe as a deliberative democracy[22] and second, the role Wallström attributed to European citizens in this vision of a democratic and deliberative Europe. Wallström's view of the role of European citizens touched upon such aspects as Wallström's conception of European civil society and the relationship between the EU and the European citizenry.

'Europe of Agorai': Europe as a Deliberative Democracy

Wallström was aware that 'reinvigorat[ing] democracy'[23] was a 'long term democratic reform process'.[24] It was a long-term process that was worth being undertaken, as 'democracy is fundamental to European society'.[25] However, when Wallström spoke of democracy she thought of a form of deliberative democracy because she believed that this was the only form of democracy that could close the 'yawning gap between the people and the policy-makers'[26] and 'improve the Commission's relationship with European citizens'.[27] It was also the only form of democracy that would allow for a consensus on the future of European integration and for European citizens being involved in the development of the European project and its future direction.[28] The key term in Wallström's approach was citizens' participation or as Wallström put it: '[D]emocracy is not a spectator sport. It requires leadership and active participation. The truth is, the symphony of European integration will be a success only if the people are involved in writing the script'.[29] What this shows is that Wallström believed European representative democracy—which we return to under the Barroso II Commission, as I will show in the following chapter—was insufficient. According to her, democracy 'does not simply mean asking the citizens of Europe to elect a European Parliament every five years. It means allowing—and encouraging—people from all walks of life to have their say in shaping EU policies'.[30] This could only be achieved through a genuine public debate[31] between EU policymakers and European citizens.

The Idea of Debate and Dialogue in the 'Europe of Agorai'

Public debate was the dominant theme in Wallström's speeches and the Commission's public communication policy documents. In these, Wallström emphasised the necessity to 'ensure that public debate finds its way into the European decision and policy-making process, that citizens get their entitled right to be heard'[32] but was vague about what topics need to be debated. All we can find are references to 'stimulating a wider public debate'[33] and encouraging 'citizens' participation'[34] with regard to general topics such as 'the future of Europe',[35] 'common European issues',[36] issues of 'common interest',[37] 'European policies'[38] and 'European integration'.[39]

The aim of such public debate was to find a consensus between citizens and policymakers or EU institutions[40] that would be 'the result of citizens' genuine interest and free choice to participate in a debate on European issues'.[41] As such, public debate was vital for a healthy democracy and democratic legitimacy: it was considered by Wallström to be 'the "lifeblood" of democracy'.[42] Public debate would help voters to grasp political issues, to vote intelligently and to get engaged with policymakers.[43] In Wallström's words, 'Informed debate and dialogue enable people to understand policy options. Understanding enables people to vote meaningfully. Democracy comes alive!'.[44]

However, European deliberative democracy could only come alive through public debate if three citizens' rights were recognised: the right to information, the right to speak and the right to be heard.

The Right to Information Presented in a Factual Style of Public Communication

The right to information, which is often seen to go hand in hand with freedom of expression, should be 'at the heart of democracy in Europe'.[45] As such, and according to Wallström, public communication represented 'an essential element of democracy, indispensable for fostering public debate. Citizens have a right to know what the European Union is doing, and why'.[46] Only if citizens were given information about 'what the decision makers are up to' would they be 'able to scrutinize them'.[47] In other words: 'political decision-makers are accountable to the public, so they must be open to public scrutiny. The transparency agenda and public communication policy are therefore essential tools for democracy and, consequently, public legitimacy'.[48] This is why in a democracy such as the EU, according to Wallström, 'the right to know is just as important a cornerstone to democracy as the right to vote'.[49]

In a democratic society, having the right to further information means to 'explain EU policies in an understandable way to European citizens'.[50] By this Wallström meant that 'the EU needs to explain its aims and policies clearly and comprehensibly. We in the Commission have to speak in plain simple language, avoiding jargon'[51] and that '[the Commission] must spell out the ways in which our proposals will actually affect people's daily lives'.[52] This is why Wallström introduced the so-called 'layperson's summary[53] [which] will explain in plain words the personal and societal benefits of a policy. The explanatory statement accompanying each Commission proposal could be useful to achieve this purpose'.[54] Once again, the Commission emphasised the need for straightforward information presented in a factual style and in a way that was appealing and digestible to a large European public. In some ways this was reminiscent of Monnet's concern for making information about European integration readily available and his notion that information was a precondition for the emergence of public sentiment and the involvement of European citizens in the political affairs of the Community. Accordingly, Wallström argued that '(…) the need to ensure citizens' equal access to information and the public sphere [are] question[s] of democracy'.[55] Equal access meant all information provided is translated into all official EU languages. The Commission has never attempted to impose a lingua franca but has always emphasised the need for information to be presented in the languages of the member states. Equal access also meant that the Commission used a variety of channels such as the factual mass media and new technologies such as the Internet (see later sections). Equal access finally meant that 'people from all walks of life in all EU countries should be helped to develop the skills they need to access and use that information. This is particularly important in the case of minorities, disabled citizens and other groups that might systematically be excluded from participation in the public sphere'.[56]

The Commission also continued to encourage institutional transparency at all levels of the European institutions[57] through several initiatives, such as the European Transparency Initiative.[58] This concern for increased institutional transparency can be explained through Wallström's[59] belief in the idea that politicians have to be democratically accountable to European citizens and that, as such, European citizens are entitled to expect efficient, open and service-minded public institutions'.[60] In this, Wallström's views were somewhat reminiscent of the Commission's rhetoric on openness and transparency during the previous representation of European citizenship 'Europe of Transparency'. However, and it is important to make this distinction, during the previous representation, the Commission considered the right to information and its attendant concern for transparency as a tool to foster support for the European project by educating European citizens. As I argued in the previous chapter, the rationale was that if European citizens had sufficient information and knowledge they could only agree that Europe was good for them. In a way, the Commission had attempted to educate them into accepting Europe. During the representation 'Europe of Agorai', access to information was seen as a precondition for democracy because access to information and institutional transparency enable European citizens to form an informed but not necessarily positive opinion about European matters and to consequently hold European politicians accountable. These European citizens were conceived of as knowledgeable and capable of scrutinising the European institutions in a constructive way.

Wallström's insistence on the democratic right to information was further connected to her belief in the political and communicative value of the straightforward factual style of public communication. During the representation of civil-spatial European citizenship in the 'Europe of Agorai', the factual style of public communication served two purposes. First, and as shown above, information in a factual style of public communication was provided to the European citizenry in order to raise awareness of EU issues, to promote European citizens' involvement in debate and to enable them to undertake civil scrutiny. Second, however, information was also, albeit only occasionally, seen as being able to 'publicize [the] added value that the EU can provide'.[61] Wallström was aware that '[t]o be more relevant to daily concerns, we must also be able to explain how we touch upon those issues; how we work; the values we stand for; and the role we play in the world'.[62] And whereas she had argued at the EP hearings before she was appointed as Commissioner that it was necessary to develop 'a common European narrative which explains the social and environmental benefits of our co-operation, as well as the economic benefits',[63] Wallström did not pursue an approach to public debate that was directed towards the achievement of a predetermined outcome but rather pursued what Tully called an open-ended approach to integration. It is an approach, as I have argued elsewhere,[64] that lacks a framing discourse and that promotes open dialogue and debate which is ongoing and open-ended.[65]

The Right to Speak and the Right to Be Heard: The Deliberative-Rational Style of Public Communication

With regard to the involvement of European citizens in debates, the Commission clearly acknowledged the European citizens' 'right to participate in the political process, through effective, two-way communication with the [European] institutions'[66] and argued that citizens' 'participation [would] further enrich this extraordinary project which was launched fifty years ago'.[67] The Commission's public communication policy was based upon the belief that European citizens were able to understand information on European issues and to critically engage with these policies in a deliberative and rational way. Its success would depend upon European citizens wanting to exercise their right to speak and to be heard. As such, the deliberative-rational style of public communication Wallström advocated was genuinely innovative in its expectations of the communicative and deliberative responsibilities (debate and dialogue) entailed in being a European citizen. She was convinced of European citizens' desire to 'have a greater say in European affairs' and equally of their ability to make valuable contributions: 'the future of the European project, what it means to be a European citizen and the common values that can create a European identity, can only be defined by the citizens of Europe debating and discussing these issues'.[68] Besides individual European citizens, Wallström also encouraged 'civil society, social partners, national parliaments and political parties'[69] to participate in the European debate.

Whereas the Commission valued the right to speak, it was equally aware of the difficulties it would face in making sure that a variety of citizens' voices was heard and that this right actually turned into more than discourse. In other words, it acknowledged that on its own it 'cannot possibly bridge the communication gap between the European Union and its citizens' but rather that it 'needs to work with the other institutions, national and regional parliaments, civil society and, of course, the media'.[70] The Commission considered itself 'primarily as a kind of "helper" to member states and civil society, through its Representations and other myriad tools'[71] and was aware that its role had to be non-interventionist if it wanted to avoid an anti-democratic top-down approach. As Wallström put it: 'Democracy is all about "bottom-up" and we must always remember that'.[72] What this meant was that the Commission had to refrain from setting the agenda for the debate but rather needed to 'give citizens and representative associations the opportunity to exchange publicly their views on all areas of Union action'[73] and to create an EU agenda which would reflect what people want.[74]

What we can see is that Wallström made a distinction between individual citizens and civil society. This distinction tells us that she considered civil society as comprised of citizens organised into civil associations, political parties and NGOs. These civil society organisations were considered, as in the previous representation, a channel to reach the wider European public, and this is why Wallström insisted on the involvement of European civil society[75] and why the Commission, subsequently began to fund deliberative European civil society projects and events (see later sections). The understanding of civil society acting as a bridge between the Commission and European citizens also tied in with the rather decentralised approach to public communication that the Commission took during the period. Notably, the Representations in the member states were expected to work with civil society organisations in order to ensure that the messages were concrete and meaningful for specific national publics.

The Right to Be Heard

For Wallström, public debate offered the EU the possibility to 'become a Union that listens'.[76] This listening-exercise was undertaken in two ways: by listening to European citizens' opinions during actual public debates and via public opinion polling. Both were meant to ensure that 'citizens get their entitled right to be heard'[77] and that their voices find their way into the European decision- and policymaking process. As such, the Commission understood that it could only increase its popular acceptance and democratic legitimacy if its 'listening exercise (...) lead[s] to clear results that are taken on board'.[78] According to Wallström, the listening exercise hadn't been taken seriously by the Commission in previous years—it is likely that she means since the idea of public debate emerged in the Maastricht crisis (1993–2004)—but rather that it has focused too much 'on telling people what the EU does: less attention has been paid to listening to people's views'.[79] In short, the Commission had been 'bad at listening'.[80] Now, the listening process was to be conceived of as a way to find out what European citizens actually expected from the EU, why they were dissatisfied and what priorities they thought should be on the EU policy agenda. In other words, 'governments and European institutions need to know what issues concern people and what policy changes people want', and this was why Wallström thought that these political bodies, and especially the Commission, had to start listening more carefully to civil society and carrying out opinion polls.[81]

Like various of her predecessors, and most notably Rabier, Wallström conceived of public opinion polling as a 'tool for democracy', one which would 'give a voice to the 'silent citizens'—the people who do not vote, do not take active part in political life, do not channel their opinions through groups of interests or citizens' organisations'.[82] In this sense, public opinion polling can be understood as a way to extend the spectrum of public opinion and to make it possibly more representative by including the views of the politically rather passive public. Wallström saw opinion polling as a way to 'put ears on the European Union'[83] and agreed with Gallup and Rae that 'public opinion can only be of service to democracy if it can be heard' and if it is dynamic and attempts to separate 'the true from the false'.[84] Public opinion had to be understood, as Alexander in reference to Gallup and Rae points out, as 'critical, not submissive; experimental, not dogmatic'.[85] Only when it takes this form can it be considered as 'the pulse of democracy'.[86] In one of her speeches Wallström referred to George Gallup Junior, who reported: "My dad thought that polls were absolutely vital to a democracy. He felt that polls were extremely important because it removed the power from lobbying groups and from smoke-filled rooms and let the public into the act. It was a way to let the public speak".[87] What Wallström's belief in public opinion shows is that she appeared to value public opinion as a democratic force based upon, to borrow JS Mill's terms, the 'antagonism of opinions'. Wallström saw the constructive value and intelligence of public opinion and in this way she was similar to Bentham but different from Tocqueville and JS Mill who, unlike her, were 'frightened democrats' and feared the tyranny of public opinion as an expression of mass conformity. She insisted that 'the Commission has to listen to people, seriously and attentively'.[88] Accordingly, a 'more systematic use of opinion polls, focus groups and citizens' panels to find out the concerns and attitudes of specific groups of people in each EU country'[89] was essential to increase civil scrutiny and to encourage institutional and political accountability. In this sense, public opinion gained 'a normative status: the government [or the EU] ought to listen to it'.[90] It ought to listen to it because, in a democracy such as Wallström imagined the EU should become, political leaders need to be ultimately 'summon[ed] (...) to the bar of public opinion'.[91] In this ideal and normative sense, public opinion as an expression of civil scrutiny forms a 'counterweight' to the political power of elite institutions such as the Commission. In short, Wallström shared in some ways the liberal tradition of valuing deliberation and diversity of views.

Recap: European Citizens in the 'Europe of Agorai'

What have we learned so far about European citizens during the representation 'Europe of Agorai'? First, and to reify the European citizen deliberately, they lived in a Europe that Wallström conceived of as a deliberative democracy and in which 'communication is more than information'.[92] It was a deliberative Europe in which the Commission via its public communication strategy established 'a relationship and initiates a dialogue with European citizens, it listens carefully and it connects to people'[93] and in which debate and dialogue between European citizens and EU policy-makers were considered vital for the advancement of European democracy. Here, European citizens had the right to information. Information itself was seen as a tool for the empowerment of European citizens, as it was through factual and comprehensible information that they would able to scrutinise rather than to 'glorify the European institutions'.[94] As Wallström stated: 'My approach is not to get people to love the EU, but to create a real dialogue with citizens and a pan-European debate. My goal is to bring the EU closer to the citizens and to bridge the gap between them and the decision-makers. To demonstrate that the EU is also a "solutions united"'.[95] Accordingly, it was necessary to ascribe to European citizens a 'right to be heard'[96] and a right to speak, which meant nothing more than to express their views. With the acknowledgement of these rights, Wallström hoped to encourage European citizens to be politically active citizens and to act 'as policy-advisors'.[97] Wallström's view showed that she conceived of the European citizen as a rational, intelligent and deliberative EU citizen, or in other words an actively engaged European citizen, who was asked to make informed choices in matters of policy contestation. And it is because of Wallström's conception of the European citizen as almost an equal partner in policy discussion that she favoured the deliberative-rational style of public communication. In this respect she was reminiscent of Tocqueville who, despite his fears of the mass, argued that 'when the right of every citizen to co-operate in the government of society is acknowledged, every citizen must be presumed to possess the power of discriminating between the different opinions of his contemporaries, and of appreciating the different facts from which the interferences may be drawn'.[98] In short, deliberative democracy and the use of a deliberative-rational style of public communication are only conceivable if one considers that citizens are rational, can deliberate and are capable of scrutinising policies and policymakers.

It was because of this belief in intelligent and interested civil-spatial European citizens that Wallström could argue and defend the view that 'a political integration project, such as the EU, can only work if people are part of writing the "script"—if it is possible to relate to and identify with the project as a commonly agreed venture. This is where Europe as a political project must improve its performance, by giving citizens ownership of the EU'.[99] Wallström believed—just like the early Commission officials did (Chaps. 1 and 2)—that the ownership of the European integration project lay with European citizens and that as such, it was their right to be able to set its agenda. To leave European citizens responsible for the agenda of the European debate showed that Wallström, in her approach to public communication of European citizenship, did not have a particular topic she favoured, that she did not steer the citizens in a particular direction neither did she prioritise one policy area more than the other. Rather she followed, as I mentioned above, an open-ended approach to European integration. In this approach to public communication, she believed, to borrow Risse's words, that 'argumentative and deliberative behaviour is not goal-oriented as strategic interaction' but that the only goal is 'to seek a reasoned consensus' rather than to 'attain one's fixed preferences'.[100] It is in exactly this way that she used the deliberative-rational style of public communication. As such, Wallström's approach was a significant change in that she moved away from the omnipresent political asymmetry of the period 1993-2004 and rather assumed that European citizens—people from all walks of life—would be able to assume their civic duties and responsibilities. In an interview Wallström insisted on the right of citizens to access information and more importantly she argued that European citizens deserved—in their role as European citizens—to be consulted on European issues more often than every five years on the occasion of the European Parliament elections.[101] Accordingly, she felt that it was the Commission's task to 'enable the citizens of Europe to set the agenda for Europe'[102] and to make sure that European citizens 'have the right channels and the right tools' to 'influence and contribute to European democracy and better European policies'.[103] Wallström said that when she started, the 'power cables (...) to communicate between the citizens and European institutions were not charged yet'[104] and that is why she made it her priority to empower European citizens.

As noted above, it needs to be borne in mind that the 'Europe of Agorai' only existed and acquired its full meaning when the lexica of the civil and the spatial lexica come together. I will now turn to the spatial lexicon and correspondingly to Wallström's multiperspectival conception of European public space.

A Spatial Lexicon

As noted in the beginning, Wallström was keen on creating 'democratic infrastructures',[105] which can be understood as places where European 'citizens can come together and meet'[106] either in 'physical meeting-places such as schools and town halls'[107] for 'face-to-face discussion'[108] or in 'virtual meeting places such as Internet websites and interactive television programmes'.[109] In short, the fourth representation of European citizenship was an attempt to create twenty-first-century high-tech agorai where giving European citizens the possibility to come together and debate European affairs was considered a rather urgent matter. This ambition came with a more sophisticated use of European space than ever before.

Physical Agorai

Wallström insisted on the creation of user friendly and easily accessible physical spaces for debate on the EU[110] and developed, together with the EP, 'a network of meeting places where people can get information, see exhibitions and films, take part in discussions and attend concerts, lectures and seminars'.[111] These meeting places should not be misunderstood 'as usual Brussels based lobbies or political elite from the Member States'[112] but rather as offering a 'programme, an education, where teachers, students, trade unionists, young people and bus drivers can come together to debate the future of Europe'.[113] Accordingly, from 2007 onward, Wallström established the so-called 'European Public Spaces'.

European Public Spaces

European public spaces can be described as joint projects run by Representations of the Commission and by the EP Information offices. The pilot project started in 2007 with European public spaces in Madrid, Tallinn and Dublin. At the time of writing, there were 13 European Public Spaces[114] across the EU. According to the Commission, European Public Spaces 'will offer new facilities, such as a conference centre, an information office, an exhibition area and a reading area'[115] and provide '(…) meeting points for citizens where they can enter into an active dialogue with the institutions'.[116] Despite having been created for the same purpose, no European Public Space ever looked same. In short, there 'is no "one size fits all"'. In fact, so the Commission official stated, 'budget and administrative resources vary considerable' and therefore '(…) programs of those European Public spaces are manifold. The European Parliament puts a lot of emphasis on cultural events, so some of the public spaces are (…) setting up cinema shows (…) where, for example, films are shown [that] participated in the so called LUX prize. [This prize] is (…) a prize granted by the European Parliament. [European Public Spaces] organise discussion (…), they organise theatre shows, lectures'.[117] European Public Spaces also varied with regard to their target audiences. As the same Commission official explained: 'In Italy, for example, the European Public space is devoted to receiving classes of school children, where they can learn about Europe, the European policies and institutions (…)'.[118] However, the European Public Spaces hosted a variety of events. In 2009, for example, 2300 events were hosted and attracted more than 300,000 visitors in total. They were designed to be places where 'the European debate can unfold'[119] and where, according to Wallström, a European public sphere could emerge.

Virtual Meeting Places

The Commission considered the use of 'internet technology to activate debates' and to establish 'virtual networks of Internet sites' vital for the creation of virtual meeting places. According to then recent studies, so the Commission claimed, 'the Internet has moved from being purely a source of information to become a tool for two-way communication and interaction'. In fact, so the Commission believed, 'the Internet has the power to bring people closer'[120] and therefore needed to be considered of 'prime importance for stimulating the debate'.[121] Therefore, the Commission said that it would begin to 'use state-of-art Internet technology to actively debate and advocate its policies in cyberspace, which has become an important opinion-forming forum of debate'.[122] And indeed, the Commission started to increasingly use the Internet. It developed its own You Tube channel 'EUTube' and Commissioners started to write blogs where discussion about specific policy areas could equally take place. With regard to her own blog, Wallström stated: 'I like the blog. It gives a lot to political debate and we have created organised feedback to the college. We now report regularly on blog comments we receive. I think it is important, to feed this into the decision-making process. (...) I wanted to do it because I find it is a way of making direct contact with European citizens'.[123]

In order to spread the word about these new opportunities for virtual European debates and encourage European citizens to participate, the Commission thought it essential to develop 'a network of civil society and private and public sector websites that promote contact with or between European citizens and stimulate debate on EU policy issues'.[124] It believed that by involving the Internet and launching online agorai it was possible to reach out to a large number of European citizens, to initiate an exchange of ideas on EU affairs and thereby to encourage the establishment of what Wallström call 'a trans-European network of humans'.[125] Accordingly, Wallström saw her task as enabling and involving a neonate European civil society with policymaking in the 'Europe of Agorai'. To encourage the participation of civil society and individual citizens, Wallström advocated a policy whereby the EU co-funds a range of European civil society projects.

Within the framework of Plan D, the Commission funded over 60 civil society projects with a budget of €6.6 million. Its follow-up programme, Debate Europe, allocated €3 million to 47 projects.[126] What all of these European civil society projects had in common was that, according to the Commission, they showed how European deliberation could work in practise by testing (1) European websites which were connected to 'a network of national debating sub-sites, combined with local, national and European debating events', (2) 'a multilingual, highly interactive website, the content of which was determined by focus groups in different EU countries and adapted according to feedback from target audience workshops', (3) 'national consultations on the same issues in all Member States, taking place more or less at the same time, leading to a European synthesis', (4) 'pan-European deliberative polling, where a random sample of the population polled gathered for three days and debated face to face' (see Fishkin 2009 for details on this project) and (5) 'local debating events in several EU Member States combined with polls and video recording of citizens' views'.[127] The Commission concluded that 'those projects showed that the development of participatory democracy on EU-related issues at local, regional, national and cross-border level is possible, both in terms of quality and logistics'.[128] All of these civil society projects played to the Commission's multiperspectival conception of European space. Let's take the example of the European Citizens' Consultations (2007 and 2009) to illustrate how Wallström's vision of deliberative democracy, the involvement of civil society, the use of twenty-first-century high-tech agorai and the deliberative-style of public communication were put into practise.

Deliberative Democracy and Democratic Infrastructures Put into Practise: The European Citizens' Consultations (EEC)[129]

In 2006/2007, the King Baudouin Foundation (KBF), with a consortium of over 40 European partner organisations, organised the first European Citizens' Consultations (ECC), which were comprised of three different phases. In the first phase, 200 randomly selected European citizens representing a demographic cross section from all of the then 27 EU member states participated at the agenda-setting event in Brussels. For two days, these European citizens discussed the political priorities EU policymakers should have. In order to communicate, they used a variety of technological gadgets such as laptops, projectors and electronic voting key pads. Translators ensured that everything was available in the then 23 official EU languages. At the end of phase 1, the participants selected three topics that would make up the deliberative agenda: (1) the environmental and economic impact of Europe's energy use, (2) the social and economic conditions for Europe's families and (3) the EU's role in the world and the management of immigration. The second phase lasted for about six weeks, and during this time all of these topics were discussed in national deliberative events which, if possible, were meant to be held at the same time in different member states. Often five to ten deliberative consultations took place at one time. These deliberative events can be seen to exemplify the use of the deliberative-rational style of public communication. In the third phase, the European citizens returned to Brussels where they had to synthesise the national results in order to create a so-called European perspective on the three topics. Ultimately, a roundtable with the European citizens, Wallström and EU policymakers took place.[130] During this roundtable the results of the national debates were discussed, once again in a deliberative-rational style of public communication, before the European citizens' perspective was handed over to EU policymakers. This was how the results of the European Citizens' Consultation were fed directly into the political process. In total, about 1800 citizens participated in the project, and feedback was collected from 1000 of the 1800 citizens involved via an evaluation survey.

Given the success of the first European Citizens' Consultation, a second round of ECC was organised in 2009 with the intention of providing European citizens with the opportunity to express their 'voice in the debate over how to respond to the current economic and financial crisis by providing a platform for pan-European dialogue on the challenges facing the EU'.[131] However, and rather than merely repeating the experience of the ECC 2007,[132] the ECC 2009 were used as an opportunity to 'develop a more structured and long-term citizens' involvement'[133] and to widen the ECC's scope to a higher number of EU citizens through the launch of online agorai in each of the member states. In the first phase, ideas on the role of the EU in the future were collected and debated in online agorai which were visited by over 200,000 European citizens. In the second phase, the ideas gathered in the online agorai 'were fed into the national consultations now taking place in all 27 Member States, over three weekends, at which a total of 1600 citizens (...) are working to produce ten recommendations for action at the EU level at each national event'.[134] Once all national recommendations had been collected the 1600 European citizens were asked to choose their top 15 European recommendations through an online vote.[135] In the third phase, about 150 European citizens made their way to Brussels for the European Citizens' Summit in order to hand the top 15 recommendations over to and discuss these with 'top EU policy-makers, including the European Commission and Parliament Presidents and the EU Presidency.'[136]

Conclusion on the European Citizens Consultation and European Space

Wallström's vision of European deliberative democracy was put into practise through the involvement of civil society and the creation and use of twenty-first-century high-tech agorai. The European citizens' consultations can be seen as the manifestation of what Fishkin referred to as 'microcosmic deliberation' in which 'a representative group of ordinary citizens, preferably constituted on the basis of random sampling'[137] debates issues of common interest. The representative sample was chosen in such a way that 'essentially, one does not need a larger sample to represent a larger population'.[138] Consequently, 'the deliberative microcosm chosen by scientific sampling, not too different in basic concept from the microcosms chosen by lot in ancient Athens, offers a middle ground, a third way, between mass plebiscitary consultation on the one hand and elite decision-making on the other, between politically equal but non-deliberative masses and politically unequal but more deliberative elites'.[139] In other words, what was shown during a 'Europe of Agorai' was that it was possible, through random sampling and a skilful way of understanding, using and creating European public space, to establish a form of pan-European deliberation. What the example of the ECC showed is that European citizens are indeed capable of engaging with the areas EU policy covers, the pressing challenges European society faces and of deciding which of these should figure on the list of EU priorities.

Wallström's understanding of a European deliberative democracy was, as noted previously, intrinsically linked to her conception of European space. In the 'Europe of Agorai', spatial manifestations were both the concretisation of a common identity and set of values and an attempt to inspire them in a particular 'European' way. Thus, the creation of 'European Public Spaces' and representation offices acknowledged the understanding that '[a]rchitecture is a part of daily life for everyone, whether or not they want it to be'.[140] Here, European citizenship was meant to become part of the physical reality of daily life. The programmes created for citizens to take place in these buildings, and particularly in the European Public Spaces, showed that architecture was used in its unique way of '[enforcing](...) social interaction, imposing a common experience despite the differences in judgment that may result'.[141] Furthermore, the organisation of space served as a way to legitimise authority through, to use Soja's words, societal integration. Soja argued that in those cases 'the emphasis is on creation and maintenance of institutions and behaviour patterns which promote group unity and cohesiveness'.[142] Such representations and articulations are, in Lefebvre's term, a 'colonisation'[143] of space. In this case, European space was inculcated with a particular meaning and specific historical story: the celebration of a peaceful and unified Europe with a common citizenry and values.

Wallström used physical and virtual space to reinforce both common identity and diversity as the above analysis of her utilisation of civil-society projects and common meeting halls shows. This statement needs qualifying: Wallström also believed and acknowledged that European citizens were first and foremost citizens of the EU member states.[144] It was her view that the European citizen should inhabit what I would call a pan-European communicative-relational virtual and physical space. It was this view that underlined her commitment to and belief in the necessity of creating trans-European democratic infrastructures that would allow European citizens to connect with each other. Ultimately, it would help the creation of a trans-European network of people from different cultures which, whilst retaining their own identity, could simultaneously be united through the Community level. In this she can be said to have endorsed Sandel's view of the citizen as someone who 'can abide the ambiguity associated with sovereignty, who can think and act as multiply situated selves'.[145] According to Sandel, 'the civic virtue distinctive to our time is the capacity to negotiate our way among the sometimes overlapping and sometimes conflicting obligations that claim us, and to live with tensions to which multiple loyalties give rise'.[146] In this sense, the EU's slogan 'Unity in Diversity' acquires a concrete meaning, which Wallström expressed (before the enlargements of 2007 and 2013) as follows: 'The European Union is a family of 25 countries (and growing). We are diverse in our languages and traditions but united in peace and in a common endeavor to build prosperity, social justice and a better world'.[147]

In conclusion, through the use of modern technology, architecture and the fixed, plastic and temporary use of spaces (European bus touring, 'European labyrinth' to be entered with a 'European passport', cultural events in the European Public Spaces, exhibitions etc.), Wallström was innovatively concerned with communicatively and relationally conceived physical and virtual civil space (audiovisual media and the Internet).

Correspondingly, she pioneered the comprehensive use of the deliberative-rational style of European public communication that attempted to create the conditions for European citizens meeting 'face-to-face' to discuss and debate issues of common concern. She thought that this could both be a model for and a facilitator of the emergence of a European public sphere (EPS). She tried through her use of space to create, in Ricœur's words, 'the conditions of plurality resulting from the extension of interhuman relations to all those that the face-to-face relations of 'I' and 'you' leave out as a third party'.[148]

There were two other things that are important for the understanding of the 'Europe of Agorai'. I have referred to them previously but thus far neglected to explain them: the role of the factual mass media and Wallström's understanding of the European public sphere. I will take each in turn.

The Role of the Media in the 'Europe of Agorai'

McNair argued that the factual mass media have five key functions in a democratic society. First, 'they must *inform* citizens of what is happening around them'[149]; second, 'they must *educate* as to the meaning and significance of the 'facts'"[150]; third, 'the media must provide a *platform* for public political discourse, facilitating the formation of 'public opinion', and feeding that opinion back to the public from whence it came. This must include the provision of space for the expression of *dissent,* without which the notion of democratic consensus would be meaningless'[151]; 'the media's fourth function is to give *publicity* to governmental and political institutions'[152] and fifth, 'the media in democratic societies serve as a channel for the *advocacy* of political viewpoints'.[153] Wallström's understanding of the factual mass media as having a democratic function was in some ways similar to McNair's. She argued that the factual mass media have the function 'that our democratic tradition has entrusted them: informing citizens in an independent, pluralistic and critical manner, on European issues as on domestic issues'.[154] For Wallström, particularly the public service broadcasters had a 'duty to scrutinise public policy', and in this role they needed to be 'at the service of democracy in Europe'.[155] During the fourth representation of European citizenship, the factual mass media were seen as a tool to empower citizens by enabling them to form an informed opinion, which in turn, would allow them to discuss policy issues and to scrutinise policy—and decision-makers. Accordingly, Wallström emphasised that she and the Commission had absolutely 'no intention of trying to tell [the media] what to say [because, as indicated above,] media freedom is essential to democracy'.[156] Subsequently, Wallström saw the Commission's role as limited to the provision of accurate and factual information—information which was relevant and avoided jargon. She also considered it essential that the Commission provided adequate technical facilities for the media to help them to cover EU news.[157] Wallström noted that 'broadcasters clearly want the Commission to help them provide informative, educational and entertaining programmes about European affairs as part of their public service mission. In all these ways, the Commission wants to encourage an informed public debate about the European Union and to engage in real dialogue with European citizens'[158] and insisted firmly on the need to 'respect completely media's editorial independence'.[159] As such, the Commission's role had to be limited to that of assisting the media in gathering information. At a conference she proposed the following: 'How about using our excellent pressroom to invite the various visiting groups from every corner of the Union that are in Brussels every week to meet with commissioners and ask them questions directly and face-to-face? We could translate into the relevant languages and send by satellite (EbS) across Europe, giving the people of Essen in Germany or Krakow in Poland a chance to see what their compatriots visiting Brussels are asking and talking about with the commissioners'[sic]'.[160] What this shows is that Wallström realised that the media could be seen as 'connective tissue of [European] democracy'[161] and concomitantly of the European citizenry. Once the media acts in this role it can be seen as able to stimulate debate. However, so the Commission argued, 'one of the factors currently constraining a citizens' debate on the European Union is the very limited coverage of EU information in the audiovisual media'[162] and as such, the Commission thought it necessary to 'increase coverage of EU affairs and thus help people to engage in a properly informed and democratic debate on EU policies'.[163]

Over the years there have been several attempts to encourage the creation of a European Public Service Broadcaster (PSB), all of which failed. Harrison argued that it is both necessary and plausible for the EU to develop an independent pan-European public news service, one which is self-conscious of the civil power of the news and which understands the news to be a public resource for people who are open to envisaging themselves in more solidarising terms in the context of the EU.[164] The series of interviews with senior Commission officials I conducted revealed a general consensus that the establishment of an EU PSB was important.[165] However, they equally listed a number of reasons for the impossibility of such an undertaking, ranging from financial issues[166] to the problem of organisation,[167] audience interest and legal issues. The latter was supported by various Commission officials who argued that (a) 'there is a challenge in doing anything about media at the European level because there is no treaty for establishing [a PSB]'[168] and that 'member states have been very careful to communitarise communication' [sic] and (b) 'you cannot just create media at an institutional level.[169] Rather, so another Commission official argued, 'media is something that is by nature (…) free and independent'[170] to which Wallström would add that 'these types of projects should be initiated but not by the EU institutions but by private partnership'.[171] Another argument was that it was much more effective to establish partnerships with national, regional and local media which citizens already routinely watch[172] than to create a PSB from scratch.

And in fact, this was exactly what Wallström encouraged: partnerships with media organisations. The Commission created EURANET, a European radio network, to 'increase the capacity to offer cross-border views of EU-related events and citizens' reactions [and to] reduce the purely national angles and allow for multilingualism and media pluralism'.[173] The establishment of EURANET was judged a success[174] and accordingly, the Commission was encouraged to extend partnerships to national, regional and local TV channels and establish a European TV network facilitating citizens' access to programmes on EU current.[175] This was considered vital because 'at present, public discussion is largely confined within national borders. The newspapers people read and the TV and radio programmes they consume are almost always produced for a national or regional audience—partly for reasons of language, of course'.[176] Consequently, partnerships with the national, regional and local public service media would, so Wallström hoped, help to bring the 'town square literally into our homes'.[177]

Wallström's understanding of the importance of factual mass media[178] for a European civil society resonated with Alexander's views, which I have previously referred to. At this point, we can add Alexander's argument that 'collective representations of such social relationships are broadcast by civil society institutions specializing in communicative (…) tasks. They institutionalize civil society by creating messages that translate general codes into situationally specific evaluation and descriptions'.[179] In other words, and following Alexander, '[F]or most members of civil society, and even for members of its institutional elites, the news is the only source of firsthand experience they will ever have about their fellow citizens, about their motives for acting in the way they do, the kind of relationships they form, and the nature of institutions they might potentially create'.[180] It was in this sense that the media could contribute to the realisation of Wallström's vision of 'human infrastructures'. Ultimately for Wallström, the factual mass media was 'a cornerstone' in helping to 'build a strengthened public sphere in Europe'.[181]

The European Public Sphere as the Manifestation of the Deliberative-Rational Style of Public Communication

One of the prime objectives of Wallström's public communication policy, which I have thus far neglected, was the creation of a European public sphere. I do not intend to review the immense literature that has been written in recent years about the public sphere and the possibility of a European public sphere[182]; instead, I want to focus on the way the Commission and Wallström understood a European public sphere and what it signified for a Civil Europe.

For Wallström, a European public sphere (or 'Europe-wide arena' or 'European public space') was synonymous with a place, to use her words again, where a 'European debate can unfold' and a 'genuine cross-border dialogue between citizens on issues of general concern, across language barriers and national borders' could be achieved. Accordingly, she argued that 'having achieved the internal market, the euro, borderless travel, we now need to fill the European idea with more democracy, genuine debate and active citizenry. This is the idea of a European public sphere'.[183] What she meant was that the hosting and conducting of pan-European debates concerned with the European project in all its diversity, which would take place in the media agorai as well as the inclusion of associative groupings (formal and informal) of (for the time being) nationally based civil societies, would contribute to the development of such a European Public Sphere. Wallström saw the ultimate expression of a European public sphere in a future 'debate and dialogue between a European civil society and European institutions'.[184] Wallström summarised these dialogues and debates within the EPS (both real and ideal) as 'informed' and the sphere as open to all, in which 'citizens are given the information and the tools to actively participate in the decision-making process and gain ownership of the European project'.[185] The term citizens meant 'the general public at large'.[186] For Wallström, as Calhoun had already argued, 'the importance of the public sphere lies in its potential as a mode of societal integration',[187] or as I would say, 'civil integration'. As a Commission official stated, the 'public sphere is a concept to create platforms either physically or virtually where people can debate and exchange their views on different topics concerning the European Union with different tools'[188] and as such a 'public sphere in modern terms [means that] people feel part of a common reality, project and (…) have the means and structures to discuss issues of common interest'.[189]

Further, for Wallström, a European public sphere was meant to provide civil-spatial European citizens in the 'Europe of Agorai' with the opportunity to feel more European by being part of the same European public sphere which would (she believed) potentially reinforce the 'imagined community' in which, 'in the minds of each, lives the image of their communion'.[190] According to Calhoun '(…) even Kantian notions of universality, cosmopolitanism, and science were constituted in the communication of rational beings' to which he added: 'When Kant called on Enlightenment thinkers to address the world, or to be men of the world, the public sphere was essential to its definition (…)'.[191] Analogically, when Wallström spoke of the public sphere she was addressing the citizens of the member states in their role as Europeans. In other words, she addressed a European public and invited it to debate in a European public sphere which, as Wallström put it, would be one 'of 27 Member States and of 23 languages (…), 3660 TV channels in Europe, of 25,000 journalists and of 480 million citizens'.[192] This was why the Commission considered it necessary that 'national public authorities, civil society, and the European Union institutions need to work together to develop Europe's place in the public sphere'.[193] It pointed to the problem that the public sphere within which political life has been taking place in Europe was largely a national sphere and that to the extent that European issues appeared on the agenda at all in those national spheres they were considered from exactly that: a national perspective. Indeed, the Commission claimed that the 'media remain largely national, partly due to language barriers; there are few meeting places where Europeans from different Member States can get to know each other and address issues of common interest'.[194] To redress this, Wallström considered it necessary not only to create physical and virtual meeting places for citizens but also 'to create space for European debate in the media (…)'.[195] As such, the media were considered part of the democratic infrastructures of Europe as a deliberative democracy and were meant to fulfil the purpose of providing citizens with the information they would need to be able to engage in debate.

Wallström's understanding of the European public sphere as a 'European debate' led to her prioritising the deliberative-rational style of public communication (in combination with the factual style of public communication) in the public communication of the 'Europe of Agorai' expressed through the idea of a constructive dialogue between European citizens and the EU institutions. According to Wallström and as already noted above, 'it is essential to speak *with* people, rather than talk *at* them'.[196] Hence, it mattered 'to engage in a dialogue' since 'communication can never be one-way'.[197] As such, the deliberative-rational style of public communication supported and put Wallström's understanding of the EU as a deliberative democracy into practise. In Wallström's words: 'My communication policy was linked to my understanding of democracy'[198] or alternatively expressed: 'Communicating Europe is not like selling socks or mobile phones. As far as I am concerned, communication is an indispensable element of democracy'.[199] In short: 'First dialogue—then decision. That's democracy—twenty-first-century democracy!'.[200]

The portrait of European citizens the Commission painted with its discourse can be summarised as follows: In the 'Europe of Agorai' (2005–2009), European citizens were understood to be intelligent and rational deliberators who were interested in and knowledgeable about European policies and who could act as a policy advisor to the Commission. The Commission imagined European citizens to be enthusiastic about the emerging possibilities in a deliberative Europe, its attendant new opportunities of involvement and about finally 'being taken seriously' by the Commission. European citizens were thought of as keenly wanting to debate Europe's future in the virtual fora and in the newly established physical European Public Spaces. In accordance with a time of network optimism and enthusiasm for its democratising potential, the Commission conceived of European citizens as sitting in front of their computer screens in deliberative virtual online fora debating the future of Europe with their fellow citizens across the EU. Sometimes, so the Commission hoped, these European citizens would readily pack their suitcases and impatiently make their way to Brussels to debate European policies and the future of the EU with relevant Commission officials. In other words, debate and dialogue in different forms of space gave, so it was thought, European citizens the possibility to debate European topics, to voice their own opinions and to reach a common consensus on the European project. Partnerships with local, regional and national radio stations and TV channels were enlisted to help bring the 'town squares of Europe' into the living rooms of European citizens so as to enable them to follow the European debate. It was further hoped by the Commission that civil society associations would also become excited about these new opportunities for involvement in European affairs. Indeed, the Commission went out of its way to sponsor and fund civil society projects that would attempt to put pan-European deliberation into practise. Civilly minded and believing to be perceived as lacking popular legitimacy and acceptance, the Commission wanted to give European citizens ownership of the European project.

The fourth representation of European citizenship 'Europe of Agorai' was short-lived and became obsolete with the end of Wallström's mandate as the following section will show.

3   From a 'Europe of Agorai' to a 'Europe of Rights'

Wallström's public communication approach was hindered by essentially four factors which ultimately led to a reinterpretation of the meaning of European citizenship and a change in the Commission's understanding of and approach to public communication.

The first factor was of a structural nature and concerned the position of DG COMM (a) within the Commission and (b) on the interinstitutional level. With regard to (a) its position within the Commission, DG COMM existed alongside the other 26 DGs and their independent and autonomous communication units and had to collaborate with all of these DGs in the attempt to issue coherent messages to the public and orchestrate public communication priorities. Whereas this collaboration could have led to 'the exchange of best practices on communication plans, tools and evaluation methods',[201] more often than not there was a risk of *'continuous fragmentation of communication activities* by insufficient coordination and planning [and] therefore losing efficiency',[202] as had been the case during the term of the Prodi Commission.[203] In order to avoid this fragmentation, Wallström asked the other communication services to ensure co-ordination with DG Communication. However, and with regard to the institutional hierarchy, DG COMM was not superior to other DGs, and as such, Wallström could not impose collaborative rules on the other communication units or control the other DGs' public communication outputs. Consequently, Wallström had to rely on the other DGs' willingness to cooperate on a voluntary basis, and accordingly her work and success depended on 'everyone else doing the right things'.[204]

With regard to (b) the interinstitutional level, DG COMM existed in parallel to the communication services of the other EU institutions such as the Council and the EP rather than being a central communication service which would formally communicate on behalf of the EU. However, and as her portfolio which gave her responsibility for Interinstitutional Relations imposed, Wallström tried to establish common rules that would help the EU to communicate with one voice. Correspondingly, in the White Paper, the Commission proposed a framework document in the form of a 'European Charter or Code of Conduct on Communication' to establish 'common principles and norms that should guide information and communication activities on European issues'.[205] The EP refused to adhere to such a code of conduct, even on a voluntary basis, because it considered that 'it [isn't] appropriate to submit the Parliament to a code of conduct that regulates its communication with EU citizens'[206] and insisted 'that any new instrument should respect the prerogatives of Parliament as an elected assembly, in particular its power to freely address citizens from across the Union'.[207] What this revealed was that the Parliament considered itself as directly legitimised by European citizens and as such disapproved of the Commission's attempts to submit the EP to common rules. Whereas these power struggles should not be overestimated, they cannot be ignored either. As noted in the previous chapter, the EP previously blocked the budget for public communication because it didn't agree with the Commission's public communication strategies and priorities. This also leads us to the second factor that hampered Wallström's public communication of the Europe of Agorai: the occasional resistance of the EP.

It appears that the EP and Wallström disagreed about whether and to what extent European citizens should be consulted and listened to in public debates. Whereas the Commission stated that 'any successful communication policy must centre on citizens' needs [and that it] should therefore focus on providing tools and facilities—the forums for debate and the channels of public communication—that will give as many people as possible access to information and the opportunity to make their voices heard', and that citizens should further 'have the opportunity for dialogue with the decision-makers',[208] the EP showed itself suspicious of the active involvement of European citizens in the European decision-making and policy-forming processes at the time and stated: 'However, it is not sensible to view citizens as the prime movers of participation and dialogue.

It would be pointless to listen carefully to what citizens had to say if they were ill informed. Before their input can serve a purpose, the European institutions have to find ways of passing on all the information that they need to involve themselves in, and identify with, the European project. Information must come first, otherwise no opinion is possible. Or at any rate, no useful opinion'.[209] Once again, the disputes need not to be overestimated. According to Wallström, it was the EP that offered more support for the Commission's approach to public communication than did the member states and the Council and as such, the EP was the institution Wallström managed to collaborate most with.[210]

Although the above factors certainly got in the way of the public communication of the 'Europe of Agorai', the remaining ones were more pertinent to the change of the representation of European citizenship.

The third factor was Wallström's lack of a legislative portfolio, which meant that she wasn't provided with any legislative power. In an interview in 2009, Wallström described the difficulties that were caused by her portfolio as follows: 'As environment commissioner, every week I had two or three files on the commission agenda [sic]. I had a given constituency. To come and do communication meant I had absolutely nothing. I did not have a legal base (...) I did not have a machinery that was up and running. I did not have the full commitment from everybody else.'[211] What the lack of legislative powers also meant was that Wallström had no competencies with regard to the formulation of public policies defining European citizenship. These were regarded as a matter for DG for Justice, Freedom and Security and remained disconnected from DG COMM. As such, Wallström was left with the task of communicating European citizenship without any political or legislative power over European citizenship policies. In other words, she hadn't any degree of influence on the area she was assigned to publicly communicate, which led to the results of citizens' deliberations having less influence on policies than Wallström had initially hoped.[212] Wallström summarised her term of office: 'I am proud of having done the sometimes boring and sometimes frustrating work of reforming the way the Commission works on [communication][213]', to which she added that she believed that 'the role of a Commissioner for Communication strategy would be strengthened if communication policy was linked to other aspects of citizenship in the Commission; the citizenship programme (EAC), citizens' rights (JLS) and relations with NGOs, and the new citizens' initiative, for example. If the next College were to name a Commissioner for Citizenship and Communication, it would be an important signal in itself that Europe is continuing to take these issues seriously'.[214]

The fourth factor was the alleged inappropriateness of Wallström's approach in the context of the European economic crisis and the ratification of the Lisbon Treaty. Through a series of interviews with senior Commission officials which I conducted in 2009 and 2011, I was able to gain insights into how the Commission understood the differences of the political, institutional and economic contexts of the Barroso I Commission (2004–09), on the one hand, and the Barroso II Commission (2010–14), on the other, and how these different contexts impacted upon the understanding and public communication of European citizenship.

There was an overall consensus amongst Commission officials that context matters for EU Politics and that the economic and political contexts often determine institutional priorities. More specifically, the Barroso I Commission started its term of office after the enlargement from the EU-15 to the EU-25, which meant that the Commission had '[to navigate in] a completely different environment, both internally as well as externally'.[215] In addition, it was the Barroso I Commission under which the ratification of the Constitutional Treaty failed and that had to overcome the subsequent Constitutional Crisis and 'the big (...) challenge (...) to communicate after the French and Dutch referendum' with European citizens in a climate where 'there was a general sort of question mark put on the democratic accountability of the EU'. This context made it 'very important to engage with the citizen, I would almost say regardless of the subject (...)'.[216]

The lack of a legislative portfolio as well as the political context meant was that Wallström had to devise an approach that would increase the democratic legitimacy, that is, the popular acceptance of the EU itself and consensus about the future course of European integration. According to Joachim Ott, a senior Commission official, the approach Wallström 'tried to stipulate was (...) much more open and (...) the ownership for the debate was meant to be much more with citizens and their organisations. The price for that was a certain vagueness'.[217] It was an approach that some Commission officials judged too theoretical and not sufficiently practically oriented: 'Wallström had a (...) broad theoretical approach. It was fine because it [established] (...) the theoretical bases [for public communication and deliberation] but it had to be implemented'.[218] What these comments point to is that there was a doubt among Commission officials about the practical sustainability of pan-European deliberation in terms of financial and human resources as well as of time investment. For example, and as Luskin who, together with Fishkin, conducted the first EU-wide deliberative poll (DP) pointed out: 'In everyday life, most people do not know or think much about politics', to which he adds that the poll shows 'what EU citizens would think (…) if they knew, thought and talked much more about these issues'.[219] Indeed, according to the DP results 72% of the participating European citizens did not think of themselves as European but '"as just being from" their own country'[220] and the reason why they participated was that the 'survey researchers would (…) stay in touch with the initial sample, offer them financial incentives to participate, pay for their transportation, meals, and hotels'. The point here is simply that deliberative democracy in the EU would need to be moderated, organised and promoted through direct contact and incentives and that any attempt to involve European citizens in debate without these incentives would only lead to events attended by professors and would-be Eurocrats.[221] In short: it would cater merely to those who are 'already interested'.

Thus, anyone committing to pan-European deliberation would face the challenge of dealing with the following criticisms: (a) deliberation is costly; (b) deliberation needs to be accompanied by substantial institutional changes and (c) pan-European deliberation can only be sustained through a long-term effort. Wallström was aware of these criticisms. She argued that deliberation could only be realised as part of a 'long term democratic reform process'[222] and that establishing a genuine European deliberative democracy would not 'simply require a little consultation for a short period [but] commitment for years to come',[223] also in terms of the gradual adjustment of current institutional structures.

In 2010, when the Barroso I Commission entered office, the political and economic context was different for two reasons: first, because of the European economic crisis and second, because of the Lisbon Treaty. Both urged the Commission to send out clear and focused messages to the European public.[224] According to a Commission official, the Commission was 'dealing with the biggest economic crisis we had in our, in some cases, in our lifetime. So priorities change and the way we communicate changes as well'.[225] Another Commission official pointed out that 'the Lisbon Treaty changed the nature of the European Union but also changed the responsibilities of the EU as the Treaty especially puts the citizens at the centre. If you look at what it is that we are doing in Brussels, everything we do, we do it for the citizens to ensure (…) that they enjoy all the rights as European citizens and that the Single Market is enjoyed for their benefit. So basically when we entered into force with the Treaty of Lisbon the time for institutional introspection was over and we needed to focus on policy delivery and results',[226] be 'pragmatic' and more concerned with 'efficiency'.[227] Alternatively expressed, the Barroso II Commission was advised to 'focus on giving concrete meaning to EU citizenship (…) to EU citizens' rights'.[228]

The entry into force of the Lisbon Treaty (2009) and the subsequent creation of an autonomous DG Justice[229] as well as the new focus on practical results led to the emergence of the fifth representation of European citizenship: civil-legal European citizenship in a what I call 'Europe of Rights'.

Notes

1. I am grateful that Margot Wallström and one of her close collaborators during her mandate (2004–2009) have read and endorsed an earlier version of this chapter in terms of its accuracy.
2. With regard to politics, Wallström's political career in Sweden included experience as a member of the Swedish Parliament (1979–1985) as well as Minister of Civil Affairs (1988–1991), of Culture (1994–1996) and of Social Affairs (1996–1998). From 1999 to 2004, Wallström served as Commissioner for Environment under the Prodi Commission and was elected EU Commissioner of the Year in 2002 by the European Voice newspaper. With regard to her media experience, Wallström was CEO of TV Värmland (Regional TV network) from 1993 to 1994, and when she retired from Swedish politics in 1998 Wallström became Executive Vice-President of Worldview Global Media based in Sri Lanka (1998/1999).
3. Wallström (2004a: 1).
4. Vitorino (personal communication 14 March 2012) pointed to the importance of interinstitutional cooperation in the Commission's public communication. In the late 1990s, the EP's dissatisfaction with the Commission's approach to public communication had led the EP to block the budget and subsequently to a deadlock in public communication—which was then solved in 2001 (see Chap. 4).
5. Commission (2012a).
6. Wallström (2004b: 3), see also Wallström (2005a).
7. Wallström (2004a: 1).
8. Wallström (2004b: 3).
9. EP (2004).
10. See Commission (2010a).

11. Barroso also estimated that the ratification of the Constitutional Treaty would 'generate a wide-ranging debate across the continent on the meaning of the Union for our peoples'; also see Commission (2010b).
12. Wallström (2004a: 2).
13. On the Constitutional crisis on the Commission's subsequent understanding of public debate and the European public, see Pukallus (forthcoming).
14. On the failure of ratification of the Constitutional Treaty, see Wallström (2006e).
15. Commission (2005a).
16. CVCE (2012).
17. Commission (2005a: 2).
18. Ibid.
19. Wallström (2004b: 9).
20. Calhoun (2003: 243).
21. Ibid.
22. I follow Wallström here in using the terms 'participative' and 'deliberative' democracy as synonyms.
23. Commission (2005a: 2).
24. Wallström (2006c: 2).
25. Wallström (2007b: 5).
26. Wallström (2007b: 4).
27. Wallström (2005c).
28. Wallström (2007b).
29. Wallström (2006a: 4).
30. Wallström (2007b: 5).
31. I use public debate and debate synonymously.
32. Wallström (2005k: 3).
33. Wallström (2005i: 3, 2005j: 5) and Commission (2005a: 2).
34. Wallström (2005i: 3, 2005j: 5) and Commission (2005a: 8).
35. Wallström (2004c: 4).
36. Commission (2005a: 8).
37. Commission (2006: 4).
38. Wallström (2005i: 3, 2005j: 5).
39. Wallström (2005d: 2).
40. Wallström (2005g) and Commission (2005a).
41. Wallström (2005k: 3).
42. Wallström (2007d: 3, also 2008a: 5).
43. See Wallström (2007d: 3).
44. Wallström (2007c: 2).
45. Commission (2006: 5).
46. Wallström (2006b: 2).

47. Wallström (2008b: 2).
48. Wallström (2009d: 2).
49. Wallström (2008b: 2, 2009a: 2).
50. Wallström (2005e: 2).
51. Wallström (2005g: 5).
52. Ibid.
53. 'Laypersons summaries' are also known as citizens' summaries. For examples of citizens' summaries, see Commission (2010c or 2012b).
54. Commission (2005b: 18).
55. Wallström (2005k: 3).
56. Commission (2006: 6).
57. Commission (2005a).
58. On the European Transparency Initiative, see Commission (2005c).
59. Wallström (2004b).
60. Commission (2005a: 9).
61. Commission (2005a: 4).
62. Wallström (2004b: 3).
63. Ibid.
64. Pukallus (forthcoming).
65. Tully (2008).
66. Wallström (2006b: 2).
67. Wallström (2007a: 3).
68. Wallström (2005k: 3).
69. Wallström (2008c: 5).
70. Wallström (2005f: 2).
71. Wallström (2005h: 3).
72. Ibid.
73. Wallström (2004c: 4).
74. Wallström (2008c).
75. Wallström (2005c).
76. Wallström (2004b: 9, 2005k, 2008c).
77. Wallström (2005k: 3).
78. Commission (2005a: 6).
79. Commission (2006: 4).
80. Wallström (2005h: 2).
81. Wallström (2005c, 2007d).
82. Wallström (2006f: 3).
83. Wallström, personal communication, 19 January 2012.
84. Gallup and Rae (1940: 15).
85. Alexander (2006: 73).
86. Gallup and Rae (1940: 8).
87. Wallström (2006f: 2).

88. Wallström (2005g: 5, 2004c).
89. Wallström (2005g: 5).
90. Taylor (2004: 88).
91. Tocqueville (2000: 216).
92. Commission (2005b: 3).
93. Ibid.: 3.
94. Wallström (2007c: 2).
95. Wallström (2009c: 2).
96. Wallström (2005k: 3).
97. Wallström (2009b: 3).
98. Tocqueville (2000: 210).
99. Wallström (2005k: 3).
100. Risse (2009: 149).
101. Wallström, personal communication, 19 January 2012.
102. Wallström (2007b: 5).
103. Wallström (2009b: 2). On the Commission's 'democratic experimentalism', see Abels (2009), on EU deliberation during see Boussaguet and Dehousse (2008), Hüller (2010), Saurugger (2010) and Kies and Nanz (eds.) (2013). It is interesting that Viviane Reding wrote the foreword to Kies's and Nanz's edited volume on EU deliberation and the experimental nature of these deliberations because, as I will show in the following chapter, by 2013 (when the book was published) she had already discontinued the Commission's 'democratic-deliberative experimentalism'.
104. Ibid.
105. Wallström (2004b, c, 2005j, k).
106. Wallström (2004c: 4, 2006a, 2007b, c) and Commission (2005a, 2006).
107. Wallström (2006a: 4, 2006d).
108. Wallström (2007d: 4).
109. Wallström (2006a: 4).
110. Wallström (2004c).
111. Wallström (2007c: 2).
112. Wallström (2004c: 4).
113. Ibid.
114. Wallström also considered turning Terezin into 'such a meeting place for people from the whole of Europe. This location in the Czech Republic was the site of the Nazi concentration camp Theresienstadt. Now it can become a place where individuals and groups can exchange views, whether they are groups of teachers, trade unionists, young people or bus drivers; in short, a people's university to discuss the future of Europe'. However, this project of a European Public Space in Terezin was never realised. (Interview with Jürgen Wettig, additional personal communication, 18 June 2011).

115. Commission (2007a: 8).
116. Interview with Jürgen Wettig, then Head of Directorate B 'Representations', 14 February 2011.
117. Ibid.
118. Ibid.
119. Commission (2006: 4).
120. Commission (2007b: 4).
121. Commission (2005a: 3).
122. Ibid.: 10.
123. Interview with Waterfield (2006).
124. Commission (2005a: 12).
125. Wallström (2004b: 8).
126. Euréval et al. (2009) and Commission (2008a).
127. Commission (2008a: 5).
128. Ibid.
129. See ECC (no date a).
130. For a report on a conference held after the EEC, see European Citizens Action Service (2007).
131. See Public Participation Case Studies (no date).
132. ECC (no date b).
133. Ibid.
134. See Public Participation Case Studies (no date).
135. Ibid.
136. Ibid.
137. Fishkin (2009: 81).
138. Ibid.
139. Ibid.: 176.
140. Goldberger (2009: xi).
141. Ibid.: 15.
142. Soja (1971 in Gale and Moore 1975: 30).
143. Lefebvre (1991).
144. Interview with Member of the Cabinet of former Vice-President Margot Wallström (date and name confidential).
145. Sandel (2005: 34).
146. Ibid.
147. Wallström (2005b: 3).
148. Ricœur (2000: 8).
149. McNair (2011: 18).
150. Ibid.: 19.
151. Ibid.
152. Ibid.
153. Ibid.: 20, all emphases in the original.

154. Wallström (2006g: 3).
155. Wallström (2006h: 1).
156. Wallström (2005e: 3).
157. See Wallström (2005f).
158. Wallström (2007c: 5).
159. Wallström (2005f: 3).
160. Wallström (2005e: 5). She further said that that she 'would also like to have a more regular dialogue with you, like this opportunity [and therefore] consider[s] inviting you [the journalists and media specialists], every year, to propose programmes aimed at national or regional audiences and describing how EU policies affect ordinary people. For 2006 we are considering significantly increasing the budget for calls for proposals of this kind, so that as many as 70 TV stations and 100 radio broadcasters could be involved. The best proposals would be awarded a contract and we would place at your disposal the Commission's technical facilities' (ibid.).
161. Mughan and Gunter (2000: 1).
162. Commission (2008b: 4).
163. Ibid.: 11.
164. Harrison (2010a, b).
165. Interviews with a member of the Cabinet of former Vice-President Margot Wallström, Commission official DG COMM Directorate B Representations, B1 Geographical Coordination; a member of the spokesperson service, Commission official DG COMM Directorate C Multimedia Communication (all of the names of the interviewees and dates of the interviews are confidential) and Michael Hager, member of the Cabinet of former Vice-President Margot Wallström, 3 December 2009.
166. Interview with a Commission official DG COMM Directorate B Representations, B1 Geographical Coordination, a member of the spokesperson service (all of the names of the interviewees and dates of the interviews are confidential) and Claus Sorensen, Director General of DG COMM until 2011, 24 January 2011.
167. Interview with a Commission official DG COMM Directorate B Representations, B1 Geographical Coordination (name of the interviewee and date of the interview are confidential).
168. Interviews with Claus Sorensen, 24 January 2011; Commission official DG COMM Directorate B Representations, B1 Geographical Coordination and a member of the spokesperson service (name of the interviewees and date of the interviews are confidential).
169. Interview with Claus Sorensen, 24 January 2011.
170. Interview Commission official DG COMM, C1 Citizens' Information (name of the interviewee and date of the interview are confidential).

171. Wallström (2005f: 4).
172. Interviews with Commission official DG COMM Directorate B Representations, B1 Geographical Coordination and a member of the spokesperson service (name of the interviewees and date of the interviews are confidential).
173. Commission (2008b: 7).
174. Member of the public communication team (DG JUS, name of interviewee and date of interview are confidential).
175. See Wallström (2009f) on this.
176. Wallström (2005e: 2 and personal communication, 19 January 2012).
177. Wallström (2006h: p. 2). In addition to these partnerships, several initiatives were addressed at media professionals such as the EU events calendar, the EU audiovisual library and Europe by Satellite (EbS). However, EbS was received in a critical way by the media and consequently, the Commission's 'commitment to explore setting up a "news agency" was dropped' (Wallström in an interview with Waterfield 2006) and media initiatives came to a halt.
178. In one speech Wallström (2005e) indicates awareness of the importance of the fictional mass media when she endorses an idea in favour of the creation of a European version of "The West Wing" TV soap opera.
179. Alexander (2006: 70).
180. Alexander (2006: 80).
181. Wallström (2005f: 4).
182. The debates on the meaning of the concept currently seem to centre on the Habermasian' conception of a public sphere as a bourgeois 'sphere of private people coming together as a public' (Habermas (1989): 27) in the 18th century and as representing a 'public which practices the art of critical-rational public debate' (ibid.: 29). For alternate approaches one can consult, for example, Benhabib (1992), Fraser (1992) and Kramer (1992). The current debate on the meaning of European public sphere (EPS) can be subdivided into four categories. The first category advocates the need for a single European public sphere and discusses its (im-)possibility (see e.g. Gerhards (1993), van de Steeg (2002, 2010), Eriksen (2005)), the second discusses the EPS as an ensemble of segmented and fragmented public spheres (see e.g. Schlesinger (1999, 2003, 2007); Baisnée (2007)), the third understands the EPS as a network of public spheres (see e.g. Eder and Trenz (2004); Friedland et al. (2006); Bello and Bee (2009)) and the fourth category primarily looks at the Europeanisation of national public spheres (see e.g. Trenz (2004); Koopmans (2007); Machill et al. (2006); Lauristin (2007); Brüggemann and Kleinen-von-Königslöw (2009)). Also McKee (2005), Bee (2014), Fishkin et al. (2014), Risse (2010) and Risse (ed.) (2014).

183. Wallström (2006a: 4).
184. Interview Commission official DG Justice, Directorate C Fundamental Rights and Citizenship (name of interviewee and date of interview are confidential).
185. Commission (2005a: 2), interview member of the spokesperson service (name of interviewee and date of interview are confidential).
186. Wallström (personal communication, 19 January 2012).
187. Calhoun (1992: 6).
188. Interview Commission official DG COMM, C1 Citizens' Information (name of interviewee and date of interview are confidential).
189. Interview Member of the Cabinet of Vice-President Margot Wallström (name of interviewee and date of interview are confidential).
190. Anderson (2006: 6) and Morley and Robins (1995).
191. Calhoun (1992: 18).
192. Wallström (2008c: 6).
193. Commission (2006: 5).
194. See ibid.: 4.
195. Wallström (2006a: 4).
196. Wallström (2004b: 6 emphasis in the original).
197. Ibid.
198. Wallström, personal communication, 19 January 2012.
199. Wallström (2009e: 2).
200. Wallström (2009b: 4).
201. Commission (2005b: 6).
202. Ibid.: 4, emphasis in the original.
203. Anderson and Price (2008).
204. Mahoney (2009) on Wallström; Wallström, personal communication, 19 January (2012). Also Smith (2007), Martins et al. (2012) and Bjismans (2014).
205. Commission (2006: 6).
206. (EP 2006: 5).
207. Ibid.: 6.
208. Commission (2006: 6).
209. EP (2006: 12).
210. Wallström (personal communication 19 January 2012).
211. Mahoney (2009).
212. Also see Smith (2013).
213. Ibid.
214. See Wallström (2009c).
215. Interview Commission official DG COMM, C1 Citizens' Information (name of interviewee and date of interview are confidential).
216. Interview Claus Sorensen, 24 January 2011.

217. Interview Joachim Ott, then Deputy Head of Unit at European Commission, DG Communication—Citizens' Policy Unit C2 of Directorate C, 12 January 2011.
218. Interview Commission official Directorate A Communication Actions (name of interviewee and date of interview are confidential).
219. Centre for Deliberative Democracy (2009).
220. Ibid.
221. Moravcsik (2005). Moravcsik makes this point with regard to the deliberative events organised in the preparation of the ratification of the Constitutional Treaty.
222. Wallström (2006c: 2).
223. Wallström (2005b: 2).
224. Interviews Commission official DG Justice, Directorate C Fundamental Rights and Citizenship and DG COMM, C1 Citizens' Information (names of interviewees and dates of interview are confidential); Claus Sorensen (24 January 2011) and Joachim Ott (12 January 2011).
225. Interviews Commission officials DG COMM, C1 Citizens' Information and DG COMM, Directorate C 'Citizens' (names of interviewees and dates of interview are confidential).
226. Interview Telmo Baltazar, Member of the private cabinet of Vice-President Viviane Reding, 2 February 2011.
227. Interview Commission official Directorate A Communication Actions (name of interviewee and date of interview confidential).
228. Interview Commission official Citizenship Unit, DG Justice (name of interviewee and date of interview confidential).
229. When the Barroso II Commission was constituted, the former DG for Justice, Freedom and Security was spilt into two separate DGs: DG Justice and DG HOME. It is to the former that 'Fundamental Rights and Union Citizenship' were attached.

References

Abels, G. (2009). Citizens' deliberations and the EU democratic deficit. Is there a model for participatory democracy? *Tübinger Arbeitspapiere zur Integrationsforschung*, TAIF Nr. 1/2009.
Alexander, J. (2006). *The civil sphere*. Oxford: Oxford University Press.
Anderson, B. (2006). *Imagined communities*. London: Verso.
Anderson, P., & Price, J. (2008). An evaluation of the press and communication reforms of the Prodi Commission of 1999—2004. With particular reference to UK Europhile and Eurosceptic journalists' perceptions of their impact. *European Journal of Communication, 23*(1), 29–46.

Baisnée, O. (2007). The European public sphere does not exist (at least it's worth wondering…). *European Journal of Communication, 22*(4), 493–503.

Bee, C. (2014). Transnationalisation, public communication and active citizenship. The emergence of a fragmented and fluid European public sphere. *Sociology Compass, 8*(8), 1018–1032.

Bello, V., & Bee, C. (2009). A European model of the public sphere: Towards a networked governance model. In J. Harrison & B. Wessels (Eds.), *Mediating Europe: New media, mass communications and the European public sphere* (pp. 128–149). Oxford: Berghahn.

Benhabib, S. (1992). Models of public space: Hannah Arendt, the liberal tradition, and Jürgen Habermas. In C. Calhoun (Ed.), *Habermas and the public sphere* (pp. 73–98). Cambridge: MIT Press.

Bijsmans, P. (2014). The Commission, the politics of information, and the European public sphere. In T. Blom & S. Vanhoonacker (Eds.), *The politics of information. The case of the European Union* (pp. 179–192). Basingstoke: Palgrave Macmillan.

Boussaguet, L., & Dehousse, R. (2008). *Lay people's Europe—A critical assessment of the first EU citizens' conferences.* (European Governance Papers, no. C-08-02).

Brüggemann, M., & Kleinen-von Königslöw, K. (2009). Let's talk about Europe: Why Europeanization shows a different face in different newspapers. *European Journal of Communication, 24*(1), 27–48.

Calhoun, C. (1992). Introduction: Habermas and the public sphere. In C. Calhoun (Ed.), *Habermas and the public sphere* (pp. 1–48). Cambridge: MIT Press.

Calhoun, C. (2003). The democratic integration of Europe: Interests, identity, and the public sphere. In M. Berezin & M. Schain (Eds.), *Europe without borders: Re-mapping territory, citizenship and identity in a transnational age* (pp. 243–274). London: Sage.

CCE (Commission des Communautés Européennes). (2005a, October 13). *Plan-D for democracy, dialogue and debate* (COM (2005) 494 final).

CCE (Commission des Communautés Européennes). (2005b, July 20). *Action plan to improve communicating Europe by the Commission* (SEC (2005) 985 final).

CCE (Commission des Communautés Européennes). (2005c, November 9). *European transparency initiative* (SEC (2005) 1300/6).

CCE (Commission des Communautés Européennes). (2006, February 1). *White paper on a European communication policy* (COM (2006) 35 final).

CCE (Commission des Communautés Européennes). (2007a, October 3). *Communication on communicating Europe in partnership* (COM (2007) 568 final).

CCE (Commission des Communautés Européennes). (2007b, December 21). *Communicating about Europe via the Internet. Engaging the citizens* (COM (2007) 1742 final).

CCE (Commission des Communautés Européennes). (2008a, April 2). *Debate Europe* (COM (2008) 158/4).
CCE (Commission des Communautés Européennes). (2008b, April 24). *Communication on communicating Europe through audiovisual media* (SEC (2008) 506/2).
CCE (Commission des Communautés Européennes). (2010a). Communicating the constitution. http://ec.europa.eu/archives/commission_2004-2009/wallstrom/pdf/communicating_constitution_en.pdf. Accessed 2 July 2011.
CCE (Commission des Communautés Européennes). (2010b). The members of the Barroso Commission (2004–2009). http://ec.europa.eu/archives/commission_2004-2009/index_en.htm. Accessed 14 July 2012.
CCE (Commission des Communautés Européennes). (2010c). Margot Wallström, Vice-President of the European Commission—Key documents. http://ec.europa.eu/archives/commission_2004-2009/wallstrom/keydocs_en.htm. Accessed 7 July 2011.
CCE (Commission des Communautés Européennes). (2012a). Culture 'European capital of culture'. http://ec.europa.eu/culture/our-programmes-and-actions/doc413_en.htm. Accessed 12 Jan 2012.
CCE (Commission des Communautés Européennes). (2012b). Summaries of EU legislation. http://europa.eu/legislation_summaries/index_en.htm. Accessed 7 July 2011.
Centre for Deliberative Democracy. (2009, June 3). *EuroPolis proves that debate does change European citizens' attitudes.* Press release.
CVCE. (2012). Declaration by the heads of state or government on the ratification of the treaty establishing a constitution for Europe (Brussels, 16 and 17 June 2005). http://www.cvce.eu/obj/declaration_by_the_heads_of_state_or_government_on_the_ratification_of_the_treaty_establishing_a_constitution_for_europe_brussels_16_and_17_june_2005-en-6f48b533-b2e1-437e-a01b-0d762b593c08.html. Accessed 25 July 2012.
Eder, K., & Trenz, H.-J. (2004). The democratising dynamics of a European public sphere. Towards a theory of democratic functionalism. *European Journal of Social Theory, 7*(1), 5–25.
EP. (2004, October 6). *Response to hearing of Wallström 2004* (AFCO (2004) D/41922). http://www.europarl.europa.eu/hearings/commission/2004_comm/pdf/lt_wallstrom_en.pdf. Accessed 5 Apr 2015.
EP. (2006, October 17). Report on the white paper on a European communication policy (Herrero Report).
Eriksen, E. (2005). An emerging European public sphere. *European Journal of Social Theory, 8*(3), 341–363.
Euréval, et al. (2009). Evaluation of the Plan D/Debate Europe citizen consultations projects. Report. http://ec.europa.eu/dgs/communication/about/evaluation/documents/2009-debate-europe_en.pdf . Accessed 15 Jan 2015.

European Citizens Action Service. (2007). Is the EU really listening to citizens? The ABC of participatory democracy methods. Report on the conference following the European Citizen Consultations in Brussels, 3 Oct 2007.
European Citizens' Consultations. (no date a). European citizens' summit. http://ecc.european-citizens-consultations.eu/74.0.html. Accessed 5 July 2012.
European Citizens' Consultations. (no date b). Project outline. http://www.vitalizing-democracy.org/site/downloads/219_265_ECC_09_Project_Description_final.pdf. Accessed 14 July 2012.
Fishkin, J. (2009). *When the people speak: Deliberative democracy and public consultation.* Oxford: Oxford University Press.
Fishkin, J., Luskin, R., & Siu, A. (2014). Europolis and the European public sphere: Empirical explorations of a counterfactual ideal. *European Union Politics, 15*(3), 328–351.
Fraser, N. (1992). Rethinking the public sphere. In C. Calhoun (Ed.), *Habermas and the public sphere* (pp. 109–142). Cambridge, MA: MIT Press.
Friedland, L., et al. (2006). The networked public sphere. *Javnost/The Public, 13*(4), 5–26.
Gale, S., & Moore, E. G. (Eds.). (1975). *The manipulated city: Perspectives on spatial structure and social issues in urban America.* Chicago: Maaroufa Press.
Gallup, G., & Rae, S. F. (1940). *The pulse of democracy: The public-opinion poll and how it works.* New York: Simon and Schuster.
Gerhards, J. (1993). Westeuropäische Integration und die Schwierigkeiten der Entstehung einer europäischen Öffentlichkeit. *Zeitschrift für Soziologie, 2,* 96–110.
Goldberger, P. (2009). *Why architecture matters.* New Haven: Yale University Press.
Habermas, J. (1989). *The structural transformation of the public sphere: An inquiry into a category of bourgeois society.* Cambridge, MA: MIT Press.
Harrison, J. (2010a). European social purpose and public service communication. In C. Bee & E. Bozzini (Eds.), *Mapping the European public sphere: Institutions, media and civil society* (pp. 99–116). Aldershot: Ashgate Publishing.
Harrison, J. (2010b). The development of a European civil society through EU public service communication. In S. Papathanassopoulos & R. Negrine (Eds.), *Towards a theory of communication policy* (pp. 81–94). London: Palgrave Macmillan.
Hüller, T. (2010). Playground or democratisation? New participatory procedures at the European Commission. *Swiss Political Science Review, 16*(1), 77–107.
Kies, R., & Nanz, P. (Eds.). (2013). *Is Europe listening to us? Successes and failures of EU citizen consultations.* Farnham: Ashgate.
Koopmans, R. (2007). Who inhabits the European public sphere? Winners and losers, supporters and opponents in Europeanised political debates. *European Journal of Political Research, 46*(2), 183–210.

Kramer, L. (1992). Habermas, history, and critical history. In C. Calhoun (Ed.), *Habermas and the public sphere* (pp. 236–258). Cambridge, MA: MIT Press.
Lauristin, M. (2007). The European public sphere and the social imaginary of the 'New Europe'. *European Journal of Communication, 22*(4), 397–412.
Lefebvre, C. (1991). *The production of space*. Malden: Blackwell.
Machill, M., et al. (2006). Europe-topics in Europe's media—The debate about the European public sphere: A meta-analysis of media content analyses. *European Journal of Communication, 21*(1), 57–88.
Mahony, H. (2009). Wallström: EU needs a commissioner for citizens [sic]. http://euobserver.com/political/28598. Accessed 18 July 2011.
Martins, A. I., Lecheler, S., & De Vreese, C. (2012). Information flow and communication deficit: Perceptions of Brussels-based correspondents and EU officials. *Journal of European Integration, 34*(4), 305–322.
McKee, A. (2005). *The public sphere: An introduction*. Cambridge: Cambridge University Press.
McNair, B. (2011). *An introduction to political communication* (5th ed.). London: Routledge.
Moravcsik, A. (2005). Europe without illusions: A category mistake. *Prospect*, Issue 112, July. http://www.prospect-magazine.co.uk/article_details.php?id=6939. Accessed 12 Mar 2010.
Morley, D., & Robins, K. (1995). *Spaces of identity. Global media, electronic landscapes and cultural boundaries*. Abingdon: Routledge.
Mughan, A., & Gunther, R. (2000). The media in democratic and nondemocratic regimes: A multilevel perspective. In A. Mughan & R. Gunther (Eds.), *Democracy and the media: A comparative perspective* (pp. 1–27). Cambridge: Cambridge University Press.
Public Participation Case Studies. (no date). European citizens consultation 2009. http://www.peopleandparticipation.net/pages/viewpage.action?pageId=27788161&showChildren=false&decorator=printable. Accessed 14 July 2012.
Pukallus. (forthcoming). The European Commission's two versions of public debate 1993–2013 and its corresponding conceptions of the EU and European citizenship. Unpublished paper.
Ricœur, P. (2000). *The just*. Chicago: University of Chicago Press.
Risse, T. (2009). Social constructivism and European integration. In A. Wiener & T. Diez (Eds.), *European integration theory* (2nd ed., pp. 159–176). Oxford: Oxford University Press.
Risse, T. (2010). *A community of Europeans?: Transnational identities and public spheres*. Ithaca/London: Cornell University Press.
Risse, T. (Ed.). (2014). *European public spheres. Politics is back*. Cambridge: Cambridge University Press.
Sandel, M. (2005). *Public philosophy: Essays on morality and politics*. Cambridge, MA: London: Harvard University Press.

Saurugger, S. (2010). The social construction of the participatory turn: The emergence of a norm in the European Union. *European Journal of Political Research*, *49*(4), 471–495.

Schlesinger, P. (1999). Changing spaces of political communication: The case of the European Union. *Political Communication*, *16*(3), 263–279.

Schlesinger, P. (2003). The Babel of Europe? An essay on networks and communicative spaces (ARENA Working Paper 22/03). http://www.sv.uio.no/arena/english/research/publications/arena-publications/workingpapers/workingpapers2003/wp03_22.pdf. Accessed 23 Feb 2010.

Schlesinger, P. (2007). A cosmopolitan temptation. *European Journal of Communication*, *22*(4), 413–426.

Smith, A. (2007). European commissioners and the prospects of a European public sphere: Information, representation and legitimacy. In J. E. Fossum & P. Schlesinger (Eds.), *The European Union and the public sphere: A communicative space in the making?* (pp. 227–245). London: Routledge.

Smith, G. (2013). Designing democratic innovations at the European level: Lessons from the experiments. In R. Kies & P. Nanz (Eds.), *Is Europe listening to us? Successes and failures of EU citizen consultations* (pp. 201–216). Farnham: Ashgate.

Soja, E. W. (1971). The political organization of space in metropolitan areas. In S. Gale & E. G. Moore (Eds.), *The manipulated city: Perspectives on spatial structure and social issues in urban America* (pp. 27–38). Chicago: Maaroufa Press.

Taylor, C. (2004). *Modern social imaginaries*. Durham/London: Duke University Press.

Tocqueville, A. (2000[1835]). *Democracy in America*. New York: Bantam Classic.

Trenz, H.-J. (2004). Media coverage on European governance: Exploring the European public sphere in national quality newspapers. *European Journal of Communication*, *19*(3), 291–319.

Tully, J. (2008). *Public philosophy in a new key: II. Imperialism and civic freedom*. Cambridge: Cambridge University Press.

Van de Steeg, M. (2002). Rethinking the conditions for a public sphere in the European Union. *European Journal of Social Theory*, *5*(4), 499–519.

Van de Steeg, M. (2010). Theoretical reflections on the public sphere in the European Union: A network of communication or a political community? In C. Bee & E. Bozzini (Eds.), *Mapping the European public sphere: Institutions, media and civil society* (pp. 31–46). Aldershot: Ashgate Publishing.

Wallström, M. (2004a). European Parliament hearings. Answers to the questionnaire for Commissioner-Designate Ms Margot WALLSTRÖM (Institutional relations & communication strategy) Part B—Specific questions.

Wallström, M. (2004b). European Parliament hearings. Speech by Margot Wallström, Commissioner-Designate for Institutional Relations and Communications.

Wallström, M. (2004c, November 25). *More democracy, more rights—We need the constitution for Europe.* (SPEECH/04/496). European Parliament, Constitutional Affairs Committee, Brussels.

Wallström, M. (2005a, January 11). *Opening remarks to the European Parliament 0070lenary, Corbett/Mendez de Vigo report* (SPEECH/05/5). Strasbourg.

Wallström, M. (2005b, March 10). *Being Irish, being European, being human* (SPEECH/05/165). Dublin.

Wallström, M. (2005c, April 6). *For better partnership with civil society* (SPEECH/05/202). Brussels.

Wallström, M. (2005d, April 7). *Why the constitution is needed for social Europe* (SPEECH/05/209). Brussels.

Wallström, M. (2005e, April 20). *Putting the EU in the picture* (SPEECH/05/246). Brussels.

Wallström, M. (2005f, May 24). *Media—A key partner in communicating Europe* (SPEECH/05/296).

Wallström, M. (2005g, June 28). *Communicating a Europe in stormy waters: Plan D* (SPEECH/05/396). Brussels.

Wallström, M. (2005h, June 30). *Relays: A central help to listen to citizens* (SPEECH/05/403). Brussels.

Wallström, M. (2005i, October 3). *Plan D* (SPEECH/05/573). Brussels.

Wallström, M. (2005j, October 4). *Need to stimulate a wider debate with the public.* (SPEECH/05/574). Brussels.

Wallström, M. (2005k, November 8). *Bridging the gap; How to bring Europe and its citizens closer together?* (SPEECH/05/668). Brussels.

Wallström, M. (2006a, January 27). *The sound of citizens—Let's hear the chorus!* (SPEECH/06/44). Salzburg.

Wallström, M. (2006b, May 2). *The white paper on a European Communication policy defining common principles—Which way forward?* (SPEECH/06/271). Brussels.

Wallström, M. (2006c, May 10). *Press conference on "citizen's agenda".* (SPEECH/06/297). Brussels.

Wallström, M. (2006d, August 28). *Meeting the communication challenge* (SPEECH/06/478). Brussels.

Wallström, M. (2006e, October 18). *The Constitutional Treaty: The way forward, Notre Europe debate on "Plan B: How to rescue the European Constitution"* (SPEECH/06/613). Brussels.

Wallström, M. (2006f, October 27). *Understanding public opinion* (SPEECH/06/639). Madrid.

Wallström, M. (2006g, November 16). *Debate on the Herrero report on the White Paper on Communication* (SPEECH/06/696). Strasbourg.

Wallström, M. (2006h, September 13). *Speech at the Nordic public service broadcasters happening* (no number). No place.

Wallström, M. (2007a, March 24). *Europe of those who are constructing Europe* (SPEECH/07/189). Rome.

Wallström, M. (2007b, April 19). *Taking the European Union forwards: The next 50 years* (SPEECH/07/239). The Hague.

Wallström, M. (2007c, October 3). *Communicating Europe in partnership* (SPEECH/07/602). Brussels.

Wallström, M. (2007d, December 8). *Today is a new beginning* (SPEECH/07/804). Brussels.

Wallström, M. (2008a, February 28). *The Lisbon Treaty: Giving more power to the people* (SPEECH/08/122). Dublin.

Wallström, M. (2008b, June 2). *The citizens' right to know—Transparency, access and outreach—Essential tools for democracy* (SPEECH/08/292). Brussels.

Wallström, M. (2008c, November 25). *Communicating Europe—Mission impossible?* (SPEECH/08/649). Berlin.

Wallström, M. (2009a, January 20). *The citizens' right to know—Time to improve openness, transparency and access* (SPEECH/09/11). No place.

Wallström, M. (2009b, May 11). *European citizens' consultations* (SPEECH/09/234). Brussels.

Wallström, M. (2009c, September 3). *Communication and democracy: The way forward* (SPEECH/09/360). Brussels.

Wallström, M. (2009d, September 8). *Transparency and clear legal language in the EU* (SPEECH/09/378). Stockholm.

Wallström, M. (2009e, October 6). *After the Irish "Yes", what next?* (SPEECH/09/462). Brussels.

Wallström, M. (2009f, November 17). *Communicating Europe: Lessons (to be) learnt from the Irish referendum* (SPEECH/09/542). Brussels.

Waterfield, B. (2006). The messenger and the message. Interview with Margot Wallström. http://www.docstoc.com/docs/967552/The-messenger-and-the-message. Accessed 12 July 2011.

CHAPTER 6

Europe of Rights (2010–2014)

1   The Lisbon Treaty and Reding's Portfolio

With the entry into force of the Lisbon Treaty on 1 December 2009, the Commission's understanding of what Europe stands for changed. Justice became the key term for EU policies and concomitantly, the Commission turned to a rights-based conception of European citizenship, with Viviane Reding as Commissioner for Justice, Fundamental Rights and Citizenship.

More specifically, three sets of stipulations are significant for understanding the fifth representation of European citizenship that was soon to emerge. The first was described in art. 61 TEU and was concerned with the EU as an area of freedom, security and justice: 'The Union shall constitute an area of freedom, security and justice with respect for fundamental rights and the different legal systems and traditions of the Member States'. Whereas the five chapters concerned with the area of freedom, security and justice in the Lisbon Treaty[1] determined the scope of the Union's competence in the policy areas of justice, it is art. 9e) that defined the Commission's role within the area of justice in general terms: 'The Commission shall promote the general interest of the Union and take appropriate initiatives to that end. It shall ensure the application of the Treaties, and of measures adopted by the institutions pursuant to them. It shall oversee the application of Union law under the control of the Court of Justice of the European Union'. What this indicated was that justice and rights as well as legal institutions were becoming key characteristics of the EU's identity and would guide its policies during the Barroso II

© The Editor(s) (if applicable) and The Author(s) 2016
S. Pukallus, *Representations of European Citizenship since 1951*,
DOI 10.1057/978-1-137-51147-8_6

Commission and possibly beyond. The second set of stipulations reinforced this aspect by granting the EU Charter of Fundamental Rights primary law status and emphasising that the Union 'shall combat social exclusion and discrimination, and shall promote social justice and protection, equality between women and men, solidarity between generations and protection of the rights of the child' (art. 2 al. 3). Therefore, the Commission, as guardian of the Treaties, had to ensure that these rights were respected within the EU and as such, it was reasonable to expect that fundamental rights would become one of the main themes in the Commission's public discourse as well as a defining feature of European citizenship. Finally, the third set of stipulations was concerned with the reinforcement of liberal democratic values and mechanisms such as the direct representation of the Union citizens at Union level in the European Parliament, the right of every citizen to participate in the democratic life of the Union and the confirmation of the principle of transparency and accountability (Title II, art. 8). Added to this, the Lisbon Treaty provided for the direct involvement of European citizens and, more broadly, European civil society in the policymaking process of the EU through a new EU citizenship right: the European Citizens Initiative. It was formulated in art. 8b as follows: 'Not less than one million citizens who are nationals of a significant number of Member States may take the initiative of inviting the European Commission, within the framework of its powers, to submit any appropriate proposal on matters where citizens consider that a legal act of the Union is required for the purpose of implementing the Treaties'. Whereas this represented the first legally binding element of direct democracy in the EU, it is an element that has been rather difficult to achieve. At the time of writing, and over four years after the entry into force of the Lisbon Treaty, there have only been two initiatives which received an answer from the Commission.[2] There was an observable change from the previous period (2005–2009) and the attendant view that any European citizen should have a say and be able to make a difference to a situation in which not one but, as Sefčovič, then European Commissioner and Vice-President for Inter-Institutional Relations and Administration, pointed out 'A million voices make a difference'.[3]

Barroso put together a Commissioner portfolio that linked together all of the three critical aspects mentioned above: Justice, Fundamental Rights and Citizenship. As for the first aspect, the Lisbon Treaty provided the Commission with competence for Justice. The Lisbon Treaty (2009) read: '[T]he Union shall offer its citizens an area of freedom, security and justice without internal frontiers, in which the free movement of persons is ensured (...)' (art. 2 al. 2). This explicit competence enabled Barroso to do two things: first, to create DG Justice, which was previously linked to DG Home Affairs, and second, to link justice and citizenship by nominating Viviane Reding as head of DG Justice with the responsibility for EU citizenship (as legally defined in the Maastricht Treaty 1992). The linking of justice and citizenship consequently enabled Reding to emphasise the dimension of justice and rights[4] in her conception of European citizenship and its subsequent public communication. The second aspect of Reding's portfolio was Fundamental Rights. The fact that the EU Charter of Fundamental Rights gained primary law status allowed Barroso to add 'Fundamental Rights' to Reding's portfolio. Correspondingly, Reding was given the responsibility for 'equality between men and woman' as well as the responsibility for 'actions against discrimination'. The third aspect, the elements of direct democracy stipulated in the Treaty, notably the involvement of civil society and the 'citizens' initiative', were linked to Reding's portfolio by giving her the responsibility for the 'Civil Society Directorate EMPL G'.[5]

It was the extent of these competences that constituted and defined the legislative side to Reding's portfolio. The communicative side of Reding's portfolio included two responsibilities: first, her political responsibility for DG COMM and second, her responsibility for the publication office (PO). The combination of both provided her with the responsibility for the Commission's public communication policy towards communicating the meaning and significance of European citizenship. In other words, Reding was given both a legislative and public communication policy portfolio, unlike Wallström, and it was on the back of this newly defined portfolio that the fifth representation of European citizenship 'Europe of Rights' emerged.

2 THE CIVIL-LEGAL REPRESENTATION OF EUROPEAN CITIZENSHIP: EUROPE OF RIGHTS[6]

A Civil-Legal Lexicon

The civil-legal lexicon that the Commission and notably Reding employed throughout the fifth representation of European citizenship was concerned with two main aspects: justice and rights. With the idea of justice, the Commission defined Europe's identity and its relationship with European citizens, whilst its emphasis on rights framed the civil-legal character of European citizenship.

As noted above, the Lisbon Treaty defined Europe as an 'area of law, rights and justice' (art. 61) and thereby rendered 'the justice revolution possible'.[7] What this 'revolution' consisted of was simply that Justice became its own policy area for which the Commission was handed explicit competencies. Given, as Reding pointed out, that '[j]ustice lies at the very heart of the European construction' and that it has been considered 'the foundation of our Union',[8] the Commission felt that this development was long overdue. According to Reding, 'justice for citizens was the "Cinderella" of EU law. For over 50 years, justice was locked away, excluded from the "community method" and left to intergovernmentalism'.[9] The Lisbon Treaty changed this, as apparent in its preamble, and 'place[d] the individual at the heart of its activities by establishing the citizenship of the Union and by creating an area of freedom, security and justice'. For Reding, this was 'a quantum leap' that made path for a 'new vision'.[10] What was this 'new vision' Reding referred to?

In Reding's terms, this new vision was best understood as 'a vision of justice for citizens'[11] that of a Europe where, Reding continued, citizens' rights became tangible, legally enforceable and easy to enjoy. In fact, the Commission set out to make sure that there was as little difference between the 'legal text' and 'its effectiveness on the ground' as possible.[12] This, in turn would, so Reding hoped, stimulate confidence amongst European citizens in the Single Market as '[e]nsuring access to justice is', after all, 'every citizen's dream'.[13] Correspondingly, she stated at the beginning of her mandate that her objective was to 'reorient [EU] policies in the field of Justice, Fundamental Rights and Citizenship, and to turn them into practical results'.[14] Concomitantly, the concept of European citizenship and its attendant rights were to become something concrete and tangible.[15] Especially, Reding added, the right to 'free movement [which] is after all a core right of EU citizens must become a concrete reality across all EU Member States, and EU law must be rigorously enforced wherever necessary'.[16] What the emphasis of the right to free movement did was to inextricably link the Commission's citizenship policies to the Single Market. This tandem of citizenship and the Single Market in combination with the Commission's focus on justice pointed to the area of justice essentially consisting of the Single Market in which European citizens used their Single Market and attendant cross-border rights. Reding argued that only if 'citizens feel at ease about living, travelling and working in another

Member State'[17] and are 'confident that their rights are protected no matter where they are in the Union'[18] will the EU be able to 'regain the hearts and minds of European citizens'[19] and to 'give [them] more trust in the [S]ingle [M]arket'.[20] She intended to achieve this by showing that the 'European Union is made for the benefit of citizens'[21] and by 'making sure that consumers can surf and shop online without worrying about the safety of their personal information'[22]. Or alternatively expressed, the Commission 'must highlight to citizens, what their EU citizenship rights are' and show them that they 'have a beneficial impact on [their] lives and open new opportunities, such as the right to move freely within the whole territory of the EU, to work, do business, study and train, and the right to participate in the political life of the EU, notably through the European elections'[23]. Reding hoped that an effective EU justice policy would inspire trust amongst European citizens because she believed that trust was 'the foundation for our European area of Justice, and only if we consolidate this trust will people and businesses be able to reap the full benefits of EU justice policy. And that has to be our aim. Justice is not for the statute books. It is for citizens',[24] to which she added that the EU justice policy had to serve 'end-users, citizens and businesses'.[25]

In this European area of justice, European citizenship could be defined via two kinds of rights: fundamental rights[26] and Single Market rights (Reding passim). However, by considering the right to free movement a fundamental right, Reding tightened the connection between both and variously conflated the distinction. She acknowledged that 'EU citizenship and fundamental rights policies are indeed closely interlinked, to the extent that the rights attached to EU citizenship form an integral part of the rights enshrined in the Charter'.[27] For reasons of clarity, I will keep the distinction and consider freedom of movement as a Single Market right, as it has existed since the beginning of European integration as a core Single Market right.

EU Fundamental Rights

With the ratification of the Lisbon Treaty (2009), the EU Charter of Fundamental Rights became 'legally binding, and [was put] on equal footing with the Treaties'.[28] The Charter in itself was, according to Reding, 'one of the most modern codifications of fundamental rights in the world [which] contains all the classic guarantees of fundamental rights, which are also enshrined in the European Convention on Human Rights, but goes beyond it. The Charter also guarantees rights and principles, including economic and social rights, which stem from the constitutional traditions common to the Member States, European Court of Justice case law and other international agreements'.[29] Reding emphasised the importance of protecting the Charter which was considered 'the basis of the Union's identity, in each and every one of the Union's activities and at the very heart of the 500 million citizens'.[30] The 'aim of the Charter of Fundamental Rights [was] to oblige the EU institutions to uphold fundamental rights in the same way as the 27 [now 28] Member States'[31] and consequently, it was to 'be the compass for all policies developed by the EU institutions, as well as for EU Member States who must respect it whenever EU law is implemented'.[32] Accordingly, Reding was 'keen to use the full potential of the Treaties, including the very strong anchoring of EU citizens' rights in the Charter of Fundamental Rights of the EU' and stressed that the Commission would continue 'to pursue a rigorous enforcement policy with a view to achieving the full and correct transposition and application of the EU free movement rules across the EU'.[33] Nevertheless, it is necessary to note that, as Reding pointed out herself, 'the Charter does not apply to all situations in which fundamental rights are at issue in a Member State. It applies only when a Member States implements EU law'.[34]

The fundamental rights enshrined in the Charter can be considered high-level aspirational statements of entitlements acquired by virtue of being a European citizen. Although the Commission stated that 'the Charter is not a text setting out abstract values' but rather 'an instrument to enable people to enjoy the rights enshrined within it when in a situation governed by Union law',[35] it was doubtful that the change of legal status of the Charter made a significant impact on, and difference for, European citizens' daily lives in a 'Europe of Rights' in terms of practical results, because these fundamental rights have been interpreted through judicial procedure and defended by legal institutions if disrespected. Reding, on the occasion of her hearings before the Reding (2010a) and in several speeches, promoted what she referred to as a 'Zero Tolerance Policy' with regard to the violation of the Charter.[36] However, whether this Charter, which has become legally binding, represented a substantive change for European policies and European citizens, and thereby provided the civil-legal representation of European citizenship with a strong and coherent element was questionable for the following reason.

The Charter did not introduce any new fundamental rights, as the Commission acknowledged by saying that the Charter 'brings together in one text all the fundamental rights protected in the Union, spelling them out in detail and making them visible and predictable'.[37] Accordingly, it is fair to say that the Charter can't be understood as 'innovative'[38] but rather as a jigsaw puzzle of rights that assembled existing fundamental rights stemming from the documents named above. Consequently, and with regard to the Charter's impact on the civil-legal representation of European citizenship, it can be said that the fact the EU Charter became legally binding did not represent in itself a substantial change. Even before the entry into force of the Lisbon Treaty, the EU had to respect these fundamental rights indirectly, as member states wouldn't have agreed to any policy proposals contradicting fundamental rights existing in the member states' constitutions. Consequently, the legally binding Charter contributed to the depth of the civil-legal representation of European citizenship only to a limited extent. However, the Charter strengthened the Commission's role of being a guardian of the Treaties. In addition, this new legal competence for fundamental rights allowed Reding to officially and publicly communicate the Commission's commitment to the Charter rhetorically through her speeches and policy statements such as her Zero Tolerance Policy.

Single Market Rights

Reding linked European citizens' rights to the Single Market with the freedom of movement being the core right[39] and, as she pointed out, the 'most cherished [right] by citizens'[40] with over 14 million EU citizens living in another EU state than their own. European citizens were understood to exercise their citizenship rights in physical and virtual cross-border situations[41]; that is, as Reding clarified, 'when they sign a contract in a cross-border situation, when they shop online, when they want to enforce a court decision cross-border, when a bi-national couple wants to get married or divorced, or when a person living outside his home country wants to write a will',[42] when European citizens travel, study, found companies, shop or inherit[43] or when they participate in ERASMUS exchanges, hold a European Health Card or ask for the recognition of their diplomas.[44] In other words, in 'an area of justice without internal borders' (Lisbon Treaty, art.2), civil-legal European citizens should know that their 'rights are protected [in any cross-border situation anywhere] in the Union'.[45]

Accordingly, Reding believed that the role of the Commission with regard to citizens' rights was to make these rights easily enjoyable and judicially enforceable, and therefore to 'progressively remove all the obstacles' which European citizens 'still encounter when trying to use their rights across national borders'.[46] In order to be able to do so, Reding was given policy instruments which included 'the responsibility for the free movement within the European Union; civil justice and contract law; consumer legislation, starting from the Package Travel Directive[47] and reaching to the proposal for a Consumer Rights Directive[48]; data protection[49]; (...)'.[50] These policy instruments were meant to enable Reding to establish the needed level of 'legal consistency in Europe to ensure that the EU's Single Market serves our citizens and our economy'.[51] Reding believed that a genuine area of justice could only exist if the 'EU institutions (...) ensure that [European] citizens are able to make use of their rights as [European] citizens in the same way as they use their rights as nationals of their respective Member States'.[52] Therefore, she said, speaking for the Commission, 'We will make it easier for citizens to work and do training in another EU country; we will reduce excessive paperwork for EU citizens living and travelling in the EU; and we will eliminate barriers to cross-border shopping'.[53] Particularly, 'red tape' meaning long and costly administrative procedures for both citizens and businesses were a matter of concern that the Commission intended to tackle quickly.[54] Overall, Reding emphasised the need for 'better European legal cooperation'[55] which entailed harmonisation of legal systems and rules such as 'consumer and contract rules'[56] as well as the enforcement of rights concerning fair trials and legal support.[57] However, it is not so much the technical detail that is important at this point but the overall objective Reding pursued through her initiatives in establishing legal harmonisation, namely the establishment of a European judicial culture which embraced all aspects of the law: 'One continent, one law', to use Reding's words.[58] This constitutes an important insight into how she conceived of European citizenship and civil society.

European Civil Society in a 'Europe of Rights'

According to Reding, 'European law is the cement binding together our Union. Our Union has, within a remarkably short period of time, emerged into a unique political entity. Its successful and peaceful rapid growth and development has only been made possible because of the force and the rule of European law. Europe is a "Rechtsgemeinschaft", a Community of law, as Walter Hallstein already said, and until today, our Union is not held together by force or armies, but first of all by the respect of the commonly created European rules'.[59] Such a European 'Rechtsgemeinschaft' needed to be understood as aspirational: Reding believed in the integrative force of law for the European Community or, in Alexander's[60] terms, the civil force of law and the primary importance of legal institutions in civil society (unlike Wallström who, it could be argued, believed in the primacy of the communicative institutions or infrastructure of civil society). Reding believed that through practical step-by-step harmonisation of law and European citizenship rights Europe could progress towards a future 'Rechtsgemeinschaft'. According to Reding, as much as law represented an integrative force for European economic and political integration, it also represented an integrative force for the facilitation of the emergence of a European civil society. Accordingly, Reding hoped that the development of effective European legal institutions would provide substance to a European civil society by enabling European citizens to enjoy their rights, deriving from EU law, freely and easily in a 'Europe of Rights'.

It is apparent therefore that Reding believed in the EU as a 'Communauté de droit', or a 'Rechtsgemeinschaft'. In this 'Rechtsgemeinschaft'—to reify the matter—lived European civil society, which based its solidarity upon the civil force of law and justice. This version of civil society conforms to Pérez-Díaz' view of what civil society should be composed of. He argued that civil society has 'an institutional and cultural dimension. As a set of practices and institutions, [civil society] brings together, in a systematic whole, the spheres of free markets; of a liberal (democratic) polity defined by the rule of law, limited and accountable government, and a public sphere-cum-free elections and a representative body (…)'.[61] In Reding's 'Rechtsgemeinschaft', the civil-legal European citizen was circumscribed by legally based rights which were institutionally promoted across the EU in an open and even-handed (universal) manner. These legally based rights allowed for European citizens to be conceived of as simultaneously a 'citizen' in a civil setting with both democratic rights (such as electoral rights and information rights) and some limited social rights[62] and as a civil actor with economic rights located in the regulation and civil force of law applied to the Single Market and designed to protect the 'citizen-consumer'. This extension of European civil activity to include the European citizen as a consumer (actively defined[63]) was designed to display the practical and daily side of the benefits of European citizenship and was as such reminiscent of the type of understanding of the European citizen as 'homo oeconomicus' of the 1950s/1960s and of the PRINCE programme during the third representation of European citizenship (1993–2004).

With Reding's conception of a legally based European civil society, the civil motives[64] that determine the dynamics and boundaries of civil society changed from the fourth to the fifth representation of European citizenship. Whereas Wallström emphasised rational and reasonable civil motives and thereby advocated a deliberative European civil society in the Kantian-Habermasian sense, Reding's emphasis lay in the recognition that an autonomous European civil society was one where civil motives were directed on a daily and practical basis towards activity in non-civil spheres, primarily the economic sphere. It is in this light that Reding talked about the European consumer as a civil actor with civil rights. To put the matter bluntly: Reding attempted to incorporate European civil rights within the workings of the Single Market—which is after all 'a commercial space for 500 million people' as she pointed out.[65] Simultaneously, she created a 'European citizen-consumer'[66] and reinforced the economic dimension of European citizenship. Interestingly, in Reding's political discourse there was a tendency to use the expression 'citizens and businesses'[67] which revealed how she linked the market sphere to the civil sphere. Alternatively expressed, it was her understanding of European citizenship as including the European citizen-consumer that enabled Reding to extol the Single Market and to move effortlessly between the European citizen as a rights holder and a consumer in a coherent way.

Concurrently and by extension of her understanding of the European citizen-consumer, Reding returned to a single-perspectival approach of European space (from Wallström's multiperspectival approach), which was based upon a precise and concretely expressed version of space as the extent of the application of EU law. In short, the EU was understood as a spatially distinct Community of law: a 'Europe of Rights'. Naturally enough, this Community of law had its fixed and concrete boundaries where EU law ceased its legal force. Correspondingly, European civil society was defined for Reding as primarily existing in accordance with the space occupied by EU law, reminiscent of Roman citizenship, or as Taylor argued: 'The ancient society was given its identity by its laws. On the banners of the legions, SPQR stood for "Senatus populusque romanus", but the "populus" here was the ensemble of Roman citizens (…). The people didn't have an identity, didn't constitute a unity prior to and outside of these laws'.[68] And accordingly, it was only within this fixed space circumscribed by law that, to borrow Alexander's terms, 'civil society can become unique and meaningful' and where 'the capacity for liberty becomes limited to those who have their feet on the sacred land (...)'[69] that was, in Reding's case, the European land. The metaphor of 'sacred land' was for Reding an area of unambiguously held law, rights and justice. In this area the Commission aimed to protect European citizens' rights and to ensure that rights could be exercised safely and be judicially enforced.[70] This protection, in turn, was hoped to facilitate and stimulate European citizens' trust in the Single Market and EU Justice.[71] It was this protection that made European citizenship, for Reding, 'the crown jewel of European integration'[72] and special in that she saw it as 'an entry door to the EU Treaty and to the rights that EU citizens enjoy'.[73]

In other words, Reding returned to a fixed and unambiguous understanding of European space which had within it European citizens of equal rights and whose particular historical stories were relegated to the unity of these rights, a unity which in her case was based upon a judicial culture. It was the civil force of this legalism and rights-based judicial culture that relegated spatial ambiguity and diversity for Reding and subordinated it to the promotion of unity.

The problem with Reding's conception of a European civil society in a 'Europe of Rights' circumscribed by European legal institutions was that Reding was prone to failing to appreciate the spontaneous nature of civil society and civil action and further, appeared to ignore the fact that legal institutions do not stimulate public reasoning when understood as the 'self-reflexive' element of civil society[74] in the same way as communicative institutions do—as Wallström so strongly emphasised.[75] Rather, legal institutions articulate public reasoning as a matter of procedural reasoning. And quite naturally, legal institutions themselves tend towards articulating highly formal versions of a so called 'enlightened public debate' around matters of justice and the interpretation of the law, but this is insufficient if one takes a broad view of public opinion (say, one which conforms to Krause's conception of 'civil passions', where reason and emotion or moral sentiments combine to express public opinion[76]) in capturing civil and non-judicial matters like 'felt identity' or 'associative membership' and very importantly, criticism of the EU project itself. In this respect, Reding's conception of European civil society could appear too disconnected from the man in the street, as it emphasised a version of European civil society as conceived of by lawyers—understood by Reding as 'rather conservative people'[77]—and included 'judges, legal practitioners, barristers, solicitors, law professors'.[78] They would express legal opinions on behalf of a European citizenry who, in turn, would accept such opinion as an expression of their public will. Reding seemed to think that there existed an idealised version of 'the court of public will formation' that would be sufficiently engaging and culturally attractive as to suffice ultimately for a Civil Europe not especially interested in 'feelings of belonging', personal identity and democratic contestation and the democratic value of public opinion, understood in its widest sense.

Evaluation: Civil-Legal European Citizenship

As noted above, Reding conceived of the civil-legal European citizen as both an individual civil actor and an active consumer. This spectrum of European citizenship was emphasised by Reding with regard to two aspects: first, the 'the privacy of our citizens in the context of all EU policies'[79] needed to be protected and, second, 'the right of citizens to move freely in the European Union'[80] needed to be strengthened.

Accordingly, the civil-legal citizen in a 'Europe of Rights' was understood as a rights bearer and as a bearer of certain specific freedoms. Reding, representing the Commission, understood freedom to mean the freedom to be an active and sovereign consumer able to decide where to work, live, travel and shop in the EU as well as to make cross-border contracts. According to Reding, citizens' rights needed to be protected and 'enforced effectively'[81] so that European citizens could act as autonomous and independent, self-determining consumers who didn't have to worry about the safety of their personal information when shopping online.[82] Therefore, it was a priority to protect civil-legal EU citizens' privacy, civil liberties and to sensibly deal with issues such as 'data retention, Passenger Name Records, wire tapping legislation or proposals for blocking Internet access for public purposes'[83] in what I call a 'Europe of Rights'.

What we have seen so far is that Reding constantly attempted to see European consumer activity as itself having a civil force. She did not share the traditional idea, expressed in Alexander, that '[t]he goal of the economic sphere is wealth, not justice in the civil sense [and that] it is organised around efficiency not solidarity, and [that it] depends more upon hierarchy than equality to meet its goals'[84]—a view where civil society and the economic sphere are regarded as clearly distinct. Rather, Reding believed the distinction was blurred and as such, she apparently didn't agree with Alexander's view that non-civil spheres can be subject 'to legal-cum-civil regulations'[85] and that the civil forces of tort law and contract law are powerful influences on, in this case, the Single Market. Rather for Reding, 'civil justice and contract law'[86] were intrinsically linked to and conditional upon each other. In other words, Reding believed that 'a well-functioning European area of justice has an important role in reinforcing the Single Market', to which she added that 'consumers and businesses may limit their investments and transactions to national markets if they lack confidence in the judicial system. That's why [the EU] must overcome barriers to cross-border trade caused by the prospect of civil litigation'.[87]

Concomitantly, Reding's civil-legal representation of the EU citizen was based upon the success of her desire to harmonise the application of EU law in all member states. Only in this way can a European judicial culture be said to be effectively in place. This was an ambitious project that faced two serious obstacles. First, in the EU there currently exist 28 different legal systems, and as Reding argued (to repeat the point), 'lawyers are rather conservative people'[88] who 'will prefer to stick instinctively to the traditional concepts of their national legal systems'[89] so that turning national lawyers into national lawyers with a European attitude and the necessary knowledge about all aspects of European law would be a Herculean task. Such a task would not only require human but also financial resources in order to introduce the necessary and probably time-consuming and presumably controversial reforms. And during Reding's term there were few signs of these resources being made available or this policy being advanced in anything but an aspirational way. Second, a progressive and increasing harmonisation of the application of EU law (or even only enhanced legal cooperation) was rendered complicated because of linguistic differences related to the field of law. Reding explained these linguistic differences as follows: 'Sometimes a word in one legal order has a similar, not the same, concept in another national legal system. Just think of the word "bona fide", "bonne foi", "Guter Glauben". (....) it is [therefore] not sufficient to translate a legal term. The concept behind it must also be well understood before one can really understand, work in and succeed in another legal system'.[90]

The above two obstacles could only have been rectified if first, as Reding emphasised, 'every national lawyer and every national judge also becomes a European law expert, capable of interpreting and effectively enforcing EU law alongside his own domestic law'.[91] Second, the EU legal order would need to be able interact with our diverse national legal traditions and systems in coherent and consistent ways. These two conditions could, however, only be fulfilled if university law courses were reformed in a way that would make it possible to have 'well informed and well trained legal practitioners, in particular judges'.[92] Consequently, Reding's reliance on the development of a European judicial culture that derived from the harmonisation of the application of EU law in the 28 member states and on its civil force would require popular 'confidence in the EU's legal system'[93]. As such, it remained problematic.

The outlined obstacles and the conditions for their resolution show the potential weaknesses in the civil-legal representation of European citizenship in 'A Europe of Rights' with regard to it being based upon a uniform European judicial culture. Reding herself acknowledged that Europe was marked more by its diversity than its uniformity.[94] And as argued above, Reding aspired to uniformity and harmonisation of EU law whilst her civil-legal representation of European citizenship showed the existence of acute problems in her understanding of citizenship and pluralism, and the realisation of the EU's motto 'Unity in Diversity'. This tension between the 'uniformity' (Reding used 'uniformity' and 'unity' seemingly interchangeably in the area of law) and 'diversity' became particularly evident with Reding's remarks on contract law. Reding stated that European Contract Law was a prime example for the need of diversity rather than forced uniformity. In her own words: 'Contract law is a field where we need particular scope for subsidiarity. And this is why in the field of contract law I do not favour full harmonisation or a compulsory European Code'.[95]

The important question to ask at this point is how Reding actually understood 'Unity in Diversity' and what the significance of her understanding was for the civil-legal representation of European citizenship. First, Reding held a narrow legalistic version of the EU's motto 'Unity in Diversity', in which 'Diversity' was to be achieved through the subsidiarity of contract law. This conception of 'Unity in Diversity' is different from the way it has traditionally been understood, since it was first used in the speeches of the early European officials of the 1950s. It was then understood as referring to different historical, cultural, political and economic traditions and the question of how to form a European society despite these differences. Reding's legal understanding of the EU motto risked losing these elements of cultural and historical diversity and their richness. Prioritising contract law was nothing other than a somewhat technical translation of 'Unity in Diversity'. This view can only be softened if one decides that Reding thought of law as a cultural and intellectual force.[96] This understanding of law as a common heritage and a common value is further expressed in the following quote, in which Reding referred to the so-called "Draft Common Frame of Reference", for the elaboration of which 'scholars from all over Europe have come together looking for what is common in our legal heritage, sharing the rich national traditions in search of a language that is European, but recognisable at the same time to national lawyers'.[97] Again we must wait and see how and whether this common legal heritage continues to be both communicated and applied across Europe.

Ultimately, though, Reding linked the legal to the civil by guaranteeing access to justice for civil-legal European citizens. In this she was closest to Marshall's conception of citizenship insofar as he considered access to justice to be a fundamental aspect of the civil dimension because access to justice allows citizens 'to defend and assert all one's rights on terms of equality with others and due process of the law'.[98] Reding's belief in the civil force of law was not limited to the pure application of law but extended beyond to the emergence of 'civil solidarity'. Alexander argued accordingly that 'to the degree that the civil sphere gains authority and independence, obedience to law is seen not as subservience to authority (...), but as commitment to rules that allow solidarity and autonomy'.[99] This belief in civil solidarity was an intrinsic element of the understanding of Europe as a 'Rechtsgemeinschaft'.

At this point it is worthwhile taking a moment to examine briefly how Reding's conception of Europe as a Community of law was linked to her understanding of Europe as a political Union and as representing a form of democracy. For Reding, democracy and the rule of law were intrinsically linked, as she emphasised accordingly, stating that the 'rule of law is the backbone of modern democratic, pluralist societies and constitutional democracies' and that the rule of law is 'one of the main values on which the European Union is founded'.[100] The rule of law, according to Reding, can be understood as 'a system where laws are applied and enforced (...) but also the spirit of the law and fundamental rights, which are the ultimate foundation of all laws'.[101] Whereas, as I have shown, Reding's conception of European citizenship was legally based and intrinsically linked to Single Market rights (some of which are indeed understood by Reding as fundamental rights), she saw no contradiction in simultaneously arguing that 'by creating a status common to all Europeans and by attaching to this status a series of additional rights (…) a clear signal was given: the EU is more than a common market'.[102] Rather, claims such as 'European citizenship must be to the Political Union what the Euro is to the Monetary Union'[103] pointed to a conception of Europe in which a political union subsumed the Single Market and democracy was likened to an area of Justice. However, and as Dunn argued: 'The rule of law (…) is not democracy. Its attractions are not those of democracy. Its irritations are not those of democracy. Its dangers are not those of democracy'[104] to which he added: 'It is not because we value or expect legality (..) that we have chosen democracy as the one ground on which we can accept subjection (…)'.[105] It appears that in the last third of her mandate, Reding began to realise that there was more to democracy and citizenship than the rule of law and the Single Market, and that civil society couldn't emerge solely based upon legal institutions but required in fact discursive engagement. I will return to this change in Reding's approach to European citizenship and its significance at the end of this chapter.

Reding's citizen-consumer can be sketched accordingly: In this representation, the civil-legal obstacles European citizens encountered when trying to exercise their rights across borders; obstacles that were found in first, the difference… and second, European citizens lack of knowledge about their European citizens' rights and how to enforce them. Accordingly, the European citizen, so the Commission believed, had for a long time been frustrated with different consumer regulations across the EU that made his online shopping difficult and left him in doubt about his rights when shopping in another EU member state. In other words, European citizens wished to utilise the benefits to be gained from the Single Market—if only they knew how to register their cars, understood European health insurance and knew more about their rights and EU legislation in matters of cross-border marriage, divorce or death. The hope was that once the Community had fulfilled its role of rendering citizens' rights easy to understand and apply, European citizens would correspondingly develop a solidarity with, and loyalty to, the EU and other European citizens.

The Public Communication of 'Europe of Rights'

Whereas Wallström believed that public communication was a policy area in its own right[106] and as such an intrinsic feature of democracy, Reding conceived of public communication as a tool,[107] as an interviewed DG Commission official pointed out, or service[108] that is first and foremost aimed at publicly communicating 'results'. Subsequently, and in contrast to the fourth representation of European citizenship, 'Europe of Agorai', Reding prioritised the factual style of public communication over the deliberative-rational style of public communication.

Informing Civil-Legal European Citizens About Their Rights

The use of the factual style of public communication in disseminating the representation 'Europe of Rights' had as its objective to increase citizens' awareness about their European citizenship rights deriving from EU law and to provide them with factual information about the rights, to explain how to enjoy them and where to go when obstacles in the exercise of European civil-legal rights are encountered.[109] This public communication approach appeared to have been endorsed by other European institutions. For example, the Council expressed the same understanding of the role of public communication in the Stockholm programme: 'The achievements in the area of freedom, security and justice are generally of great importance to citizens, businesses and professionals. The European Council therefore calls on all Union institutions, in particular the Commission as well as the Member States, to consider ways to better communicate to citizens and practitioners the concrete results of the policy in the area of freedom, security and justice. It asks the Commission to devise a strategy on how best to explain to citizens how they can benefit from the new tools and legal frameworks, for instance through the use of e-Justice and the e-Justice Portal'.[110] Although the Commission emphasised the need for factual information, it nevertheless pursued an informative-affective objective, which was to increase European civil solidarity and civil-legal European citizens' attachment to and trust in the European Community as a 'Europe of Rights'. It did so through the public communication of practical results and through the use of personal stories in, for example, the EU Citizenship Reports 2010 and 2013.[111]

By communicating practical and concrete results, the Commission aimed at evoking civil solidarity with Europe amongst European citizens which was grounded in Europe's usefulness for European citizens' daily lives. As a member of Reding's private cabinet explained, raising awareness needed to be done by communicating results: 'We need to make sure that we transform this institutional creation [the EU] into producing policies that do have a positive impact and that we explain the contribution [these policies make] to improving the lives of citizens—this can be done by looking at institutional proposals, by picking up fact sheets[112]—say, for example, the roaming [where] Miss Reding brought the prices down. Do you want anything better?'.[113]

Thus, instead of trying to create European civil solidarity through the coming together in a 'Europe of Agorai' as Wallström attempted, Reding tried to build European citizens' identity on civil-legal rights and their practical significance for European citizens' daily lives. This is reminiscent to some extent of Roman legalism whereby Roman citizens were characterised and distinguished from others by having more rights than the others.[114] It was the exercise of these rights that made Roman citizens' daily lives more comfortable across the empire within the geographical space in which Roman law applied. However, and as an extension of a somewhat abstract Roman legalism, Reding wished to help the EU develop into a 'Rechtsgemeinschaft'. Such a 'Rechtsgemeinschaft' should enable civil-legal European citizens to feel part of the Community by virtue of the fact that because all European citizens have the same civil-legal rights, this alone should generate a feeling of European civil solidarity. This feeling of civil solidarity would ultimately extend beyond a simple legalism and become a cultural, social and intellectual force. As such, Reding's practical approach to demonstrate the value of concrete rights to the daily lives of European citizens was finally nothing more than a springboard or a first step towards a 'Rechtsgemeinschaft'.

With regard to the use of individual stories in the public communication of the representation 'Europe of Rights', the Commission intended to create a sense of identification and solidarity of European citizens with each other across Europe who might encounter the same problems in the Single Market or have the same questions about the use of civil-legal European citizenship rights as oneself. In the EU citizenship report 2013, we can find the following story (amongst others): 'Monika, who is Lithuanian, works in a hotel in an Austrian ski resort five months a year. As the annual roadworthiness test for her car is due in March, when she is in Austria, she has to interrupt her stay and drive all the way back to Lithuania just to present her car for the periodic test. It would be so much easier if she could do the test in Austria and have the roadworthiness certificate automatically recognised in Lithuania, and elsewhere in the EU'.[115] The personal story represented one of the many questions European citizens could have with regard to their Single Market rights, and the Commission hoped that European citizens could recognise themselves in the individual in the example and that this, in turn, would help generate a feeling of European civil solidarity through the recognition of shared benefits based upon a common European identity amongst those who derive these benefits. In Alexander's words: 'What the legal bonds of civil society reflect, rather, is "a sort of anonymous collaboration amongst men"'.[116]

Ultimately then, Reding used the factual style of public communication in the representation of 'Europe of Rights' to reach out to the affective aspect of European civil solidarity based upon a common loyalty to the EU and pride in the achievements of the European project. Her approach was reminiscent of Hallstein's ambition to have European citizens say proudly: 'Civis Europaeus sum'[117] ("Homo Oeconomicus (1951–1972)"). It is derived from the Roman expression 'Civis Romanus sum' which was used by Roman citizens to indicate their pride in Rome and its achievements. As such, this style, so Reding hoped, would act as a catalyst and trigger of European loyalty and pride and an increased sense of European civil solidarity. As Reding pointed out: 'Jacques Delors once said that nobody falls in love with a single market' but 'we need to change this and make the EU's Single Market more lovable for citizens and businesses alike. By making it work in their interest'.[118] The terms 'love' and 'lovable' need to be understood in the sense of 'loyalty' and 'pride' achieved through an effective European legal system producing concrete results for its civil-legal European citizens. In short, Reding's approach can be understood under the formula of factual legal information wrapped up in personal stories as a means to stimulate affective aspects of European citizenship and commonality.

The Deliberative-Rational Style of Public Communication

Reding's use of the deliberative-rational style of public communication was limited especially in the first two-thirds of her mandate and bound to specific and structured occasions such as the 'citizens' initiative'.[119] She 'inherited' a policy which favoured the use of the deliberative-rational style of public communication from the Lisbon Treaty (art. 8b): first, 'institutions shall, by appropriate means, give citizens and representative associations the opportunity to make known and publicly exchange their views in all areas of Union action'; second, 'maintain an open, transparent and regular dialogue with representative associations and civil society' and third, 'the European Commission shall carry out broad consultations with parties concerned in order to ensure that the Union's actions are coherent and transparent'. The European Council endorsed the general idea of holding consultations and 'encourages the Union institutions, within the framework of their competences, to hold an open, transparent and regular dialogue with representative associations and civil society. The Commission should put in place specific mechanisms, such as the European Justice Forum, to step up dialogue in areas where such mechanisms are appropriate'.[120]

With that said, Reding's approach to consultation and deliberation was different from the one taken by Wallström. The deliberative-rational style of public communication was merely used to pursue a pragmatic purpose, as Reding herself emphasised: 'So let's be practical. Let's avoid ideological debates and work through the text chapter by chapter, and article by article, to make the progress we need'.[121] This was also reinforced by a member of her private cabinet: 'in Brussels everything we do, we do it for the citizens to ensure, you know, that they enjoy all the rights as European citizens and that the single market is enjoyed for their benefit'.[122] On the back of these two statements it is reasonable to surmise that Reding remained doubtful about the value of discussing the democratic future of Europe, helping the emergence of an EPS—in fact, one of her close collaborators said that if the European public sphere was not in the Treaty, then it was not a concern for the Commission[123]—or even strengthening the communicative infrastructures for deliberative democracy. My argument can further be supported by Reding's narrow vision of European civil society as circumscribed by legal institutions—a vision which neglected the importance of communicative institutions for the emergence of a potential European civil society. Rather, she remained pre-eminently concerned with demonstrating the direct relevance of the EU and especially its legal institutions, civil-legal rights in the Single Market and these civil-legal rights impact on the daily lives of the European citizens here and now in a 'Europe of Rights'. As such, her approach was characterised as practical or pragmatic,[124] focused[125] and realistic[126] by some of the Commission officials I interviewed.

3   A Change Within 'Europe of Rights'?

Whereas 'Europe of Rights' was the dominant representation of European citizenship throughout Reding's mandate 2010–2014, and the references I have given testify to this, it was possible to see an emphasis of the need to involve European citizens in the 'democratic life' of the Union through the European elections and through citizens' deliberations from 2012 onwards. I believe that the emergence of this new emphasis was occasioned by three things: first, the Eurozone crisis and the subsequent call for greater European fiscal and monetary integration, which led Reding to believe in the advent of greater political integration; second, the then upcoming 2014 European elections and third, the Commission's general realisation that', as one of the interviewed DG COMM officials pointed out, communication cannot be done one-sided, that if we forget about engaging in a dialogue with the citizens our approach won't work'.[127] Examining these reasons will help evaluate the extent to which there really was a substantial change in the meaning of European citizenship and/or the approach to public communication.

The Eurozone Crisis, the European Elections and a Greater European Political Union

During the second half of her mandate, Reding started to focus more on the EU as an economic force. She described Europe as the biggest economy on the world scene and illustrated its economic success by listing the 'Single Market and an area of freedom for 500 million citizens', Europe's 'trade power [which] represent[s] 20% of world trade—by only 7% of the world population'[128] and by pointing out that the 'The European Union is the world's biggest development aid donor'.[129] According to Reding, the Euro was a major part of the reason for this economic success. She described it as 'an extremely strong and stable currency' and as an 'undeniable success which deserves our confidence and pride'.[130] Further, so she added, 'the Euro is the currency of the European Union, and it is irreversible. It is the second reference currency in the world in terms of reserves and a currency that has ensured low interest rates and delivered a decade of low inflation and stability in Europe'.[131] Consequently, Reding considered the then current economic crisis as solvable, and importantly, as the 'beginning of a stronger, more united Europe'[132] which would be accomplished through greater fiscal harmonisation. According to Reding, the Eurozone crisis has made clear the fault lines with economic arrangements across the Eurozone with regard to independently pursued budgetary aims.[133] Specifically, Reding argued that there were four essential shortcomings. The first was that 'financial supervision was too narrowly concentrated on domestic developments, which was incompatible with the international nature of the operations of large financial institutions'; second, 'economic surveillance was too narrowly concentrated on fiscal developments, leaving non-fiscal economic imbalances outside the scope of surveillance'; third, 'fiscal surveillance suffered from some weaknesses in design but especially from insufficiently rigorous implementation' and fourth, 'the surveillance process was backward-looking, and its outcomes were ex-post feedback rather than ex-ante guidance'.[134]

However, Reding pointed out that this crisis had provided Europe with the possibility of deepening European integration through even more common economic and financial mechanisms and policies. Accordingly she argued that 'following the turbulence in the sovereign debt markets in [2010], the EU created financial backstops for countries under market pressure: the European Financial Stability Mechanism (EFSM) and the European Financial Stability Facility (EFSF), as temporary mechanisms for rapid response, and the European Stability Mechanism (ESM), as a permanent mechanism for the future'.[135] In fact, Reding advocated (alongside other Eurozone leaders) further European integration brought about by greater fiscal unity through strong fiscal supervision of domestic budgets, an increased role for the European Central Bank (ECB) and the establishment of the European Stability Mechanism (ESM). According to Reding, these reforms would represent a deepening of the integration process which, in turn, would lead to a European Confederation rather than 'a centralised, uniform State [which she believed] would never fit Europe'.[136] This confederation, or political union, should be discussed on the occasion of the EP election in 2014 where the questions of whether 'we [should] move towards a full-fledged political union' and whether 'we do it with all Member States or just with euro area countries'[137] should also be on the agenda.

Overall, Reding's call for a European political union—a stronger political union—was economically motivated.[138] It was actually not quite clear what this political union she advocated would concretely look like. Indeed, all we were left with is a vague statement by Reding that such a political union would be 'at the heart of everything'[139] and serve to enhance 'democratic legitimacy at the European level'.[140] Reding considered EU citizenship a milestone in the development of a political union.[141] One of the rights of EU citizenship was the right to directly elect the European Parliament, and this was, for Reding, one of the ways to involve European citizens in the shaping of the future of the EU.

According to Reding, 'the time is ripe for parliamentary democracy at EU level'.[142] She claimed that 'the next European Parliament elections are an opportunity to give our European Union a true parliamentary regime, where each citizen sees what their vote does and exercises democratic control over the executive'.[143] However, in order for European Parliament elections to become a meaningful democratic tool, it would be necessary to overcome European citizens' disenfranchisement with EU Politics. Only then could it become, what Reding called 'the decisive moment for citizens to have their say in this debate'.[144] This debate concerned at the time, as Reding's list showed, questions of 'whether Europe should take a more social or a more market-oriented direction', whether Europe opens its borders or becomes 'a Fortress Europe', 'whether [the EP] will defend free movement rights of all EU citizens or focus on new rules against poverty migration', 'whether company boardrooms will have women quota or not', 'whether we are tough with the U.S. when it comes to data protection, or whether we will instead favour the economic benefits of free trade'.[145] According to Reding, it was essential that citizens understood that there was a lot at stake and that in fact, as Reding claimed, 'European Parliament elections are more important than national elections [because] they decide on the direction a whole continent will take'.[146] What this showed was that Reding considered European elections to be fundamentally important—however, whether one considers that one vote every five years can effectively give a citizen's perspective on all of these issues and increase democratic legitimacy is a matter of conjecture.

Despite its emphasis on the importance of European citizens' participation in elections, the Commission nevertheless realised that it would need to put other mechanisms in place that might be able to make engaging in EU politics more salient for European citizens and that would also provide opportunities to involve European citizens more frequently and more directly in the political consultation and decision-making processes of the Union.

In other words, the Commission started to doubt that its one-sided approach to public communication was efficient in gaining citizens' support for the EU, in stimulating a feeling of belonging and in generating a sense of civil solidarity. As argued above, Reding's practical approach to the harmonisation of legal rights had thus far produced a narrow legal version of European civil society in which the civil force of the media was continuously downplayed[147] and in which there was no place for the development of a European public sphere. In fact, the development of a European public sphere was dropped as a policy priority, as one of Reding's colleagues pointed out.[148] This decision showed that Reding did not acknowledge the importance of a public sphere for civil society in the same way Calhoun would. He understood the 'public sphere as an arena of cultural creativity and reproduction in which society is imagined and thereby made real and shaped by the ways in which it is understood. It is because public life can help to constitute a thicker, more meaningful and motivational solidarity that it can help to underpin a modern democratic polity'.[149] Consequently, a thick political culture, seen as democratically necessary by Habermas,[150] was unlikely to be encouraged by a public communication strategy that, once again, focused on the rights and benefits that civil-legal European citizens gained from the Single Market, and thereby reduced citizens into the category 'citizen-consumers'. Such a Single Market-oriented public communication strategy which treated European citizens as citizen-consumers can easily be perceived as a communicative strategy that either has given up on or lacks the confidence to attempt to engage European citizens more broadly than via their economic self-interest.

However, appearing to realise the shortcomings of this approach, the Commission changed the way it spoke about European citizens and its relationship to Europe. In fact, Reding admitted that '(...) democracies cannot function without the link between the citizens and those who govern' and that fading confidence needed to be restored,[151] thereby announcing an approach to European citizenship and public communication more akin to Wallström's. Indeed, as one senior Commission official put it: 'A year ago I would have said that there are big changes from Wallström to Reding but now I don't think so anymore because gradually we start using a lot of elements which were characteristic of Wallström's approach', such as 'organis[ing] more physical debates, town hall meetings, and also listening to citizens'.[152] This Commission official was certainly correct in his/her observation.

Beginning in 2012 and then increasingly in 2013, the Commission returned to the idea of public spaces, citizens' deliberation and public debate, and thereby reintroduced characteristics of the vocabulary used by the Commission, and notably Wallström, during the 'Europe of Agorai'. Against the background of the Eurozone crisis, Barroso began to argue in favour of 'a serious discussion between the citizens of Europe about the way forward'[153] in order for Europe to be 'ever more democratic'.[154] He further argued for the creation of 'platforms where culture debates Europe'[155] and where 'a European public space, where European issues are discussed and debated from a European standpoint'[156] could emerge.

Accordingly, the Commission started a series of 'townhall meetings'[157] and online consultations 'to debate with citizens, to respond to their questions and to listen to their fears and dreams'. Whereas this indicated a broadening of topics, the focus largely remained Single Market rights rather moving to the topics that Reding considered fundamentally important and which included topics such as immigration, women's quota, democratic structures within the EU or how to redress the Eurozone crisis. This remaining focus on Single Market rights can be illustrated by the EU Citizenship Report 2010 in which the Commission expressed its intention to 'open a debate and exchange on how EU citizenship can fulfil its potential in terms of enhancing Europeans' life chances by delivering concrete benefits that will have a visible impact', to which is added that 'to launch an open and constructive dialogue will be a crucial part of building a Europe that protects citizens' rights and serves their needs'.[158] This intention was concretely put into practise with an online consultation (a form of debate) entitled 'EU Citizens: your rights, your future'. It ran from May to September 2012 and was, according to the Commission, the 'biggest ever EU public consultation on citizens' rights'.[159] With this initiative, the Commission hoped to provide European citizens with the opportunity to share their experiences of the benefits of their citizens' rights in the Single Market. On its website the Commission stated: 'The European Commission likes to know about any obstacles you might be facing in your daily life as a European citizen living, studying, working, shopping or simply travelling within the EU. We would also like to hear your ideas about how to remove these obstacles and further develop EU citizenship'.[160] For Reding, this online consultation was a success that testified to the Commission's ambition for more democratic engagement and to listen to European citizens more carefully. She summarised the success with the following statement (which is worth quoting at length): 'I have listened to citizens: we have carried out public consultations on citizens' rights (...). We have had over 1 million enquires from EU citizens on their rights over the past year; we have conducted Eurobarometer polls and we have participated in citizens' dialogues. The results: although two thirds of EU citizens feel European only one in three citizens (36%) say they are well informed about their EU rights. People also tell us that they still run into problems when working or studying, living, travelling or shopping in the EU, or when they want to use their vote to take part in the EU's decision-making process'.[161] Whereas this can be believed to be true, it needs to be recognised that the agenda for the online consultation had been set by the Commission. In this way, the Commission controlled the agenda and limited the choice of topics for citizens and where they could actually have a say. What this meant was that European citizens might have got a say in how a certain area was to be 'decorated' rather than being able to decide what areas the Commission needed to focus on, 'design' or improve. In this way, Reding's approach was similar to that of the 1990s but remained different from Wallström's who, as argued in the previous chapter, limited the Commission role in citizens' deliberations to that of an organiser or sponsor. This role did not include any agenda-setting powers. Similarly to the 2012 online consultations, the European Year for Citizens (EYC) 2013, which had been advertised by the Commission as providing an opportunity for a European debate on European issues,[162] remained equally focused on Single Market rights. The Commission stated that the 'EYC sets out to redress the lack of knowledge amongst European citizens by both 'raising Union citizens' awareness of their right to move and reside freely within the European Union and more generally, the rights guaranteed to Union citizens in cross-border situations' by 'raising Union citizens' awareness of how they can tangibly benefit from EU rights and policies while living in another Member State, and [by] stimulating their active participation in civic fora on Union policies and issues'.[163]

Nevertheless, and to be fair, not all of the Commission's initiatives were centred on the Single Market, as can be seen in both the use of websites and civic fora and the increased diversity of topics addressed. However, what this broadening of topics revealed was a fundamental disconnect between the topics debated and the EU policy agenda. Specifically, what was revealed was a pluralism of topics that masked the difference between high-level issues and issues of pressing concern. For example, the website 'Debating Europe'[164] claimed to offer the opportunity for European citizens to give their opinions on a variety of topics ranging from energy prices, tourism welfare and the EU's space exploration to CO_2 emissions, greener cities in Europe and the war in Syria and yet, at the height of the Eurozone crisis, 'Debating Europe' was more focused on the question of whether we should abolish monarchies in the EU[165] than on tackling the Eurozone crisis via new, and to many controversial, common European economic, fiscal and monetary policies. Equally, the civic fora that have thus far taken place have often shown the same distinction between the high-level and the immediately pressing. For example, the civic forum in Dublin focused exclusively on 'concrete needs of families, working women, consumers, young job-seekers as well as on issues like resource efficiency, climate change or fundamental rights'—in short, economic issues that exist independently of the Eurozone crisis—whilst the participants of the citizens' forum in Berlin at least marginally addressed the question of solutions to the Eurozone crisis, preferring to debate in favour of deeper European political-federal integration and en passant only noting that they expected the EU to 'do more' in order to overcome the Eurozone crisis.[166]

What is striking is that these civic fora or citizens dialogues had been 'advertised' as 'laying the foundations for a pan-European debate', especially 'by making the European elections more transparent' and as such, were considered 'a prime occasion for European citizens to make their voices heard'.[167] And yet, to what extent Citizens' dialogues had the potential to increase European elections' transparency remained rather unclear. It was also telling that various speeches concerning 'main messages from (here you can fill in the names of the cities the 'Citizens dialogues' were held in)' were in fact a collection of what the Commission said and the messages it wanted to get across in terms of what the EU had been doing and had achieved in a variety of areas rather than a collection of citizens' views expressed at those Citizens' dialogues.[168]

Reding's overall judgement of her mandate and initiatives in the field of citizen involvement was the following: 'By putting our citizens at the heart of everything we do, Europeans will be empowered individually, more protected legally and more involved politically than ever before and more listened to'. The claim that citizens were more politically involved than ever before can only be seen as political rhetoric given that the European Parliament elections were not innovative but, as shown in "Homo Oeconomicus (1951–1972)", had been envisaged since the early days of European integration and were put into practise in 1979. Equally, the claim that citizens' engagement was substantial and at an all-time high could hardly be upheld if compared to citizens' engagement in the 'Europe of Agorai'. It would be a mistake to think that this emphasis on civic fora marked a return to the way Wallström wished to create 'European Agorai' since that would be to attribute to the Commission a deep and abiding interest in democratic deliberation that it has not been showing since 2010.

Indeed, between 2010 and 2014 the blueprint for European citizenship remained the Lamassoure Report (2008) on the importance of the easy enjoyment of cross-border citizen-consumer rights. My judgement can be further supported by the fact that the EU Citizenship Report 2013, which came out after the 'Citizens Dialogues' had started, still focused on removing obstacles in the Single Market.[169] As such, I think it is fair to say the emphasis of the need to involve European citizens in the 'democratic life' of the Union through the European elections and through citizens' deliberations did not change Reding's understanding of European citizenship or public communication in any substantial way. After all, Reding said herself that she would always be a first pillar girl.[170] Reding linked political participation to the Single Market. This can be illustrated by Reding, who stated that participation in the democratic life of the EU is essential for the European project and then continued with a five-page long text on the necessity of making citizens' rights—again Single Market rights—more tangible by removing the obstacles citizens' encounter in cross-border situations.[171] Consequently, we are left considering the extent to which, unlike her predecessors, she was perhaps a realist where Europe as a deliberative democracy was concerned, or whether she was doing a disservice to the progress of political contestation and democratic change in Europe by confining her attention to a rather realistic and pragmatic approach of ensuring that people felt the daily benefits of European citizenship.

Either way, one thing is certain, and that is that the context of European integration, which continues to shape the Commission's understanding of what European citizenship is and how it is represented, has once again been changing with, as yet, indeterminate outcomes. The European political, economic and cultural landscape has been changing, and with this, how European civil integration has been understood and championed. The aspiration (or 'dream') of a 'real' European civil society is at the time of writing held as keenly as ever.

Notes

1. These chapters are concerned with: Chapter 1: General provisions, Chapter 2: Policies on border checks, asylum and immigration, Chapter 3: Judicial cooperation in civil matters, Chapter 4: Judicial cooperation in criminal matters, Chapter 5: Police cooperation.
2. Commission (2015a).
3. Sefčovič (2013).

4. Reding's approach to European citizenship and her emphasis on rights, the removal of obstacles when citizens exercise their rights and the public communication of results was based on the Lamassoure Report (2008), 'The citizen and the application of Community law', which pointed out the existing obstacles to the enjoyment of citizens' rights in the single market. Barroso agreed with this report and accordingly asked Reding to follow his ideas during her mandate as Commissioner for Justice and Citizenship (see Reding 2010j). Thus, this report provided the 'blueprint' of her EU citizenship policies 2010–14.
5. This Civil Society Directorate remained within DG EMPL but was put under Reding's responsibility.
6. I am grateful that a senior Commission officials of DG COMM read and endorsed an earlier version of this chapter in terms of accuracy.
7. Reding (2013f: 7).
8. Ibid.: 4.
9. Ibid.: 2.
10. Reding (2013f: 3).
11. Reding (2013f: 4).
12. Reding (2012d: 2).
13. Ibid.
14. Reding (2010a: 3).
15. Reding (2010a, j, 2011d, 2012c, 2013a, e, f).
16. Reding (2010a: 3).
17. Reding (2010c: 2).
18. Ibid., Reding (2014g).
19. Reding (2012b: 4).
20. Reding (2010h: 2).
21. Ibid.
22. Ibid.
23. Reding (2013a: 2).
24. Reding (2013l: 2).
25. Ibid.: 3.
26. See Reding (2010a, d, h, i, j, k, 2012b, d, 2013a, f, i, k, 2014d, e, f, g).
27. Reding (2013a: 3).
28. Reding (2010a: 2).
29. Reding (2010k: 2, 2010b).
30. Reding (2012d: 4).
31. Reding (2010k: 9).
32. Reding (2011f: 2).
33. Reding (2013a: 3).
34. Reding (2011f: 2).
35. Commission (2010b: 3).

36. See, for example, Reding (2010d).
37. Ibid.
38. Ibid.
39. See Reding (2010a, h, j, 2011d, 2012c, 2013a, d, e, f, g, k, l, o, 2014b, c, d, f, g)
40. Reding (2014c: 3).
41. See Reding (2013m).
42. Reding (2010e: 2).
43. See Reding (2011g: 3, 2013a, e, g, k).
44. Reding (2011c: 3, see also 2013a).
45. Reding (2010c).
46. Reding (2010j: 4).
47. Commission (2015b), see also Reding (2010j, 2013g).
48. Directive 2011/83/EU, see also Reding (2010j, k, 2012c, 2013k).
49. Commission (2014b), see also Reding (2010j, k, 2013k).
50. Reding (2010j: 2).
51. Reding (2010e: 2).
52. Reding (2010a: 4, 2012a, see also 2013f, m, o, 2014g).
53. Reding (2013e: 2).
54. See Reding (2013d, e, f).
55. Reding (2010e: 3).
56. Reding (2010h: 4, 2011e, h).
57. Reding (2013l, m, o, 2014f).
58. Reding (2013k: 2).
59. Reding (2010e: 4, see also Reding 2010f, 2011g, 2012d, 2013f, i).
60. Alexander (2006).
61. Pérez-Díaz (2009: 28).
62. The EU social agenda, although it had a strong start in the 1960s, can be understood as underdeveloped nowadays. According to Liddle (2006: 280), 'Social Europe has stalled' and therefore would need 'both a new level of social ambition and a new model of European integration' (ibid.). Giddens (2006: 14) argued along the same lines by saying that the '[European social model] (ESM) is currently under great strain, or even failing' but qualifies this statement by putting the ESM into the complex context of reality. He argued that 'unlike other major achievements of the European Union (...) the ESM has been only minimally shaped by the EU itself', to which he added that 'the welfare state was built by nations, not by international collaboration' (ibid.: 20 f.) and accordingly in the area of social policy 'most real change will have to come from within nations' (ibid.: 21). On Social Europe, see Majone (2009, 2014), and on European social policy, see Geyer (2000), Daly (2006, 2007), Giddens (2006), Barbier (2012), and de la Porte and Heins (2014). Daly (2006:

462) divided the bulk of literature on EU social policy into three strands. The first strand of literature evaluated EU social policy by comparing it to nation-state social policy. Subsequently, EU social policy has been characterised as 'hollow and, over time, halting and limited'. The second strand of literature acknowledged that the EU has developed an 'articulated social policy in a number of key domains (for example, worker protection, health and safety in employment, equal opportunities between women and men)' (ibid.: 463). In the third kind of literature, the 'EU is represented as carving out a social space for itself which allows it to fashion key aspects of social identity, institutions and social relations in the Member States, as well as a social sphere that transcends national boundaries' (ibid.). See also Commission (1989, 1994).
63. Harrison and Woods (2007: 25) drew a distinction between citizens and consumers whereby they defined the latter as implying 'a concrete economic activity that is defined and de-limited by the structure, workings and efficiency of the market'. Based on this definition, an active consumer can be characterised as being able to choose between goods and services that are offered in any of the EU member states, effortlessly knowing that his consumer rights—about which the active consumer is well informed— are enforceable, protected and progressively reinforced, notably by the Commission in the case of the EU.
64. For more information on Alexander's understanding of the 'civil motives', see Alexander (2006: 57).
65. Reding (2013f: 6).
66. On consumer citizenship, see Everson and Joerges (2006) and Shuibne (2010).
67. Reding (2010c, e, 2013g, j, k, l, m, 2014e, g).
68. Taylor (2004: 92).
69. Alexander (2006: 196).
70. Reding (2010c, k, 2013f, g, j, k, n, o, 2014f, g).
71. Reding (2010a, h, 2012b, 2013i, k, o, 2014e, f, g).
72. See Reding (2013e).
73. Reding (2014b: 3).
74. Keane (2003: 6).
75. Reding adopted this approach of tending to neglect the communicative institutions and focusing on the legal institutions by choice, as her portfolio would allow her to focus on both.
76. Krause (2008).
77. Reding (2010e: 3).
78. Ibid.
79. Reding (2010a: 3).
80. Ibid.

81. Ibid.
82. See Reding (2010h).
83. Reding (2010j: 2).
84. Alexander (2006: 203).
85. Ibid.: 154.
86. Reding (2010j: 3).
87. Reding 2010c: 2).
88. Reding (2010e: 3).
89. Ibid.
90. Ibid.: 4.
91. Ibid.
92. Ibid.
93. Ibid.: 4.
94. Ibid.
95. Reding (2011h: 10 and 6). The reason why Reding did not want unified contract law was probably of a practical legal nature, but maybe this was also an entry point for civil activity? If one believes that 'contracts are a primary medium through which civil society actually enters into the economic realm' (Alexander 2006: 156), one could understand Reding in her attempt to apply the principle of subsidiarity to contract law as following this logic; the principle of subsidiarity in the domain of contract law would foster more civil-legal activity because of contract law being more flexible than other legal areas.
96. A reference to Hallstein's belief in the cultural force of law can be found in Reding (2010g).
97. Reding (2010e: 4).
98. Marshall (1992: 8).
99. Alexander (2006: 152).
100. Reding (2013i: 3).
101. Ibid.
102. Reding (2013a: 2).
103. Reding (2012c, 2013e).
104. Dunn (2014: 33).
105. Ibid.: 32.
106. Wallström passim and interview Commission official DG COMM, C1 Citizens' Information (name of interviewee and date of interview are confidential).
107. Interview Commission official DG COMM, C1 Citizens' Information (name of interviewee and date of interview are confidential).
108. Although, Reding's approach to public communication was different from Wallström's, both agreed on the importance of the professionalisation of the Commission's approach to it, and this is why Reding continued the professionalisation of public communication initiated by

Wallström with further training modules for staff. For example, a brochure entitled 'Learning and development opportunities for communication professionals' issued by DG ADMIN A3 Learning and Development shows all the training modules that are offered to Commissioners and senior civil servants in order to improve their public communication skills. In an email exchange, a Commission official noted that the courses started being developed under the Barroso I Commission under Wallström but that about '70% of the courses are new', that is, developed since 2010, and hence under Reding and the Barroso II Commission. Further, Reding allowed journalists to travel with the President of the Commission, Barroso, and has overseen the establishment of a new team of speechwriters in DG COMM who 'draft master speeches for Commissioners and senior level civil servants on cross-cutting issues, such as the Europe 2020 strategy, the financial crisis, the Lisbon Treaty or the EU's consumer policy, thereby establishing the coherency of messages across the Commission on cross-cutting issues (see Reding 2010l).

109. Commission (2010a, b, 2011, 2013, 2014a) and Reding (2010e, 2011d, f, 2012a, c, d, 2013a, e, 2014g).
110. The e-Justice Portal is a one-stop desk and addressed to citizens, businesses and law practitioners.
111. Reding referred to the 2013 EU citizenship report as the second report (2013e) and to the 2010 EU citizenship report as the first, as does the Commission (2014a). However, this is incorrect. The first report on EU citizenship was published in 1993 (Commission 1993, the second in 1997 (Commission 1997), the third in 2001 (Commission 2001), the fourth in 2004 (Commission 2004), the fifth in 2008 (Commission 2008). The one Reding referred to as the first report was effectively the sixth citizenship report published by the Commission.
112. For a list of factsheets on the policy areas that were within Reding's responsibility, see Commission 2012a).
113. Interview Telmo Baltazar, Member of the private cabinet of Vice-President Viviane Reding, 2 February 2011.
114. Interview Paul Magnette, then Minister in Belgium Government; Professor of Political Science ULB until 2007, author of: La citoyenneté européenne (1999), 19 May 2011.
115. Commission (2013: 13).
116. Alexander (2006: 172).
117. Interview Paul Magnette, 19 May 2011; Hallstein (1964: 26).
118. Reding (2010l: 3).
119. It needs to be noted for reasons of accuracy that the citizens' initiative did not fall into Reding's competences but into the competence of the Secretariat-General. If the citizens' initiative concerned, however, an aspect that was part of Reding's portfolio, then she would have to address

the concern European citizens voiced through the citizens' initiative. For recent analyses of the citizens' initiative and its significance, value and problematic nature, see De Clerck-Sachsse (2012), Monaghan (2012) and Szeligowska and Mincheva (2012).
120. European Union (2010).
121. Reding (2010j: 6).
122. Interview Telmo Baltazar, 2 February 2011.
123. Ibid.
124. Interviews Commission officials DG Justice, Directorate C Fundamental Rights and Citizenship and Directorate A Communication Actions (names of interviewees and dates of interviews are confidential), Paul Magnette, 19 May 2011.
125. Interviews Claus Sorensen, 24 January 2011 and Joachim Ott, 12 January 2011.
126. Interview Commission official Directorate A Communication Actions (name of interviewee and date of interviews are confidential).
127. Interview Commission official DG COMM, Directorate C 'Citizens' (name of interviewee and date of interviews are confidential).
128. Reding (2011c: 2).
129. Reding (2012b: 2).
130. Reding (2011c: 3).
131. Reding (2012b: 2).
132. See Reding (2011b).
133. On the coverage of the Eurozone crisis by the British Press, see Baranowska (2014). For various analytical approaches to the Eurozone crisis, see Bruno de Witte, Adrienne Héritier and Alexander H. Trechsel (eds.) (2013) and the special issue 'The Effects of the Eurozone Sovereign Debt Crisis: Differentiated Integration between the Centre and the New Peripheries of the EU' in *European Politics and Society* 2014, 15(3).
134. Reding (2011b: 3).
135. Ibid.
136. Reding (2012a: 5).
137. Reding (2012b: 5).
138. See Reding (2012c, d).
139. Reding (2012c: 4).
140. Ibid.
141. See Reding (2013a).
142. Reding (2013h: 4).
143. Ibid. and 2012c.
144. Reding (2014a: 2).
145. Ibid.: 3.
146. Ibid.

147. It needs to be noted, though, that during Reding's mandate the creation of a Euronews studio in Brussels financed by the EU was envisaged. However, views about Euronews are divided. Whereas some Commission officials believed in its quality (interview Telmo Baltazar, 2 February 2011), others considered it boring and inappropriate to report on EU affairs (interview Member of the Cabinet of Vice-President Margot Wallström; name and date confidential).
148. Interview Telmo Baltazar, 2 February 2011.
149. Calhoun (2003: 249).
150. Habermas (2001).
151. Reding (2012a: 3).
152. Interview Commission official DG COMM, Directorate C 'Citizens' (name of interviewee and date of interview are confidential).
153. Commission (no date).
154. Barroso (2012: 12).
155. Commission (2014c).
156. Barroso (2012: 9).
157. Reding (2012c: 4).
158. Commission (2010a: 23).
159. Commission (2012c).
160. Commission (2012b).
161. Reding (2013e: 2).
162. Commission (2011, 2013) and Reding (2012c, 2013a).
163. Commission (2011: 3). For a discussion of whether the EYC promoted market citizenship (or not), see Vogiatzis (2014).
164. Commission (2015b).
165. Ibid.
166. Representation of the European Commission in Berlin (personal communication, 14 January 2013).
167. Reding (2013f: 9).
168. See Reding (2013b, c, p, q, r, s, t, u, v, w, 2014h, i, j).
169. Reding (2013e, f).
170. See Reding (2013n).
171. Reding (2011a: 83).

References

Alexander, J. (2006). *The civil sphere*. Oxford: Oxford University Press.
Baranowska, P. M. (2014). The coverage of the Eurozone economic crisis in the British press. *Perspectives on European Politics and Society*, 15(4), 500–517.
Barbier, J.-C. (2012). Tracing the fate of EU "social policy": Changes in political discourse from the "Lisbon strategy" to "Europe 2020". *International Labour Review*, 151(4), 377–399.

Barroso, M. (2012, September 12). *State of the Union 2012 address* (SPEECH/12/596). Strasbourg.

Calhoun, C. (2003). The democratic integration of Europe: Interests, identity, and the public sphere. In M. Berezin & M. Schain (Eds.), *Europe without borders: Re-mapping territory, citizenship and identity in a transnational age* (pp. 243–274). London: Sage.

CCE (Commission des Communautés Européennes). (1989, November 29). *Communication from the Commission concerning its action programme relating to the implementation of the community charter of basic social rights for workers* (COM (89) 568 final).

CCE (Commission des Communautés Européennes). (1993). Report from the Commission on the citizenship of the Union. 21 December, COM (93) 702.

CCE (Commission des Communautés Européennes). (1994, July 27). *European social policy—A way forward for the Union. A white paper* (COM (94) 333 final).

CCE (Commission des Communautés Européennes). (1997, May 27). Second report from the Commission on the citizenship of the Union. (COM (97) 230).

CCE (Commission des Communautés Européennes). (2001, September 7). *Third report from the Commission on the citizenship of the Union* (COM (2001) 506).

CCE (Commission des Communautés Européennes). (2004, October 26). *Fourth report on citizenship of the Union (1 May 2001–30 April 2004)* (COM (2004) 695).

CCE (Commission des Communautés Européennes). (2008, February 15). *Fifth report on citizenship of the Union (1 May 2004–30 June 2007)* (COM (2008) 85).

CCE (Commission des Communautés Européennes). (2010a, October 27). *EU citizenship report 2010. Dismantling the obstacles to EU citizens' rights* (COM (2010) 603 final).

CCE (Commission des Communautés Européennes). (2010b, October 19). *Strategy for the effective implementation of the Charter of Fundamental Right by the European Union* (COM (2010) 573 final).

CCE (Commission des Communautés Européennes). (2011, August 11). *Proposal for a decision of the European Parliament and of the council on the European Year of Citizens (2013)* (COM (2011) 489 final).

CCE (Commission des Communautés Européennes). (2012a). Viviane Reding, Vice President of the European Commission—Making citizens' lives easier. http://ec.europa.eu/commission_2010-2014/reding/factsheets/index_en.htm. Accessed 15 Aug 2011.

CCE (Commission des Communautés Européennes). (2012b). Growth—European commission—Public consultations. http://ec.europa.eu/enterprise/newsroom/cf/itemdetail.cfm?item_id=6074&lang=en. Accessed 4 Feb 2012.

CCE (Commission des Communautés Européennes). (2012c). European commission launches public consultation on citizens' rights. http://ec.europa.eu/unitedkingdom/about_us/office_in_northern_ireland/2012/120509_en.htm. Accessed 4 Feb 2012.

CCE (Commission des Communautés Européennes). (2013, May 8). *EU citizenship report 2013. EU citizens: Your rights, your future* (COM (2013) 269 final).

CCE (Commission des Communautés Européennes). (2014a, March 12). EU citizenship: European Parliament supports Commission's efforts to foster EU citizens' rights. Memo, Strasbourg.

CCE (Commission des Communautés Européennes). (2014b). Protection of personal data. http://ec.europa.eu/justice/data-protection/. Accessed 12 Mar 2015.

CCE (Commission des Communautés Européennes). (2014c). President José Manuel Barroso. Speeches and statements. http://ec.europa.eu/commission_2010-2014/president/news/speeches-statements/index_en.htm. Accessed 4 Oct 2012.

CCE (Commission des Communautés Européennes). (2015a). Closed initiatives. European citizens' initiative. http://ec.europa.eu/citizens-initiative/public/initiatives/finalised/answered. Accessed 12 Mar 2015.

CCE (Commission des Communautés Européennes). (2015b). Package travel. http://ec.europa.eu/consumers/consumer_rights/travel/package/index_en.htm. Accessed 25 Mar 2015.

CCE. (2013, May 8). EU citizenship report 2013. EU citizens: Your rights, your future, COM(2013) 269 final.

CCE (Commission des Communautés Européennes). (no date). Citizens' dialogues. http://ec.europa.eu/citizens-dialogues/, http://ec.europa.eu/european-debate/index_en.htm. Accessed 4 Oct 2012.

Daly, M. (2006). EU social policy after Lisbon. *Journal of Common Market Studies, 44*(3), 461–481.

Daly, M. (2007). Whither EU social policy? An account and assessment of developments in the Lisbon social inclusion process. *Journal of Social Policy, 37*(1), 1–19.

De Clerck-Sachsse, J. (2012). Civil society and democracy in the EU: The paradox of the European citizens' initiative. *Perspectives on European Politics and Society, 13*(3), 299–311.

De la Porte, C., & Heins, E. (2014). Game change in EU and social policy: Towards more European integration. In M. Rodrigues & E. Xiarchogiannopoulou (Eds.), *The Eurozone crisis and the transformation of EU governance: Internal and external implications* (pp. 157–172). Farnham: Ashgate Publishing.

De Witte, B., Héritier, A., & Trechsel, A. (Eds.). (2013). *The crisis and the state of European democracy*. Florence: European University Institute, Robert Schuman Centre for Advanced Studies, European Union Democracy Observatory.

Dunn, J. (2014). *Breaking democracy's spell*. New Haven: Yale University Press.
European Union. (2010, May 4). *Official Journal of the European Union*, C115.
European Union. (2011). Directive 2011/83/EU of the European Parliament and of the Council of 25 October 2011 on consumer rights.
Everson, M., & Joerges, C. (2006). *Consumer citizenship in postnational constellations?* (EUI Working Paper LAW, No. 2006/47).
Geyer, R. (2000). *Exploring European social policy*. Cambridge: Polity.
Giddens, A. (2006). A social model for Europe. In A. Giddens, P. Diamond, & R. Liddle (Eds.), *Global Europe, social Europe* (pp. 14–36). Cambridge: Polity.
Habermas, J. (2001). Why Europe needs a constitution. *New Left Review, 11*, 5–26.
Hallstein, W. (1964). *The unity of the drive for Europe*. Address by Professor Dr. Walter Hallstein, President of the Commission of the European Economic Community, at the opening session of the seventh conference of European local authorities. Rome, 15 October.
Harrison, J., & Woods, L. (2007). *European broadcasting law and policy*. Cambridge: Cambridge University Press.
Keane, J. (2003). *Global civil society?* Oxford: Oxford University Press.
Krause, S. (2008). *Civil passions: Moral sentiment and democratic deliberation*. Oxford: Princeton University Press.
Lamassoure, A. (2008). *The citizen and the application of Community law*. Report to the President of the Republic. http://www.alainlamassoure.eu/liens/975.pdf. Accessed 13 July 2011.
Liddle, R. (2006). A common social justice policy for Europe. In A. Giddens, P. Diamond, & R. Liddle (Eds.), *Global Europe, social Europe* (pp. 279–298). Cambridge: Polity.
Magnette, P. (1999). *La Citoyenneté européenne: droits, politiques, institutions*. Bruxelles: Editions de l'Université de Bruxelles.
Majone, G. (2009). *Dilemmas of European integration: The ambiguities and pitfalls of integration by stealth*. Oxford: Oxford University Press.
Majone, G. (2014). *Rethinking the Union of Europe post-crisis: Has integration gone too far?* Cambridge: Cambridge University Press.
Marshall, T. H. (1992). *Citizenship and social class*. London: Pluto Press.
Monaghan, E. (2012). Assessing participation and democracy in the EU: The case of the European citizens' initiative. *Perspectives on European Politics and Society, 13*(3), 285–298.
Pérez-Díaz, V. (2009). Markets as conversations. Markets' contributions to civility, the public sphere and civil society at large. In V. Pérez-Díaz (Ed.), *Markets and civil society. The European experience in comparative perspective* (pp. 27–76). Oxford: Berghahn Books.
Reding, V. (2010a, January 11). *Opening remarks at the European Parliament hearing in the Committee on Civil Liberties, Justice and Home Affairs (LIBE)*. (SPEECH/10/). Brussels: European Parliament Hearing.

Reding, V. (2010b, February 18). *Towards a European area of fundamental rights: The EU's Charter of Fundamental Rights and accession to the European Convention of Human Rights* (SPEECH/10/33). High Level Conference on the Future of the European Court of Human Rights Interlaken.

Reding, V. (2010c, March 15). *Making the single market work for Europe's citizens and businesses: Reforming international litigation* (SPEECH/10/92). Brussels I Conference on the Reform of International Litigation in Europe, Madrid.

Reding, V. (2010d, March 18). *Next steps for justice, fundamental rights and citizenship in the EU* (SPEECH/10/108). European Policy Centre Briefing, Brussels.

Reding, V. (2010e, April 10). *A European Law Institute: An important milestone for an ever closer union of law, rights and justice* (SPEECH/10/154). Speech at the European University Institute Florence.

Reding, V. (2010f, April 29). *Auf dem Weg zu einem Europa der Bürger—Neue Perspektiven durch den Vertrag von Lissabon* (SPEECH/10/198). Podiumsdiskussion, Berlin.

Reding, V. (2010g, Mai 14). *Die Bedeutung einer wirksamen Kommunikation des Europäischen Unionsrechts für die Herausbildung eines starken Europäischen Justizraums*. Rede vor dem 61 (SPEECH/10/239). Deutschen Anwaltstag 2010, Aachen.

Reding, V. (2010h, June 2). *Building citizen's rights into the single market*. 2nd Consumer Rights Forum 2010 (SPEECH/). Brussels.

Reding, V. (2010i, June 22) *How to make the Charter of Fundamental Rights the compass for all EU policies?* (SPEECH/10/324). Hearing of the Committee on Civil Liberties, Justice and Home Affairs, Brussels, European Parliament.

Reding, V. (2010j, July 1). *Effectively tackling obstacles faced by EU citizens: The need for a new approach and a new ambition, EU citizens' rights conference—The way forward* (SPEECH/10/353). Brussels.

Reding, V. (2010k, September 17). *The importance of the EU Charter of Fundamental Rights for European legislative practice* (SPEECH/10/463). Lecture given at the German Institute for Human Rights, Berlin.

Reding, V. (2010l, June 21). Letter to Barroso, D (2010) 36.

Reding, V. (2011a). Justice et citoyen: mettre le citoyen au cœur du projet européen. In B. Fauvarque-Cosson, et al., (Eds.), *La citoyenneté européenne. Collection trans Europe experts* (pp. 83–87). Paris: Société de législation comparée.

Reding, V. (2011b, September 8). *The end of Europe? No, the beginning of a stronger, more united Europe* (SPEECH/11/566). Economic Policy Seminar, Helsinki.

Reding, V. (2011c, September 14). *La crise vue comme une chance—Vers un nouveau plan Schuman* (SPEECH/11/573). Conférence Débat Sciences-Po Paris—Notre Europe, Paris.

Reding, V. (2011d, September 15). *Justice et citoyens: Mettre le citoyen au cœur du projet européen* (SPEECH/11/XXX). Conseil supérieur du notariat, Paris, le.

Reding, V. (2011e, September 21). *Auf dem Weg zum optionalen Europäischen Vertragsrecht: Welche Regeln brauchen Europas Unternehmen und Verbraucher im grenzüberschreitenden Handel?* (SPEECH/11/593). Vertretung des Landes Nordrhein-Westfalen, Brüssel.

Reding, V. (2011f, October 6). *Know your rights: Applying the Charter of Fundamental Rights* (SPEECH/11/638). Seminar on the application of the Charter of Fundamental Rights: Handling of citizens' petitions and complaints on fundamental rights, Brussels.

Reding, V. (2011g, Oktober 15). *Die supranationale Rechtsgemeinschaft als Fundament der künftigen Confoederatio Europaea* (REDE/11). Festakt, 60-Jahrfeier des Europa-Instituts der Universität des Saarlandes, Saarbrücken.

Reding, V. (2011h, June 3). *The next steps towards a European Contract Law for businesses and consumers*, no place indicated.

Reding, V. (2012a, February 1). *20 years after Maastricht—Quo vadis, Europa?* (SPEECH/12/58). Speech on the occasion of the 1st anniversary of the Press Club Brussels Europe, Brussels.

Reding, V. (2012b, March 14). *A new deal for Europe* (SPEECH/12/184). Deutsche Bank's 13th women in European business conference, Frankfurt.

Reding, V. (2012c, November 28). *Building the future with Europeans in the European Year of Citizens* (SPEECH/12/886). Brussels.

Reding, V. (2012d, December 6). *A European Union grounded in justice and fundamental rights* (SPEECH/12/918). Brussels.

Reding, V. (2013a, February 19). *EU citizenship: A new impetus—Towards the 2013 EU citizenship report* (SPEECH/13/139). Brussels.

Reding, V. (2013b, July 2). *Situation of fundamental rights: Standards and practices in Hungary* (SPEECH/13/603). Strasbourg.

Reding, V. (2013c, March 22). *Main messages of Vice-President Viviane Reding at the Citizens' Dialogue in Thessaloniki, Greece* (SPEECH/13/254).

Reding, V. (2013d, April 24). *Cutting red tape for citizens and businesses* (SPEECH/13/362). Brussels.

Reding, V. (2013e, Mai 8). *EU citizenship report: 12 new actions to make EU citizens' rights a reality* (SPEECH/13/393). Brussels.

Reding, V. (2013f, Mai 24). *From vision to action: Putting citizens at the heart of Europe* (SPEECH/13/458). Luxembourg.

Reding, V. (2013g, July 9). *Modernising EU rules on package travel: Plan your summer holiday with peace of mind* (SPEECH/13/620). Brussels.

Reding, V. (2013h, September 3). *Seizing the big day in 2014: A European parliamentary democracy in action* (SPEECH/13/670). Brussels.

Reding, V. (2013i, September 4). *The EU and the rule of law—What next?* (SPEECH/13/677). Brussels.

Reding, V. (2013j, October 7). *Building a true European area of justice that works for citizens and businesses* (SPEECH/13/782). Luxembourg.
Reding, V. (2013k, October 22). *An important moment for European democracy* (SPEECH/13/845). Strasbourg.
Reding, V. (2013l, November 21). *From Maastricht to Lisbon: Building a European area of justice in small steps and great bounds* (SPEECH/13/960). Brussels.
Reding, V. (2013m, November 22). *Mapping the road towards a true European area of justice* (SPEECH/13/963). Brussels.
Reding, V. (2013n, November 21). *I am just a first pillar girl* (SPEECH/13/964). Brussels.
Reding, V. (2013o, November 27). *Three steps and a leap forward: Building fair trial rights across the EU step by step, day by day* (SPEECH/13/986). Brussels.
Reding, V. (2013p, June 16). *Main messages: Citizens' Dialogue in Heidelberg* (SPEECH/13/639). Heidelberg, Germany.
Reding, V. (2013q, July 23). *Main messages: Citizens' Dialogue in Sofia* (SPEECH/13/655). Sofia, Bulgaria.
Reding, V. (2013r, September 13). *Messages principaux: Dialogue avec les citoyens à Namur* (SPEECH/13/696). Namur, Belgium.
Reding, V. (2013s, September 16). *Main messages: Trieste Citizens' Dialogue* (SPEECH/13/706). Trieste, Italy.
Reding, V. (2013t, September 24). *Main messages: Helsinki Citizens' Dialogue* (SPEECH/13/738). Helsinki, Finland.
Reding, V. (2013u, October 15). *Main messages: Citizens' Dialogue in Stockholm* (SPEECH/13/813). Stockholm, Sweden.
Reding, V. (2013v, November 14). *Main messages: Citizens' Dialogue in Marseille* (SPEECH/13/924). Marseille, France.
Reding, V. (2013w, December 13). *Main messages: Citizens' Dialogue in Vilnius* (SPEECH/13/1077). Vilnius, Lithuania.
Reding, V. (2014a, January 7). *2014: Time to make a choice* (SPEECH/14/1). Brussels.
Reding, V. (2014b, January 15). *Citizenship must not be up for sale* (SPEECH/14/18). Strasbourg.
Reding, V. (2014c, January 15). *Upholding the right to free movement and fighting cases of abuse* (Strasbourg). SPEECH/14/23.
Reding, V. (2014d, January 21). *Freizügigkeit im Binnenmarkt: gemeinsam für den Schutz eines unverzichtbaren Grundrechts* (SPEECH/14/47). Brussels.
Reding, V. (2014e, April 2). *Quo vadis, European justice policy?* (SPEECH/14/273). Brussels.
Reding, V. (2014f, April 15). *Making sure European area of justice works for international couples and their children* (SPEECH/14/329). Strasbourg.
Reding, V. (2014g, June 20). *Justice past, justice present and justice future—Three messages to the European Council* (SPEECH/14/481). Brussels.

Reding, V. (2014h, February 10), *Main messages: Citizens' Dialogue in London* (SPEECH/14/118). London, UK.

Reding, V. (2014i, February 23). *Main messages from the Citizens' Dialogue in Barcelona* (SPEECH/14/153). Barcelona, Spain.

Reding, V. (2014j, March 14). *Main messages from the Citizens' Dialogue in Amsterdam* (SPEECH/14/224). Amsterdam, Netherlands.

Šefčovič, M. (2013, April 23). *A million voices make a difference: The power of the European Citizens' Initiative* (SPEECH/13/356). Brussels.

Shuibne, N. (2010). The resilience of EU market citizenship. *Common Market Law Review, 47*(6), 1597–1628.

Szeligowska, D., & Mincheva, E. (2012). The European Citizens' Initiative—Empowering European citizens within the institutional triangle: A political and legal analysis. *Perspectives on European Politics and Society, 13*(3), 270–284.

Taylor, C. (2004). *Modern social imaginaries.* Durham/London: Duke University Press.

Vogiatzis, N. (2014). A 'European Year of Citizens'? Looking beyond decision 1093/2012: Eyeing the European elections of 2014. *Perspectives on European Politics and Society, 15*(4), 571–588.

CHAPTER 7

Summary

European Citizenship 1951–2014: An Uninterrupted European Civil Narrative

The five representations of European citizenship that I have identified and analysed in the previous chapters—Homo Oeconomicus (1951–1972), A People's Europe (1973–1992), Europe of Transparency (1993–2004), Europe of Agorai (2005–2009) and Europe of Rights (2010–14)—enable us to understand the meaning of the concept of European citizenship better. They revealed three things: first, that European citizenship has its own nature and that this nature cannot be fully understood if it is conceived of or compared to national or universal cosmopolitan citizenship. Indeed, European citizenship cannot be examined as a static concept with pre-fixed categories; rather it needs to be understood as a dynamic, diachronically evolving concept—it is open to interpretation and meaning making. Second, the five representations of European citizenship showed that the Commission has reinterpreted the meaning of European citizenship on five separate occasions and that each particular meaning of European citizenship depended on the institutional, political, economic and historical contexts at the time. The evolution of European citizenship and the European integration process thus occur in parallel and have been interlinked. In other words, they haven't occurred in vacuums or disconnected from each other. As Shaw pointed out, '[T]he development of citizenship is related in different ways to other changes of both an institutional and an ideational nature which can be seen within the scope of European integration processes',[1] or to put the matter another way, 'European citizenship was conceived of as a dynamic status whose content was to evolve in parallel to the key stages of European integration'.[2] Third, the five representations of European citizenship testified to the fact that the Commission has since 1951 realised the value of public communication in facilitating the development of a solidary European civil society marked by a unity of interests and civil dispositions within its own plurality. It has in fact, experimented with three different styles of public communication in order to engage European citizens, to appeal to them, to effectively tell them their story and to give them their own place in European integration history.

Indeed, when combined, the five representations of European citizenship form an uninterrupted European civil narrative, though, as noted in the preface, this narrative is not a story of unmitigated success. Rather it is a story of ambition, unachieved goals, adaptation and reinvention. The continuous need for change and adaptation can be understood as pointing to a certain inadequacy of the representations expressed through their temporary character. This lack of stability and permanence indicates, so one could argue, failure and incompletion.

Notwithstanding all shortcomings, the representations of European citizenship constitute an uninterrupted European civil narrative that can testify to the Commission's persistent civil ambitions. The narrative, its successes and failures, can be briefly and summarily characterised in the following way:

Homo oeconomicus[3] (1951–1972) was a male qualified coal and steel worker (from 1957 a worker *per se*) of French, German, Dutch, Luxembourgian, Italian or Belgian nationality. The Commission imagined that such a worker would happily use his newly acquired right to free movement in order to find work in another member state. However, the Commission well understood that homo oeconomicus would only move across Europe if he could take his family with him and be sure that the Community also provided for his wife and children. And the Community did. Through housing projects and initiatives to facilitate the children's schooling, the Community tried to make homo oeconomicus and his family feel at home 'in Europe'. Homo oeconomicus was portrayed as a responsible family father who was concerned about keeping a comfortable standard of living for himself and his family. And in order to show him that moving to another member state would not threaten his standard of living, the Community concerned itself with the harmonisation of social security schemes across Europe where necessary. Once homo oeconomicus and his family had become familiar with their new European way of life and settled in their new home, the Community expected homo oeconomicus to become more curious about the European Community and his fellow European citizens. Accordingly, the Community provided homo oeconomicus and his family with a financial bonus to go travelling across Europe. The new opportunities the European Community offered homo oeconomicus would, so the Community hoped, encourage him to inform himself about the Community, to develop curiosity and ultimately acquire a European civil consciousness. However, the representation of homo oeconomicus wasn't able to capture as wide a European public as had been hoped for by the Commission. Whereas the Commission had been keen to provide workers' families with the same rights to freedom of movement and establishment as fast as possible, the concrete realisation of these rights took longer than expected—the directive concerning the abolition of restrictions on movement and residence within the Community for workers of Member States and their families was created in 1968, and the one regarding the schooling of workers' children took another decade and saw the light only in 1977. Concomitantly, by the late 1960s it became apparent that 'Homo Oeconomicus' was soon to become obsolete. The rights ascribed to homo oeconomicus were too narrowly conceived and couldn't keep pace with the Commission's pressing ambition to push for greater political integration. In other words, homo oeconomicus lacked political rights necessary for democratic citizenship. Consequently, in the context of the political challenges of the early 1970s and the Community's optimism and aspiration to internally democratise the European Community, the appellation 'European citizen' acquired a new meaning. 'Homo oeconomicus' was 'morphed' into a specifically political-federal European citizen residing in 'A People's Europe' (1973–1992). At that time the Community imagined the European citizen to be a member of a liberal democratic Community and accordingly provided European citizens with electoral rights and encouraged them in 1979 for the first time to make their way to the polling stations, as part of the 180 million European voters, to directly elect the European Parliament. The introduction of European electoral rights marked the first concrete step in providing European citizens with the opportunity to actively participate in the democratic life of the Community. But there was more to a 'People's Europe' than just electoral rights, namely the use by the Commission of a single-perspectival conception of Community space, the introduction of specifically European cultural events and the use of European political-federal symbolism. I'll take each of these in turn. First, the way the Community publicly communicated Europe as a single-perspectival space was as a 'homeland', a Europe conceived of as a single political-federal, economic-social and cultural unity buttressed by European economic and social rights. Second, there was an increasing emphasis by the Commission on certain aspects of a 'European culture' mainly, sport and music. Third, political-federal European symbols such as the flag, the anthem and the emblem were promoted and adopted at exhibitions and fairs, at the seats of the institutions, public buildings or outside the Community's information offices and delegations in an attempt to become part of the daily experienced reality of European citizens, who were also further encouraged to celebrate the birthday of the European Community on 9 May 9 (the day of the Schuman Declaration in 1950).

Whereas the Commission had been confident about the suitability of this new representation of European citizenship and had seen it as a version of European citizenship which, a majority of Europeans could and would want to identify with, they failed to communicate its significance in anything like a reassuring way. Rather, the European public viewed the Commission's intentions with suspicion and became increasingly concerned about the Community becoming a top-down superstate where nationally based citizenship was at risk of being marginalised. In other words, the Community was seen as a threat to Europeans national identity, which led to the near failure of the Maastricht Treaty in 1992.

Following the difficult ratification of the Maastricht Treaty (1992), the Commission felt that European citizens were at odds with what they perceived to be the secretive bureaucracy of the European institutions. It believed that European citizens desired both transparency and easy access to official information and documents in order to be able to hold European politicians accountable and, more hopefully, to obtain opportunities to enter into a dialogue with the European institutions. In response, the Commission attempted to create opportunities for European citizens to enter into what they referred to as 'debate and dialogue' with Commission officials. Accordingly, the third representation of the 'political-dialogical European citizen' was a version of the ideal civil actor in a 'Europe of Transparency' (1993–2004). European citizens were to be well-informed rational discussants deeply concerned with all forms and sorts of policy matters. In short: European citizens who were perceived as helping to bring about the civil arena of a European public sphere.[4] The idea of debate and dialogue led to a multiperspectival conception of Community space in which the Commission started to increasingly and progressively use both physical and virtual space on different levels, namely on Community, national, regional and local levels. At the same time it was recognised that public communication needed to become more inclusive and to be deepened and extended in order to genuinely involve European citizens. What that meant was that if the Commission was to realise its agenda of debate and dialogue with the European citizenry in a meaningful way rather than merely one rhetorically appealed to, it had to make European citizens' direct engagement with and participation in the European project genuine. However, and as pointed out in chapter "Europe of Transparency (1993–2004)", the European citizens' discursive engagement in debate and dialogue was confined to a narrow range of topics chosen by the Commission. Debate and dialogue were further seen by the Commission as a possibility to encourage agreement through 'educating' European citizens rather than to stimulate genuine contestation—an 'essential element of even the "thinnest" theories of democracy', according to Hix and Follesdal.[5] The aim and hope for discursive involvement was to a certain extent compromised by the Commission's apparent lack of ability or courage to encourage and manage disagreement as much as agreement. This lack was to be addressed and rectified in the next representation.

Indeed, the need to generate a more meaningful debate gained in urgency when in 2004/2005 the Commission (supported by the European Parliament) set itself the challenge to devise a public communication strategy that would lead to the successful ratification of the Constitutional Treaty. To help with this, Barroso appointed Margot Wallström as Commissioner for Communication Strategy. It was the combination of the context of the upcoming ratification challenge of the Constitutional Treaty and Wallström's understanding of European citizenship and European democracy that led to the emergence the fourth representation 'Europe of Agorai' as a form of civil-spatial European citizenship.

In this representation (2005–2009) the European citizen was understood as an intelligent and rational deliberator who was interested in and knowledgeable about European policies and who could (at least in theory) act as a policy-advisor to the Commission. The Commission imagined European citizens to be enthusiastic about new opportunities of involvement and about 'being taken seriously'. Such citizens, it was thought, would be keen on debating European policies and correspondingly would utilise the virtual and physical European agorai that the Commission had built. The Commission imagined that European citizens would sit in front of their computer screens whilst engaging in deliberative virtual online fora with their equals from across the EU and/or happily meet their peers face to face in the European public spaces to discuss the future of 'their' Europe. Sometimes, so the Commission hoped, these European citizens would readily pack their suitcases and impatiently make their way to Brussels to debate European policies and the future of the EU. In other words, the Commission believed that debate and dialogue facilitated by these virtual and physical European public spaces gave European citizens the real possibility to debate European topics, to voice their own opinions and to reach a common consensus on the European project. Furthermore, through partnerships with local, regional and national radio stations and TV channels, the Commission attempted to bring the town squares of Europe into European living rooms and to enable European citizens to follow the European debate from their homes. But even this was not enough: the Commission also duly tried to give 'ownership' of Europe to its citizens via the involvement of civil society associations. The shortcomings of this representation were essentially threefold: first, it relied entirely on the assumption that European citizens were genuinely interested in EU politics and desired to be more actively involved in decision-making processes. This judgement stood in contradiction to European citizens' apathy for EU politics that had been demonstrated in various studies and academic research during the 1990s/2000s. Second, Wallström believed that even those who weren't quite as interested in EU politics could become interested if they were encouraged. However, this would entail an immense investment of financial and human resources without much guarantee of success. Third, and directly linked to the second, it was impossible to assess the cost-benefit of pan-European deliberations, and as such, the approach was thought not to be sufficiently effective in the short term (if at all). Overall, the fourth representation of European citizenship can be seen as too ambitious and accordingly it was soon replaced.

With the Lisbon Treaty (2009) and the Barroso II Commission taking office, the emphasis on deliberative democracy almost disappeared completely. Instead there was a new emphasis on Europe as an area of freedom, security and justice. With this change in emphasis, the fifth representation emerged as a 'Europe of Rights' (2010–2014). In this representation, European citizenship was understood as defined by civil-legal rights and accordingly, the European citizens were represented in the form of citizen-consumers who gained their rights from the Single Market and who should be able to easily enjoy these rights. The Commission's objective was therefore to remove all obstacles that European citizens encountered when trying to exercise their rights across European borders. One of these obstacles lay in the lack of knowledge about these cross-border rights. What the Commission believed was that European citizens had for a long time been frustrated with different consumer regulations across the EU that made their online shopping difficult. In short, it was felt, above all else, that European citizens wanted to do nothing other than move freely and travel effortlessly across European borders, know how to register their car in another member country, know more about health insurance across Europe, understand their rights and legislation when it came to cross-border matters relating to marriage, divorce or death—that is, European citizens wanted to utilise the quotidian benefits gained from the Single Market. Once the Community has fulfilled its role of rendering citizens' rights understandable and easily enjoyable, European citizens would, so it was imagined, develop a solidarity with and loyalty to the European Union and fellow European citizens. 'Europe of Rights' can be seen as the most extreme form of market citizenship in the European Union so far. Deliberative engagement was marginalised and European citizenship was essentially reduced to a form of consumer-citizenship. In short, the Commission did not manage to strike a balance between a Single Market and a deliberative-democratic approach to European citizenship.

To conclude, despite the shortcomings, failed ambitions and the short-lived character of particularly the last two representations, this uninterrupted European civil narrative is significant in three ways. First, this civil narrative sheds light on the limited diversity of meanings attached to European civil identity by the Commission. There have been five representations of European citizenship between 1951 and 2014. To put the matter rather differently, two aspects combine under what we might call (following Harrison)[6] Europe's invariant civil concern of identity: namely that European citizenship has been both an enduring category and an utterly plastic and historically contingent category. In short, this civil narrative reflects both an enduring concern and the diverse meanings variously attached to it. European citizenship as a civil identity should be a banal concern that accompanies us wherever we are and go and whatever stage of life we are at. But as yet it is not. This has been the problem the Commission (and the EU) has persistently struggled to resolve—

with the net result that historically, being European has no fixed meaning and has meant different things at different times. As Yuval-Davis argued, 'Identities are narratives, stories people tell themselves and others about who they are (and who they are not)'. At the same time, identity is always in transition, 'always producing itself through the combined processes of being and becoming, belonging and longing to belong'.[7] This 'duality' is reflected in the present narrative of European civil identity.

Second, the study of this European civil narrative goes some way towards rectifying the neglect that some European scholars and theorists display when attempting to understand European integration in exclusively political or economic terms, especially when discussing the first two decades of European integration. In fact, it testifies to the Commission's continuous and persistent aspiration and attempts to facilitate the emergence of a European civil society through the public communication of European citizenship. It has actively and with perseverance attempted to facilitate what I call a Civil Europe. The public communication of European citizenship is just one of many civil initiatives that the Community pursued since the 1950s in order to stimulate a European civil consciousness and ultimately the emergence of a European civil society. Such a European civil society has been consistently understood by the Commission as an 'arena not of solidarity narrowly defined in a communitarian and particularistic way'[8] but rather as 'the kind of mutual identification that unites individuals dispersed by class, race, religion, ethnicity, or race'.[9] Ultimately, the Commission envisaged the emergence of a European civil society sustained by 'Unity in Diversity', the EU's motto. Significantly, the achievement of 'Unity in Diversity' requires civil legitimacy to bring the two (unity and diversity) together through a form of civil legitimacy which constructs civil boundaries that circumscribe a pluralistic Europe at ease with itself. Civil legitimacy cannot simply be derived from the political or economic sphere; it requires civil society equipped with civil force, a civil force[10] that maintains the cultural and psychological boundaries that define who is a European and who is not. And this was just as well understood by Monnet as it was by Reding. Nevertheless, it is clear that such a European civil society hasn't emerged yet and that in this way the Commission's attempts haven't had as much success as they hoped for.

Third, the study of this uninterrupted European civil narrative shows that European citizens have their own place in the European integration process and that we can tell stories about their belonging. The history of this belonging must be reflective and concern itself with European identities (and cultural heritages) as they are assembled together under the rubric of citizenship, solidarity and diversity. The history of the way European citizens are represented and understood speaks of Europe's contingent changing circumstances as well as its abiding concern for who we as Europeans might actually be and what we might actually belong to.

Notes

1. Shaw (2007: 41). Diez (1999: 601) also recognised the link between European integration and citizenship, as he noted that 'a most interesting story in this respect is how citizenship developed from concerns about Europe's political future and role in the world, via the necessity to regulate membership of a single market, to being a response to questions about legitimacy and democracy within the EU'.
2. Magnette (1999: 205).
3. Throughout this section, the European citizen and the representations of European citizenship have been intentionally reified.
4. Here understood in the Habermasian sense, that is, as a forum for rational debate.
5. Follesdal and Hix (2006: 533).
6. Harrison (forthcoming).
7. Yuval-Davis (2006: 201). This passage is taken from Andrews (2007: 9).
8. Alexander (2006: 43).
9. Ibid.
10. A civil force is both ideological, in the sense of consisting of the ideas we have about ourselves, and institutional, consisting of the factual media, the law, parties and formal voluntary associations.

References

Alexander, J. (2006). The civil sphere. Oxford: Oxford University Press.
Andrews, M. (2007). Shaping history: Narratives of political change. Cambridge: Cambridge University Press.
Diez, T. (1999). Speaking 'Europe': The politics of integration discourse. Journal of European Public Policy, 6(4), 598–613.
Follesdal, A., & Hix, S. (2006). Why there is a democratic deficit in the EU: A response to Majone and Moravcsik. Journal of Common Market Studies, 44(3), 533–562.
Harrison, J. (forthcoming). The civil power of the news. Unpublished manuscript.

Magnette, P. (1999). La Citoyenneté européenne: droits, politiques, institutions. Bruxelles: Editions de l'Université de Bruxelles.

Shaw, J. (2007). The transformation of citizenship in the European Union: Electoral rights and the restructuring of political space. Cambridge: Cambridge University Press.

Yuval-Davis, N. (2006). Belonging and the politics of belonging. Patterns of Prejudice, 40(3), 197–214.

Bibliography

Beck, U., & Grande, E. (2007). *Cosmopolitan Europe*. Cambridge: Polity.
Bossuat, G. (1998, Juin). *Entretien avec Jacques-René Rabier*. http://www.eui.eu/HAEU/OralHistory/pdf/INT609.pdf.
CCE (Commission des Communautés Européennes). (1969, Octobre 16). *Orientations sur la politique d'information de la Commission pour 1970* (SEC (69) 2697 final).
CCE (Commission des Communautés Européennes). (1987, March). *European identity: Symbols to sport* (European File 6/87).
CCE (Commission des Communautés Européennes). (2010). Vice-President Margot Wallström. http://ec.europa.eu/archives/commission_2004-2009/wallstrom/index_en.htm. Accessed 10 June 2012.
Cubitt, G. (Ed.). (1998). *Imagining nations*. Manchester: Manchester University Press.
D'Oliveira, H. U. J. (1994). European citizenship: Its meaning, its potential. In R. Dehousse (Ed.), *Europe after Maastricht: An ever closer union?* (pp. 126–148). München: Beck.
De Angelis, E., & Karamouzi, E. (2015). *Une entité politique, une véritable communauté: Building the EC's democratic identity through the enlargement lens*, paper under review, obtained via personal communication.
Delanty, G. (2008). European citizenship: A critical assessment. In P. Isin et al. (Eds.), *Citizenship between past and future* (pp. 61–70). London: Routledge.
Dewey, J. (1927). *The public and its problems*. Ohio: Ohio University Press/Swallow Press.
Joergensen, K., et al. (Eds.). (2007). *Handbook of European Union politics*. London: Sage.

Monnet, J. (1972). *L'Europe Unie: De l'utopie à la réalité*. Allocution prononcée au Congrès International de la Friedrich-Ebert-Stiftung. Centre de recherches européennes Lausanne, no date.

Rabier, J. R. (1989). L'opinion publique et l'intégration de l'Europe dans les années '50. In *ll Relancio dell'Europa E I Trattati Di Roma*. Actes du Colloque de Rome 25–28 mars 1987. Brussels: Bruylant.

Reding, V. (2013, December 2). *EU citizenship—Anno 2013* (SPEECH/13/1003). Leuven, Belgium.

Schuman, R. (1980). Pour l'Europe. Textes de Robert Schuman. In *Ce jour-là l'Europe est née* (pp. 29–33). Lausanne: Fondation Jean Monnet pour l'Europe et Centre de recherches européennes.

Varsori, A. (2007). The emergence of a social Europe. In M. Dumoulin (Ed.), *The European Commission, 1958–72. History and memories* (pp. 427–441). Luxembourg: Office for Official Publications of the European Communities.

Wallström, M. (2004). European Parliament hearings. Answers to the questionnaire for Commissioner-Designate Ms Margot WALLSTRÖM (Institutional relations & communication strategy) Part A—General questions.

Wallström, M. (2006, May 16). *Listening to citizens and delivering results: A way towards the constitutional settlement* (SPEECH/06/305). Strasbourg.

Wallström, M. (2008, April 7). *Ireland and Lisbon: Giving people the facts* (SPEECH/08/180). Brussels.

Wallström, M. (2009, May 6). *Looking ahead: A new treaty for a more democratic Europe* (SPEECH/09/226). Strasbourg.

Index

A
access to information, 138, 141, 142, 147–9, 159n52, 159n56, 160n57, 176, 177, 197
Adam, 44, 68n4
Adenauer, 41, 63
Agence Europe press agency, 61
'agora,' to the Ancient Greeks, 173
Aldrin, 110
Alexander, Jeffrey, 3, 4, 15, 46, 47, 50, 51, 65, 108–10, 112, 141, 180, 192, 225, 227, 228, 231, 235, 248n95, 250n133
Alsace, 42
America, 3
Amiel, 40
Amsterdam Treaty, 146, 157n17
Anderson, 155, 156, 163n132, 163n133
Arab countries' oil supplies, 93
Assembly, 7, 46, 69n15, 78n117, 95, 173, 197
asymmetric power relationship, 145
Athens, ancient, 188

B
Baldoni, 49
Barroso
  I Commission public communication reforms, 156, 169, 199, 200, 249n108
Barroso
  II Commission, 175, 199, 201, 209n29, 249, 264
Baudouin Foundation, King, 186
Beck, 13, 26n98
Beethoven, 105, 111
Belgium, 15, 42, 45, 56, 69n15, 71n30, 249n114
Bentham, 72n60, 181
Berlin, 243
Billig, 49, 104
Birmingham Council, 136
bottom-up approach, 174
Britain, Great, 69n15, 94
Brugmans, 5, 70n21
Brussels, 95, 151, 170, 184, 186–7, 191, 195, 200, 236, 251n147, 264
Building Europe together, 145–7
Burke, 46, 47, 77n113

C

Calhoun, 173, 194, 240
Campine region, 15
cards
    health, 101, 223
    identity, 27n120, 49, 55, 72n55
    (*see also* passports)
Caron, 63, 71n36
Churchill, 39, 67n2
citizenry, 12, 18, 46, 53, 60, 96, 105, 106, 111, 113, 115n23, 116n33, 123n152, 135, 137, 140, 144–6, 149, 151, 159n47, 174, 177, 189, 191, 193, 228, 263
Citizens First, 145, 146, 160n78
citizenship. *See under* European
Citizenship report, viii, 19, 233, 234, 241, 244, 249n111
civil
    consciousness, vii, 1–9, 21, 50, 57, 59, 65, 108, 112, 113, 124n156, 261, 266
    identity, 27. *See also*
    (European Citizenship)
    identity, vii, viii, 14–16, 20, 21, 65, 96, 138, 265, 266
    narrative, 1, 15, 21, 259–67
    scrutiny, 20, 138, 141, 177, 181
    servants, 2, 5, 6, 249n108
    society, 2–4, 7, 15, 21, 46, 47, 51, 52, 62, 65, 75n92, 108–10, 112, 113, 121n128, 139–41, 147, 151, 153, 158n35, 158n46, 159n47, 172, 174, 179–80, 185, 186, 188, 189, 192–4, 196, 218, 219, 224–8, 232, 235, 236, 240, 244, 248n95, 260, 264, 266
    (*see also* demos)
    solidarity, 3, 4, 18, 112, 113, 131, 231–5, 239
    sphere, 4, 51, 226, 231

Civil Europe, A, 1–28, 45, 47, 96
Cohen, 98, 120n106, 139, 161n88
Cold War, 39, 44, 48
Collowald, 41, 69n14, 75n92, 76n103, 78n117, 120n108
Commission, *passim*
Commissioner for
    Communication strategy, 156, 169, 198, 263
    Justice, Fundamental Rights and Citizenship, 217, 218, 220
common market, 26n112, 45, 53, 64, 73n66, 78n117, 99, 118n66, 232. *See also* single market
communication. *See* public communication policy
communication services. *See* Directorate General
Community (EC), 4, 5, 7, 10, 12, 14, 17, 22n5, 22n8, 22n14, 26n112, 39, 49, 50, 57, 61, 63, 72n60, 74n82, 75n92, 76, 78n114, 98, 111, 112, 114n22, 124n156, 135, 145, 150, 159n56, 225, 233, 261, 262. *See also* European Union (EU)
    homo oeconomicus's Europe, 17, 39–67, 72n60, 74n82, 75n92, 76n104, 78n114, 261
    A People's Europe, 93–113, 114n22, 121n133, 124n156, 150, 261
Community holiday, 5, 105
Community institutions. *See under* European Coal and Steel Community (ECSC)
Constitutional Treaty, 156, 169–73, 199, 202n11, 209n221, 263
Consultative Committee, 50–2
Copenhagen Declaration, 94, 95
Coppé, 24n60, 45

Council of Ministers, 46, 73n66
Court of Justice, 46, 47, 51, 52, 217, 222

D
Davignon Report, 67, 80n168
De Clercq Report, 18
De Gaulle, 41, 65, 66, 78n115
deliberative democracy, political theory, 139
Delors, Jacques, 115n23, 120n108, 235
democracy
  bottom-up approach, 179
  deliberative; Europe of Transparency, 137, 139, 140, 143, 147, 153, 161n89, 178–9, 186–8, 193–6
  liberal, 7, 81, 94, 218, 225, 261
  'life-blood' of, 175
  participatory/ deliberative; Europe of Agorai, 153, 172–5, 178–9, 181, 182, 186–8, 193–201, 204n103
  representative, 94, 96, 137, 139, 172, 175, 179, 180, 188
  'the pulse' of, opinion polls
  top-down approach, 179
democratic
  rights, 225
  society, 176, 190
  values, 218
demos, 96, 97, 99, 101, 106, 107, 109, 112, 139–41, 158n35
Denmark, 94
DG COMM. *See* DG Communication
DG Communication (DG COMM), ix, 24n74, 161n80, 196–8, 206n165, 209n217, 209n224, 219, 237, 248n106, 249n108

DG X (the Directorate General for Information and Communication), 104, 116n33, 154–6, 163n131
Directorate General
  Communication (DG COMM), ix
  Home Affairs (DG Home Affairs), 219
  Information and Communication (DG X), for, 154, 163n131
  Justice (DG Justice), ix, 201, 219, 250n124
  Justice, Freedom and Security, for, 198, 209n229
  Press and Communication, for, 156, 163n131, 170
Dryzek, 139, 161n88
Dunn, 232

E
EbS. *See* Europe by Satellite
EC. *See* European Community
ECB. *See* European Central Bank
ECC. *See* European Citizens Consultations
Economic and Monetary Union (EMU), 80n163, 137, 152, 157n17
Economic and Social Committee, 52, 73n66
EDC. *See* European Defence Community
education, 2, 4, 13, 53, 57, 74n84, 76, 102, 113, 119n72, 119n77, 147, 160n75, 162n101, 163n131, 184, 191
EFSF. *See* European Financial Stability Facility
EFSM. *See* European Financial Stability Mechanism
e-Justice (Portal), 233, 249n110

274 INDEX

EMU. *See* Economic and Monetary Union
Engaging Citizens', 188, 228, 237, 239, 264
Enlightenment outlook, 103
EP. *See* European Parliament
EPC. *See* European Political Community
EPS. *See* European public sphere
ESF. *See* European Social Fund
ESM. *See* European Stability Mechanism
Etats-Unis d'Europe, 41
EURANET, 192
Eurjus, 149
EUR-LEX, 149
Euro, 12, 107, 145, 146, 149, 193, 232, 237, 238
Eurobarometer. *See* opinion polls, public
eurojargon, 142
EUROPA website, 149, 158n46
European
 Central Bank (ECB), 118n62, 238
 Defence Community (EDC), 6
 Financial Stability Facility (EFSF), 238
 Financial Stability Mechanism (EFSM), 238
 Justice Forum, 236
 Political Community (EPC), 6, 147
 Political Cooperation (EPC), 93, 94
 Social Fund (ESF), 54
 Stability Mechanism (ESM), 238
 Year for Citizens (EYC), 242
European Citizens
 Consultations (ECC), 186–8
 Initiative, 218
European Citizenship
 in constant transition, 266
 in daily life, 188, 241
 definition, 8–11, 45, 52
 democratic, 13, 14, 41, 51, 66, 67, 96, 103, 110, 138, 143, 173–7, 179, 180, 183, 186–91, 194, 199, 218, 225, 228, 231, 236, 237, 240, 244, 265
 membership criteria, 49
 national, and, 10–11, 48, 94, 95, 137, 140, 143, 150, 178, 229, 239, 259, 262–4
 rights, 225, 233, 234
 Roman, and, 7, 64, 101, 163n131, 226, 234, 235
European citizenship, theoretical approaches
 cosmopolitan post-national, 10, 13–21
 national, 10–11
 socio-historical policy analysis, 10–13
European City of culture, 102, 105
European Coal and Steel Community (ECSC), ix, 26n104, 44, 45, 51, 54, 57, 58, 61, 71n30, 74n84, 79n126, 107
 institutional foundations; Assembly, 46; Council of Ministers, 46; Court of Justice, 46, 47, 51; High Authority, 46, 54, 58, 107
European Commission. *See* Commission
European Community (EC), viii, 4, 5, 7, 10, 12, 14, 17, 22n5, 22n8, 22n14, 26n112, 39, 49, 50, 57, 61, 63, 72n60, 74n82, 75n92, 76n103, 78n114, 98, 111, 112, 114n22, 124n56, 135, 145, 150, 159n56, 225, 233, 261, 262. *See also* Community (EC); European Union
European Economic Community (EEC), 24, 45, 51, 61, 71n31, 118n72, 186

INDEX 275

European Parliament (EP), ix, 22n9, 46, 58, 60, 62, 66, 72n43, 72n44, 78n114, 78n115, 78n117, 95, 96, 99, 103, 106–10, 112, 114n22, 115n33, 116, 135, 136, 138, 140, 142–145, 146, 151, 159n56, 163n131, 170–2, 175, 178, 183, 184, 197, 198, 218, 238, 239, 243, 261, 263
European public spaces. *See* European public sphere (EPS)
European public sphere (EPS), 75n92, 184, 190, 193–6, 207n182, 236, 240, 262
European Union (EU)
  A Europe of Agorai, 144, 146, 153–6, 169–201, 233, 234, 243
  A Europe of Rights, 196–201, 217–44
  A Europe of Transparency, 19, 135–56
European Union institutions. *See* European Coal and Steel Community (ECSC)
Europe by Satellite (EbS), 99, 162n99, 191, 207n177
Europe Direct, 149, 161n96, 162n98
A Europe of Agorai period, representation
  European public spaces, 21, 174, 184, 188, 189, 195
  mass media, 61–80, 106–8, 177, 190, 192, 193, 207n178
  open-ended integration, 178, 182
  participatory democracy, 172, 173, 186
  political deliberation, 21
  public debate, rights, 175, 176, 179, 180, 197
  virtual/ physical agorai, 173, 183–6, 189, 194, 195

Wallström, Communication Strategy, 156, 169, 181, 198, 240, 263
A Europe of Rights period, representation
  civil–legal lexicon, 21, 219–21
  Eurozone crisis: fiscal harmonization, 237–44
  informative-affective communication style, 233
  'Rechtsgemeinschaft': a Community of Law, 225, 231
  rights-based citizenship, 14, 217, 227
  Single Market consumer rights, 21
  a single-perspectival Europe, 21, 226, 261
A Europe of Transparency period; representation
  agenda, Commission's, 137, 143, 145–8, 152, 153, 176, 263
  communication policy reorientation, 135–8, 140, 144, 154–6, 163n131
  debate and dialogue, 19, 113, 137–9, 141–8, 150–3, 262–4
  deliberative civil society, a, 139–41, 147, 153, 218
  disengaged citizen, the, 135–7
  online/ Info centres, 149
  right of scrutiny/ open access, 138, 141
euro, the, 12, 146, 193, 232, 237
Eurozone crisis, 8, 237–44, 250n133
EUtube, 185
EYC, *See.* European Year for Citizens

F
Fishkin, 141, 152, 161n88, 161n89, 186, 188, 200, 207n182
Follesdal, 147, 157n4, 263

Fontainebleau Council, 101
Fontaine, François, 2, 68n4, 70n16
Foret, 63
Fortress Europe, 239
France, 22n15, 39, 40, 42–5, 63, 66, 68n12, 78n115, 79n117, 118n62, 123n152, 172
Froschmeier, 104
Fundamental Rights, Charter of, 218, 219, 221, 222

G
Gallup, 108, 122n138, 152, 180
Gaudet, Michel, 2
Gazzo, 61, 62, 122n133
Gerbet, 19n15, 43
Germany, 15, 39, 40, 42–5, 56, 68n5, 71n30, 191
Gfeller, 94, 114n7
Greece, 8, 114n22
Griffiths, 66

H
Haas, 1
Habermas, 75n92, 207n182, 226, 240
Hague Summit (1948), 39
Hague Summit (1969), 66, 67, 80n163
Hallstein, Walter, 1–5, 24n60, 45, 46, 48, 53, 60, 62, 63, 65, 78n116, 78n117, 95, 225, 235, 248n96
Harrison, 70n24, 77n112, 121n127, 121n128, 191, 247n63, 265
High Authority. *See* Commission
Hirsch, Etienne, 41, 42
Histoire d'un Traité documentary, 63
Hix, 147, 157n4, 263
Hobbes, Thomas, 14

Homo Oeconomicus period; representation, 17, 20, 39–67, 72n59, 76, 95, 96, 100, 139, 159n47, 226, 235, 243, 259–61, ix. *See also* Schuman Declaration
economic and social rights, 20, 139
economic pragmatism, 41
ECSC, context of, 45–8
mass media, factual, 61–3, 106–8
Treaties; of Paris, Rome, 48, 50, 51, 53, 54, 71n31

I
identity
a civil concern, 61, 77n112, 265
European, viii, 2, 4, 5, 13–16, 18, 20, 21, 27n116, 27n117, 49, 61, 65, 72n55, 94, 96–8, 101, 104, 105, 113, 114n22, 119n72, 119n78, 123n152, 124n156, 138–53, 178, 188, 189, 219, 226, 234, 235, 247n62, 262, 265, 266
European civil, 1–9, 15, 16, 65, 113, 139–41, 224–8, 234, 259–67, vii
national, 5, 10–11, 13–21, 61, 124
Ifestos, 94, 114n2
imago. *See* visual imagery
Information Service, 57, 59, 60, 65, 75n103, 76, 77n106, 78n117, 107, 108, 116n33. *See also* Directorate General
integration
civil, 1, 2, 8, 15, 74n84, 244, 294
open-ended, 178, 182
process, vii, viii, 10–12, 15, 17, 44, 48, 57, 59, 75n103, 95, 110, 114n23, 115n23, 137, 152, 238, 259, 266
project, 182

Israel, 7
Italy, 15, 19, 45, 56, 71n30, 72n54, 184

J
justice
  civil, 224, 229
  court (*see* Court of Justice)
  DG (*see under* Directorate General)
  EU, area of, 217, 220, 221, 224, 229, 232, 233, 264
  social, 74, 94, 189, 218

K
Kant, 194
Kohnstamm, Max, 2, 5, 48
Kostakopoulou, 11, 12
Krasner, 47
Krause, 227

L
Lamassoure, 112, 124n156, 224, 245n4
layperson's summary, 176
Lefebvre, 102, 189
Lejeune, 43, 44
lexicon
  civil-legal, 16, 21, 219–21
  civil-spatial, 16, 21, 174
  economic-social, 16, 20, 48–61
  political-dialogical, 16, 20, 138
  political-federal, 16, 20, 96–7, 110
Lisbon Treaty, 27n121, 199–201, 217–21, 223, 235, 249n108, 264
listening-exercise, 179
Lodge, 137
Lorraine, 42, 69n15
Ludlow, 4, 78n114, 80n163, 112, 115

Luskin, R., 200
Luxembourg, 42, 56, 61, 65, 66, 69n15, 74n84

M
Maas, 11, 12, 49
Maastricht Treaty, 9, 10, 19, 96, 97, 111–13, 115, 119n72, 122n146, 123n152, 135, 136, 142, 151, 152, 160n75, 169, 219, 262
Magnette, 11, 12
Mansholt, Sicco, 2
Marshall, 10, 231
Mayer, René, 2, 5, 44, 46, 54
McNair, 190
media, mass, 61–6, 106–8, 110, 177, 190, 192, 193, 207n178
Middle East situation (1973), 93
Mill, J.S., 181
Monnet, Jean, 1, 2, 5, 6, 8, 39–45, 48, 54, 58, 60, 61, 63, 68n4–5, 68n11–12, 69n16, 70n24, 71n30, 75n102–3, 76, 77n110, 78n117, 121n115, 149, 176, 266. *See also* Homo Oeconomicus
  leadership, 5
  press relations, 61
  public communication strategy, 8, 48, 54, 58, 60, 63, 176, 266
  toward a civil association, 48
Moravcsik, 53, 95, 147, 157n4, 158n46
Murville, Maurice Couve de, 65

N
nation-state
  and citizenship, 94, 95, 103, 112
  citizen's rights, 95
  and manufacturing, 44
  media influence, 103

nation-state (cont.)
  parliamentary elections, 95
  and passports, 95, 105
  social provisions, 53–4
  visible symbols, 105
Nesti, 58
Netherlands, the, 45, 71n30, 93, 172
New York Council on Foreign
   Relations, 5
Nixon-Kissinger European Year, 93
Noël, Emile, 104
non-civil sphere, 4, 226, 229

O
Official Journal of the European
   Communities, 145
Olsen, 11, 12
OPEC, oil embargo, 93
opinion polls, public, 4, 63, 108–10,
   160n75, 179, 180
  Eurobarometer, 108–10, 121n133
  pulse of democracy (see Gallup)
  tool, as a, 108, 180
Ortoli, 108
O'Shaughnessy, 105
Ott, Joachim, 199

P
Paoli, 109, 121n133
Paris Summit 1974, 95, 98
Paris, Treaty of (ToP). See Treaty
passports, 18, 49, 95, 98, 105,
   117n50, 189
pax Europa, 41, 44, 103
A People's Europe period,
   representation
  affective style and symbols, 18–20,
     98, 103–5, 111–13, 115n23,
     118n70, 120n108, 121n115,
     124n156, 261

democratisation, 95
'demos,' an active, 96, 97, 101,
   106, 107, 109, 112, 139–41
Eurobarometer, role of, 108,
   122n133
identity reinforced, 123n152, 226,
   247n63
space, cultural and territorial, 20,
   96–103, 110, 111, 117n57,
   118n66, 118n70, 148–51,
   188–90, 204n114, 261
Pérez-Díaz, 225
Perrin, 99
physical/virtual space, 16, 20, 148,
   149, 152, 173, 189, 195,
   263, 264
Plan-D/Debate Europe projects,
   172, 174, 183, 185, 195, 264
Pleven, René, 44
Poidevin, 54
Pompidou, George, 66, 114n7
portraits of the European citizen,
   15, 110, 195
  Europe of Rights, the consumer and
     justice, 221, 224–6, 228, 229,
     232, 240, 243, 244
  high-tech Agorai, access and
     deliberation, 183, 186, 188
  Homo Oeconomicus; coal/
     steelworker moving family,
     54–6
  a People's 'homeland' Europe with
     an active demos, 96, 97, 99,
     101, 106, 107, 109, 112,
     139–41
  Transparency right of scrutiny,
     debate/dialogue, 20, 138,
     141, 153, 176
PRINCE information progamme,
   145–7, 152, 226
Prodi-Commission, 155–6, 163n131,
   170, 196, 201n2

INDEX 279

public communication activities.
See media, mass; opinion polls,
public; quasi-fictional/quasi-
factual public communication
tools
public communication policy
awareness-raising, 109
to educate, 17, 144, 150, 177
to inform, 59–63, 109, 121n115,
143, 171
under Monnet's leadership, 4–5
Reding's use of, 219, 248n108
Wallström, primacy, 225
public communication style
affective, 17–21, 111–13, 118n70,
121n115, 103–105
deliberative-rational, 17, 19–21,
110, 142, 143, 146, 178–9,
182, 187, 190, 193–6, 233,
235–6
factual, 17–21, 59, 61, 105, 106,
110, 121n115, 147–8, 176–8,
195, 233, 235

Q
quasi-fictional/quasi-factual public
communication tools, 63, 64
quasi-fictional representations.
See portraits

R
Rabier, Jacques-René, 2, 6, 41, 46,
67n2, 71n41, 75n92, 76n103,
78n114, 108, 109, 122n132,
122n136, 122n138, 180. See also
Eurobarometer
press, and the, 76n103, 108
Rae, Gallup and, 152, 180
Rechtsgemeinschaft (a community
of law), 225, 231, 234

Reding, Viviane, 204n103, 217–44.
See also Europe of Rights period,
representation
the citizen-consumer European,
225, 226, 232, 240, 244
justice, key to civil society, 217, 219,
220–5, 227–9, 231–3, 236,
245n4
practical approach to harmonization,
224, 225, 229, 230, 237, 240
public communication as a tool,
163n131, 219, 233–7, 239,
240, 244, 245n4, 248n108
role as Commissioner, 163n131,
217, 245n4, 249n108
representations of European
citizenship. See under the
following periods
A Europe of Agorai, 21, 169–201
A Europe of Rights, 217–44
A Europe of Transparency, 135–56
Homo Oeconomicus, 39–67
A People's Europe, 93–113
Representations of the
Commission, 184
Reuter, Paul, 41, 42, 70n16
Rey, Jean, 2, 5, 63, 66, 67
Ricœur, interhuman relations, 190
Rights, 9, 50, 94, 137, 175, 217–44.
See also Europe of Rights period,
representation
of access to information, 142
citizenship, 221, 223, 225, 233,
234
civil-legal, 50, 51, 56, 67, 72n59,
233, 234, 236, 264
consumer, 9, 21, 99, 100, 224,
247n64
electoral, 96, 97, 109, 110, 225, 261
human, 94, 221
to scrutiny, 20, 67
socio-economic, 9

Risse, 182, 207n182
Rome, Treaty of (ToR). *See* Treaty
Ronan, 54, 56, 105
Ruggie, concept of space, 16
Runciman, 45, 64, 68n11

S
Saarland, 15, 42, 56
Sandel, 4, 189
Sandri, Levi, 54, 73n82
Santarelli, 115n23, 123n152, 155
Santer
  Commission and the press, 140, 154–6
  Commission President, 140
Scarascia-Mugnozza, 109
Schulz-Forberg, 7, 70n24
Schuman Declaration
  collaborating writers, 42
  drafting the, 42, 67, 68n5
  economic solidarity, 44
  ensuring peace, 39, 41, 42, 48
  need for secrecy, 41, 43
  objectives, 45, 66, 102
Schuman, Robert, 39, 41–5, 48, 60, 63, 66, 67, 68n5, 68n12–14, 75n92, 102, 105, 111, 262
Shanahan, 100
Shaw, 11, 259, 267n1
Shore, 100, 109, 112
Signpost, 149, 161n97
Single Market, 13–15, 21, 99, 100, 112, 145, 147, 151, 201, 220, 221, 223–7, 229, 232, 234–7, 240–2, 244, 245n4, 265, 267n1. *See also* Europe of Rights period, representation
Skinner, 14, 15
Soja, 189
solidarity, 2–4, 18, 19, 43, 44, 48, 51, 69n12, 74n84, 98, 104, 112, 113, 218, 225, 228, 231–5, 239, 240, 265–267. *See also* integration
solidary sphere, 2, 3
Soviet Union, 39
space concept for 'Homo Oeconomicus'
  horizontal, Community level, 75n92
  imaginary, as an, 102, 103
  territory, geographic/political, 47, 49, 52, 53
space concept in a Europe of Agorai
  European Public Spaces, 188
  multi-perspectival, 21, 153, 183, 186
  physical and virtual high-tech, 173, 189, 194
space concept in a 'Europe of Rights'
  single-perspectival, 21, 150, 226
  territory, geographic/ legal, 221
space concept in a 'Europe of Transparency
  network of levels, 148–50
  physical and virtual, 148, 152, 263
space concept in 'A People's Europe
  commercial/ an 'imaginary', 100
  cultural dimensions, 146
  events, 18, 66, 93, 94, 101, 102, 105, 106, 111, 261
  'homeland,' EC, 97, 111
  horizontal perspective, 16
  symbols, 18, 103, 105, 111–13, 115n23
Spain, 8, 114n22
Spierenburg, 54
Sternberg, Schrag, 16, 25n81
Stevenson, 13
Stockholm programme, 233
symbols, 2, 16–18, 49, 57, 98, 103, 105, 111, 113, 115n23, 118n70, 120n108, 124n156, 262. *See also* People's Europe period, representation
community, 17, 120n108

economic-social, 57
political, 49, 113

T
Taylor, 99, 102, 226
television, 61, 76, 107, 108, 149, 162n99, 169, 170, 183, 192, 194, 196, 201n2, 206n160, 264
Television Without Frontiers Directive (TVWF), 107
Thucydides, 14
Tindemans, 100–2, 118n72
Tocqueville, 78n113, 144, 181, 182
ToP (Treaty of Paris). *See under* Treaty
top-down approach, 179
ToR (Treaty of Rome). *See under* Treaty
transparency initiatives, 141
Treaty
  of Amsterdam, 118n62, 142
  of Lisbon, 201
  of Paris, 8, 39, 45, 48, 50, 51, 53, 54, 159n47
  of Rome, 24n60, 45, 48, 54, 118n72
TVWF. *See* television

U
UK, 61, 64, 72n46
United Europe, a, 39, 45, 74n84, 237
Unity, 2–6, 8, 18, 27n117, 39, 48, 93, 97, 111, 118n71, 123n152, 189, 227, 230, 231, 238, 260, 262, 266. *See also* integration
Unity in Diversity, 27n117, 189, 230, 231, 266
Uri, Pierre, 2, 41, 42
US, 39, 68n5, 114n7, 122n138

V
Valentini, 58
Van Bjisterveld, 151
Van Helmont, 5, 60, 68n4, 70n16, 75n102
visual imagery, 15
Vitorino, 140, 144, 145, 163n131, 201n4

W
Wallström, Margot, 116, 153, 156, 161n87, 161n89, 169, 170–200, 201n1–2, 204n114, 206n165, 207n177– 8, 219, 225–7, 233, 234, 236, 240, 242, 243, 248n108, 251n147, 263, 264. *See also* Europe of Agorai period, representation
Weber, 3, 141, 153
Westphalian nation state ideal, 47, 103
White Paper on European Governance, 142, 148, 163n131
Wiener, 11, 12, 25n98
Worldview Global Media, 170, 201n2
World War II (WWII), 22n14, 40, 44, 71n30

Y
Yom Kippur War, 93, 114n2
Yuval-Davis, 266

Z
Zero Tolerance Policy, 222, 223